Crossroads

The Multicultural Roots of America's Popular M

Second Edition

ELIZABETH F. BARKLEY

UPPER SADDLE RIVER, NEW JERSEY 07458

Library of Congress Cataloging-in-Publication Data

Barkley, Elizabeth F.
Crossroads: the multicultural roots of America's popular music / Elizabeth F. Barkley.— 2nd ed
p. cm.
Earlier edition was published in 2003 under the title: Crossroads: popular music in America. Includes bibliographical references and index.
ISBN 0-13-193073-7
1. Popular music—United States—History and criticism. I. Title.

ML3477.B35 2007
781.640973

2005056571

Editor-in-Chief: Sarah Touborg
Acquisitions Editor: Richard Carlin
Editorial Assistant: Evette Dickerson
Marketing Manager: Andrea Messineo
Director of Production & Manufacturing: Barbara Kittle
Managing Editor: Lisa Iarkowski
Production Editor: Jean Lapidus
Manufacturing Buyer: Benjamin D. smith
Image Permission Coordinator: Craig A. Jones
Color Scanning: Cory Skidds
Copy Editor: Laura A. Lawrie
Indexer: Murray Fisher
Cover Design: Kiwi Design
Cover Photo: © Raeanne Rubenstein
Cover Printer: Phoenix Color/Hagerstown
Compositor: Integra–India
Printer/Binder: Bind-Rite Graphics

Credits and acknowledgments borrowed from other sources and reproduced, with permission, in this textbook appear on appropriate page within text.

Pearson Education LTD.
Pearson Education Singapore, Pte. Ltd
Pearson Education, Canada, Ltd
Pearson Education—Japan
Pearson Education Australia PTY, Limited
Pearson Education North Asia Ltd
Pearson Educación de Mexico, S.A. de C.V.
Pearson Education Malaysia, Pte. Ltd

10 9 8 7 6
ISBN 0-13-193073-7

This book is dedicated to my students, whose multicultural diversity challenged me to look beyond "classical music" and explore and celebrate the musical contributions of America.

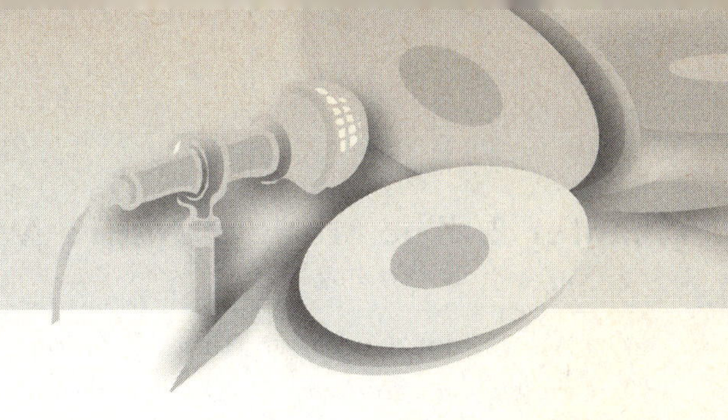

Contents

PART III: EXCURSIONS IN NEW DIRECTIONS

Preface

"The Crossroads"—the juncture where two paths intersect— has been an enduring symbol for encounters between people throughout history. America has, in some ways, been a continental crossroads, a destination to which people have traveled from all over the world. Meeting at the crossroads has often been full of hope and joyous expectation of arriving and starting anew. But it has also been a place of collision, a place to where people were dragged against their will, a place where once here, they yearned to return home. Just as the people who came to America were challenged by their interactions at the crossroads, so were the music traditions that they brought with them. Some immigrants sought to preserve their old world music in its original form as much as possible despite being transplanted to a new country. These "ethnic" musics have contributed to the rich, multicultural music mosaic in the United States. But cross-fertilization of immigrant music styles has also led to the creation of entirely new musics such as blues, jazz, Gospel, Cajun, zydeco, salsa, rock 'n' roll, hip-hop, rap and Tejano. These uniquely American musics were created by the critical convergence of different immigrant traditions in this country, and it is these genres that are the subject of this book.

Written to meet the needs of today's more diverse students, *Crossroads: The Multicultural Roots of America's Popular Music* uses ethnicity and race as a central organizing principle. It traces a variety of contemporary musical styles such as rap, hip-hop, rock 'n' roll, salsa, gospel, blues, jazz, Cajun, zydeco, and Tejano from their roots in the music traditions of immigrant groups to their hybridization and development into uniquely new American musics.

Perspectives on American history, experiences with race, the development of ethnic identity, and preferences for musical style are complex issues. The safest strategy is to ignore them, and continue to focus on the monocultural European-based music that has been the mainstay of American higher education for centuries. But this is ultimately self-defeating: the population of the United States is characterized by increasing and unprecedented ethnic diversity, and the traditional approach, although important, needs to be balanced by alternatives. European-based classical music is only a portion (and now an increasingly smaller portion) of all American music. Besides, we are no longer a colony. Isn't it time to start celebrating our own significant contributions to the world's music? Understanding that it is often difficult for instructors who are not trained in ethnic studies to deal in the classroom with the issues and vocabulary of multiculturalism, this text provides instructors and students with the information and tools to discuss music from a multicultural perspective even if they have had no prior experience in this area.

ORGANIZATION

The book is organized in three parts:

Part I: The Journeys Begin (Chapters 1–5)

Immigrants have brought with them the music traditions of their home country starting with the earliest journeys to America. Part I begins with an overview of key concepts in acculturation, assimilation, race, and ethnicity, followed by an introduction to the vocabulary required to discuss music. After establishing this context, subsequent chapters introduce four of the broad constituent groups that became the earliest Americans: Native Americans, European Americans, African Americans, and Hispanic/Latino Americans. It provides an overview of when and how these groups arrived here, the music traditions that they brought with them, and the initial ways in which these traditions were adapted to meet the needs of the new environment.

Part II: Encounters at the Crossroads (Chapters 6–11)

Although music traditions had been hybridizing through contact with other ethnic and racial groups from the earliest years in America, changes accelerated after the Civil War. Part Two explores some of the most important and influential musics that emerged in the last half of the nineteenth and early twentieth centuries as a result of interaction with other ethnic groups. Jazz, Gospel, and the blues are some of the earliest and direct results of the emancipation of African-American slaves and their expanded contact with the European-based music traditions of whites. Cajun music and zydeco are further examples of encounters between groups, specifically the French Acadian immigrants and the Blacks in areas of Louisiana. "Hillbilly music" provided some of the first recordings that were broadcast on the new radio transmissions of the 1920s, delivering the folk music of the primarily British immigrants in rural Appalachia to the ears and attention of people across the nation. As this music traveled out of the remote hills and into the city, it developed into many different styles of "country music "and launched the urban folk revival.

Part III: Excursions in New Directions (Chapters 12–17)

Following World War II, the ethnic and racial demographics of the United States started to change drastically. The egalitarian political climate that was created by the Civil Rights movement of the 1960s also led to more cultural interaction between ethnic and racial groups. Furthermore, the Immigration Act of 1965 abolished discriminatory national origins quotas, and led to substantial increases in the percentage of Asian and Hispanic immigrants. With refinements of recording technology and the rapid growth of the music industry, the sharing of different musical styles of various groups was accelerated. Part III explores the heritage of Asian Americans, and some of the new genres of American music that developed in this radically changed social and historical context.

Key Features

Structural Characteristics: Designed for students with no prior musical training, this book develops a global-based vocabulary to identify and describe the musical elements (rhythm, melody, harmony, texture, form, and instrumentation) that characterize each ethnic group's musical traditions and the genres that developed out of these traditions.

Stylistic Categories: Many genres have evolved over time and include multiple stylistic categories. For example, "jazz" includes ragtime, New Orleans style, Dixieland, Big Band/Swing,

Kansas City style, Big Band, Bebop, Cool Jazz, Hard Bop, Avant-Garde, Free Form, Fusion, and Acid Jazz. In addition to a full discussion of a genre's stylistic evolution, each chapter includes a brief, introductory description of each stylistic category, explaining each category's characteristics, representative artists, and the basic historical context in which that style developed.

Context: Music is more than the sum of stylistic elements, and often its power comes from the less tangible qualities that are the result of that music's interiority and its creation in a particular time and place. Thus, each chapter provides a framework that enables students to identify the similarities and differences between musical traditions both from the perspective of stylistic elements *and* from the perspective of the aesthetic, expressive and functional qualities that are the result of that music having been created in a particular historical and social context.

Boxed Features

Three kinds of breakout sections provide students with optional sources of additional information to deepen their learning.

Listening Guides: A significant challenge for most students is being able to connect the information that they read about a musical style with the music that they hear. To assist students in making these connections, we provide listening examples with commentary as well as description of that selection's structural characteristics (rhythm, melody, harmony, texture, form, and instrumentation).

In-Depth Focus or Insight: These provide additional information to help students understand more clearly and intuitively the nature of a complex topic, event, or trend.

Profile: Extensive biographical information about selected representative performers helps students associate what they are learning with what they listen to in their everyday lives.

Through a blended historical, ethnic, and musical approach, with a strong contemporary focus and the inclusion of a wide variety of musical styles from American society's five broad ethnic constituent groups (Native Americans, European Americans, African Americans, Latino/Hispanic Americans, and Asian Americans) this text hopes to better meet the needs of the new generation of faculty and students by more accurately reflecting, and encouraging appreciation for, the diverse musical traditions of the United States.

About the Author

Elizabeth Barkley holds a BA and MA from the University of California at Riverside and a Ph.D. from UC Berkeley. She has worked at Foothill College since 1977, including nine years as Dean of Fine Arts and Communications. As a faculty member at Foothill she has taught piano, music history and literature, and music theory and composition. Her books include *Collaborative Learning Techniques: A Handbook for College Faculty* (co-authored with K. Patricia Cross and Claire Howell Major, Jossey-Bass, 2004), the earlier edition of *Crossroads: Popular Music in America* (Prentice Hall, 2003), and a three-volume series, *Great Composers and Music Masterpieces of Western Civilization* (co-authored with Robert Hartwell, Pearson Custom Publishing, 2001 and 2002).

She has been the recipient of several honors, including the Carnegie Foundation for the Advancement of Teaching's California's Higher Education Professor of the Year, the Chair Academy's Outstanding Leadership Award for work with Learning Outcomes Assessment, Innovator of the Year in conjunction with the National League for Innovation, the Gerald Hayward Award for Educational Excellence, the Center for Diversity in Teaching and Learning in Higher Education's Faculty Award, the Foothill College President's Special Achievement Award, and the California Community College League's Out-of-the-Box Thinker Award. She has also served as a Leadership Fellow through the American Council on Education and has been named a Carnegie Scholar in the discipline of music by the Pew Charitable Trusts in conjunction with the Carnegie Foundation. Additionally, the California Virtual Campus selected her course Music of Multicultural America as the Best Online Course.

Chapter One

Music in Multicultural America

Music is an integral component of contemporary society. Car radios, boom boxes, laptops, and portable CD and MP3 players enable us to listen to our favorite music nearly every place we go. Even if we don't take music with us, we still hear it when we participate in the myriad activities that comprise our daily lives. Music, for example, is often played in the background when we shop, exercise, eat in restaurants, or even wait on hold on the telephone. The pervasiveness of music combined with the global nature of today's media ensures we are exposed to many different musical styles. Most of these styles are categorized as "popular music" (as distinguished from "classical music") because these styles don't require any specialized musical training and they appeal to a large number of people.

Within this broad category of popular music, there are many styles and substyles. The chart below shows one approach to categorizing a sample of contemporary popular styles:

A Sample Organization of a Few Contemporary Popular Styles

Modern Rock	Electronica	R&B	Hip Hop
Alternative Rock	Acid Jazz	Funk	Old School
Experimental	Ambient	Disco	Pop Rap
Rock en Espanol	Big Beat	G-Funk	Gangsta
Indie Rock	Breakbeat	Gospel	Independent
Brit Pop	Downbeat	70s Soul	Turntablist
Grunge	Electro Funk	Contemporary	Abstract
Jam Rock	House	Motown	Bass
New Wave	Industrial	New Soul	
Post Punk	Intelligent Dance Music	Quiet Storm	
Power Pop	Techno		
	Trance		

Source: http://www.audiogalaxy.com/list/glossary.php, *accessed 1-12-05.*

Each style is defined by a unique set of structural characteristics—the typical manner in which that style treats rhythm, melody, harmony, form, and instrumentation. But each style is also defined by a set of values, practices, and behaviors—a "culture"—that is associated with the performers and fans of that style. Some of our musical preferences or dislikes are based solely on a style's structural characteristics. For example, if we like a really strong rhythmic beat, we are more likely drawn to hip-hop than New Age. But some of our tastes are also shaped by our response to the culture surrounding that style. Fans of country music generally find the positive emphasis on traditional family values in their songs appealing and find the socially critical, sometimes angry, lyrics of gangsta rap distasteful, and vice versa. To truly understand a musical style, therefore, it is important to look at its "culture" as well as its structural characteristics.

This book addresses music as a vehicle for multicultural studies as well as music as an art form. It celebrates the diversity of American popular music through coverage of a wide spectrum of musical styles, including folk music, blues, jazz, Cajun, zydeco, rock and roll, rap, salsa, and Tejano. Each music style is discussed in terms of its: (1) roots in the ethnic traditions of a specific immigrant group, (2) development into a uniquely American music, and (3) evolution into new forms that retain vitality and relevance in contemporary society. This book looks both at the elements that make that style distinctive from a purely musical perspective as well as the cultural context that originally created and currently sustains that style.

It is not intended to be comprehensive. For example, it does not cover American music of composers such as Charles Ives and Leonard Bernstein in the "classical" European-based style, because this music has been amply covered in other books. It also does not cover "ethnic" music in America, such as Arab music in Detroit. This is because although such ethnic music is important and contributes significantly to the richness of the American multicultural mosaic, if the music has managed to survive essentially intact despite being transplanted to U.S. soil, it is not yet truly "American" music. (It is highly possible, however, that these "ethnic" musics may be the seeds of future "American" musics.)

With the exception of Native American music traditions (which are included because of the American Indians' unique claim as the original inhabitants of this continent), this book confines its study to selected musics that have strong ethnic and racial roots and that have "hybridized" with other musics to form unique, new American musics. It further restricts its study to those musics that have gone on to play a significant role in shaping our national music identity. Thus, through recognition of the contributions of non-European immigrants and Native Americans as well as European immigrants, the book hopes to more accurately reflect the diversity of contemporary and historical American culture. At the same time, it looks for the commonality that holds these musics together, for out of these varied traditions we have created the exciting, unique, and new traditions that constitute "American" music. To provide a framework for this exploration, we begin by looking at the unique characteristics and circumstances that shaped America and established the environment that encouraged the development of these popular music styles.

The Components of American Multiculturalism

What is it that makes the United States so unique? It is that it is a country of immigrants. Although there was an indigenous population, that population was almost immediately marginalized. When the new U.S. government decided to take stock of its citizens in the first official census of 1790, Native Americans were not even counted. Over two hundred years later, in the 2000 census, they comprised less than 1 percent (.9) of the total population. Most of the 281.4 million people who currently call themselves Americans are either immigrants themselves or they are the descendants of immigrants. It is this unique history of being a country of immigrants that has led to the development of a "multicultural" America. To understand the implications of being

Break-Out One

INSIGHT *The "United States" or "America"?*

Throughout this book, when we talk about "America," we are referring to the "United States." This is because, most commonly, people from the United States are known around the world as "Americans." Yet this is seen by many as presumptuous and ethnocentric because the history of the United States and the history of the music of its peoples must be placed in the context of the geography and history of the Western Hemisphere. The Western Hemisphere cannot be studied without taking into context sixteenth-century European expansion. Therefore, let us take a brief moment to review the geography and history of this hemisphere.

The Western Hemisphere is a slice of the planet Earth that is made up of the two continents known as North America and South America. These are geographic areas separated by the Panama Canal. Geographically and politically, North America includes three large nations (Canada, the United States, and Mexico) as well as the smaller nations in the area of Central America (Guatemala, El Salvador, Belize, Costa Rica, Panama, and Nicaragua) and the island nations to the West (such as Cuba and Jamaica). South of the Panama Canal, the continent of South America includes the nations of Colombia, Venezuela, Ecuador, Peru, Brazil, Bolivia, Paraguay, Chile, Argentina, and Uruguay. Another name for the Western Hemisphere is "the Americas," in effect making anyone from all of these nations on the two continents "American."

In addition to the geographic frontiers and political borders, there also are cultural regions in the Americas. We speak of "Latin America" to refer to the vast majority of countries south of the United States. The term, though not the most accurate, groups those countries under the common experience of having been colonized by European countries with Latin-based languages, especially Portugal and Spain. In contrast, we speak of "Anglo-America" (although not as common a term) when we refer to the United States and Canada, as those countries were colonized by Anglos—another name for the English, who are descendants of Anglo-Saxons. Incidentally, Anglo-Saxons were themselves descendants, along with such peoples as the Scandinavians and the Dutch, of Germanic tribes who apparently migrated into northern Europe from western Asia.

History in the Americas is an ever-evolving story. Hundreds of civilizations thrived in the lands of the Western Hemisphere before European colonization. Where the peoples of these civilizations came from continues to be debated, and will be addressed in the next chapter on Native Americans. But at this point, it is important to remember that when we speak of "America" in the context of this book, we are speaking of the United States, recognizing that the United States itself is only one political and geographic entity within a much larger historical and geographic context that is also "America."

a "multicultural" nation, we need first to understand what is meant by the word "culture."

Culture

Culture is the combination of beliefs, customs, and practices that are characteristic of a nation or people. It includes the products of human work and thought such as art, music, literature, language, and religion. It is a way of life that organizes social experience and shapes the identities of individuals and groups. Culture provides the glue that binds individuals together into a group that has a "sense of peoplehood," a group that is recognized as a group because the individuals all possess certain common characteristics. Because of the large variety of possible groups,

Break-Out Two

IN-DEPTH FOCUS *America as the "New World"*

Before the arrival of Europeans and colonization in the Americas in the fifteenth and sixteenth centuries, the Western Hemisphere was home to hundreds of civilizations. Although there had been small European, Asian, African, and Polynesian expeditions to the Americas before 1492, the hemisphere had existed in relative isolation from the rest of the world. Trade of all types was taking place between peoples in Europe, Asia, and Africa, whereas the Americas evolved independently. We refer to the peoples who lived in the Americas as "Native Americans" because they are the original inhabitants of the Americas.

History books speak of the "Old World" and its "discovery" of the "New World." Most recent historians feel that these terms have a European perspective that frequently disregards the Native American view. Many Native Americans vehemently oppose the continued use of these terms. They feel that the term "discovery" implies to locate or identify something unclaimed or unknown, and that one cannot discover a land that is already occupied and already claimed. Likewise, the "New World" was only new to invading Europeans, and clearly not new to the inhabitants of the Americas. It is important to make these distinctions as we continue to promote greater understanding and appreciation for the diversity of people within the United States and all of the Americas.

there is also a large variety of cultures. When discussing how to increase tolerance for cultural diversity, we speak of the cultures associated with gender, differences in physical ability, and sexual preference. We refer to the differences between urban and rural social cultures, "Southern" and "Western" regional cultures, and even "community college" and "research university" campus cultures. In music, there are clear differences in the cultures surrounding symphony orchestra players, folksingers, and pop stars.

Ethnicity and Culture

One type of a group that possesses a culture is an ethnic group. Ethnicity refers to a group with a shared culture based on ancestral national origin (German) or religion (Jewish). In the most recent national census, U.S. citizens categorized themselves into over two hundred different ethnic groups. Thus, Americans possess a complex blend of the larger "American" culture (sometimes referred to as "mainstream" culture) and one or more ethnic cultures. The degree to which one identifies with the larger American culture or one's more specific "ethnic" culture is a combination of many variables such as whether an individual is a first generation immigrant or a fifth generation descendant of immigrants. It also is shaped by the degree to which an individual or that individual's immigrant group or family chose to retain their ethnic culture or assimilate into the mainstream culture. Indeed, the development of an individual's ethnic identity is an intricate process that is continually influenced by a wide range of social and environmental factors.

Race and Culture

Another type of group that possesses a culture consists of individuals belonging to the same "race." Race has traditionally been defined as a biological category as opposed to ethnicity, which is a sociological category. The concept of race developed in the eighteenth century when scientists were attempting to categorize human beings (as they were attempting to categorize all living things). Scientists based their categorization on physical traits such as skin color or eye shape. Scientists observed that the proportions of certain physical traits were differently distributed from one part of the world to another. This variance in distribution is believed to be a result of inbreeding within a geographic region. In the past, people traveled less and marriages were likely to be between neighbors. This resulted in the people of that geographic area developing and retaining similar physical characteristics.

The physical characteristics that a group in a particular geographic area possessed may reflect adaptations to the different environments in which the ancestors of that group of individuals lived for many generations. Although the concept of genetic adaptation is still debated, most scholars agree that it is probable that human beings have adapted biologically to such conditions as climate, disease, and diet. For example, the physical response of humans to a hot environment is to cool off through perspiring. Although all humans seem to have the same number of sweat glands, peoples of hot, dry climates where it is especially important to be able to cool off tend to be tall and slim, with a maximum of skin available for potential cooling by sweating. In Arctic regions, stocky body builds are more common, and these traits may help to conserve heat. Also, tightly curled head hair and darker skin may provide more protection against direct sunlight. Conversely, long, straight hair may provide more warmth and lighter skin may be less susceptible to frostbite. Although it seems probable that regional physical characteristics are the results of adaptation to different geographical environments, efforts to explain the present distribution of physical traits on this basis are still speculative and rigorously debated.

Problems with Classification by Race

There are several significant problems with classifying individuals into races.

This painting by Samuel B. Waugh shows immigrants disembarking at the harbor in New York City in 1855. The round building on the left is Castle Garden, the city's first immigration center. *Source: Samuel B. Waugh,* The Bay and Harbor of New York, *circa 1855. Gift of Mrs. Robert M. Littlejohn, Museum of the City of New York, 1855. 33.169.1*

Many Americans Are Multiracial. One of the first problems is that many individuals can be classified into more than one race. For example in general, American "blacks" average about four fifths African origin and the rest European or Native American. The golf champion Tiger Woods coined the term "Cablinasian" to describe his white, black, Thai, Chinese, and American Indian heritage, a heritage he shares with 10,671 Americans. In the 1990 census, half a million Americans taking the census refused to check only one race, forcing the 2000 census to allow for multiple racial responses. Seven million Americans took advantage of this change in racial reporting. Conversely, some groups do not fit into a race at all. The people of present-day India fit most closely in terms of biological characteristics with those of Europe, except that many of them have dark skin. The aborigines of Australia are also dark-skinned but do not in other ways appear closely related to the peoples of Africa.

Individuals Have Many Common Ancestors. Although races are defined as persons with the same pool of ancestors, no individuals have precisely the same ancestors except for brothers and sisters. Each of us has two parents, four grandparents, eight great-grandparents, and so on, expanding to a very large group of ancestors. Yet, there are more people living today than have lived in the history of humankind combined. Thus, if each of us were able to trace our ancestors back through time, we would find that we have many ancestors in common and we are all probably descendants of a small group of very early ancestors.

Classification by Race Is Not Scientifically Useful. The concept of race is of limited usefulness. Although it is supposed to be a biological-based categorization, it is in fact not very effective in explaining current biological responses. Although it is possible that one human group may have some genetic advantages in response to such factors as climate and dietary resources, these differences are small and are greatly outnumbered by commonalities. With social disadvantages eliminated, there are no differences in native intelligence or mental capacity that cannot be explained by environmental circumstances. Race is sometimes used to trace the origins of ethnic groups, but because ethnic groups are based on sociological characteristics, race and ethnicity are more or less independent of one another. For example, individuals who are racially classified as "black" or "Asian" have a wide range of ethnic backgrounds. Trying to separate "racial" and "ethnic" influences such that all humans can be divided into a small enough number of discrete groups that would result in every individual belonging to one and only one group is impossible and ultimately not useful or effective. Thus, scientists have generally abandoned using racial classifications in favor of geographic or social criteria in their study of human variability.

The Concept of Race Has Been Historically Misused. Fourth, and perhaps most problematic, is that the concept of race has traditionally been misapplied, with one race acting as if they were superior to another. In the late nineteenth century, "scientific" racialism asserted the superiority of Caucasians (specifically Anglo-Saxons) and this was used as justification for genocide, imperialism, and immigration restriction.

It is now generally accepted that humans cannot be scientifically classified into races based on biological factors, and, hence, race is now seen as a social construction, similar to ethnicity. Although race as a viable biological construct largely has been abandoned by the scientific community, race continues to shape culture and society. American citizens are still identified and categorized into races, and racial identity plays a fundamental role in their opportunities and social experiences. For immigrants, it influences their experience of acculturation and assimilation.

Acculturation and Assimilation into American Society

Acculturation is the process whereby immigrants absorb American cultural attributes, by assuming, for example, the English language and the manners and values of the mainstream society. They change their behavior and thinking because they now live in a different mainstream culture. Assimilation is the process by which these immigrants are integrated into the social networks—such as work and residence—of the mainstream society. The essential difference is that the immigrants do the acculturation, whereas society assimilates the immigrants. Many immigrants have experienced only limited acculturation and assimilation because of a variety of factors. Sometimes the immigrants themselves are determined not to be acculturated, but instead wish to hold on to their old world traditions, languages, and beliefs. When they immigrate to the United States, they regroup in cities and towns in ways that are designed to help them maintain their customary ways. If a group is strongly opposed to acculturation, it is likely that the group will have difficulty being assimilated. More often, however, the dominant group has set up impediments to assimilation.

IMPEDIMENTS TO ASSIMILATION

At different times throughout U.S. history, impediments to assimilation have been based on social class, gender, religion, and national ethnicity. For example, at one time, Catholics were strongly discriminated against partly because the predominant Protestant group felt that Catholics would be slavish followers of the Roman Catholic pope and not be able to think independently. Although impediments have fluctuated throughout U.S. history, one impediment has remained consistent, and that is the impediment of race.

Race, especially skin color, has probably been the single most important obstacle to acceptance and assimilation into mainstream American society. This has been the case since the nation's founding: soon after the United States became an independent country, the Naturalization Act of 1790 specified that citizenship was available to "any alien, being a free white person." Thus, Native Americans, African Americans, Asians, and

This photograph of Mulberry Street, New York in 1900 shows the bustling community of Russian Jewish immigrants in New York's lower East Side. As with many other immigrant communities, the neighborhood reflects the customs and styles of the homeland. Gradually, immigrants became acculturated and assimilated and a blend of immigrant and American traditions emerge. *Source: Courtesy of the Library of Congress.*

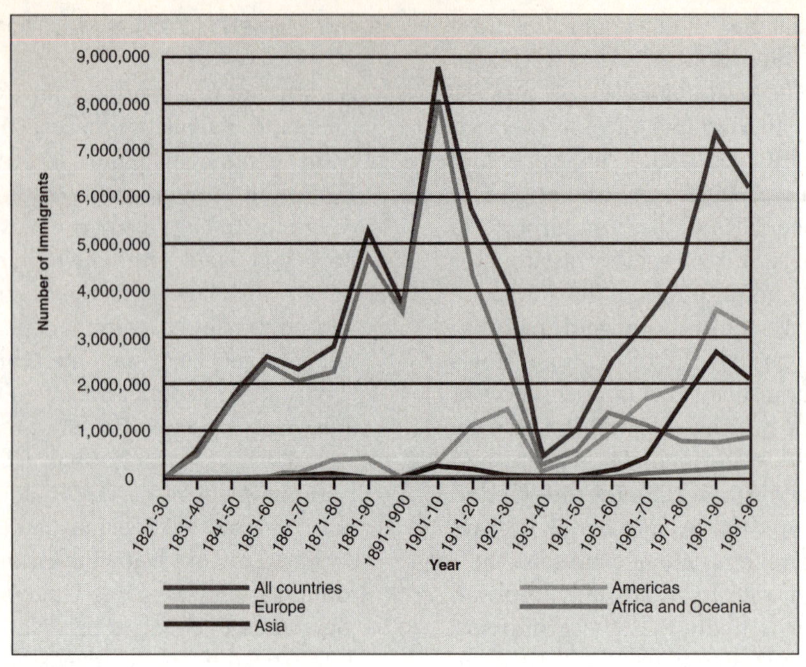

Immigration Statistics 1821–1996.

Hispanics faced barriers to assimilation from the earliest years of this country's history.

The Role of Race and Ethnicity in Immigration Policies

Although *citizenship* was restricted to free whites, the United States initially welcomed all newcomers with minimal regulation. In 1882, however, two laws were passed that started a period of steadily tighter immigration restrictions. The first law established qualitative health and moral standards by excluding "criminals, prostitutes, lunatics, idiots, and paupers." The second law, the Chinese Exclusion Act, denied admission to Chinese immigrants. This law led to further agitation for exclusion of Asians in general, culminating in the Immigration Law of 1924. This law essentially limited immigration of specific groups and denied entry to aliens ineligible for citizenship—those who were not "free whites." One of the results of this law was the implementation of the National Origins Act in 1929, which put in place quota systems designed to allow residents of favored countries to immigrate while restricting immigration from nonfavored countries with "inferior" races (at the time, southern and eastern Europeans as well as Asians).

The United States maintained this restrictive, racially based policy for several decades until the Immigration Act of 1965, which attempted to respond to increased national sensitivity to civil rights. This law eliminated the national origins quota system and opened the country to immigration from throughout the world. Although it maintained numerical quotas by hemisphere (120,000 annual visas from the Western Hemisphere, 170,000 from the Eastern Hemisphere), it exempted immigrants seeking family reunification with American citizens or resident aliens. This greatly increased the "chain migration" of people seeking to join relatives already in the United States and resulted in Asian immigrants becoming the fastest growing ethnic group. Asian immigrants included highly skilled professionals as well as low-skilled, impoverished Asians, many seeking political refuge from countries such as Cambodia, Laos, and Vietnam. At the same time, desperate economic and political conditions in Mexico and Central America enlarged the flow of legal and illegal immigrants from these areas.

As a result of all these factors, over sixteen million new immigrants have come to the United States since 1965, mostly from Asia and Latin America rather than Europe. It is this extensive influx of non-European immigrants that has been the most significant factor in creating the diverse population in the United States today. The chart below shows the changes in racial composition since the implementation of this act:

Racial Composition Changes in the Population (in thousands)

Year	White	Black	Indian	Hispanic	Asian
1960	158,732	18,872	(NA)	(NA)	(NA)
1970	178,098	22,581	(NA)	(NA)	(NA)
1980	194,713	26,683	1,420	14,609	3,729
1990	205,710	30,486	2,065	22,354	7,458
1996	219,749	30,503	2,288	28,269	9,743

Source: U.S. Bureau of the Census, U.S. Census of Population 1940, vol. II, part 1, and vol. IV, part 1, 1930, vol. II, part 1, vol. I, part I, 1970. vol. I, part B, and Current Population Reports P25-1095 and P25-1104, Statistical Abstract of the United States (1997), and unpublished data. Excerpted from Out of Many: A History of the American People, *3rd edition (New Jersey Prentice Hall, 2000) Appendix A-18*

Illegal (or "undocumented") immigration has become a growing concern. Many immigrants came from Europe and Asia on student or tourist visas and simply decided to stay. Others came into the United States by crossing over the Canadian or Mexican border. In 1986, the government attempted to address the issue with the Immigration Reform and Control Act. This law extended amnesty for undocumented immigrants under certain conditions but imposed penalties on employers who hired undocumented immigrants.

Nativist sentiment can run strong in states such as California that have absorbed the bulk of these new immigrants. Thus, California voters approved Proposition 187 in 1994, which declared all undocumented immigrants ineligible for any welfare services, public schooling, and nonemergency medical care. A federal court overturned this law in 1998. Appeals for tighter immigration controls have continued to be part of the political landscape, fueled by security concerns following terrorist attacks on the United States on September 11, 2001. Yet "how" to deal with illegal immigration continues to be problematic.

In 2005, for example, the House of Representatives passed Bill 261–161, attempting to tighten controls by barring states from issuing driver's licenses to illegal immigrants, enhancing border patrol between California and Mexico, and increasing the burden of proof for political asylum. This bill has been described as signaling a "potentially bruising congressional battle," reflecting a country and legislature divided over immigration policies and reform.[1] Meanwhile, statistics propose that eight million illegal immigrants are believed to be living in the United States.[2]

The United States Today

The United States is now in its third century of existence, and although many Americans still feel their closest cultural allegiance is to Western Europe, there is a growing number of Americans who do not. Furthermore, race is still an important factor in U.S. society. American citizens continue to be identified and categorized into races, and racial identity continues to play a fundamental role in shaping

[1] Ibid.

[2] Curtius, May, "House Passes Bill Cracking Down on Illegal Immigration." *Los Angeles Times,* reprinted in *San Jose Mercury News,* February 11, 2005, p. 5A.

This group of school children demonstrates the diversity that characterizes many communities in the United States today. Studio shot of multi-ethnic group of 13 smilings junior high kids.
Source: Photo by David Young-Wolff. PhotoEdit.

their opportunities and social experiences. It is challenging to measure the growth or decline of racial groups since 1990 because Census 2000 used both different and more racial categories, but of the foreign-born Americans counted in the 1990 census, fewer than one in eight came from Western Europe. The vast majority of immigrants came from Asia, the Caribbean, or one of the countries of Latin America, particularly Mexico.

Thus, America continues to be a country of immigrants, but now these immigrants are coming from all over the world, creating the most diverse population of any nation on Earth. A brief glance at almost any American city, classroom, or workplace powerfully reinforces this point. Many Americans have become alarmed at these changes in the country's demographics. They have voiced concerns that the unity of the nation is being threatened by its diversity, that there are more powerful centrifugal forces pulling the country apart than there are centripetal forces holding it together. One of the challenges the country continues to face is to find the means to forge a national identity that embraces this multicultural diversity while also celebrating the ties that bind us together as Americans.

American Multiculturalism and American Music

How does multiculturalism affect America's music? Like the population of the United States, music in the United States is diverse and eclectic, drawing from the many different cultural traditions of its people. Paralleling its immigrant patterns, the early history of American music reflected the primary Western European culture. At first, the colonists simply transplanted European music, but later, American musicians such as Heinrich, Gottschalk, Sousa, and Ives composed their own American versions of these European traditions. As the flood of immigrants diversified, as the new nation expanded its territories to absorb new lands (such as what had been the northern provinces of Mexico), and once African Americans were freed from slavery, American musicians began creating a whole range of hybrid musical genres. Examples of these uniquely American multicultural musics include spirituals, Gospel, blues, jazz, Cajun, zydeco, salsa, banda, Tejano, rhythm and blues, soul, and rap.

The Building Blocks of Music

Although there are many different kinds of music, these different musics share similar structural elements, or building blocks. Regardless of the style, all musics are made up of some combination (or conscious exclusion) of rhythm, pitch, melody, harmony, texture, instrumentation, and form. In fact, it is the special and unique way a style assembles these building blocks that makes each style unique. What are these building blocks?

Rhythm

At the basis of all music is a sense of movement through time. Although this sense of motion is accomplished through a variety of means, one of the most elemental is the pulse, which is also called "the beat." When we listen to music and tap our foot, we are tapping to the beat. In most styles of popular music these beats are further organized into groups of predictable patterns of strong and weak beats called meters. Generally, meters come in one of three categories: duple, triple, and quadruple. Duple meter organizes the beats into recurring patterns of **1** 2. Triple meter organizes the beats into recurring patterns of **1** 2 3. Quadruple meter organizes the beats into recurring patterns of **1** 2 3 4. In notated music, the meter is indicated at the beginning of the piece. Because the overall beats are divided into a series of repeated beat patterns, this approach to rhythm is called "divisive." Whether the piece is played fast or slow—called the "tempo"—the rhythm and meter remain the same.

It is this combination of beats, meters, and the microlevel of different durations of long and short notes that creates "rhythm" and that helps propel a piece of music forward. Sometimes musicians create interesting rhythmic effects by purposefully displacing the microrhythm, putting these beats before or after the main beats of the meter. This shifting to a weak beat rather than emphasizing the normal, strong beat pattern of the established meter is called syncopation.

Although rhythm is a fundamental building block in music in general, it is particularly pronounced in American popular music. This is largely because of the influence of African Americans, because rhythm is *the* essential component of traditional African music. For example, the heavy syncopation in jazz is a direct result of the fusing of European divisive and African additive rhythmic traditions that occurred early in the twentieth century.

Another approach to rhythm is found, for example, in traditional Native American and African music, where the music can be described as accumulating beats rather than dividing beats into the regular, repeating patterns of meters. This approach is called "additive," and the accumulation of beats rather than division into regular patterns can create extraordinarily complex rhythms.

Whether the beats are felt as accumulating or as dividing into meters, there is another level of rhythmic motion that exists. This is the varied duration of the individual sounds that are layered over and under the beat, creating patterns in which some notes are shorter or longer than the basic beat. Try to distinguish between these three different levels of activity in the opening phrase of "Happy Birthday."

Pitch

A second basic element of music is pitch. Acoustically, pitch is a certain number of vibrations per second. The higher the pitch, the more vibrations per second. Every musical system has its own culturally defined set of pitches. Since the eighteenth century, pitches in European-based music have been the group of twelve equidistant tones that divide up the octave (the same pitch at different levels of high or low) and called by letter names from A to G. To recognize how other pitch systems are different, we need first to understand "intervals."

"Intervals" is the term used to describe the distance between pitches. Intervals can be measured in units called cents, with twelve hundred cents per octave. The typical intervals of Western music are multiples of one hundred cents, but in other musical cultures intervals of

		Hap-py		**Birth-day**	**to**	**you**			
Beats	/	/	/	/	/	/	/	/	/
Meter:	**1**	2	3	**1**	2	3	**1**	2	3
Microrhythm:			Long short long		long	long	long		

other combinations of cents, such as 50, 150, and 240, are also found. One of the striking characteristics of African-American music is the way musicians expand the repertoire of conventional Western pitches with notes in between the pitches (for example, the "blue" notes achieved by a guitarist bending a string or a singer sliding up to the note). This approach comes from the African tradition of using different pitches and smaller intervals than those used in Western music.

There is another method for measuring intervals in Western music. In the Western pitch system, the distance between the pitches A and B is called the interval of a "second," because these pitches are two consecutive pitches apart. The distance between the pitches A and C is called the interval of a "third," because the distance between these pitches is three consecutive pitches. Sometimes melodies are described in terms of their interval range. For example, the pitches in many folk songs and Native American melodies span an interval of a fifth (creating a melody with a narrow range), whereas a jazz melody might span an interval of a twelfth (a much wider range).

Melody

When rhythm is combined with pitch in some logical progression and order, we have melody. Melodies can have different qualities depending on how they integrate these two elements. Melodies in which the pitches move upward in a slow and stately rhythmic pattern can be heard as "soaring," such as the final phrase of "The Star Spangled Banner," in which we sing, "Oh say does that star spangled banner yet wave, o're the land of the free and the home of the brave." Melodies can be simple, catchy, and easily singable, or they can be complex and require several "hearings" to recall.

Harmony

The pitches a melody uses typically come from a scale, which consists of a series of tones in a specific pattern of interval relationships. Some common Western scales are the major scale and the minor scale. The different scales contribute to a melody's character. For example, the melodies for the songs "Happy Birthday" and "We Shall Overcome" are drawn from the major scale and both songs have a positive, uplifting feeling to them. The folk songs "Greensleeves" and "House of the Risin' Sun" have a more somber quality, largely derived from the fact that their melodies are based on the minor scale. Melodies from non-Western cultures, such as the traditional melodies of Asians or Native Americans, use different scales based on different pitch systems. This, combined with different rhythm organizations, can make these melodies sound very exotic or foreign to Western ears.

When three or more pitches are combined together, they form a chord. In any given piece these chords are typically constructed from the same scale as the melody. There are many different kinds of chords, ranging from simple chords (such as a three-note triad) to very complicated chords (such as a five-note "ninth" chord, called a "ninth" because the top note is an interval of a ninth away from the root of the chord). A simple piece or song such as a European folk song will often have a few simple chords, and long sections of the melody will be constructed over the same chord. A more complex piece such as a jazz tune will have many complicated chords, and these chords will change very rapidly. Thus, the harmony provides musical support to the melody, giving the piece depth and structure.

Texture

The combination of all of the above elements creates a piece's texture that can be described as thick or thin, simple or complex. Hence, folksingers accompanying themselves on guitar would produce a simple, thin texture. A large jazz "big band" with several different instruments playing in a variety of groupings would produce a thick texture.

A second way of organizing and describing texture is by its combination of melody and chords. From this perspective, a texture comes in one of four categories: monophony, heterophony, polyphony, and homophony. Monophony is a texture that refers to a single, unaccompanied melody (such as Christian, Buddhist, and Islamic religious chant). Heterophony refers to the simultaneous sounding of slightly different versions of the same melody (such as would be created by a group of slaves singing a spiritual). Polyphony is two or more melodies that are played simultaneously but are independent, although they may be related. This texture predominates during certain periods of European art music and is also a distinguishing characteristic of some traditional Asian music. And, finally, homophony refers to a texture in which there is a primary melody with the other melodies and voices (or instruments) providing harmonic or chordal accompaniment. This is the texture to which we are most accustomed, and characterizes a wide range of music traditions from European art music to R & B. Texture is another important characteristic of a piece that helps us place that piece in a cultural context. For example, early folksingers simply sang their melodies without instrumental accompaniment, creating a monophonic texture. Later, when they accompanied themselves on guitar or banjo, they created a homophonic texture. Still later, if they composed complex arrangements with many different voices and instruments (such as occurred in the "Urban Folk Revival"), they created polyphony.

A third way of describing texture is associated with the way a piece is performed. Responsorial performance (often referred to as "call-and-response") is when a leader sings or plays a melody and a group responds or answers with a melody. Direct performance is when a soloist or a group performs the piece straight without alternation. Antiphonal performance is when one group alternates with another group. For example, responsorial performance is very common in African music and this influence can be clearly seen in the interaction between lead singer and backup vocalists in African-American music ranging from Motown to Gospel.

INSTRUMENTATION

The choice of the specific instruments or voices used in a performance or a composition is called the instrumentation. Besides singing, most societies seem to produce music through four different basic groups of instruments. These four groups are cordophones, aerophones, membranophones, and idiophones. Cordophones are instruments that produce their sound through stretched string such as a guitar or a piano. Aerophones are instruments that produce their sound through the blowing of air. Aerophones include trumpetlike instruments that create the sound through buzzing the lips into the instrument (like a trumpet) and flutelike instruments that create the sound through blowing air either into the mouthpiece (recorder) or across a hole on the instrument (transverse flute). Mebranophones are instruments that produce tone through a stretched skin or membrane, and are primarily drums. Idiophones are instruments that create the sound through the resonating of the body of the instrument itself, such as castanets and the marimba. Idiophone instruments can be struck, scraped, or rattled. In the twentieth century, we have added a fifth category of instruments called electronophones, in which the sound is produced through electronic circuits (digital keyboards and sound synthesizers).

FORM

The overall organization of a piece of music is called its form. This is often achieved through a balance between unity and variety. Examples of form include theme and variations, where the basic theme or melody is altered in successive versions of it. Another important form is ternary form, represented by the folk song "Twinkle, Twinkle Little Star," in which the first and last phrases of text have the same melody (and incidentally, the same words):

A Twinkle, twinkle, little star how I wonder what you are

B Up above the world so high, like a diamond in the sky

A Twinkle, twinkle, little star, how I wonder what you are.

There is virtually an infinite range of possible forms, and another contributing factor to the

Black gospel music is a glorious blend of European- and African-based music traditions. Gospel choir in church, portrait, clevaged view. *Source: Photo by Andy Sacks. Getty Images Inc.- Stone Allstock.*

uniqueness of a musical style is that different cultures tend to favor specific forms. Throughout this book, we will return continually to discussion of these building blocks as we attempt to describe and understand the unique qualities that characterize each musical style.

Conclusion

The population of the United States is a fascinating and complex mixture of Native Americans, immigrants, and the descendants of immigrants. Immigrants have brought the music traditions of their home countries with them and, as immigrants from one country came into contact with immigrants from other countries, they were exposed to different music traditions. Uniquely American musics such as spirituals, blues, jazz, Gospel, Cajun, zydeco, rock 'n' roll, and Tejano are the results of the merging of different immigrant music traditions and styles. Studying these styles from a cultural perspective involves paying attention not only to the sound itself but also to the human behavior that produces and values that sound.

In this book, we will examine selected, uniquely American music styles on two levels: the sound, and the historical and social context in which those sounds are created. Within the "sound" category, we will continue to develop and apply the vocabulary of structural building blocks introduced in this chapter so that we can see what is universal or specific to each culture's music. From the perspective of "context," we will see how that music emerged from the historical experiences of one of the five broad American constituent groups: Native Americans, European Americans, Latino Americans, African Americans, and Asian Americans. Through study in this combined historical and musical approach, it is hoped that you will develop greater appreciation for, and understanding of, the diverse and eclectic musical traditions of the United States.

Bibliography

"Audiogalaxy." http://www.audiogalaxy.com/list/glossary.php. Accessed 11-23-04.

Crawford, Richard. *America's Musical Life: A History.* New York: Norton, 2001.

Curtius, May. "House Passes Bill Cracking Down on Illegal Immigration." *Los Angeles Times,* reprinted in *San Jose Mercury News*, February 11, 2005, p. 5A.

Faragher, John Mack, Mari Jo Buhle, Daniel Czitrom, and Susan H. Armitage. *Out of Many: A History of the American People.* Combined Edition Third Edition. Upper Saddle River, NJ: Prentice Hall, 2000.

George, Diana and John Trimbur. *Reading Culture.* New York: Harper and Collins, 1995.

Handlin, Oscar. "Immigration" and "Immigration and Naturalization Service." *Encarta Multimedia Encyclopedia*, 1994.

Lasker, Gabriel W. "Classification of Races." *Encarta Multimedia Encyclopedia*, 1994.

Lee, Sharon M. *Using the New Racial Categories in the 2000 Census.* Baltimore, MD: Annie E. Casey Foundation and the Population Reference Bureau, March 2001.

Mather, Mark. *Census 2000: U.S. Population Grew 13 Percent; 12 Seats in U.S. House Will Change.* Washington, DC: Population Reference Bureau, 2001. http://www.prb.org/press/census2000/USHouseSeatsChange.html

———. *The Complex Stories from Census 2000 about America's Diversity.* Washington, DC: Population Reference Bureau, 2001.

Omi, Michael and Howard Winant. "Racial Formation," in *Racial Formation in the United States from the 1950s to the 1990s.* New York: Routledge, 1994.

Perry, Marc J. and Mackun, Paul J. *Population Change and Distribution 1990 to 2000: Census 2000 Brief.* Washington, DC: U.S. Census Bureau, Census 2000; 1990.

Roberts, Sam. *Who We Are: A Portrait of America Based on the Latest U.S. Census.* Revised and Updated. New York: Times Books, Random House, 1995.

U.S. Census Bureau, Population Division. *Population by Race and Hispanic or Latino Origin for the United States: 1990 and 2000* (PHC-T-1). Washington, DC: U.S. Census Bureau, maintained by Laura K. Yax, April 3, 2001. http://www.census.gov/population/www/cen2000/phe-tl.html

U.S. Department of Commerce, U.S. Census Bureau. *Resident Population of the 50 States, the District of Columbia, and Puerto Rico: April 1, 2000 (Census 2000) and April 1, 1990 (1990 Census).* Washington, DC: U. S. Department of Commerce, U.S. Census Bureau, December 28, 2000. http://www.census.gov/population/cen2000/tab05.txt

Vecoli, Rudolph J. "Introduction." *Gale Encyclopedia of Multicultural America.* Two Volumes. Judy Galens, Anna Sheets, and Robyn V. Young (eds). New York: Gale Research Inc., An International Thomson Publishing Co., 1995.

Chapter Two

The Music of Native Americans

When Douglas Spotted Eagle and Tom Bee won the first Native American Grammy Award for their album, *Gathering of Nations Powwow* in 2001, it drew attention to the essential issue that has concerned many American Indians for years: how can they balance the traditions of their ancestral heritage and still thrive within the contemporary world? The new "Native American Music" category was established and then presented in 2001 after a ten-year struggle for recognition led by the Native American Music Association with the help of prominent Native Americans such as Robbie Robertson and Val Kilmer. But the category itself falls within the folk music field and is therefore governed by strict traditional principles. To qualify for nomination, the recordings cannot incorporate the sounds, instruments, and influences of contemporary rock or of other ethnic traditions, such as those of European Americans or African Americans.[1]

Yet much of Native American music, like the music of other American ethnic and racial groups, *does* reflect the influence of other traditions. Furthermore, Native Americans today are creating contemporary rock, blues, country, hip-hop, funk, electronic, and New Age releases as well as attempting to preserve the music traditions of their past. Reconciling the past with the present is a particularly poignant challenge for Native Americans because of their unique history on the American continents. We therefore start our exploration of Native American music by looking at answers to the question, "Who are Native Americans, and how and when did they arrive here?'

Native American Origins

Native American Creation Stories

Native Americans possess a rich tradition of creation stories describing the beginnings of their people. Although the stories told by various Indian tribes differ, and some stories speak of arriving here after a long journey from an ancient homeland, many stories state that the ancestors came "out of this very ground." Native Americans treasure their cultural history, and many feel deeply offended when non-Native anthropologists and historians insist on an alternative origin.

[1] "Native American Music Is Getting Attention" (Knight-Ridder/Tribune News Service) Richard Chang; 01-16-2001.

Break-Out One

PROFILE *Douglas Spotted Eagle*

Douglas Spotted Eagle is a musician, dancer, singer, producer, recording engineer, and writer of American Indian descent. As a musician, Spotted Eagle is an acclaimed performer of the Native American flute. He strives to meld traditional Native instruments with contemporary themes, and was the first artist to appear on the Billboard New Age charts as a solo performer with the Native American flute. He also was named debut jazz artist of the year in 1996. He has received multiple Emmy and Grammy nominations. His music and sounds have been heard on several major recording labels and in conjunction with many film and TV projects. Following thirteen albums of his own recording, he coproduced *The Gathering of Nations Powwow* with Tom Bee and the album received the first Native American Recording Grammy Award in 2001.

He has organized several hundred powwows and produced many forms of Native American music, including music for powwows, Native American Church, country, rap, New Age, rock and spoken word. His recording group, Native Restoration, has developed methods for live powwow recordings that have transformed recording techniques in large area performance venues. With Tom Bee, he founded the Native American Restoration Studios and SOAR Records. Spotted Eagle is actively involved in film and new media productions, and in 2003 produced *Toubat,* a new historical documentary film on the Native American flute. In Spotted Eagle's own words,

Tom Bee and Douglas Spotted Eagle (right) accept their Grammy Award for Best Native American Album at the 43rd annual Grammy Awards in Los Angeles, February 21, 2001. The Grammy was presented for the album *Gathering of Nations Pow Wow.* *Source: CORBIS-NY. Photo by Gary Hershorn.* *© Gary Hershorn/CORBIS. All Rights Reserved.*

> Native music is timeless ... the music comes from the earth; from the heartbeat of our Mother. From the time that our early ancestors began to communicate with the earth, through the use of drums, to the time that the flute was given to the people, the music has been a major participant in ceremony and daily life ... the basic rhythms have not changed, only the voices and words. True, modern music forms have influenced the vocal structures, even to the point of harmonies being found from time to time among modern drum groups, yet the overall styling and arrangements of the songs are the same today, as they were hundreds of years ago.[19]

[19] Eagle, Douglas Spotted. *Voices of Native America: Instruments and Music.* Liberty, UT: Eagle's View Publishing, 1998, pp. 6–13.

PREVAILING MIGRATION THEORIES

The prevailing explanation for the origin of the first Americans is that they migrated here from the continent of Asia. Anthropologists and historians have proposed this migration theory for two main reasons. First, unlike on other continents, no evidence has yet been found of prehuman hominids anywhere in the Americas. Skulls, bones, and teeth of the earliest humans found here so far indicate that America's first inhabitants were fully developed *homo sapiens.* Thus, working within the framework of evolutionary theory, most scholars believe that the indigenous peoples migrated here from somewhere else. Second, physical traits (including genetic information encoded in DNA) and cultural traits (such as similarities in myths) indicate that native peoples have much in common with tribal peoples of northeastern Siberia. This, along with reconstruction of the advances and retreats of glaciers, physical evidence, and analysis of Indian languages has led to the dominant theory of migration.

This migration theory proposes that the ancestors of Native Americans came from Asia during the last Ice Age sometime between thirteen thousand and thirty thousand years ago. At that time, so much water was frozen in the huge glaciers covering North America and northernmost Eurasia that the sea level had fallen to the point where Siberia and Alaska were connected by a stretch of dry land called Beringia. It is believed that these early immigrants traveled over this "land bridge" between the two continents. But direct evidence of a trail or indirect evidence of human existence such as stone tools along this route across Beringia has not been found. Anthropologists say this is because evidence was covered by the rising sea as the ice

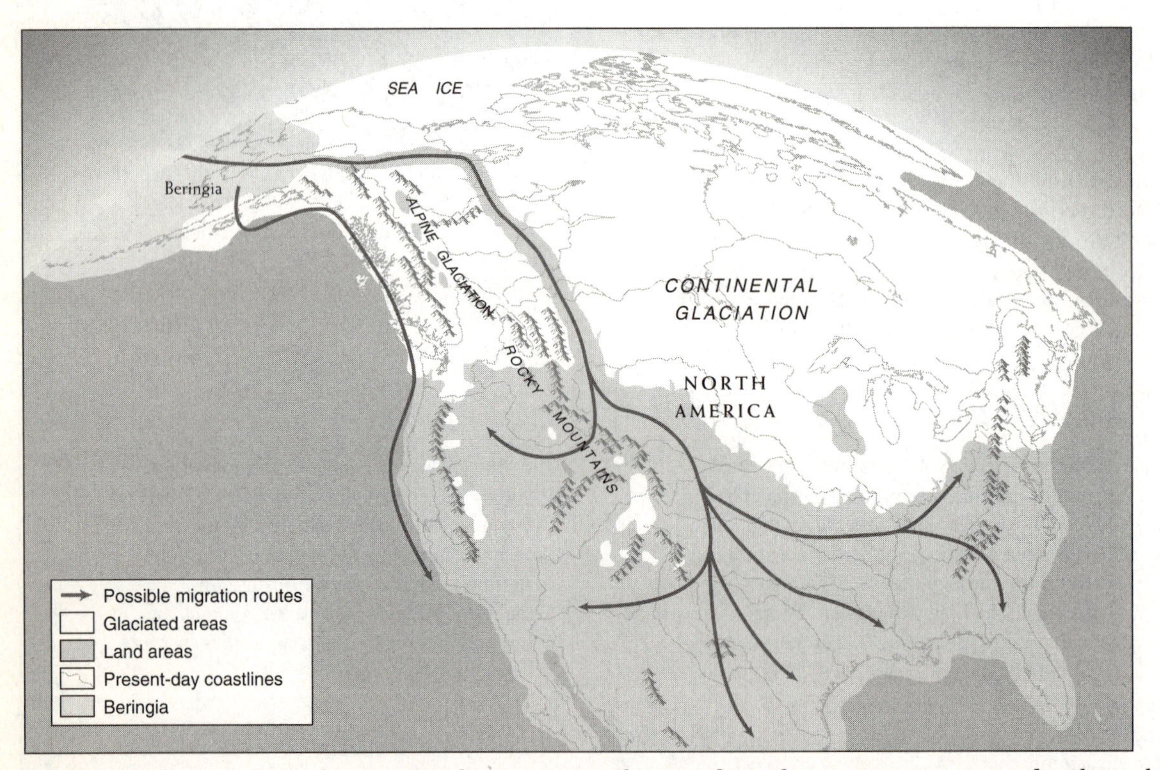

The "Bering Straits" that today separate the continents of Asia and North America were covered with ice thirty thousand years ago. The dominant theory on the origins of Native Americans proposes that hunting peoples migrated over this ice or by boats along the coast or through a corridor between the glaciers.

melted; some Native Americans say it is because evidence does not exist.

Having crossed over Beringia and Alaska, anthropologists propose that these earliest settlers continued down along the Pacific Coast or followed a thin, ice-free corridor between two huge ice sheets along the eastern base of the Rocky Mountains that opened up thirteen thousand years ago. At various points, some Indians spread out across the continent, whereas others continued migrating south.

Alternative Migration Theories

The origins of Native Americans continue to be debated. Until the 1970s, the earliest secure evidence of humans in the Western Hemisphere was a site in Clovis, New Mexico, where stone spear points were found. But the discovery of the Meadowcroft rock shelter in Pennsylvania, which has been dated at seventeen thousand years old, challenged and eventually replaced Clovis as the most ancient site. In 2000, an ancient campsite known as Cactus Hill in Virginia was conclusively dated at around eighteen thousand years old. A new interpretation based on tools found there that resemble even older tools found in Spain and France has led some archaeologists to propose that at least some of the ancestors of Native Americans came in boats across the Atlantic from Europe.[2]

Geneticists studying DNA propose another theory. This theory is based on the study of mutation patterns in DNA and the fact that native Siberians lack a peculiar mutation that appears in the six- to ten-thousand-year-old skeletal remains of many Native Americans. To explain this discrepancy, some geneticists working with anthropologists have suggested that a group of ancient peoples moved out of China into Malaysia where they became sailors and populated the islands of the South Pacific. Then, in one way or another (perhaps across the Pacific Ocean) these ancient mariners made it to Central and South America.[3] Of course, new discoveries will continue to be made that may lead to new theories.

Whatever their true origin, the earliest known inhabitants were augmented by two waves of immigrants coming from Asia around nine thousand years ago and again seven thousand years ago. These first Americans thrived in all habitable areas of North America. As they migrated to different regions, they adapted to the environments they found, with distinct cultures emerging as early as 4000 B.C.E.

Overview of Pre-Conquest Music Traditions

Challenges to Studying Pre-Conquest Native American Music

There are many challenges to studying Native American music traditions as they were before European invasion and colonization. First, their music was passed on from generation to generation orally as an integral part of ancestral tradition. They had no need for musical notation and hence there are no "pieces" of music that have been preserved. Second, they did not have a music theory (as far as we know) that could provide secondary insights into their music traditions. Third, their music was primarily vocal; instruments were not very important and the ones that have survived do not provide us with much information. Fourth, by the time scholars were interested in studying Native American music at the end of the nineteenth century, the Native American population and culture had been decimated. Many tribes had completely disappeared and those that had survived had had considerable contact with the music traditions of other tribes as well as European Americans and African Americans. Fifth, some Native Americans purposefully misled non-Native collectors in order to protect their traditions. Sixth, we depend largely on European descriptions of Native American music, and these accounts rely on perceptions that were formed within a whole framework of colonization, conquest, and a very different music aesthetic. European observers and collectors had difficulty comprehending, documenting, and

[2] Dorfman, Andrea, "New Ways to the New World." *Time Magazine,* April 17, 2000, p. 70.
[3] Bishop, Jerry E., "Strands of Time." *Wall Street Journal,* September 10, 1993, p. 1, col. 1.

describing music that was so entirely different from their own.[4]

Nevertheless, scholars have developed hypotheses based on recordings made in the 1890s, references by early observers such as Jesuit missionaries, knowledge of the movements of tribes and the distribution of certain musical features and song forms, and the preservation of traditions within the Native American community itself. This information has led to the following generalizations about early Native American music.

Commonalities among Native Music Traditions

Music Was Functional

Native American music was functional, consisting primarily of songs and dances that were related to various needs such as ensuring a successful hunt, effecting healing, or celebrating victory in battle. Music was part of an organic process, an element within a much larger context, not a separate aesthetic entity. One of the most important functions of music was its use in worship, both as accompaniment to sacred rituals and as the art of worship itself. Music also was used for social purposes, such as in calendar rituals and ceremonies marking rites of passage and other events in the life cycle.

Music Had Strong Spiritual Associations

In many tribes, music possessed spiritual power that was given to human beings through songs. Some tribes believed that all songs were given to them "in the beginning." Others believed that the songs existed in the spiritual world and were brought into the human realm through dreams or visions. Some individuals appeared to have a special relationship with music, and retreated into isolation until they received a song through visions. Because of the powerful connection between music and the spiritual world, music was judged not by its musical characteristics, but by how effective it was in contributing to the larger context, such as restoring personal health or sustaining the fertility of crops. Similarly, musicians and composers were not valued for their musical expertise, technical competence, or aesthetic creativity, but for their expertise in spiritual matters. Many songs were valued for their power and were owned by individuals who needed to protect the power of the songs by not performing them except under special ritualistic or ceremonial circumstances.

Music Was Primarily Vocal and Strongly Correlated with Text and Dance

Native American music was primarily vocal and there was a strong correlation with text. For example, in the setting of a poem to music, the musical phrase bore a close relationship in rhythm and contour (the shape created by the pitches rising and falling) to the textual lines. There also were many native cultures that used verbal structures that do not normally occur in spoken language. The primary example of this is called "vocables," nontranslatable syllables such as *hey, ya,* and *ho,* which conveyed an emotional meaning or identified a particular song or kinds of songs. These structures were interpolated into otherwise translatable text. In addition to text, because many rituals also involved dance, the musical structure also was closely related to the structure of the dance.

Structural Characteristics

Rhythm, Melody, and Harmony

Rhythmic organization was additive rather than divisive, such that there was a steady, uniform beat

[4] Also, other obstacles impeded collectors. For example, Natalie Curtis, when she began her comprehensive task of collecting Native American music at the beginning of the twentieth century, found that native songs were absolutely forbidden in the government schools, and she was told to do her collection secretly or she would be expelled from the reservation. Curtis, Natalie, *The Indians' Book: An Offering by the American Indians of Indian Lore, Musical and Narrative, to Form a Record of the Songs and Legends of Their Race.* 1907. Dover Publications: New York, 1968.

(often referenced to the heartbeat) serving as the foundation for the piece. Most melodies were constructed in a small range, rarely over an octave, and were frequently downward terraced or descending in contour, breaking off on an open vowel syllable. They frequently began on a high note and then moved downward, ending an octave or a minor third below the octave. The melodies used pitches that were closer together than our current Western pitch system, with scales that were different than the major and minor system with which we are most familiar today.

Texture, Form, and Instrumentation

Textures were monophonic or heterophonic, and performance styles were usually direct or responsorial. Music was heard as sound occupying space, with great value placed on sound coming from multiple directions, such as singers moving around and engulfing their listeners with song. The formal structure of a piece was closely related to text and dance. There also was considerable use of incomplete repetitions in which a second iteration of a phrase did not include the beginning notes of the first iteration of the phrase.

Singing was the dominant form of musical expression. The singing of the song incorporated aspects of performance that included vocal embellishment (such as gutturals and slurs), a wide range from high falsetto to extremely low bass, and frequently pulsations (rapid quivering of the voice). Additionally, the sounds of birds and animals were imitated in many songs.

Most Indian instruments were percussive, used mainly as accompaniment. These included idiophones made from a variety of materials including tree bark, planks, and logs that were struck or rubbed, and rattles made from materials such as gourds, sewn leather globes, baskets, and turtle shells that were filled with seeds or pebbles. Suspension rattles were another important type of idiophone and consisted of a series of perforated objects such as deer hooves, bird beaks, bones, and animal claws that were strung together and shaken. Membranophones included the single-headed frame drum, which was held in one hand and struck with the other like a tambourine, and medium-sized drums that were beaten with wooden sticks whose ends were left uncovered or sometimes padded with rawhide.

The most important melodic instrument was the flute, an instrument in the aerophone category. Indian flutes were made from wood, cane, bark, bone, and pottery and were mostly end-blown (as distinguished from the European flute, which is "transverse," or blown across a whole on top of the flute). Men of some tribes played courtship songs on flutes. The only chordophone was the musical bow, in which a regular hunting bow was adapted to musical use by plucking the string, but very little information is available on this instrument.[5]

Native American Music within a Historical and Social Context: The Fifteenth–Nineteenth Centuries

Native American Cultural Diversity

When Europeans came to colonize at the beginning of the fifteenth century, North America was home to a thriving native population estimated from one to eighteen million, with most recent estimates ranging from 4.5 to 10 million. The numbers vary widely because precise figures are impossible to ascertain. When Europeans began keeping records, the native population had already been drastically reduced by war, famine, forced labor, and epidemics of disease. What is clear, however, is that when the Europeans came to "The New World," the land was already occupied by millions of people. Although all these people were called "Indians" (See Breakout: Native American or

[5] Nettl, Bruno, "Indian Music, Instruments." *The New Grove Dictionary of Music and Musicians*, V. 13, pp. 302–304: Edited by Stanley Sadie. 1980 Macmillan Publishers Limited, London Grove's Dictionaries of Music Inc., New York, N.Y.

Indian?), the people who lived in North America were extremely diverse.

Anthropologists have determined that indigenous peoples were organized into one to two thousand different tribal nations, with almost as many languages divided into approximately sixty independent language families. In addition to not having a single language, there was not a single religion, social structure, arts tradition, or even history to bind them together. Just as Europeans typically identify themselves as Germans, Irish, or Italians, most Native Americans refer to themselves by their tribal ancestry, such as "Hopi," "Cree," or "Blackfoot." Thus, even before European immigration, the area we currently call the United States was multicultural.

Anthropological Organization into "Culture Areas"

In an effort to study this diverse native population more efficiently, scholars have organized the thousands of different tribal groups into "culture areas." Anthropologists have divided the Americas into several different culture areas, with one generally accepted model dividing the United States into the following nine: Arctic, Subarctic, Northwest, California, Great Basin, Southwest, Great Plains, Northeast, and South.

Each culture area began as a geographical region with characteristic climate, land, and water forms, plants, and animals. Humans who lived in the region adapted to these characteristics as they developed their way of life. For example, in the arid Southwest region, the ancestors of the present-day Pueblo Indians learned to build extensive irrigation systems to bring water to their cultivation of maize, beans, and squash. They lived in towns of terraced stone or adobe blocks, some of which had windowless walls facing the outside of the town for protection. In the lush Northeast region, a defining characteristic was the abundance of a single wild plant known as "wild rice" (not truly a rice but, rather, a wild grass). Much of the social structure was organized around the harvesting, drying, roasting, threshing, and preserving of this wild rice.

Thus, each culture area possessed certain natural resources that in turn inspired the humans who lived there to develop specific technologies and social systems. Neighboring peoples learned from one another and, over time, societies within one culture area resembled each other and differed from societies in other culture areas. Even within a culture area, however, each tribal group had distinct histories and traditions.

The Diversity and Distinctiveness of Native American Music

Just as anthropologists have used similarities and variations between clusters of tribal groups to organize tribes into culture areas, enthomusicologists have used music characteristics and identified regional music styles. These regional music styles correspond generally to cultural areas. For example, the tribes that inhabited the Great Basin area that had retained what archeologists refer to as the Archaic life-style of hunting and gathering, created music that was relatively simple, which some scholars suggest may be remnants of very ancient musical practices. By way of contrast, the music of many tribes in the South tended to be quite complex, correlating to the complex cultures of Indians such as the Aztecs from present-day Mexico.

An Example of a Regional Style: The Plains

Of the different regional styles, the music of the Plains peoples is the source of the predominant musical styles heard at present-day powwows. "Powwow" is the Anglicized version of the Algonquin word *pau-au*, which means a "gathering of holy men and spiritual leaders." As was true with many other words, non-Indians mispronounced and misused the word. At first "powwow" was used to refer to a Plains Indian assembly, but it eventually became a word to describe any gathering of native peoples, and is now used to symbolize unity among Native Nations across the continent. Today, powwows are social gatherings held for all sorts of

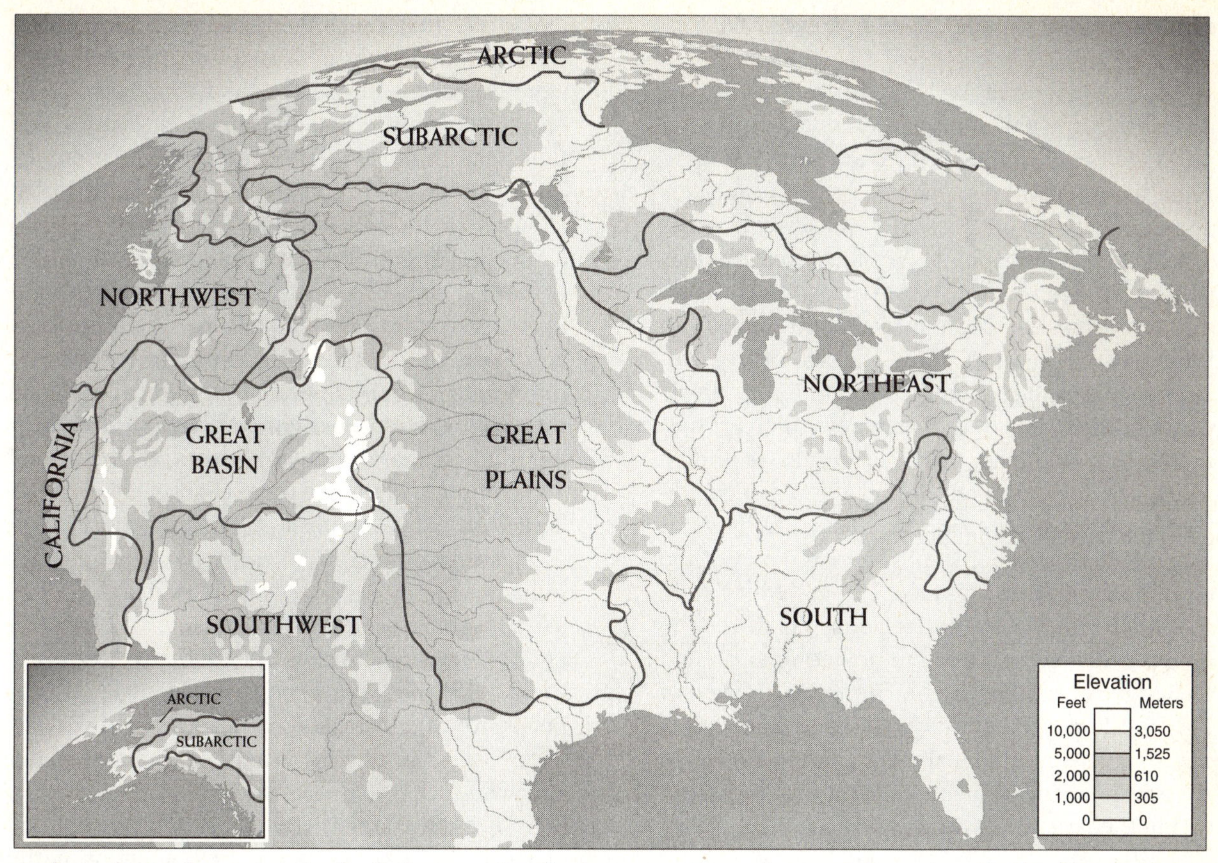

Anthropologists have organized tribal groups into "culture areas" in order to study more easily the diverse Native American population.

reasons, from birthday celebrations to occasions to honor elders to memorials of the deceased.[6] The fact that this Plains peoples gathering was eventually expanded to include and represent all Native peoples is largely a result of the history of the Plains culture area.

In the nineteenth century, the Plains became home to Indians who had been forced to relocate from many other regions as Europeans took more and more land. It is therefore more difficult to identify earlier traditions before this intertribal and European contact. In the Plains style, men's voices predominate, but the singing is in high falsetto and in an extremely tense, forceful style with dynamic pulsations (women achieve a similar effect by slightly altering the pitch). Melodies are in a wide range, and there is a typical terraced-contour of starting out high and gradually descending as the song progresses. There is a predominance of pentatonic (five note) scales and use of vocables. Plains Indians often accompany their songs with the drumming of a group of men sitting around a large, double-headed drum played with drumsticks, and their rhythm is distinguished by slightly off-the-beat drumming, with the drumstrokes appearing just before or after the beats of the melodic rhythm. There is extensive use of a form called "incomplete repetition," which consists of two sections, with the second section being an incomplete version of the first. Also, the first half is usually comprised of vocables and the second half of translatable words.

[6] Spotted Eagle, Douglas, *Voices of Native America.* Liberty, UT: Eagle's View Publishing Company, 1997, p. 13.

Native American Music as a World Music

Despite the fact that Native Americans possessed a vital and ancient music tradition, their music never strongly influenced European colonists. Even today, traditional Native American music is generally treated as a "world" music that exists outside the boundaries of Western culture. This is largely because Native American music is so different from European music in both sound and function and because it did not hybridize with European music traditions to create a new music genre in the same way that many other groups' music did. Although partly a result of Indian resistance to acculturation and their determination to preserve their distinct cultural heritage, it also reflects a lack of receptivity on the part of the early European immigrants. These settlers were frequently in a hostile relationship with the natives, dismissing their culture as inferior and having little value to the immigrants. A review of the most important events in American Indian history may further illuminate why traditional Native American music remains separate and distinct within the larger American mainstream.

Contact with Europeans in the Colonial Period

The first Europeans to arrive in America were welcomed by the natives. Natives were intrigued by European white complexions, beards, and clothing styles and by the technology of sailing ships, steel knives, gunpowder, mirrors, and copper and brass cooking implements. This early friendliness soon gave way to more negative feelings and early records include several comments on European character flaws. Whites were seen as stingy and avaricious with a seemingly insatiable desire for furs and hides. They were considered to be amazingly intolerant of native religious beliefs, sexual and marital arrangements, eating habits, and other customs. European architectural traditions of building permanent structures of wood and stone that precluded the ability to relocate when needed was seen as absurd. And Natives were especially repelled by the Europeans' apparently antagonistic relationship with nature and their materialistic view of natural resources.

European action also significantly contributed to the deterioration of relationships. In a practice begun by Christopher Columbus and continued by English explorers, Indians were kidnapped and transported to serve as curiosities in European courts. When the Spaniards discovered the wealth of natural resources, particularly gold, they combined exploration with conquest, enslaving the Indians, depriving them of their land and culture, and forcing them to submit to Spanish authority. The Spanish soldiers and English colonists also brought disease, especially smallpox, pulmonary ailments, and gastrointestinal disorders, all of which were unknown prior to European contact and for which the Indians were not immunologically prepared.[7] (Incidentally, Europeans returned to their countries with syphilis, a disease that they apparently picked up from Indians.)

French contact with Indians in present-day Canada and Louisiana was more benign, primarily because the French commercial interests were focused on the fur trade, and the Indians with their knowledge of the land and their specialized hunting skills were invaluable partners in the business enterprise. The French also needed a positive relationship with the Indians so that they would have allies in their wars with the British. Additionally, the French encouraged intermarriage, which also facilitated cross-cultural communication. The children of these marriages created a whole population of Métis (people of mixed French and Indian blood) that are still a recognized social group in present-day Canada.

The English, by contrast, scorned the Indians and actively discouraged intermingling. Furthermore, unlike the Spanish (who needed the Indian labor population) and the French (who needed the Indians' hunting expertise), the English colonial economy was not dependent on

[7] Interestingly, this did not seem to be such a problem in contact with the French, perhaps because the French were fewer in number and the colonization took place in areas that were not densely populated and in wide open places.

natives. As a result, the English generally viewed the native population as an obstacle, except when they needed them as allies in their fight with the French. This antagonistic English-Indian relationship of the seventeenth and eighteenth centuries was marked by a series of wars, all won by the English who had superior weapons. The inevitable result was the mandate that the vanquished tribesmen give up land and submit to English sovereignty, and either confine their activities to extremely limited areas or move away from the colonies' ever-expanding borders.

Native Americans and the United States of America

Eighteenth-Century Federal Policies

When the colonies rebelled against England in 1776 and formed the new nation of the United States of America, one of the many problems facing the new government was what to do with the Indians. The Treaty of Paris (1783) that formally ended the American Revolution completely ignored the Indians, leaving the founding fathers to determine their own policy. The early government's decision is reflected in Article I, Section 8, of the Constitution, which states "Congress shall have Power to regulate commerce with foreign nations, and among the several States, and with the Indian tribes." This statement in the Constitution became the basis for over two hundred years of federal legislation.

Inspired by the ideals of the Enlightenment that had given the revolution and the new government its moral and conceptual power, Washington policy makers were genuinely interested in pursuing a just and humane policy toward the Indians. One of the first full declarations of the U.S. Congress under the Constitution stated:

> The utmost good faith shall always be observed toward the Indians, their lands and property shall never be taken from them without their consent; and in their property, rights, and liberty, they shall never be invaded or disturbed, unless in just and lawful ways authorized by congress; but laws founded in justice and humanity shall from time to time be made, for preventing wrongs being done to them, and for preserving peace and friendship with them.[8]

The Trade and Intercourse Acts. Some of the initial legislation guiding interaction with Native Americans was a series of programs and policies collectively called The Trade and Intercourse Acts. The primary aim of this legislation was to reduce fraud and other abuses by whites who conducted commerce with the Indians. A second goal was to establish that the new Congress would acquire land for white settlement by purchasing it based on treaty agreements arrived at through peaceful negotiations. Between 1778 and 1871 (when the treaty process was abandoned) some 370 treaties were signed.

The treaties acquiring land quickly led to white expansion. The first wave of white settlers expanded into present-day Kentucky and Tennessee. At the outset of the American Revolution, there were only about four hundred settlers in this region, but by 1790 there were seventy three thousand. The second wave focused on Ohio. In 1790, there were about three thousand settlers there, but, by 1805, there were 230,000.[9] In 1803, the purchase of Louisiana from the French further encouraged expansion. Other treaties, purchases, and annexations followed, forcing tribes to continue relocating further north and west.

Although many Washington policy makers had hoped that these land transfers would occur without violence and in a fair and just manner, in actuality Indians were usually victimized in the process. Whites on the frontiers did not subscribe to the attitude of humanitarian tolerance but, rather, viewed the Indians as subhuman savages who should be exterminated. Dispossessing the Indians of their land was considered almost

[8] *Encyclopedia Britannica,* "North American Peoples and Cultures." vol. 13, p. 221.
[9] Hornbeck Tanner, p. 72.

a spiritual duty, as the Indians had not cultivated the land "properly" and hence were "wasting" God-given resources. Ridding the area of the "savages" would free up the land for "Americans" to cultivate in much more productive and efficient ways. Brutal treatment of Indians and raids on their land were not uncommon, and Indians were often tricked or coerced into signing treaties.

Nineteenth-Century Federal Policies

By the early nineteenth century, it was evident that the Trade and Intercourse Acts were not successful in terms of promoting peaceful and fair interactions between whites and Indians. Policy makers therefore concluded that the solution was to remove the Indians to territories west of the line of frontier settlement.

The Indian Removal Act. The Indian Removal Bill was passed in May 1830 and it empowered President Andrew Jackson of the United States to move eastern Indians west of the Mississippi to so-called Indian Territory (now essentially Oklahoma). There they would be free of white hostility and pressures to run them off of the land, and they could live as they chose and assimilate into mainstream society at their own pace. Removal was supposed to be voluntary, but it became mandatory whenever Indians resisted. In the decade that followed, approximately one hundred thousand Indians were moved westward. One of the bitterest examples of the implementation of this policy was the "Trail of Tears," in which about sixteen thousand Cherokee were forced to walk in the dead of winter from their homelands in Georgia to "Indian" territory in present-day Oklahoma. Walking barefoot and without blankets during stormy weather, about a quarter of their population died along the way.

Events in the mid-nineteenth century made it increasingly apparent that the United States was going to expand into "Indian Territory" west of the Mississippi as well. Mormons pursuing religious freedom migrating to the Utah territory (1846) and the discovery of gold in California (1848) intensified expansion that had already begun by farming settlers in Oregon (beginning 1842). As thousands of wagon trains bearing white settlers moved along the Oregon, Santa Fe, and California trails, Washington policy began carving the undefined tracts of Indian territory into smaller and more sharply defined reservations. As the white settlers both took Indian land and scared away or slaughtered the mountain and prairie game Indians depended on for subsistence, some Indian tribes resisted by attacking the wagon trains and the settlers' farms and ranches. The consequence was that the U.S. Army was sent to round them up and force them onto the reservations.

The Allotment Act (The Dawes Severalty Act). By 1870 it became clear that a new government policy was needed. Natives appeared to be on the brink of extinction, and several congressmen also had come to feel that it was absurd to view Indian tribes as independent sovereign nations with which the federal government should make treaties. In 1871, Congress decided to abandon the treaty process and deal with Indians as wards of the state, simply legislating on their behalf. This policy shift led to the General Allotment Act that went into effect in 1887. The Allotment Act aimed at assimilating Indians by attacking tribalism through parceling out communally owned reservation land to individual heads of family.

By making the lands ineligible for sale for twenty-five years, the government hoped to protect the Indians from land-grabbing whites and give them a period of time to transform into independent farmers. The hundreds of thousands of acres that remained after the individual 160-acre allotments had been made were then sold to whites. But the allotment program that was designed to speed the assimilation process actually turned out to be a disaster, as the Indians lost not only their surplus land but often their allotted land as well, despite the twenty-five-year government trusteeship (a safeguard that was later rescinded). Thomas Morgan, Indian affairs commissioner during implementation of the act, estimated that in 1891 alone, Indian land had been reduced by 17,400,000 acres.[10] One hundred eighteen reservations were allotted in this way and in the process, Indians lost 86,000,000 acres, or 62 percent, of the land they owned before the Allotment Act.[11]

The Plains Wars. The antagonistic relationship between whites and Indians was manifested in the Plains Indian Wars. These wars consisted of over one thousand battles during the last half of the nineteenth century. Some of the most notable events of these tragic wars included the brutal suppression of a Sioux uprising in 1863; the forced walk of eight thousand Navajos three hundred miles to a camp guarded by Fort Sumner in 1864; the Sand Creek massacre in 1864; the massacre led by Sioux Chief Sitting Bull of General Custer and his U.S. cavalry troops at Little Bighorn, Montana, in 1876; the seventeen-hundred-mile chase by the Army to corner and capture Nez Perce Chief Joseph forty miles south of the Canadian border in 1877; the Apache warrior Geronimo's attacks that led to his capture and imprisonment in 1886; and the final massacre by the U.S. Seventh Cavalry of more than two hundred Sioux men, women, and children shortly after Christmas at Wounded Knee, South Dakota, in 1890.

By this time, Americans had settled the continent all the way to the Pacific and had formed most of the conterminous forty-eight states. The Indians who had survived battles, disease, and relocation were confined to about a dozen large reservations and numerous smaller ones all across the country. The millions of natives that had populated the land before European contact had been reduced to about 250,000 by 1900.[12] Furthermore, whereas they had begun their relationship with Europeans and the U.S. government as an independent people in control of a wealth of natural resources, they were now among the nation's poorest, living as wards of the state in restricted areas primarily on the country's least desirable land.

Impact of Europeans on Native Culture and Music Traditions

General Cultural Decimation

From the very beginning, European contact altered native cultures and societies. For example, Indian acquisition of manufactured articles such as metal utensils, axes, knives, blankets, and cloth led to a decline of the native arts and crafts. The introduction of the horse by the Spanish completely revolutionized the hunting of buffalo, and whole tribal nations such as the Cheyenne and Arapaho abandoned their traditional patterns as farmers and village dwellers to become nomadic horse Indians. Fur trade led to changes in social organization: because women dressed the hides, successful hunters secured more and more wives to do this required ancillary work, thereby increasing polygamy.

When Indians were confined to reservations, further changes to their culture occurred. Tribes that had been hunters or herdsmen were now transformed into farmers. Those who had been farmers were transferred to reservations where they often found the land unsuitable for agriculture and were forced into finding wage-earning jobs. Traditional patterns of property exchange were altered when officials insisted on listing families by surnames (which Indians did not possess) and on changing inheritance rules. Schools were established both on and off the reservation to facilitate the learning of American language and customs. Christian missionaries continued conversion efforts that had been part of the earliest European contact, and as Indians accepted or incorporated aspects of this new cosmology, many of the old rituals and traditions were abandoned and replaced with new religious practices.

[10] Takaki, Ronald, *A Different Mirror*. p. 236.

[11] "North American Peoples and Cultures, Radical Land Allotment Legislation," in Encyclopedia Britannica, Inc., Chicago. 1979, p. 222.

[12] Davis, Mary, "Population." In *Native Americans in the Twentieth Century: An Encyclopedia,* p. 462.

This poster from Buffalo Bill's "Wild West Show" (1899) vividly reflects the impact of European culture on Native Americans. The theatrical show reenacted battles and included Native American dances, touring the United States and Europe for decades. Buffalo Bill was the army scout and showman William Frederick Cody (1846–1917). *Source: Getty Images, Inc. Hulton Archive Photos.*

Impact on Music

In the face of such drastic changes in Native cultures and societies, Native music traditions also changed. It is impossible now to ascertain specifically what was changed, and what was lost, because whole tribal nations were wiped out, or the survivors assimilated into other tribal groups or into mainstream white society. Generalizations must suffice. First, because music had played such a significant role in a wide range of social and religious functions, when these functions were abandoned or changed, so was the music that originally accompanied them abandoned or changed. Additionally, there was increasing incidence of intertribal music, where the music traditions of tribes that had been separate before European invasion were blended.

Native American music also incorporated influences from European traditions. In terms of instruments, the Apache fiddle and Navaho violin were apparently hybrids of Western string instruments and the Indian musical bow. The large double-headed drum popular in Plains ceremonies is believed by some to be a result of exposure to European-style percussion instruments known as timpani (others, particularly Native Americans, insist that this is not true). Indians were also systematically taught European music traditions by Christian missionaries and by teachers in reservation schools, and although they generally tried to keep their own music traditions separate, some European characteristics were assimilated. For example, two important late-developing traditions, the Peyote religion (early eighteenth century, renamed Native American Church in the twentieth century) and the Ghost Dance (late nineteenth century) both reflected the influence of Christianity.

When interest in native traditions as entertainment became a whole industry beginning in the frontier days of the nineteenth century (Buffalo Bill's "Wild West Show," for example, was begun in the 1880s), traditional music performance style was replaced by European-style concerts intended for tourists. Hence, by the time scholars began studying Native American music traditions in the 1890s, many traditions had been vastly altered and their stylistic variety and repertories greatly reduced.[13]

Native Americans at the End of the Nineteenth Century

The massacre at Wounded Knee, South Dakota, in 1890 was the last major confrontation between whites and Natives. That same year, the U.S. Census Bureau announced that there was no longer a frontier line on the map, for all land had now been settled and the Indians had been relocated to reservations. The decade that followed represented the nadir in Native American history. The population had been reduced from many millions to about 250,000 and the culture had been decimated. However, the destructive pattern that had begun several centuries earlier with the first European contact finally began to reverse in the twentieth century.

Native Americans in the Twentieth Century

Following centuries of population decline that began in the fifteenth century, the population of Native Americans began to slowly but steadily increase in the twentieth century. Federal policy makers still believed that the answer to the "Indian problem" was to assimilate Indians into mainstream America, and great effort was made to "civilize" the tribes and to teach them Christianity and other aspects of Western culture. In an effort to accomplish this, young Indian children were often taken from their tribes and families and sent to distant government- or church-run boarding schools, sometimes thousands of miles away from their homes. By the 1930s, however, the federal government acknowledged the failure of this approach and stopped expecting that Indians could be coaxed or coerced into abandoning their traditional tribal ways.

Break-Out Two

LISTENING GUIDE *Title: "Rabbit Dance"*

This is a social dance of the Northern Plains Indians. It is one of the few dances in which women and men dance together. Couples dance in a clockwise circle around the drum, holding hands crossed in front of them. Notice the "fusion" aspect of Native American musical characteristics and vocables with the English words, "Hey Sweetheart, I always think of you . . . "

Rhythm	Additive, but with an underlying triple feeling.
Melody	Terraced, descending, conjunct motion in relatively small range (one octave).
Harmony	Pentatonic. The pitch framework moves down about a tone during the song.
Texture	Call-and-response; heterophonic.
Form	Basic stanzas repeated four times.
Instrumentation	Voice and drum. Notice the pulsation and glides and relatively high tessitura.

[13] Nettl, Bruno, "Indian Music, Western Influence" Groves, Vol. 13, p. 304.

The government boarding school on the Pine Ridge Reservation in South Dakota was designed to force Indian youths to acculturate and assimilate into mainstream America by separating them from their elders and culture. Pine Ridge Boarding School, 1891. *Source: Photo by Grabill. Courtesy of the Library of Congress.*

The Indian Reorganization Act. In 1934, the passage of the Indian Reorganization Act acknowledged the enduring power and value of tribal organization and encouraged tribes to organize their own governments and to adopt their own constitutions and bylaws (subject to approval by the U.S. Department of the Interior). In addition, the act provided for the reacquisition of tribal lands and incorporated preferential treatment for the hiring of Indians to work within the U.S. Bureau of Indian Affairs. Progress under this act, however, was slowed once the United States entered World War II in 1941. After the war, preoccupied with other postwar issues, policy makers decided it was time to end federal responsibility for Indian tribes.

The Termination Period. In 1953, Congress resolved to work toward withdrawal of all federal support and responsibility for Indian affairs, beginning what is referred to as the "Termination Period." In the following two decades, federal services were withdrawn from about 11,500 Indians and federal protection was withdrawn from about 1.5 million acres. Funds acquired from the selling of the land were divided among tribal members. Unfortunately, as in so many of the earlier policy decisions, this had a devastating effect on many Native Americans. For example by 1961, most members of one of the largest tribes affected by termination policies—the Wisconsin Menominees—were almost totally dependent on welfare.

1970s Activism and Self-Determination. In 1970, Indian activists led by Russell Means and others organized the American Indian Movement (AIM) and publicly protested the condition of Native Americans by occupying Alcatraz Island in San Francisco Bay. That same year, President Nixon officially repudiated termination as a policy and issued in an era of "self-determination." These new policies encouraged Indians to determine their own future by emphasizing tribal administration of programs dealing with health, education, welfare, housing, and law enforcement. At the same time, Indian activists continued to fight for Indian rights. Some continued active protest, such as occupying the Bureau of Indian Affairs in Washington, DC, in 1972, and conducting a seventy-one-day armed siege at the site of Wounded Knee in 1973. Others took legal action, testing the extent of Indian jurisdiction on reservations and asserting long-ignored treaty rights to land, water, and off-reservation hunting and fishing.[14] In the late 1980s, because Indian tribes were now seen as

[14] Encarta article.

In November 1972, members of the American Indian Movement (AIM) dramatized their struggle for civil rights by leading a march of Indian peoples along the "Trail of Broken Treaties" before occupying the offices of the Bureau of Indian Affairs in Washington, DC. They occupied offices for a week, and are shown here guarding the door. AIM, Native American group protesting (Russell Means, Dennis Banks). *Source: Photo by Bettmann. Corbis/Bettmann,©Bettmann/CORBIS.*

sovereign nations and not under state jurisdiction, many tribes established gaming casinos on reservations in many states. Today, there are over 310 gaming operations run by more than 200 of the nations' federally recognized tribes. These tribal gaming operations have had both positive and negative effects. For example, the increase in economic activity has brought many young adults back to the reservations and decreased unemployment, but it also has increased the rate of bankruptcy and violent crime.[15]

[15] "The Social and Economic Impact of Native American Casinos." The National Bureau of Economic Research, http://www.nber.org/digest/feb03/w9198.html, accessed 1-18-05.

Native American Music in the Twentieth Century

Pan-Indian Music

Cultural decimation combined with the placement of previously unrelated tribes on single reservations has contributed to the development of a new movement in the twentieth century known as "pan-Indian" music. Pan-Indian music is partly the result of various resistance movements that had urged Indians to submerge tribal divisions in favor of ethnic unity, believing that Indians would survive only through solidarity. Pan-Indian music is also the unavoidable consequence of previously unrelated tribes on single reservations. There are several consequences of this development.

First, because the music is intertribal, the earlier distinctions between different tribal traditions have been blurred. Second, there has been an increase in songs using vocables that may have come originally from a different tribe's language, from Indian languages that have since disappeared, or are archaic words whose meanings have been forgotten. Fourth, the music has incorporated characteristics of other traditions, particularly European traditions. Yet, perhaps one of the most profound effects of the pan-Indian music movement is the addition of a large body of music that is secular and social in function.

Music for Powwows

Pan-Indian music is performed primarily at social events such as powwows. Members of more than one tribe typically attend powwows, and even interested peoples of other races and ethnicities who may participate occasionally in the dancing and singing. Secularization also has led to the development of a class of professional or semi-professional Indian singers and composers, with new emphasis on their compositional and music performing expertise, as opposed to nonmusical characteristics such as their spiritual power. Similarly, there has been a change in performance practice in that some of the music at these social events is now performed for an audience as entertainment.

Sacred Music

In addition to the social music of the pan-Indian movement, there also is religious and sacred music. This category contains a wide range of pan-Indian, tribal, and individual music. For example, it contains music of the Native American Church, which has its own songs generally referred to as "peyote" music because of the use of peyote in some of the church's spiritual ceremonies. There is also religious function music such as the Sundance, Yuwipi, Stomp dance, or harvest songs. Discussion of religious and sacred music has been left out of this chapter out of respect for the sanctity of these traditions.

Other Developments in Twentieth-Century and Contemporary Native American Music

With the general social changes and the Civil Rights movement in the 1960s, Native American musicians such as Buffy Sainte Marie and the members of the band "Redbone" attempted to reconcile their traditions with societal changes. Tom Bee and his Native American rock group XIT became the anthem group of AIM during their sieges at Wounded Knee and Alcatraz. In the 1970s, a few major record companies and several independent record companies provided new opportunities for Native American musicians. By 1980, over one hundred traditional and contemporary recordings were available. Then in 1988, Tom Bee (the lead singer of XIT) founded SOAR Records, which has become a major label for recording Native American and Native American–influenced music.

Native flautists such as Douglas Spotted Eagle, Tom Machaughty-Ware, and R. Carlos Nakai have become celebrated performers and also have helped contribute to the use of Native traditions in New Age music. "New Age" is a term

Break-Out Three

IN-DEPTH FOCUS *Style Categories of Powwow Music*

Traditional Drum Groups: Drum groups, an important ensemble at most contemporary powwows, consist of a group of people who sit around a single, large, round drum that is covered top and bottom and suspended among four posts. Each member of the group has a stick similar in weight and length. It is most common to have one or two lead drummers or singers who establish the beat and the melodic structure of the song. The rest of the members follow the rhythmic pattern of the leaders and frequently join in at the second line of the song.

Drum Groups sing in two basic styles, Northern Traditional and Southern Traditional. The Northern Traditional song style tends to be for men only and begins at a high pitch, then descends in a clearly contoured melodic phrase. Southern Traditional style songs begin at a lower pitch and stay within a narrow range, creating a chantlike melody that is repeated and becomes more powerful as the song progresses. Women join in singing an octave higher than the men, but rarely participate in the actual drumming.

Flag and Retreat Songs: These songs begin powwow ceremonies and vary tremendously by geographical locale and tribal group. A Flag Song is used at the grand entry at a powwow, when the dancers are in the arena and are circling the eagle staff and flags (which may include the American flag, various military service flags, state flags, and tribal or nation flags). The audience stands, and there is no dancing. After the Flag Song, the Retreat Song is sung and dancing is appropriate and done at this time.

Dance Songs: There is a variety of dance songs, many of which are used in competition at powwows. Songs are distinguished by a rhythmic style that corresponds to a particular dance form. Depending on the geographical region, songs may bear names such as "Northern Men's" or "Southern Men's" or "Ladies' Fancy." Some songs are "Trick" songs, in which the object of the song is for the drum group to trick the dancers into moving their feet when there is no struck beat and hence be disqualified. A subset of Trick songs is the "Shake" song, in which dancers shake their jingles and feathers to rhythmic patterns that change in tempo and rhythmic pattern.

Forty-Niner Songs: These are heard late at night after the main powwow and include songs that are of a lighter, more social character. The lyrics may generally contain words about a lost love or they may be a man entreating a woman to come home with him.

that began being applied in the mid-1980s as a catchall designation for various fusions musics that did not fit in other music industry categories. The term itself was applied because this kind of music was very successfully sold in "alternative" places such as bookstores, massage and meditation centers, health food stores, and other locations in which the "New Age" movement thrived. Native American music traditions have been incorporated into the New Age genre in several ways. One way is to integrate selected musical characteristics into recordings that provide music designed to induce a sense of therapeutic calm, spiritual transcendence, or physical healing. In this manner, aspects of Native American music such as steady drum beats, vocables, airy and loosely structured melodies that are chanted or perhaps played on flute provide a kind of "aural ambience."

Another of the New Age subcategories in which Native American music has thrived is identified as "technotribal." In technotribal music, contemporary artists juxtapose the otherwise contradictory styles of "primal" musical expressions (typically field recordings of aboriginal cultures in

Africa, Australia, South America, and North America) with the contemporary technology of synthesized sounds. There also are a variety of fusion efforts, in which Native American musicians incorporate characteristics from non-Indian musical genres, including country, rock 'n' roll, and jazz.

The Nammys. In 1998, the Native American Music Association founded the Nammys, the Native American Music Awards. These awards honor both Native American musicians creating traditional music and those who create music in a variety of contemporary genres. The awards include, for example, categories in Rap/Hip-Hop, Blues/Jazz, Pop/Rock, New Age, and Gospel/Christian. The organization also strives to educate the general public about the diversity of contemporary Native American music. Additionally, it maintains a Hall of Fame, and brings attention to the many well-known musicians who have Native American ethnicity, including Hank Williams, Kitty Wells, Crystal Gayle, and Jimi Hendrix.

Break-Out Four

INSIGHT *Native American or Indian?*

Several ethnic and racial groups in the United States struggle with finding appropriate names by which to identify themselves. The name "Indian" comes from Christopher Columbus's term for the Arawaks of the Caribbean, whom he called *Indios* because he thought he had landed in the East Indies. This Spanish word passed into English as "Indians." By the middle of the sixteenth century, it was widely used to refer to all peoples of the Americas, sometimes expanded to American Indian or Amerindian to distinguish them from the people of India. With the increased ethnic consciousness brought about by the 1960s Civil Rights movement, "Native American" began to replace the older, colonial-imposed "Indian," emphasizing that Indians had been the original inhabitants of what was now called America. Although this term generally gained acceptance, some people felt the new term was artificial and contrived. Others pointed out that although these first Americans had been here when Europeans arrived, they were not strictly "native" or "indigenous" as they had not originated on this continent, but had migrated here from Asia. Today, some individuals prefer Indian or American Indian, others prefer Native American, whereas others prefer "First Nations" or even simply "Native." After considerable debate and reflection, the ethnic/racial category in Census 2000 was "American Indian and Alaskan Native."

Many Indians refer to themselves by their tribal name, such as "Blackfoot" or "Hopi." But educated and sensitive people should be aware there are even problems with tribal names. For example, the tribal nation generally known as the "Sioux" were the most numerous of any Indian tribe, but they call themselves "Dakota" (meaning "the allies") or "Lakota" (meaning "many in one"). The name "Sioux" is apparently the ending of the word *Nadowessioux,* an Algonquian word for "snakes," meaning enemies. Similarly, Cheyenne comes from *Sha-hiyena,* meaning "people of strange speech," whereas the Cheyennes called themselves *Dzi-tsistas,* meaning "our people." Mohawk comes from the Algonquian *Mohawaúuck,* meaning "man-eaters," whereas the Mohawks called themselves *Kaniengebaga,* "people of the place of the flint." Thus, the common names of very large, well-known tribal nations such as the Sioux, Cheyenne, and Mohawk were not names they called themselves but were names probably originally told to Europeans by tribes hostile to these peoples.

Native Americans Today

Indians are now increasing faster than any other ethnic group in the United States. By 1990, the steady and steep increase in Indian population that had begun at the turn of the century had expanded from 250,000 to 1.8 million.[16] Data collectors for Census 2000 began their counting of Americans symbolically with Native Americans in Alaska, and when the nation's results were tabulated, the census showed that the American and Native populations had grown by 26 percent using the single-race definition, and by 110 percent if combined with multiracial American Indian groups. Results of the census indicate that the current Native population can range from 2.5 million to 4.1 million, depending on how they are counted.

More than 550 American Indian tribes are now recognized by the federal government and receiving service by the U.S. Bureau of Indian Affairs. The policies of earlier centuries, however, continue to affect Indians. Today, Indians rank lowest in almost all measures of economic well-being. They also continue to suffer from poor health standards, and have the highest rates of infant mortality, disease, and suicide in the nation. Their life expectancy is twenty-five years lower than the national average.[17] Despite these grim statistics, Indian culture and the music that is such an integral part of that culture continues to survive and to resist pressure to Americanize.

Although contemporary statistics of health, education, unemployment rates, and income levels continue to show Native Americans as disadvantaged, the revitalization in the population and the increased political activism have created a resurgence of pride in their cultural heritage. By the late 1990s, more than two hundred institutions had been established to preserve Native American history and culture. The Native American Graves Protection and Repatriation Act of 1990 is providing Indians with the legal basis to prod museums into returning thousands of Indian artifacts and bones to the tribes and sites from which they were taken. Tribal languages and traditional arts, including music, are enjoying renewed vigor.

Conclusion

With greater population numbers and with the gains of several decades of political activism, there has been a resurgence of interest among Indians in their musical traditions. On the one hand, this has led to attempts to recreate music in traditional styles. It also has led to a variety of fusion efforts. Native American musicians are proud of their tribal heritage and they are interested in making music that is relevant and appealing in today's world. The growth of the Nammy Awards and the fact that the recording academy has established the Native American Grammy Award music category attest to the increasing power and appeal of Native American music. Indian music traditions continue to survive as more and more young Native Americans use music to express both their individual and their group pride in their ethnic heritage. In the words of the musician R. Douglas Nakai, "We've survived all this. We are still here."[18]

Bibliography

Author not available, *Native Americans Take Home First Grammy.* Reuters, 02-22-2001.

Author not available, *Native American Music Experiences Growth, Growing Pains.* Morning Edition (NPR), 07-01-1996.

Bishop, Jerry E. "DNA & Native American Origin: Strands of Times." *Wall Street Journal,* September 10, 1993, p. 1, col. 1.

[16] Some scholars have suggested that as much as 60 percent of this number, however, is a result of changing definitions of what constitutes a Native American.

[17] Goldfield, David, et al. *The American Journey*, p. 622.

[18] http://www.nammys.com/mediaroom.cfm, accessed 1-15-05.

Burton, Bryan. *Moving Within the Circle: Contemporary Native American Music and Dance.* Danbury, CT: World Music Press, 1993.

Calloway, Colin G. (ed.). *Our Hearts Fell to the Ground: Plains Indian Views of How the West Was Lost.* Boston: Bedford Books, St. Martin's Press, 1996.

———. *The World Turned Upside Down: Indian Voices from Early America.* Boston: Bedford Books of St. Martin's Press, 1992.

Champagne, Duane. *Native America: Portrait of the Peoples.* Detroit: Visible Ink Press, 1994.

Chang, Richard. "Native American Music Is Getting Attention." *Knight-Ridder/Tribune News Service,* 01-16-2001.

Curtis, Natalie. *The Indian's Book.* New York: Dover Publications, Inc., 1950.

Davis, Mary B. (ed.) *Native Americans in the Twentieth Century: An Encyclopedia.* New York: Garland Publishing, Inc., 1994.

Densmore, F. *The American Indians and Their Music.* New York: Johnson Reprint Corporation, 1970.

Dorfman, Andrea. "New Ways to the New World." *Time Magazine.* April 17, 2000, p. 70.

Faragher, John Mack, et al. *Out of Many: A History of the American People.* Third Edition. Upper Saddle River, NJ: Prentice Hall, 2000.

"Ghost Dance," in *The Encyclopedia of Religion,* Mircea Eliade (Ed.-in-Chief), vol. 5, pp. 544–547. New York: Collier Macmillan Publishers, 1987.

Goldfield, David, et al. *The American Journey.* Second Edition. Upper Saddle River, NJ: Prentice Hall, 2001.

Heath, Charlotte. "Music." In Davis, Mary B. (ed.). *Native America in the Twentieth Century: An Encyclopedia.* New York: Garland Publishing, Inc., 1994.

Herndon, Marcia. *Native American Music.* Hatboro, PA: Norwood, 1980.

Highwater, Jamake. *Ritual of the Wind; North American Ceremonies, Music, and Dance.* New York: A. Vander Marck Editions, 1984.

McAllester, David P. "North America/Native America" in *Worlds of Music: An Introduction to the Music of the World's Peoples.* Jeff Todd Tilton (General Editor). New York: Schirmer Books, 2nd ed., 1992.

Means, Andrew. "Ha-ya-ya, weya ha-yya-ya!" *World Music, The Rough Guide,* vol. 2. Simon Broughton and Mark Ellingham, eds. London: Rough Guides Ltd., 2000.

Nettl, Bruno. "American Primitive Music North of Mexico," in *Music in Primitive Culture.* Cambridge, MA: Harvard University Press, 1977.

The New Grove Dictionary of Music and Musicians, Edited by Stanley Sadie. 1980 Macmillan Publishers Limited, London. Grove's Dictionary of Music, Inc. New York, N.Y.

———. *North American Indian Musical Styles.* Philadelphia: American Folklore Society, 1954.

———. "The American Indians," in *Folk and Traditional Music of the Western Continent.* Third Edition. Englewood Cliffs, NJ: Prentice Hall, 1990.

Roberts, Helen. *Musical Areas in Aboriginal North America.* New Haven: Publications for the Section of Anthropology Department of the Social Sciences, Yale University Press, 1936.

Spotted Eagle, Douglas. *Voices of Native America: Native American Instruments and Music.* Liberty, Utah: Eagle's View Publishing, 1998.

Swanson, Tod D. "Indian, American." *Encyclopedia Americana.* Danbury, CT: Grolier International, 1995.

Takaki, Ronald. *A Different Mirror: A History of Multicultural America.* New York: Little, Brown and Company, 1993.

Tanner, Helen Hornbec (ed.). *The Settling of North America.* New York: Macmillan, 1995.

Thornton, Russell. "Population," in *Native America in the Twentieth Century: An Encyclopedia.* Mary B. Davis (Editor). New York: Garland Publishing, Inc., 1994.

Wallace, William J. "Music and Musical Instruments." In *Handbook of American Indians,* vol. 8, pp. 642–648. William C. Sturtevant (General Editor). Washington, DC: Smithsonian Institution, 1978.

Women in North American Music. Urbana, IL: Society for Ethnomusicology, 1989.

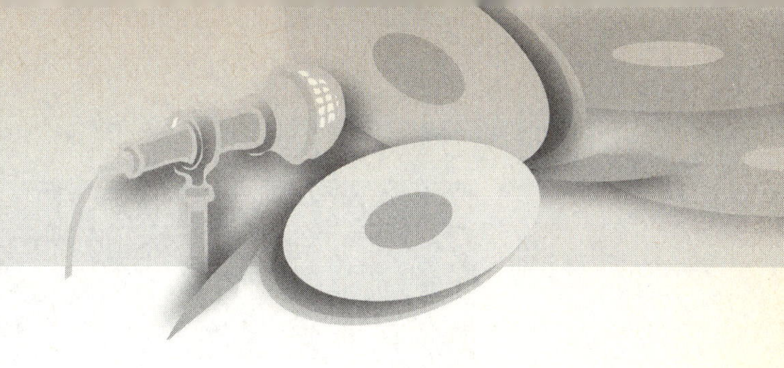

Chapter Three

The Roots of European/Anglo-American Music

A quick glance at any mainstream American entertainment magazine or online CD site demonstrates quickly the impact of changing demographics on the music industry. Many of today's most popular musicians are of mixed ethnic and racial ancestry. Yet a "snapshot" of top pop sellers taken in early 2005 shows that most solo musicians (such as Madeleine Peyroux and Alison Krauss) and group members (such as those in Greenday and Maroon5) continue to be of European descent. This should not be too surprising, as citizens of European descent still constitute the vast majority of people in America. In the last census, whites accounted for 75.1 percent of the total resident population. The large percentage of European Americans exists primarily because during much of its history, the United States had an official policy of admitting more European immigrants than Asian, African, and Latin American immigrants. Changes in immigration policy during the 1960s resulted in large numbers of non-European immigrants entering the United States. This trend has continued, contributing to the multicultural dimensions of contemporary American life. Nevertheless, European Americans continue to play a dominant role in shaping mainstream American culture.

European American Origins

Early European Visits to North America

Europeans had been making sporadic visits to the North American continent for centuries before they came as colonists. Norseman traded strips of crimson cloth in exchange for animal skins with "Skraelings" along the North Atlantic coast by 1000 C.E. Whalers and fishermen from a variety of northern European ports had occasional contact with Native Americans over the subsequent centuries. There also were probably numerous unrecorded contacts between the peoples of the Americas and Europe. In 1492, Christopher Columbus sailed on behalf of the monarchs of Spain, and after three months of sailing, approached a small, flat island in the Bahamas that most scholars now believe was Samana Cay (about 150 miles northeast of present-day Cuba). He continued to explore other islands, capturing several Taino natives to take back as curiosities for the Spanish court before heading home. He made his second trip to the Americas in 1493 to begin colonization of several islands in the Caribbean. This was followed by French, Italian, and English

Columbus kept a journal of his travels, and this image accompanied his account of his voyage that was widely distributed throughout Europe. The picture shows Spanish King Ferdinand directing the voyage, with natives fleeing in terror, demonstrating Columbus's impression that Native Americans were vulnerable to conquest. The earliest depiction of Columbus landing in the New World: Colored woodcut from Giuliano Dati's Narrative of Columbus, Florence, 1493. *Source: The Granger Collection.*

explorations on both the Atlantic and Pacific coasts throughout the sixteenth century, with Spain combining exploration with conquest.

The first attempts at colonization by Europeans other than the Spanish soon followed, but the colonies did not survive. The Spanish massacred French Huguenots who had established a community on the coast of Florida in 1565. The English, under the leadership of Sir Walter Raleigh, established another colony named Roanoke on an island off North Carolina in 1585. It consisted of a few hundred men, women, and children, but the group was evacuated the following year and their replacements, who arrived in 1587, completely disappeared before a delayed rescue ship arrived four years later. Despite the disaster of Roanoke, Sir Walter Raleigh continued to finance expeditions, naming the area Virginia in honor of Elizabeth I, the Virgin Queen. These early expeditions also failed. The English defeat of the Spanish naval fleet in 1588 ended Spain's attempts to colonize the North Atlantic coast and opened the way for new attempts by non-Spanish colonists.

The Establishment of Non-Spanish European Colonies

Finally, in 1607, an English settlement survived. This was Jamestown, Virginia, a community to protect the

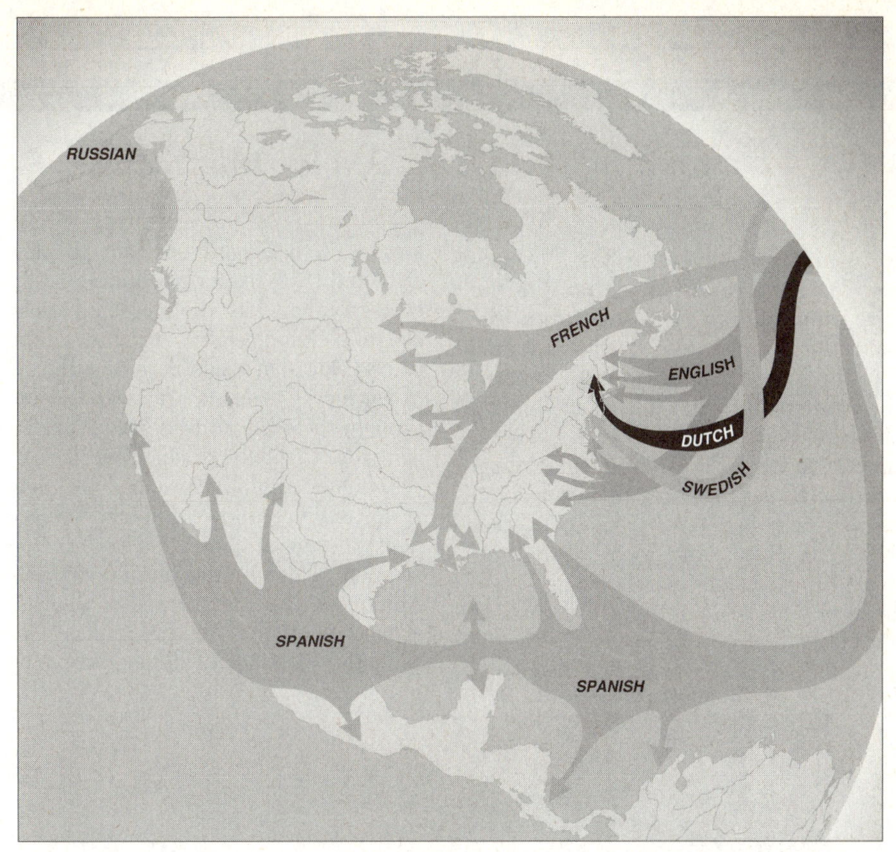

Starting in the late fifteenth century, the Spanish were the first Europeans to invade and conquer the Americas. Other European countries followed in the seventeenth century. In the nineteenth century, the Russians, entering from the northern Pacific, constituted the final colonial invasion.

London Company, a joint-stock company chartered for the purpose of trading and colonizing. Part of the reason that the Jamestown colony survived was that Pocahontas, the daughter of the chief of a powerful coalition of Native American tribes in the Chesapeake Bay region, intervened and asked her people to help the colonists. During the decade that followed, France and the Netherlands entered the competition for North American territory. In 1608, the French founded Quebec in order to control the Saint Lawrence River, the best available route to the interior. This brought vast areas of North America, including the entire Mississippi River Valley, under nominal French ownership. Henry Hudson, an English explorer in the employ of the Dutch East India Company, claimed as New Netherlands the area that is present-day New York, founding the town of New Amsterdam (now New York City) in 1609 and sending permanent colonists beginning in 1624.

Meanwhile, English colonizing activity had continued and in 1620, a group of forty-one English Separatists, a dissident sect that had previously withdrawn from the Church of England, received permission from the London Company to settle in Virginia. Because of a navigational error, their ship, the *Mayflower*, entered Massachusetts Bay instead. This group is known as the Pilgrim Fathers, and they founded Plymouth Colony on a site near the head of Cape Cod. Eight years later, another religious Separatist group known as the Puritans founded the Massachusetts Bay Colony. Then in 1635, the English founded the colony of Connecticut, and in 1636, the colony of Rhode Island. By 1640, twenty thousand English had migrated to "New England." Thus, by the middle of

Break-Out One

INSIGHT *Understanding the Term "Anglo-American"*

"Whites" are sometimes called "Anglo-Americans." The term "Anglo" comes from "Anglo-Saxon," the names of two Germanic tribes (the Angles and the Saxons) who began invading England in the second half of the fifth century. These tribes were participating in a general migration of Germanic peoples into what had been the powerful, but now steadily weakening, Roman Empire. By the seventh century, they had dominated the area and had driven out the earlier Romanized Celtic Britons into Wales. "England" was originally "Engle lande," which means "Angle land." The term "Anglo-Saxon" began to be used as early as the eleventh century to refer to the people who now lived there, and it eventually became a loose term for English-speaking peoples. Between 1815 and 1850, the term acquired racial overtones, corresponding with the increased scientific interest in defining, classifying, and ranking human races. Caucasian Anglo-Saxons, as the descendants of ancient Germanic tribes that had originally brought the seeds of free institutions to England, were now said to be the best race in the world.

Only Anglo-Saxons had the energy, work ethic, and innate love of liberty to succeed in the new experiment to create a free, democratic government. This superior racial pedigree gave white Americans the natural and God-given right to expand westward—their "Manifest Destiny"—to carry the blessings of democracy and progress.[1]

In this 1872 painting by John Gast, the spirit of America's Manifest Destiny forces Native Americans to relocate as she guides white settlers west to spread American civilization. John Gast (active 1870s). *American Progress*, © 1872.
Source: Christie's Images, Inc. © Christie's Images, Inc. 2004.

[1] Goldfield, David, Carl Abbot, Virginia DeJohn Anderson, Jo Ann E. Argersinger, William L. Barney, and Robert M. Weir, *The American Journey: A History of the United States.* Combined Volume, Second Edition. Upper Saddle River, NJ: Prentice Hall, 2001.

the seventeenth century, Western Europeans—particularly British Europeans—had established the colonial presence that would profoundly influence the course of American cultural and political history.

Overview of European-American Music Traditions

As with every other ethnic and racial group, European Americans are diverse, coming from many different countries, each with its own history, language and cultural heritage. European Americans rarely self-identify as being "European," but, rather, as being of (for example) "German" or "French" or "mixed" ethnicity. Yet just as commonalities can be identified in the music traditions of the other broad ethnic and racial constituencies, so can commonalities be identified in the traditions of European Americans.

Commonalities of European-American Music

Music Can Be Organized into Three Main Categories

The music of European immigrants can be roughly organized into three main categories: religious music, "art" music (popularly referred to as "classical" music), and popular music.

Religious Music. Religious music was among the earliest forms of music brought by European settlers to America. The music reflected the diversity of European religious practices, but was organized into two broad categories, Catholic and Protestant. Early immigrants from Spain, Italy, France, and Ireland—countries with strong Catholic affiliations—brought the religious music that had been shaped by the liturgical music of the Roman Catholic Church. The music for Catholic services had its roots in the stylistic period known as the Renaissance (1450–1600), a period that was characterized by a sound ideal of richly woven polyphony into a single smooth composition of modal harmonies. Immigrants from Great Britain, Germany, and the Netherlands—countries that had participated strongly in the Protestant revolution—brought the religious music shaped by composers for Protestant services. Protestant music had its roots in a new musical style referred to as the "Baroque" (1600–1750), a period that was characterized by a sound ideal that valued diversity and the juxtaposition of contrasting elements. Baroque music retained the polyphony of the Renaissance but added the new homophonic textures. Composers also shifted from the earlier modes to the major and minor harmonic system.

"Classical" Music. Among the early European immigrants, "classical" music was generally the music of the middle- and upper-class people who lived in the cities. The first settlers brought with them the tradition of Renaissance group singing, especially a popular type of secular song called the madrigal. Madrigals were clever, sophisticated poems set to music in polyphonic texture, consisting of five or six distinct and independent melodies. They were generally sung without instrumental accompaniment, and the singers found both aesthetic and intellectual pleasure in the clever manner in which the madrigal composer captured the meaning of the words in the music.

The early colonists also brought instruments with them to perform in amateur concerts in colonial churches, halls, and homes. The most popular instruments were the ones that were portable and could be transported easily on the long journey to America: a type of end-blown flute called a recorder, and string instruments of the viol or violin family. Later settlers also brought keyboards such as clavichords, harpsichords, and spinets, and as communities matured and travel and shipping routes became more dependable, immigrants brought a great variety of European-made instruments.

At first, American musicians simply transplanted European musical styles. In fact, many of the colonial and early American composers were born and trained in European countries. Eventually, American-born classical composers attempted to create their own styles based on their European heritage. This classical music tradition is amply covered in other books, so we will not discuss it further here.

Popular Music. This is a rubric for a wide range of music that is distinct from classical music in that it is music that is created for all people, regardless of their position in society. It is the music that is part of our everyday environment. In contemporary music, it includes everything from alternative rock to the music that provides background for films and television shows. During the first century of American existence, popular music was frowned on because it was considered to be potentially immoral. But one kind of popular music was brought in despite religious scruples, and that was "folk music." Folk music is the songs and instrumental pieces of the common people that have been passed on from generation to generation. Because in early periods the common people were generally illiterate, folk music was traditionally transmitted orally through performance and learned through hearing rather than through reading notation. Transmitted orally from one generation to the next, music in the folk genre tends to be musically simple and easily performed by nontrained musicians.

Music Is Generally Based on Notation

The method used for writing down music is called notation. Notation must be able to represent two main properties of musical sound: pitch and duration. Attempts had been made to devise symbols for each of these properties throughout the early Middle Ages. By the late Middle Ages, pitch and duration began to be integrated into one symbol, and this became the basis for European notation. Notation had been developed primarily in order to write down the increasingly complex music of the Roman Catholic Church. By the time of the first colonies, European music notation had become fairly standardized and contained the basic elements that are used in the notation system we use today. One of the books brought over by the first pilgrims was a book of musically notated religious songs. Notated music continues to be a hallmark of the European musical style and is now used to compose and transmit all types of music.

There Is a Separation Between Composer and Performer

A notated tradition encourages the specialization of people who compose music and people who perform music. In European music, the composers may not be very good performers, and performers need not be able to compose their own music. This specialization was the basis for the growth of the virtuosic performer in the nineteenth and twentieth centuries. Furthermore, except in the genre of folk music, composers are individuals who consider the music that they compose an expression of their personal identity. The early years of the European colonies in America coincided with the Baroque period in music history. During this period (1685–1750), composers were considered to be craftsmen, and they worked in the employment of the aristocracy or the church. The Baroque period was followed by the Classical period (1750–1825), a period that saw the gradual shift from the patronage system to the freelance composer. During the next period, the Romantic Period (1825–1900), audiences and consumers began to look at composers as special human beings who were gifted with unique and innate musical talent.

European-Based Music Tends to Have Similar and Familiar Structural Elements

Although there is a great deal of diversity geographically, and there have been changes throughout time, there are several commonalities within the structural building blocks of European-based music. Because European immigrants have been most influential in shaping mainstream American culture, it is not surprising that European-based music is also most familiar to Americans.

We will now turn our attention to a more specific European-American music tradition. Because the settlers who were most influential in shaping early European-American culture came from Britain, we will focus on the music traditions of British or "Anglo" Americans in this chapter.

Early Anglo-American Music Traditions

The Structural Characteristics of Anglo-American Folk Music

Rhythm, Melody, and Harmony

The earlier, rural versions of folk songs are often in a free rhythm derived from the text, a characteristic that is related to the fact that many of these were sung without instrumental accompaniment. Most melodies are simple, so that they could be easily learned and easily remembered. Their notes typically span a rather limited range. The earlier versions of folk songs use older scales known as the ecclesiastical modes. These modes are the predecessors of our major and minor system, and bear names such as Dorian, Phrygian, Lydian, and Mixolydian. The Dorian and Mixolydian modes appear to be particularly common in the folk songs of English origin.

Texture, Form, and Instrumentation

The early performance of folk song was in a monophonic texture. Sometimes a drone (a drone is one note or chord repeated or sustained under a melody) accompanied the single melody. The musical arrangements of later folk songs often added vocal harmonies to create homophonic texture, and are accompanied by an instrument, usually the guitar or banjo. The most common folk song form is strophic, in which the various stanzas of text are set to the same music. A very popular stanza type consists of four lines of text set to four musical phrases, sometimes all different (ABCD) but more frequently, incorporating some level of repetition (such as AABA, AABC, AABA, etc.). The fiddle was the most popular instrument originally in colonial America, but it was used mostly for dance tunes and not for accompanying singers. Instruments to accompany singers, in the approximate order of when they were introduced into the folk song tradition, are the dulcimer, banjo, autoharp, guitar, and stringed bass.

Anglo-American Music Within a Social and Historical Context

Religious Music of the Colonial Period

The Pilgrims and the Puritans

The Pilgrims who established their colony in 1620 had come from Leyden, Holland, because the church to which they had belonged in London had been forced to flee Britain. The Pilgrims brought with them to Plymouth a tradition of singing unaccompanied settings of the psalms, which are sacred poems in the Old Testament of the Christian Bible. The first settlers were quite competent musically, and they used as their psalm book, the *Ainsworth Psalter,* which had been published in Amsterdam in 1612. This Psalter is particularly interesting in that it contained an international (for that time) collection of settings from England, France, and the Netherlands, and its settings used a variety of different meters. These settings reflected the emerging Baroque style.

In 1630, the Puritans (who came directly from England) brought with them a similar psalm-singing tradition, although they used a different book called the *Sternhold and Hopkins Psalter.* Dissatisfied with the translations of the psalms in this book, the Puritans produced their own, called *The Whole Booke of Psalmes Faithfully Translated into English Metre* in 1640, which soon became known as the *Bay Psalm Book.* This was the first book to be printed in the British colonies of North America, and it is particularly interesting in that it contained no music, just the psalm words. Users were told to sing the words to "very neere forty common tunes." Their main interest was not the music (later editions added melodies for reference) but the words, and they tried to create translations of the psalms that flowed naturally in the English language.

THE DETERIORATION AND REFORM OF RELIGIOUS MUSIC

These first Pilgrims and Puritans were good musicians, but the later settlers were not, so subsequent collections of psalm settings reduced the number of melodies and replaced the varied meters with common time. Furthermore, most of the later colonists could not read music, so the settings were taught by oral tradition rather than notation, and by the practice of "lining out." Lining out was a process by which a deacon would assist the congregation by reading or singing each line of the psalm before it was sung by the group. By the beginning of the eighteenth century, the deterioration in the musical ability of the congregation was disturbing enough to inspire the religious leaders to launch a vigorous program of reform.

The reform of religious music was achieved through the establishment of singing schools. The singing schools used two kinds of books: theory books and tune books. Theory books taught the rudiments of music theory so that people could learn to read music. Several early instruction books were published, such as *The Grounds and Rules of Musick Explained* in Boston in 1721. The second type of book, called a tune book, provided the melodies. One of the most famous and successful musicians associated with the reform movement was William Billings, who was a singing schoolmaster, a tune book compiler, and a composer. He published a collection of his own tunes called *The New England Psalm-Singer: or, American Chorister* in Boston in 1770.

RELIGIOUS MUSIC BECOMES MORE COMPLEX

Although Billings was the most prominent and influential composer, several others followed, including Supply Belcher, Jeremiah Ingalls, Oliver Holden, and Samuel Holyoke. More than three hundred tune books were produced between 1770 and 1820. These tune book compositions were the first pieces by Europeans born in the United States, and constitute what has since been designated as the first New England "school" of music. As time went on and the congregation became more musically capable, the music became more complex. The later tune books included four basic types of compositions. The first was the "plain tune," which was a melody set in a homophonic texture of syllabic setting in four voices. This setting also was "strophic," in which the same melody was used for a series of different verses of text.

The second type of composition was the "fuging tune." The fuging tunes were generally in three parts, following an ABB form. The "A" section consisted of a plain tune harmonized in homophonic texture leading to a cadence. A cadence is a chord formula that serves a function analogous to punctuation in the written language. A "half cadence" is similar to a comma; a "full cadence" is similar to a period. The "B" section, which was repeated, was in polyphonic texture. The type of polyphony is called "imitative" polyphony, as each voice enters separately but imitates the previous voice. "Rounds" such as "Row, Row, Row Your Boat" are examples of imitative polyphony.

A third category of composition was the "set piece," which was a "through-composed" setting. Through-composed is the opposite of strophic. Rather than having the same melody used for difference verses of text, through-composed means that new melodies are composed throughout the text. The final category of music was the "anthem." It also was the most elaborate. Like the set piece, anthems also were through-composed, but they were more extended and complex.

The teaching of vocal music through singing schools that used theory books and tune books containing music of religious character was a pattern that dominated American music until 1820, thus bridging the periods of colony to independence. The method was very successful, and even before the end of the eighteenth century, churches in the larger towns and cities contained singers capable of performing the most difficult Baroque and early Classical religious music. There also was another category of music that was important: folk music.

In the Blue Ridge Mountains of the southern Appalachian chain, people maintained British folk traditions by singing folk songs to accompany work and to provide recreation. Settlers' log cabin in the Blue Ridge Mountains (Appalachians). Hand-colored woodcut.
Source: North Wind Picture Archives.

Folk Music of the Early Settlers

Most of the first colonists who had come to New England came to escape religious persecution. Both the Pilgrims and the Puritans were different sects of the same English Separatist movement (later known as the Congregationalists) that encouraged its members to practice an extremely rigorous and pure (hence, "Puritan") moral code. They had come to the colonies to find a place where they could practice their religion in peace. Religion was extremely important to them and they generally disapproved of secular music. Yet, as time went on, different kinds of settlers with different values and motivations began pouring into New England. These colonists were attempting to escape poverty; some were criminals sent away from Great Britain to relieve the British Isles from having to care for them, and some were refugees of political change. These settlers were often from the lower classes. Most were illiterate, and they came to the colonies as indentured servants, farmers, and laborers. They were not so inclined to pay attention to the religious disapproval of secular music, and they brought with them a thriving folk music tradition.

Folk Song

Folk songs are songs of the common people. They express the thoughts and feelings of ordinary human beings, and although individuals may compose songs, historically those individuals have tended to remain anonymous. In the New England colonies, the folk songs were sung without accompaniment unless someone happened to have an instrument such as a fiddle or a dulcimer. Most of the words of the songs were in English, but the melodies came from England, Scotland, and Ireland. There were several kinds of folk songs, and following are the basic types.

Members of the original Carter Family grew up in the Applachian Mountains and knew hundreds of folk songs dating back to the earliest British immigrants. Their recordings, begun in the late 1920s, were heard all over America. Carter family—Maybelle, Alvin P., wife Sara; country harmony singers, Appalachian folk songs circa 1937. *Source: Getty Images, Inc. Hulton Archive Photos.*

FOLK SONG CATEGORIES

Ballads. These are songs that tell a story, such as "Barbara Allen." An important category of ballads is the "Child Ballads," named after the American-born Harvard scholar Francis James Child (1825–1896), who made the study of English and Scottish ballads his lifelong work. His complete collection of 305 traditional ballads catalogued related versions of the same song into one group that he then gave a number. "Barbara Allen," for example, is Child Ballad 84 and contains 198 variants of the basic ballad. "The Elfin King" is Child Ballad 2 and contains fifty-five variants. We will return to the discussion of Child Ballads momentarily.

"Broadside Ballads" is a special category of ballads that flourished in the eighteenth and nineteenth centuries. These ballads had their origins in England in the sixteenth century, and they acquired their name because in England (and later in the United States) they were customarily printed and circulated on a large sheet of paper called a broadside. Sometimes just the text would be printed, sometimes the text would be printed with an indication of which well-known melody the text should be sung with, and sometimes the melody also would be printed. Many American folk songs have been traced back to these popular broadside ballads.

Lyric Songs. Instead of a story, lyric songs convey a particular feeling or mood. They tend to be more private and introspective in nature than the dramatic and entertaining ballads. Many of them are love songs, with a favorite topic being unrequited love. Examples of lyric songs include "Careless Love" and "The Water Is Wide."

Work Songs. These songs originated as songs to work by, and include railroad songs, lumber songs, and sea chanteys designed to move to a beat similar to the rhythm with which one would strike with a sledge hammer, wield an ax, or row with an oar. "I've Been Working on the Railroad" is an example of a railroad song. "Michael Row the Boat Ashore" is an example of a type of sea chantey, which originated in the Georgia Sea Islands where early transportation was provided by small boats; it is likely that the song was first composed to accompany the rowing between islands.

Children's Songs. Simple songs sung by and for children, these songs are typically associated with a function. This category includes lullabies to help children fall asleep, songs to accompany games, and nonsense and humorous songs to provide children with amusement. "Twinkle, Twinkle, Little Star," "Skip to My Lou," and "Rock-a-Bye Baby" are examples of children's folk songs.

The Americanization of British Folk Songs

The British songs were first simply transplanted on to American soil. But as successive generations became native-born, the songs became Americanized. Passed on from one generation to the next through oral tradition, and because there was not the motivation to preserve a song precisely (as there was in many indigenous cultures because of the connection of song to sacred ritual), change was encouraged. Singers attempted to "localize" the songs, to make the lyrics more relevant by changing the geographical names or the names of the participants to something more familiar. Additionally, there might be a kind of conscious or unconscious censorship in which singers selectively remembered according to their own moral standards or those of the society within which they were singing. In terms of the words, singers might have misunderstood the words, or misunderstood the meaning of the words or phrase, because they were no longer in current usage or in usage in a particular locale.

Two Examples of Change and Continuity

Child Ballad 2: "The Elfin King". In the massive collection of British folk songs, *The Traditional Tunes of the Child Ballads,* there are fifty-five versions of a famous ballad that has the category name of "The Elfin King" but that is also known by other names, including "Scarborough Fair" and "The Cambric Shirt." The oldest version of this ballad is dated 1670. Following is a series of variations on the phrase, "Savory, sage, rosemary, and thyme," in approximate order of presumably increasing distance from the original refrain:

> Savory, sage, rosemary, and thyme.
> Save rosemary and thyme.
> Rose Mary in time.
> Rose de Marian Time.
> Every rose grows merry in time.
> Every leaf grows many a time.
> So sav'ry was said come marry in time.
> Whilst every grove rings with a merry antine.
> Green grows the merry antine.[2]

In 1966, Simon and Garfunkel made the folk song famous with yet another version of this line in the song "Scarborough Fair/Canticle" on their album *Parsley, Sage, Rosemary, and Thyme.* Just as the words changed, so did the melodies, and for many of the same reasons. A singer may not have heard the melody accurately from the person from whom he learned it. They might modify it to fit

[2] Kingman, Daniel, *American Music: A Panorama.* New York: Schirmer Books, 1979, p. 8.

Break-Out Two

LISTENING GUIDE *"Barbara Allen"*[3]

Performing Artists: J. D. Cornett, Jean Ritchie, Pete Seeger

One of the most popular kinds of folk songs is the ballad, a song that tells a story. This is one of the ballads collected by Francis Child (1825–1895), who made the study of English and Scottish ballads his lifelong work.

Originating on the British Isles (the English and Scottish both claim it), it has remained popular, and now there are hundreds of versions of the song.

These three versions demonstrate changes in words and the evolving style from the early rural traditions to the urban folk revival.

J. B. Cornett, a traditional singer from Masons Creek, Kentucky, performs Example 1.

Example 2 is a version performed by Jean Ritchie. Born in Viper, Kentucky, in 1922, Jean was the youngest of fourteen children. (Members of the Ritchie family were famous as singers of traditional music, and had been visited by collector Cecil Sharp in 1917 in one of his song-collecting tours of Appalachia). Ritchie made her first recording in 1948. After getting a degree in social work, she moved to New York, where she recorded some songs for another famous collector of traditional music, Alan Lomax. She went on to an impressive career, with frequent radio and television appearances, as well as extensive performance tours of both the United States and the United Kingdom. She has made numerous recordings, and is regarded as one of the foremost singers of traditional mountain music.

Example 3 features Pete Seeger, one of the most important figures in American folk music, and central to the folk music revival of the 1960s. Pete was raised in a musical family: his father was the prominent musicologist Charles Seeger, his stepmother was composer Ruth Crawford Seeger, and his half-brother and sister were folk singers Mike and Peggy Seeger. Pete Seeger left Harvard in 1938, traveling throughout the United States singing and collecting songs with Alan Lomax for the Library of Congress Archive of Folk Music. Seeger was part of two important folk groups, the Almanac

[3] Santelli, Robert, Holly George Warren, and Jim Brown (Eds.) *American Roots Music.* New York: Rolling Stone Press, Published for Harry N. Abrams, Inc., 2001, p. 20.

current aesthetic tastes (such as changing an originally modal melody to a more contemporary major or minor melody). They might take new words and affix them to a melody that they already know or a melody with which their audiences were familiar (a practice frequently used in the broadside ballads of the eighteenth and nineteenth centuries).

Child Ballad 84: "Barbara Allen". Changes in the melody over time are evident in the ballad "Barbara Allen," one of the most popular ballads in both Great Britain and later in America. The first written reference to this folk song was in 1666, when the English author Samuel Pepys made the January 2 entry into his diary describing how he had just heard it sung by an actress. The editor of Child's collection of ballads, B. H. Bronson, begins his discussion of "Barbara Allen" with the comment, "This little song of a spineless lover who gives up the ghost without a struggle and of his spirited beloved who repents too late, has paradoxically shown a stronger will-to-live than perhaps any other

singers and the Weavers. Because of his politics, he was among those investigated by the House Un-American Activities Committee during the 1950s, but he was later exonerated. An American institution, Seeger was awarded the National Medal of Arts in 1994.

Rhythm	Compare the rhythm between all three versions. Notice that the first two more "authentic" rural versions use a very flexible, free rhythm derived from the text. The third version maintains a steady beat with the guitar, but Seeger uses a flexible rhythm for the vocal melody and sometimes drops beats so that his rendition retains a certain quality of rhythmic flexibility.
Melody	All three of the melodies are related, but each one sounds somewhat different due to the use of different scales and rhythms.
Harmony	The melody in Cornett's version is derived from a scale that does not have a clear identification, primarily because it is comprised of only six pitches. It sounds like the Dorian mode, but with a missing sixth scale degree. The melody in Ritchie's version is derived from a pentatonic scale. The melody in Seeger's utilizes a clear Bb major scale and reinforces the harmony with chordal accompaniment that is limited to the I, IV, and V primary triads. His melody also utilizes a clear major scale, this time B, and expands the tonal language of the basic primary chords by adding the vi chord.
Texture	The first two examples are in a monophonic texture, consisting of unaccompanied melody. Seeger's is in homophonic texture, consisting of melody with chordal accompaniment.
Form	This is an example of a ballad—a song that narrates a story—and it is one of the most popular types of folk songs. This ballad uses a strophic form, consisting of various stanzas of text set to the same music (represented by the same letter for each stanza, such as A A A A . . .). Each stanza is comprised of four lines, and these lines are set to four musical phrases with the pattern abcd.
Instrumentation	Cornett's is solo male voice, Ritchie's is solo female voice, and Seeger's is solo male voice with guitar.

ballad in the canon."[4] Because of its enduring popularity, the ballad provides a great example of changing melody. Bronson provides 198 versions of the song. The Library of Congress Archive of American Folk Song had, by 1962, already collected 243 versions from 27 states.

The American music scholar Daniel Kingman likens the changes that occur in the words and the music of folk songs to what happens to buildings: none survive the passage of time intact. Those of exceptional strength may have only a few parts replaced here or there; others have whole new sections that expand them or that replace lost or ruined parts; and yet others have been so completely rebuilt that only a fragment is left to remind people of its existence in a much earlier age.[5]

[4] Bronson, Bertrand Harris, *The Traditional Tunes of the Child Ballads.* Princeton: Princeton University Press, vol. II, p. 321 (first published 1959. Reprinted 1971).

[5] Kingman, Daniel, *American Music: A Panorama.* New York: Schirmer Books, 1979, p. 9.

Break-Out Three

IN-DEPTH FOCUS *Famous Patriotic Songs*

One of the most famous American songs derived from a folk ballad is the national anthem, "The Star Spangled Banner." As was the case with many other American ballads, the melody for the anthem was originally known in England as another song. This song—"The Anacreontic Song"—was a popular song in a London tavern called The Crown and Anchor. In the late eighteenth century it became popular throughout England and America. This melody was used as the setting for about eighty-five different printed American poems between 1790 and 1820. To understand how it eventually became the national anthem, it is fascinating to know the context in which that version was written.

In the early 1800s, a group of traditional Shawnees led by a warrior named Tecumseh attempted to escape white encroachment by moving further west. Tecumseh had a brother named Tenskwatawa, known as the Prophet, who began to preach a message of Indian revitalization through rejection of all American cultural attributes. Tenskwatawa promised, "The land will be overturned so that all the white people will be covered and you alone shall inhabit the land."[6] This powerful message attracted a significant pan-Indian resistance movement with a strategy that was initially defensive, but eventually became aggressive. In 1811, an American army with one thousand soldiers surrounded a pan-Indian village of Tecumseh's followers called Tippecanoe; the Indian warriors attacked and in the ensuing battle there were many casualties on both sides. Although the Americans claimed victory, the angry followers of Tecumseh attacked American settlements throughout Indiana and Michigan. Many Americans blamed the British for Tecumseh's attacks because the British had been supporting the western Indians in various disputes and encouraging them to resist. Hostilities increased, and on June 1, 1812, the American government declared war against Britain. Battles occurred on both land and sea, and in the summer of 1814, the British were able to invade the Chesapeake Bay and march to, and burn, the American capital of Washington, DC. On the night of September 13–14, the English attacked Fort McHenry near Baltimore, Maryland.

During the attack on Fort McHenry, an American named Francis Scott Key (1780–1843) was on board an English ship trying to secure the release of a friend who had been captured. As long as the bombardment continued, Key knew that the fort had not

[6] Faragher, John Mack, Mari Jo Buhle, Daniel Czitrom, and Susan H. Armitage, *Out of Many: A History of the American People.* Combined Edition, Third Edition. Upper Saddle River, NJ: Prentice Hall, 2000, p. 246.

NEW AMERICAN FOLK SONGS

As the years passed, not only were the British songs modified to suit American tastes but also there were newly composed American ballads and songs. In these songs, the theme and speech are American in character, but the form and melodies retain their clear connection to British traditions. The earliest ones were probably American words to British melodies, such as "The Buffalo Skinners," which was American words sung to a tune popular among British seamen known as "Canaday-i-o." Later American folk songs, such as "Sweet Betsy from Pike," used both original words and melodies, but their basic style was still British.

Instrumental Music of the Early Settlers

In addition to folk song, the new British immigrants also brought with them the tradition of

surrendered. But suddenly the bombs ceased, and Key paced the deck of the ship the entire night worrying over whether the English attack had been successful. At dawn, he turned his telescope to the fort and saw that "our flag was still there," and was assured that the Americans had won. He was released, and he wrote the poem on board the tender boat back to shore.

> Oh say, can you see
> By the dawn's early light
> What so proudly we hail at the twilight's last gleaming?
> Whose broad stripes and bright stars through the perilous night
> O'er the ramparts we watched were so gallantly streaming,
> And the rocket's red glare, the bombs bursting in air
> Gave proof through the night that our flag was still there.
> Oh say does that star spangled banner yet wave
> O'er the land of the free, and the home of the brave?

The poem was published a few days later as a broadside under the title "Defence of Fort M'Henry," with the instructions that it should be sung to the tune of "Anacreon." A few weeks later, it was published as "The Star Spangled Banner," and it became immensely popular. The gigantic shell-holed flag that Francis Scott Key saw flying over Fort McHenry is now one of the principal attractions at the Smithsonian Institution in Washington, DC. The song itself became the official anthem in 1931.

The patriotic song "My Country 'Tis of Thee" also was written as a broadside. The lyrics for this song were a poem, "Celebration of American Independence," written in 1831 by Samuel Francis Smith, a clergyman and hymn writer from Boston (1808–1895). Again, the melody for this poem had a much earlier history. Ironically, the melody is also the melody to the British national anthem, "God Save the King," which in turn was based on an older melody that was probably a folk ballad.[7]

Patriotic songs change popularity as the mood of the country changes. For example, for several decades there has been an ongoing debate regarding "The Star Spangled Banner" and its status as the national anthem. A vocal group of Americans has argued for change from this battle-based song to the more pacifistic song "America the Beautiful." "America the Beautiful" was originally a poem by Katherine Lee Bates (1859–1929), a professor of English Literature at Wellesley College, which she wrote one day in 1895 as she stood on the summit of Pikes Peak in Colorado. The earliest known joining of this poem with the melody—originally a nineteenth-century Christian hymn entitled "O Mother Dear, Jerusalem"—was 1910.

[7] *The Book of World-Famous Music;* Fourth Edition, Revised and Enlarged, James J. Fuld, Dover Publications, Inc. Mineola, N.Y. 1966; 1995.

communal social dancing. Peasants of the British Isles had for centuries entertained themselves in taverns and at events such as weddings and outdoor gatherings with dances that they accompanied with a fiddle. A fiddle is the same instrument as a violin, but it is played in a folk style. Fiddle playing uses little or no vibrato (an important characteristic of classical violin playing), short, quick strokes of the bow (as opposed to the long, lyrical bowed notes of most classical violin playing), and a full, deep sound (to provide the volume needed to accompany dancing). Furthermore, fiddle players up until the twentieth century played with the instrument held against their chest rather than under their chin (which is customary for classical violin players).

In the mid-seventeenth century, the cultured classes in England developed a fancy for dancing in styles patterned after those done by peasants. One or two fiddles accompanied these "country dances" playing music modeled after the peasants' music. In the country dances, the

The fiddle—a European violin played in a folk style—was one of the most popular instruments of the early British settlers. A fiddler from the Blue Ridge Mountains plays next to a guitar player. Asheville, North Carolina, 1937.
Source: Corbis/Bettman.

dancers faced each other in two rows with men on one side of the room and women on the other. The couple at the head of the line would dance moving down the center between the two rows and take their place at the end of the line, while the next couple followed suit. These dances had several attractions: any number of people could participate, individuals didn't have to be part of a couple, the dances were less disciplined than couples dancing, and inexperienced dancers could observe and then imitate the more capable dancers. Thus, country dancing was a fun, social, participatory affair and not an aristocratic display of grace and skill. In England, John Playford's *The English Dancing Master; or Plain and Easie Rules for the Dancing of Country Dances,* first published in 1651, contained the music for over one hundred dances. This music was notated on a single line without accompaniment and played on the fiddle.

Both the original peasant dances and the country dances modeled after the peasant dances were popular in the colonies. The country dances, particularly, became a favorite pastime of the more literate classes, especially after the Revolution. The first book of dance music to be published in the United States was brought out in 1788 by John Griffith, and titled *A Collection of the Newest and Most Fashionable Country Dances and Cotillions.*

Hence, the instrumental folk music was passed on in a combination of oral and written traditions. Many fiddlers were nonliterate, learning the tunes by ear and teaching the tunes to others

Break-Out Four

INSIGHT *The American Tradition of Square Dance Calling*

In the early "country" dancing of the colonies, each fiddle tune was associated with a given dance comprised of specific dance steps, or "figures." If the fiddler announced the name of the tune, this was sufficient information to tell the dancers which of the sequence of figures should be danced. At some point in the early nineteenth century, a new practice of having someone shout out, or "call" the sequence of movements for each dance began. Following is a description of a dance in the mountains of Kentucky:

> Eight hands up, circle to the left! Half way back on a single line! Lady before and gent behind! First gent lead out and swing his partner! First to the right and then to the left! Don't forget the two-hand swing! Break to the left on the Wild Goose Chase, and around that lady! Back to the right, and around that gent! Take on four and circle to the left! Half way and back on a single line! Lady before and gent behind! Swing your opposite partner, and promenade your own![8]

This American innovation of "calling" was very amusing to Europeans. In 1832, a Mrs. Trollop wrote in her *Domestic Manners of the Americans,* "the figures are called from the orchestra in English, which has a very ludicrous effect on European ears." But despite the fact that visitors to the United States found the practice funny, the tradition of "calling" flourished, and is an integral part of square and line dancing today.

[8] Quoted in Hamm, Charles, *Music in the New World.* New York: W.W. Norton and Company, 1983, p. 75.

in the same way. Others were able to read music, although performance practice required them to always play from memory. Thus, like the folk songs, the repertory of fiddle tunes was constantly growing and subtly changing, and the identity of whoever initially composed a tune was lost in obscurity.

Conflict and the Road to Revolution

The English colonies continued to be affected by developments in England. Persecution of the Puritans by Charles I drove numerous refugees to America and, in England, provoked the English Revolution in 1642 that eventually led to Charles's execution and the founding of the Commonwealth. As Parliament replaced the monarchy as the real ruler, the English government began instituting a series of increasingly stringent laws designed to regulate the colonies and to prevent them from working with any nations other than English nations. Because colonial prosperity was dependent on free commercial interchange, there was growing resentment against the home government, and smuggling and other illicit activities became fundamental features of American trade and industry.

In 1660, following the death of Oliver Cromwell (the political ruler of the Commonwealth), Charles II was restored to the throne. The new government seized New Netherlands (present-day New York) from the Dutch and increased attempts to curtail the independent attitude of the colonies. In 1689, with the Glorious Revolution in England and the accession of William and Mary and the later succession of Anne, the countries of Scotland and Wales were politically united with England, forming Great Britain. This new union challenged its French rival for colonial power in North America. The ensuing struggle, lasting for nearly three quarters of a century and fought in many parts of the world, manifested itself in North America with the French and Indian War (1754–63) in which the British, with the assistance of the powerful Iroquois, fought the French and their many Indian tribe allies.

The French and Indian War was just one manifestation of what had become a contest between the different European powers for domination of the entire North American continent. France was severely hurt by Great Britain and its allies in the European extension of the conflict (Seven Years' War). The British colonials, aided by the Iroquois, enjoyed an almost unbroken sequence of victories leading to French capitulation in 1763. Under the terms of the treaty, French holdings in the region east of the Mississippi and in what is now Canada were ceded to Great Britain. Spain—an ally of France during the war—surrendered Spanish Florida but was granted control of French territories west of the Mississippi.

The Founding of a New Nation

The British colonies emerged from the French-Indian war with all of the attributes required to create their own nation. They had the informal unification that resulted from their having to cooperate with each other during the war, and they had the confidence that came from victory in battle. By contrast, the British government, now technically the most powerful European government in both hemispheres, had greatly extended itself in order to win the war and had doubled the national debt. In order to recover financially, the government started looking for ways to increase revenues. In the colonies, they revived direct taxes and instituted other revenue-producing legislation such as the Stamp Act, which required Americans to validate transactions by buying and applying royal-issued stamps. These actions aroused widespread opposition among the colonists. In 1770, British soldiers dispersed a crowd of hecklers in Boston with gunfire, producing the first bloodshed of the conflict (the Boston Massacre).

As tensions increased, colonial leaders gathered together in 1774 in the First Continental Congress and drafted a petition to the British sovereign, George III, requesting redress of their various grievances. The petition was denied, the protest was seen as a rebellion, and on April 18, 1775, colonial leaders such as John Hancock and Samuel Adams were arrested. The following day, British troops fought colonial militia at Lexington and Concord, the first battle of the American Revolution. The Second Continental Congress convened in Philadelphia on May 10, 1775, and formally invested itself with intercolonial governmental authority. The idea of becoming an independent country gained hold, and on July 4, 1776, members of the Congress signed the Declaration of Independence, heralding the creation of a new nation. The Revolutionary War went on for seven years, formally ending on September 3, 1783, with the signing of the Treaty of Paris. Through the terms of this treaty, Great Britain was forced to recognize the former colonies as a new independent nation—the United States of America—and to acknowledge the new nation's boundaries as extending west to the Mississippi, north to Canada, and south to the Floridas.

Yankee Doodle

One of the most famous songs associated with the American Revolution is the song "Yankee Doodle." The melody for this song seems to have come from England, where it was called "Fisher's Jig." Legend has it that when Oliver Cromwell, the leader of the Commonwealth in England, rode his horse (this would have been about 1650), he wore an Italian-style hat with a long feather known as a "macaroni," and Cromwell's enemies sang the words "stuck a feather in his cap and called it macaroni" to the melody of this jig. The word "Yankee" was a contemptuous nickname the British soldiers gave to the colonists, and it is derived either from the Dutch word "Janke" meaning "Little John," or from the Indian pronunciation of the word "English"—"Yenghis." The word "doodle" was a derisive term that meant "idiot" or "fool." The first version of the song seems to have appeared during the French and Indian War (1754–1763) among the soldiers. Meanwhile, the melody returned to England where it became a children's folk song to accompany a game called "Lucy Locket."[9]

The written history of this song begins in 1767, when an American comic opera titled *The Disappointment: or The Force of Credulity* by the composer Andrew Barton was published in New York City. In the opera, there are stage directions informing the chorus to "Exit, singing the chorus, yankee doodle." No music for the song was provided, so it must have been well known in the colonies during this time. "Yankee Doodle" developed into the most important song of the American Revolution, as colonist soldiers added lyrics that eventually became their battle cry. They sang it at their Concord victory (1775) as well as other victories, especially in Yorktown (1781) when General Cornwallis surrendered to George Washington.[10]

The first printing of the music was in England in 1782. Because almost no secular music was printed in the colonies until five years after the conclusion of the Revolutionary War in 1783, it is not surprising that the first printing of the music was published in England.[11] Hence the song "Yankee Doodle" appears to have been created in the typical folk song process: someone whose name is now unknown created words to an older melody on a topic of much interest at the time, the strife between the English and the American colonials. The song became popular, various versions of the words were transmitted or created, the song was disseminated, and became part of the ever-evolving repertoire of folk songs that is passed on from generation to generation.

Conclusion

Following the Revolutionary War, the nation grew quickly. In the two decades between the first census in 1790 and the third in 1810, the total number of people nearly doubled from 3,900,000 to 7,224,000, an average growth rate of more than 35 percent per decade. With rare exceptions, these colonists had been British immigrants, and hence the population by 1830 was still remarkably homogeneous. The citizens shared the same basic religion (Congregationalist Protestant), language, social organization, and general outlook.

But conditions in Europe, such as the political repression following the end of the Napoleonic Wars in 1815 and a series of agricultural problems in Ireland that began in 1816, gave Europeans new reasons to migrate to America. The settlers who were fleeing the political crackdown following the Napoleonic Wars were primarily from Germany, but they also came from Belgium, the Netherlands, Switzerland, and Scandinavia. They brought to America their own language and their own musical traditions. The Irish settlers, although from the British Isles, were Roman Catholics. Both groups of settlers challenged the historical homogeneity of the English colonies.

As the new nation stabilized, and with the increasing industrialism and urbanization of the nineteenth century, an educated middle class and a wealthy upper class of self-made entrepreneurs developed. The religious music of these two groups absorbed the changes that were occurring in religious music throughout Europe. The "classical" music tradition that was originally simply transported to American soil continued to develop and become Americanized. As time went on, new immigrants—especially German and French immigrants—established their own music societies, orchestras, opera companies, and conservatories, which in turn gave birth to American composers and music traditions. The middle and upper classes of the now dominant urban society placed a strong value on refinement and the accoutrements of aristocratic culture, including "classical" music. Hence, these classical music traditions, and the lighter, popular music versions of the classical traditions, became the dominant music in America.

[9] Ralph, Theodore, *The American Song Treasury*. 1964, p. 35.

[10] Ibid.

[11] Fuld, James J., *The Book of World-Famous Music: Classical, Popular and Folk*. 4th Edition. New York: Dover Publications, Inc., 1995, pp. 659–660.

Break-Out Five

PROFILE *The Carter Family*

Members of the original Carter Family were born and raised in the Clinch Mountain area of Virginia, where they grew up singing the old folk ballads of their British ancestors. Alvin Pleasant (A. P.) Delaney Carter (1891–1960) was one of nine children in a very musical family. He was a restless character, and would often wander through the sparsely populated mountains and valleys, collecting songs from the occasional people he'd meet. On one of his journeys he met a young girl named Sara Dougherty (1898–1979). Sara was an orphan, and had a quiet, withdrawn personality, but she enjoyed singing the typically melancholy ballads that were part of the Appalachian tradition. The couple married in 1915 and settled down near Maces Springs. Sara had learned to play autoharp, banjo, and guitar and would sing lead or accompany A. P.'s bass singing or fiddle playing. The couple entertained neighbors with mostly traditional folk songs or folk song variations. Sara's cousin Maybelle (1909–1979) occasionally joined them, playing guitar in a style in which she plucked the melody or bass line on the lower strings with her thumb while she strummed the chords on the upper strings with the backs of her fingertips. This style, called "the Carter scratch" or "lick," has been emulated by many folksingers.

In the early days of radio, when stations were searching for recorded material to play, an A & R (artists and repertoire) executive for Victor Records named Ralph Peer came out from New York and set up a temporary recording studio in an old hat factory on the Virginia-Tennessee border town of Bristol. He circulated fliers that he would be willing to pay $50 per song (a large sum at the time) for any "hillbilly" musicians he decided to record. The Carter Family heard of the offer, and traveled down from the mountains to audition. When Peer first met them, he was not impressed; they were truly "hillbillies" in both dress and manner. But when they sang and played, his doubts vanished. "As soon as I heard Sara's voice," he recalled years later, "I knew it was going to be wonderful."[11] This recording made history, and over the next seventeen years, the Carter Family recorded approximately three hundred songs in ever-widening genres. As they popularized and preserved the folk music traditions they had grown up with in the mountains, they laid the foundations for what would become the Urban Folk Revival (influencing musicians such as Woody Guthrie, Pete Seeger, and Bob Dylan) and country music (influencing musicians such as Chet Atkins, Johnny Cash, and Waylon Jennings).

The folk music traditions that had thrived with the earlier colonials receded into the backwoods rural communities such as the Appalachian Mountains, or went west with the pioneers. By the end of the nineteenth century, scholars and musicologists were concerned that folk music would disappear forever, and in 1898, the American Folk Song Society was created specifically for the purpose of preserving folk music. This new interest in folk music inspired several individuals to become folk song collectors, and starting at the turn of the century, these people gathered thousands of songs such as "Barbara Allen" and "On Top of Old Smokey" from different parts of the United States. The subsequent publication of collections and anthologies of folk music such as John Lomax's *Cowboy Songs and Other Frontier Ballads* (1910), Cecil Sharp's *English Folk Songs of the Southern Appalachians* (1917), and Carl Sandburg's *The American Songbag* (1927) fueled a resurgence of general appreciation for American folk music. We will explore later how this interest laid the foundation for a revival in folk music later in the twentieth century.

BIBLIOGRAPHY

Abrahams, Roger D. and George Foss. *Anglo-American Folksong Style.* Englewood Cliffs, NJ: Prentice Hall, 1958.

Baggelaar, Kristin and Donald Milton. *Folk Music: More Than a Song.* New York: Thomas Y. Crowell Company, 1976.

Borroff, Edith. *Music Melting Round: A History of Music in the United Sates.* New York: Ardsley House, Publishers, Inc., 1995.

Bronson, Bertrand Harris. *The Singing Tradition of Child's Popular Ballads.* Princeton: Princeton University Press, 1976.

———. *The Traditional Tunes of the Child Ballads.* Princeton: Princeton University Press, 1959–1971.

Chase, Gilbert. *America's Music: From the Pilgrims to the Present.* Third Edition. Urbana and Chicago: University of Illinois Press, 1987.

Child, Francis James. *The English and Scottish Popular Ballads.* 5 vols. Boston and New York: Houghton, Mifflin Company, 1882–1898.

Coffin, Tristram P. *The British Traditional Ballad in North America.* Philadelphia: The American Folklore Society, 1963.

Faragher, John Mack with Mari Jo Buhle, Daniel Czitrom, and Susan H. Armitage. *Out of Many: A History of the American People.* Combined Edition. Third Edition. Upper Saddle River, NJ: Prentice Hall, 2000.

Filene, Benjamin. *Romancing the Folk: Public Memory and American Roots Music.* Chapel Hill: University of North Carolina Press, 2000.

Fuld, James J. *The Book of World-Famous Music.* Fourth Edition. New York: Dover Publications, 1995.

Goldfield, David with Carl Abbot, Virginia DeJohn Anderson, Jo Ann E. Argersinger, William L. Barney, and Robert M. Weir. *The American Journey: A History of the United States.* Combined Volume, Second Edition. Upper Saddle River, NJ: Prentice Hall, 2001.

Graves, Anna Hunt. *Folk: The Life, Times, and Music Series.* New York: Friedman/Fairfax Publishers, 1994.

Hamm, Charles. *Music in the New World.* New York: W.W. Norton and Company, 1983.

Kingman, Daniel. *American Music: A Panorama.* New York: Schirmer Books, 1979.

Lomax, John, and Alan Lomax. *American Ballads and Folk Songs.* New York: Macmillan Company, 1934.

Lornell, Christopher. *Introducing American Folk Music.* New York: McGraw-Hill Higher Education, 1992.

Nettl, Bruno. *Folk Music in the United States: An Introduction.* Third Edition. Detroit: Wayne State University Press, 1976.

Sandburg, Carl. *The American Songbag.* New York: Harcourt and Brace, 1927.

Santelli, Robert, Holly George Warren, and Jim Brown (Eds.). *American Roots Music.* New York: Rolling Stone Press, Published for Harry N. Abrams, Inc., 2001.

Sharp, Cecil J. *English Folk Songs from the Southern Appalachians.* Maud Karpeles, editor. London: Oxford University Press, 1932.

"Southern Music in the 20th Century," from The Southern Music Network. http://www.southernmusic.net/carterfamily.htm Accessed 01-20-05.

Stambler, Irwin and Lyndon Stambler. *Folk and Blues: The Encyclopedia.* New York: St. Martin's Press, 2001.

Willoughby, David. *The World of Music.* Third Edition. Madison: Brown and Benchmark Publishers, 1995.

Chapter Four

The Roots of African-American Music

African-American musicians have arguably had the greatest general impact on the creation of uniquely new American musics. Spirituals, Gospel, blues, jazz, R & B, rock 'n' roll, hip-hop, and rap are all deeply rooted in African-American history and creative culture. African Americans are citizens of African or part African ethnic heritage. For the last several decades, they have been counted in the United States census under the racial category "blacks." Blacks, or African Americans, now comprise the second largest minority in the United States, accounting for 12.1 percent of the total resident population. They had been the largest minority up until the most recent census, when Hispanics took over that position with 12.5 percent of the population.

African-American Origins

The first immigrants of African descent arrived in North America in 1619, landing at Jamestown along with the English entrepreneurs who were looking to find fortune in the colonies. These twenty immigrants were either free or semi-free indentured servants, a quasi-legal status for limited servitude preceding slavery that was shared by some Native Americans and whites. But as additional colonies were established, especially with the development of the plantation system in the southern colonies, the need for cheap agricultural labor increased, and there were insufficient indentured servants available to meet the demand.

The modern slave trade had already been in effect for almost two centuries, having been started by the Portuguese in 1444. England had joined the slave trade in 1562, so bringing slaves to America seemed a logical solution to the colonies' labor shortage. At first, such a small number of slaves were brought in that it did not seem necessary to even define their legal status. But the number increased steadily and by the time of the American Revolution in 1776 there were no longer African-American indentured servants but African-American slaves in the fullest sense of the term, with their legal, political, and social status in relation to their masters carefully articulated. Hence, the ancestors of most African Americans were forced to immigrate to the United States as captives during the slave trade of the seventeenth and eighteenth centuries.

Challenges to Retaining African Culture

When Africans came to the United States, they brought with them many of their native traditions,

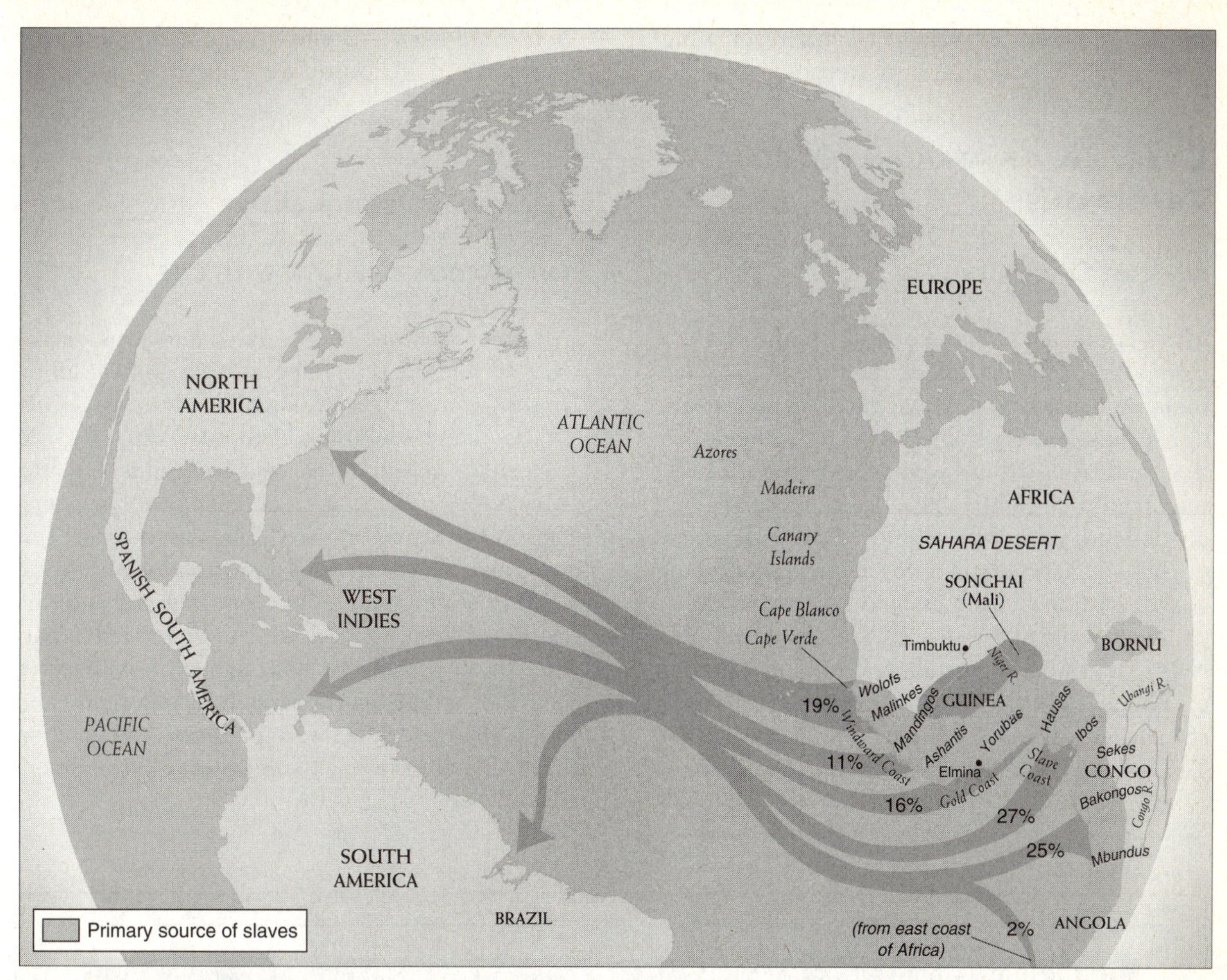

Although the earliest African immigrants were free or semifree, they were increasingly brought in as slaves to meet the colonies' need for cheap labor. Most enslaved Africans came from the many different tribal groups that populated the western areas of the African continent.

although the extent to which they were able to retain these traditions varied. This variation was a result of four main reasons.

1. Many Africans who were brought to the United States were second-generation Africans, unlike their counterparts in Latin America. They were brought first to the West Indies for "seasoning," a term to describe a process by which the slave owners tried to acclimate the slaves to the tropical climate and get them accustomed to a life of hard labor.
2. Slave owners intentionally tried to supplant African cultural roots because they felt that by making the slaves more dependent on the new white culture, it would be easier to foster the compliant attitude required for slave labor.
3. There were aspects of African culture, such as a foreign language and the ability to communicate through drumming, that slave owners prohibited because they feared slaves would use them secretly to plan insurrections and escapes.
4. European Americans regarded Africa as backward and uncivilized, and unfortunately many blacks assimilated this attitude and did not always actively attempt to retain their African heritage.

Despite these inhospitable conditions, slaves did manage to retain many of their African customs, habits, and traditions. They "Africanized" the English language, the Christian church, and other aspects of their society and culture, creating a new fusion of African-American culture.

Overview of African Music Traditions

African Diversity

Africa is a huge continent, roughly four times the size of the United States. At the time of the slave trade, it consisted of a vast number of "village states" and "family states," forming at least two thousand tribal groups who spoke somewhere in the vicinity of eight hundred distinct languages divided into twenty-four hundred dialects.[1] Each of these social units had its unique history, language, pastimes, customs, and music traditions. Although most of the slaves were taken from the relatively confined coastal areas around the Gulf of Guinea, thousands of separate tribal constituencies existed, including the Ashanti, Wa, Twi, Akan, Ga, Ewe, Kwa, Yoruba, Mandingo, Tshi, and Ibo. Acknowledging this incredible diversity, there also were several areas of commonalities.

African Commonalities

Integration of Music with Life

Music was thoroughly integrated into all aspects of society, serving as an important component in the observation and celebration of nearly every activity of the life cycle from birth to death, work to recreation, sowing to harvest, and hunts to feasts. Music also played an essential role in providing cultural cohesion, as most tribes used songs, stories, and dances to transmit important historical and social information from one generation to the next. Music was an essential and inseparable part of African life, heard in conjunction with other activities rather than separately as entertainment.

These elements were prescribed by tradition but blended according to the needs of the occasion,

Break-Out One

INSIGHT *"African Americans" or "Blacks"?*

African Americans have been identified by a series of names, many assigned to them by whites. "Blacks" replaced the earlier appellations "Negro" and "colored" in the civil rights era of the 1960s as a term of pride and in conjunction with the Black Power movement. Many people eventually objected to the designation "black" because they felt it concentrated on racial characteristics and did not address their ethnic heritage. Furthermore, it was generally inaccurate in terms of skin color hue. The term "Afro American" followed, but was eventually displaced because of the association with the "Afro" hairstyle. The current most popular term is simply "African Americans". This term is still somewhat inaccurate, as in terms of ethnic background, the vast majority of contemporary African Americans possess a mixture of ethnic heritages. Although some African ethnicity is a common denominator, throughout the Americas there was substantial mixing with people of European and Native American (particularly Cherokee and Seminole) heritage. Thus, most African Americans today share a combination of ethnic and racial backgrounds.

[1] Roberts, John Storm, *Black Music of Two Worlds.* New York: Praegar Publishers, 1972, p. 4.

taking into account the age, sex, and status of the participants. The mixture of these elements was so thoroughly melded that excising a single element would render that element meaningless. For example, a master drummer might call people together to celebrate a successful harvest by beginning with a specific rhythmic pattern based on the inflection of words describing the harvest. This would then serve as the inspiration for participants to dance, sing, and act out the meaning of the words that the pattern conveyed. Music was such an integral part of being human that, in some of the languages, there is no indigenous word for "music"; there was no reason to give it a separate name.[2]

Close Relationship between Performer and Community

A second common characteristic was the close relationship between the performer and the community. In Western traditions, it had been most common for specially trained musicians to perform for passive (though appreciative) audiences. In Africa, although there were professional or semi-professional musicians and, for example, Ewe and Yoruba master drummers were highly skilled musicians who had spent years practicing and perfecting their art, there was not the strong separation between musician and audience. Most members of African societies took part in the musical activities. The master musicians might provide the drumming or singing leads, but everyone else participated in the musical performance by singing choral parts, dancing, or adding to the general rhythmic texture with their own drums or handclapping.[3]

Based in Oral Tradition and Improvisation

A third shared characteristic was the importance of oral tradition. Although written language existed, most Africans depended on oral and aural tradition for the transmission of music. This means that the music is taught through performance and learned through hearing, as opposed to taught and learned through notation. This method of transmission encourages change. As the music passes from one generation to the next and is transported from one locale to another, the probability increases that song lyrics are misunderstood, melodies misremembered, or there are conscious attempts to change the music to make it more locally relevant. Perhaps more important in the context of African music, however, is a different concept of the function of performance and methods for creating music.

The European tradition values composition of "masterpieces" with precise directions conveyed in notation that ensure that the music can be accurately reproduced in the future and in different geographic locations. In West African traditions, oral transmission was used to preserve the general elements of the music, but what was valued was the "master" improvisations that appropriately fulfilled the function and met the aesthetic needs of the particular moment. Hence, unlike Westerners, Africans had no intention of reproducing precisely that specific music or performance at another time or in another location. Thus, it was expected that musicians and participants would improvise melodic ornamentation, rhythmic accompaniment, song forms, and dance movements that reflected the inspiration of the moment.

Importance of Text

An additional commonality was the importance of the text in music. One of the reasons is that African languages themselves are musical, based on inflection and requiring a specific relation of pitches for correct communication. The importance of language was reflected in African drumming. In fact, there is a Dogon legend that it was through the drum that God gave man the gift of speech.[4] Drum idioms imitated speech patterns through the use of high and low drum timbres performed on female and male instruments whose

[2] Ibid., p. 6.
[3] Ibid., p. 7.
[4] Ibid., p. 6.

relative size produced different levels of pitch sounds. In this manner, drums could convey something as complex as a poem or as simple as a warning that a lion was near. For example, the phrase "Wo ho te sen?" (How do you do?), which consists of four tone levels in a specific rhythmic pattern, could be conveyed as follows:[5]

Tone Levels:	Wo	ho	te	sen?
	Low	High	Low	High
	Short	Long	Short	Long

In this manner, rhythm and pitch were used to effectively communicate text and convey messages, and these messages then served as the basis around which were formulated other musical elements such as harmony, form, and timbre.

The Essential Role of Rhythm

Rhythm provided the very foundation for African music, and it flowed out of the words and the movement of human activities. Consequently, it was very fluid and could be either simple or complex. On a simple level, the short-long combination evident in the "Wo ho te sen?" example was a favored rhythmic pattern. But these and other patterns could be combined in such a manner as to create richly complex rhythmic textures. Following are examples of some of the most common rhythmic devices familiar to African-American slaves.

- **Multimeter** is a style in which the overall metric pattern consists of a series of measures that are each heard as having a different meter.
- **Polymeter** consists of two or more meters occurring simultaneously.
- **Prolongation** is a technique in which the duration of the beats gets progressively longer, obscuring the metric pulse.
- **Additive** is a technique in which there is no regular metric pulse because beats are continually added.

Prolongation and additives represent what some consider to be the essential difference between African and Western rhythm: in traditional Western rhythm, there is a consistent regular pulse that is organized into a recurring pattern (meter), which is then subdivided into smaller beats. In African rhythm, there is a consistent pulse, but it is organized into more fluid patterns that are perceived as accumulating rather than being subdivided.

Predominance of Human Voice and Percussion

A further commonality was the predominance of human voice and percussion. The human voice was used extensively and in a great variety of styles. For example in Ghana, the Akan used an "open" vocal quality that is similar to Western European styles, whereas the Frafra used a more intense tone, and others preferred falsetto.[6] Additionally, when singing melodies, singers would employ different techniques to provide variation and ornamentation, such as extending vowels over several different notes, wavering the pitch in a manner which resembles trills or vibrato, treating pitch as a continuum in slides and glissandos (like a siren as opposed to discrete notes), and using "grace" notes which are very short notes preceding the main note. Hence, the human voice was used in a great variety of ways to create music. In addition to voice, West Africans relied heavily on percussion instruments. Of the many different kinds of percussion instruments, some were instruments in the conventional sense, including many different drums, bells, gongs, rattles, and xylophones. But West Africans also used other means to contribute to the percussive texture, such as rhythmic use of vocal sounds and handclapping.

Use of Call-and-Response

Another common tradition was the reliance on an antiphonal performance practice termed "call-and-response." In this practice, a leader sings (or "calls")

[5] Roach, p. 10.

[6] Roberts, p. 8.

Break-Out Two

LISTENING GUIDE *"Drum Rhythms"*

Performing Artist: Field recording in Té village, Canton de Gan, Sous-Préfecture de Biankouma

This was recorded during a circumcision festival in the north of the Dan country. The Dan inhabits the western part of the Ivory Coast, and at the time of this recording the area included about two hundred thousand individuals of the Yakouba tribe.

Rhythm	Complex polyrhythms
Melody	Not applicable
Harmony	Not applicable
Texture	Dense texture of layered rhythmic patterns
Form	The drummer begins alone and is joined by two other drummers who provide a rhythmic ostinato.
Instrumentation	Variety of percussion instruments, including membranaphones and idiophones; some voice in background. The "master drummer" plays a drum that is a single-skinned main drum to which are attached four smaller drums so that the musician can play rhythms at various levels of pitch.

a phrase and the group responds with the same phrase or an answering phrase. This method of performance was important in the European tradition of responsorial psalmody, which consisted of a soloist alternating with a chorus in the singing of chant. It also developed in the United States in a practice called "lining out" in which psalms or hymns were taught to the members of a congregation by a leader who would sing the phrase first and then the congregation would repeat it. The African practice differed from these two on several counts. First, although the leader certainly fulfilled an important role, it was the response that was considered the essential part of the tune. Second, in European and American practice, the leader's phrase was a complete unit, whereas in the African tradition, the response provided the necessary completion of the phrase. And third, the leader's part and the responsive part might overlap.[7]

TUNING AND TONAL SYSTEMS

A shared approach to tonality in African systems was the use of microtones within a tonal framework. Let us look at microtones first. In Western music, the octave has been divided into twelve equal parts, using eleven different pitches. This "equal temperament" tuning system is the basis for Western scales and harmonies. But in African music, the approach to the octave could be described as a continuum in which the entire span of frequencies is used. These microtones were used primarily by vocalists, who would use them to embellish and ornament melodies.

The African tonal framework used heptatonic scales (seven-toned scales that were modal rather than Western major or minor), hexatonic scales (sounding like major or minor scales but with one of the scale degrees absent, usually the fourth or fifth),

[7] Brooks, Tilford, *America's Black Musical Heritage.* Englewood Cliffs, NJ: Prentice Hall, 1984, p. 15.

and pentatonic scales (scales that use five tones). Several theorists have suggested that the superimposition of African scales on European diatonic scales resulted in two ambiguous tonal areas that, in turn, created the "blue notes" popular in blues and jazz. Musicians achieve these notes through "bending" the pitch either higher or lower. These blue notes may be the result of attempts to preserve the microtonal West African traditions within the equal temperament tuning context of Western music.

African-American Music Within a Historical and Social Context

Colonial America

Africans resisted enslavement from the time of capture in Africa and throughout slavery in the Americas. Estimates of the number of Africans that were exported in the slave trade range from ten million to twenty million, but that does not take into account the Africans who died resisting capture or who managed to commit suicide during the journey. About sixty thousand slaves successfully escaped over the three-century period of bondage. Slaves also fought back through feigning illness, destroying crops, animals, machinery, and houses, and even poisoning or killing their masters. There also were organized revolts. Beginning as early as the seventeenth century, the number of revolts exceeded 250 before the U.S. Congress abolished the slave trade in 1808. But, rather than leading to freedom, revolts generally led to death and bloody reprisals, and escapes led to recapture and often brutal punishment. Hence, most Africans were forced to resign themselves to a life of slavery. There were three main kinds of vocal music that were maintained or developed during the period of slavery.

Male and female African Americans, accompanied by some children, carry large loads of cotton that they have picked in the fields in this photograph from the 1860s. G. N. Bernard *Returning from the Cotton fields in South Carolina*, © 1860. Stereograph. *Source: © Collection of the New York Historical Society, negative number 47843.*

Work Songs

Slaves were used to meet the labor needs of the specific colony, such that in the northern colonies, slaves were used for domestic work and in trade, and in the South, slaves were used for domestic and agricultural work. Slaves did have some rights granted them by both law and by custom. For example, there were legal rights for support in age or sickness, limited instruction in religion and, in special cases, the right to file a suit and provide evidence. Custom also awarded slaves the rights to private property, marriage, free time, and, for females, the right to work in domestic areas or do lighter work. But masters were not bound to respect these rights and, in actual practice, slaves lived an unbelievably harsh life. Furthermore, although atrocities such as branding, mutilation, chaining, and murder were forbidden by law, masters were not in much danger of prosecution if they broke the law, and instances of cruelty were common.

Because slaves' lives were centered on labor, some of the earliest African-American songs were work songs developed to accompany labor. Typically sung in a responsorial manner between a leader and the rest of the workers, these songs served the function of motivating laborers, providing a sense of community, ensuring that the work progressed at a steady pace, and coordinating movements so that when axes or hoes were used, accidents were avoided.

Work songs had been an integral part of African culture long before Africans were forcibly brought to America as slaves. In both West and Central Africa, large and informal labor groups gathered together for mutual assistance, and music was used in a variety of ways to enhance and coordinate everyone's work. When Africans were brought to America as slaves, this tradition was deeply embedded in their culture. Of course, working voluntarily within one's native culture is quite different from working as a forced laborer in a foreign land, and hence the work song tradition of Africa was altered to adapt to the new environment. For example, references to gods and the religions of West Africa were suppressed, and there was no drumming, as drumming was generally prohibited because of its communicative powers.

But the African tonal language and the traditions of melodic ornamentation, improvisation, and call-and-response were retained. Additionally, the slaves' work songs continued to serve the same basic function that they had in Africa. These responsorial work songs died out when the plantation system broke up and was replaced by small farms after the Civil War, but they were retained in the prison system to coordinate the labor of work gangs, and their influence can still be heard in prison work gangs and in the work drills of military groups.

Cries, Calls, and Hollers

Hollers, calls, and cries are terms often used synonymously to describe a melodic tradition that was used as a means for communicating across the fields and even to nearby plantations. This tradition was common in West Africa and it was also used with the slaves to convey a great variety of messages, from calling people to work to bringing them in from the fields, from conveying news to attracting attention of a girl. Field hands did not usually need to coordinate their movement with other workers (as, for example, did laborers who were wielding axes and hammers) and hence cries were sometimes used spontaneously to express a range of emotions from loneliness and homesickness to contentment or exhilaration. Often these chantlike expressions were rhythmically free and began on a high note (because the singer would be able to project over longer distances if he at least began singing at the top of his range) and descended in patterns emphasizing the interval of a third.

Spirituals

Black spirituals include three types of songs: spirituals, jubilees, and shouts. Spirituals acquired their name because they were religious songs that bore a close relationship to the "holy spirit." The texts focused on the Christian themes of faith, love, humility, and salvation. Jubilees tended to be more exuberant than spirituals, because their origins were the jubilant expressions of "the heart" rather than "the spirit." The texts tell God of the singer's happiness. Shouts are songs used to accompany a specific type of dance in which the "shouters" formed and moved in a circle. Because these three types of songs are often difficult to distinguish from each other, in this chapter they are all discussed under the rubric "spirituals."

There has been much discussion on whether the black spirituals originated as copies of white spirituals or whether they had their own unique origins in Africa. The American music scholar Gilbert Chase describes spirituals as "the most controversial body of music in the cultural history of America."[8] Proponents that Black spirituals derived from white Protestant traditions cite evidence that blacks were exposed to Anglo-American psalmody and hymnody as early as the mid-eighteenth century. They offer specific examples of slaves being given religious instruction, which, at the time, would have naturally included singing instruction. They point out that during the first Great Awakening (the religious revival that occurred in the colonies between 1720 and 1750) a Presbyterian minister named Samuel Davies distributed religious songbooks and Bibles to slaves. They provide quotes of whites who heard slaves singing psalms and hymns, such as in the following quote from the southern colonies in the 1760s:

> My landlord tells me . . . they heard the Slaves at worship in their lodge, singing Psalms and Hymns in the evening, and again in the Morning, long before break of day . . . [9]

Proponents that black spirituals have independent origins point out that although there is solid evidence that black and white spirituals coexisted, there is no evidence of the preexistence of white spirituals. Furthermore, they emphasize that the conditions of slavery were brutal and African Americans would have naturally sought to express through song their feelings of grief and outrage and their hope for a better life, just as they had expressed the whole gamut of emotions through song when they had not been slaves. Thus, in America, the slaves' songs became the spirituals, field hollers, and other works songs that expressed their feelings in a wide variety of everyday endeavors. Advocates for this interpretation also cite accounts that demonstrate the differences between slave singing and white singing:

> The voices of the colored people have a peculiar quality that nothing can imitate; and the intonations and delicate variations of even one singer cannot be reproduced on paper.[10]

Recent scholarship, especially by African-American researchers, suggests that black spirituals were in existence by the end of the seventeenth century, earlier than the systematic exposure of slaves to white hymns and almost a century before the development of white spirituals.

Some scholars also have suggested that many of the spirituals were actual African melodies that were brought to the American shores. Kolinski has demonstrated that thirty-six of the spirituals he examined are identical to, or resemble closely, songs of West Africa. As an example, the spiritual "No More Auction Block" is almost identical to an Ashanti song of Ghana.[11] New spirituals developed out of the spontaneous singing tradition and were "composed" by talented individuals. If these spontaneous songs were particularly effective, they were remembered and passed on through oral transmission. But there was little interest in slave music until after the Civil War, and black spirituals were not known to the outside world generally until the second half of the nineteenth century.

[8] Chase, Gilbert, *America's Music: From the Pilgrims to the Present,* Third Edition. Urbana and Chicago: University of Illinois Press, 1987, p. 213.

[9] Kingman, Daniel, *American Music: A Panorama.* New York: Schirman Books, 1979, pp. 32–33.

[10] Ibid., p. 39.

[11] Brooks, Tilford, *America's Black Musical Heritage.* Englewood Cliffs, NJ: Prentice Hall, 1984, p. 33.

Break-Out Three

INSIGHT *The Double Language of Spirituals*

The African-American leader Frederick Douglass (c. 1817–1895), born and educated as a slave, recalled spirituals in his autobiography:

> I did not, when a slave, fully understand the deep meaning of those rude and apparently incoherent songs. . . . They breathed the prayer and complaint of souls overflowing with the bitterest anguish . . . [12]

He and other former slaves such as Sojourner Truth also indicate that the language of the spirituals, in addition to conveying sincere emotional grief and spiritual piety, also held concealed meanings. Douglass recalled,

> A keen observer might have detected in our repeated singing of "O Canaan, Sweet Canaan, I am bound for the land of Canaan" something more than a hope of reaching heaven. We meant to reach the *North* and the North was our Canaan.[13]

Hence, the texts of the spirituals were replete with double meanings: "de Lord" could serve as a collective embodiment of the North that might intercede and help save the slaves from their bondage; "Heaven" (the North) or "Canaan" (Canada) also might refer to the location to which slaves hoped to escape; "Go down in the lonesome valley" might inform slaves to gather together in a secret meeting.[14]

There is evidence that Nat Turner (1800–1831), a slave who served as the leader for a revolt in Southampton County, Virginia, in 1831, may have written the spiritual "Steal Away" and that he intentionally imbued it with double meanings. Whether or not Turner actually wrote it, it is known that he used the spiritual to convene the meetings at which his rebellion was planned. The lyrics, which urge people to "steal away to Jesus," to "steal away home" and that "I ain't got long to stay here" may have conveyed the message to come to a meeting, to take a risk to acquire freedom, and perhaps even to return to Africa, and that the meeting was illegal and dangerous and must understandably be kept short. Turner's rebellion lasted several days. Fifty-seven whites were killed and sixteen of the conspirators were killed during the insurrection or hanged afterward, as was Turner himself. In the suppression that immediately followed, at least one hundred blacks were killed.

Turner's rebellion was one of several that occurred throughout the years of bondage. But, rather than resulting in freedom, such rebellions typically resulted in bloody reprisals. Hence, slaves were forced to continue to find solace in religion and in the singing of spirituals. Whether or not the lyrics of spirituals conveyed precise double meanings, there is no question that the vast majority of texts (e.g., "Swing low, sweet chariot, coming for to carry me home," "Deep river, my home is over Jordan" and "I am a poor wayfaring stranger, wandering through this life of woe . . .") reflect the sorrow and sense of displacement Africans felt as slaves in America.

This tradition of double meanings in African-American spirituals is evident in many forms of African-American music. For example, the lyrics of early blues and work songs also carried hidden meanings, asking about family members and providing information that was helpful in planning escape. Finally, the use of musical lyrics to disguise communication continues to be evident in the double entendre sexual language and multilevel messages in blues, rhythm 'n' blues, jazz, and rap.

[12] Roach, p. 5.

[13] Groves

[14] Kingman, Daniel, *American Music: A Panorama.* New York: Schirmer Books, 1979, p. 38.

Structural Characteristics of Early African-American Music

Rhythm, Melody, and Harmony

African-American hollers and the early performance of spirituals use primarily a free and fluid rhythm, derived from the text. Work songs tend to be more rhythmic and repetitive because of their frequent use to coordinate both physical movements and the response of the group to the leader. The melodies of spirituals, work songs, and hollers incorporate traditions of indigenous African music. These include use of microtones and improvising notes around the melodic line through ornamental devices such as swoops, slurs, smears, and glides. Most spirituals as we have inherited them use the major scale. Several use natural minor. But they also use a variety of scales and pitches that have their origins in African scales. These include pentatonic scales, hexatonic scales (lacking either the fourth or the seventh tone), and variations on the major or minor scale (such as major with lowered seventh tone). Brooks stresses that these variations of scales come from the use of microtones in African music and that the pitches that are used are the result of those that could only be approximated by European notation.[15]

Texture, Instrumentation, and Form

The early spirituals were monophonic, consisting of unaccompanied melody. Later settings of spirituals are homophonic, consisting of melody with chordal accompaniment. The work songs, hollers, and early spirituals were strictly vocal. But guitars, banjos, or anything that could produce percussive sounds (such as spoons, woodblocks, and washboards) would be added if available. Work songs, hollers, and spirituals use a variety of different forms to organize the music, but a strong unifying formal element with clear African roots is the predominance of variations of call-and-response. For example, in work songs and spirituals, the leader or soloist often sings various lines and the group of laborers or the chorus answers with a specific response.

Leader: Oh, poor sinner,
Chorus: Now is your time,
Leader: Oh, poor sinner,
Chorus: Now is your time,
Leader: Oh, poor sinner,
Chorus: Now is your time,
What you going to do when your lamp burns down?[16]

The American Revolution and Striving for Freedom

During the American Revolution, thousands of slaves responded to an offer from England for freedom for those who fought on the side of the British. When the war was finished, these blacks had to escape along with thousands of white Loyalists. Most went to Canada, with many of them settling in Nova Scotia. Five thousand blacks also participated in the revolution, serving in the Continental army. After the war, the revolutionary ideology of the freedom of man and Quaker pietism contributed to growing antislavery sentiment, particularly in the North. By the time of the first U.S. census in 1790, although more than 90 percent of blacks were still slaves, others were "freed" and established their own social institutions, including African-American churches, schools, political organizations, militant pamphlets, and newspapers.

But many of the gains were reversed, particularly in the South, after whites realized the potential of the new cotton gin invented by Eli Whitney in 1793. This simple machine combed the seeds out of the cotton and greatly increased the efficiency of processing cotton and the possibility for profits. With the subsequent growth of the big cotton plantations, the demand for slaves increased. Additionally, an archconservative political order developed in the South based on the plantation

[15] Ibid, p. 37.
[16] Ibid, p. 35.

The Old Plantation, an eighteenth-century painting of slave quarters on a South Carolina plantation, in which the slaves are celebrating with a dance known as "jump the broomstick", accompanying themselves with music performed on the African *mbanza*, the predecessor of the banjo. *Source: Abby, Aldrich Rockefeller Folk Art Museum, Williamsburg, VA. The Colonial Williamsbury Foundation.*

system and slavery. As a result, there was intense discrimination against the manumitted (freed) slaves even in the North, and laws were enacted that restricted black political participation, land ownership, and social contact with whites. There were attacks of white mobs on black communities, such as the attack on a Cincinnati black community in 1829. Hence, most freed blacks lived on the margins of society, unable to take advantage of the increasing public education facilities, housing, and legal protection afforded whites.

As the nineteenth century progressed, more attempts were made by both white abolitionists and blacks to eliminate slavery and improve the situation for African Americans. In 1833, the abolitionist William Lloyd Garrison founded the American Anti-Slavery Society. Frederick Douglass, the eloquent black orator and runaway slave, joined with others to establish an independent black journal, the *North Star.* Ex-slave Harriet Tubman was one of many courageous blacks and whites who fought slavery by helping slaves escape through the Underground Railroad, a network of backroads and hideouts leading from the South to the North in which volunteers "conducted" the slaves to freedom. But white resistance to abolition also increased, and the Fugitive Slave Act of 1850 made many blacks pessimistic about the end of slavery.

The Civil War, Reconstruction, and the Late Nineteenth Century

When the Civil War broke out in 1861, African Americans were anxious to help the North fight because they hoped that one of the results of the war would be that they would acquire freedom. The black leader Frederick Douglass wrote a stirring editorial and urged, "Men of Color, to Arms!" Many African Americans, both freedmen and slaves, offered their services to the Union.

President Lincoln was at first very reluctant to bring African Americans into the Union army for several reasons, not the least of which was his fear that by doing so he might anger the border states of Maryland, Delaware, Kentucky, and Missouri. These states still maintained slaves and Lincoln knew that if he alienated them he might drive them into joining the Confederate side. But by November 1862, with casualties rising, he did admit some blacks. On January 1, 1863, he issued the Emancipation Proclamation, declaring freedom for all slaves in those states or portions of states still at war against the United States. In 1865, with the war ended and an amendment to the Constitution was passed that abolished slavery, the South entered a period known as the Reconstruction.

In March 1865, the Freedmen's Bureau was established to help the freed slaves and destitute whites through activities such as providing food and shelter. The Freedmen's Bureau also worked with other groups to establish schools to assist blacks. Fisk School was one of the first of these endeavors, established in 1866 in Nashville, Tennessee, by the American Missionary Association and the Cincinnati Western Freedmen's Aid Commission.

The Fisk Jubilee Singers

Opened in an abandoned Union Army barracks and named for General Clinton B. Fisk (1828–1890), the school began to experience financial difficulties within the first five years of its operation. In an effort to raise money, the school's treasurer and music instructor, George L. White, proposed that he take his chorus called "The Colored Christian Singers" on a concert tour. The school's Board of Directors rejected the idea, but White was adamant and decided to do the tour anyway. He borrowed money to get started, contributed some of his own funds to the project, and took his students on a daring tour in 1871.

It was a dangerous and difficult tour. The group's performances were in towns and cities in the Reconstructionist South at a time when the anger and frustration of whites at losing the war was erupting in racial hatred through the recently

The Fisk Jubilee Singers were very important in exposing whites to black spirituals. ca. 1880. *Source: Corbis/Bettman.*

formed Ku Klux Klan. Although George L. White was Caucasian, all nine of the members of the choir were black, and all but two had been slaves. It was not easy to find accommodations for the group, and most people they met were either hostile or noncooperative. Furthermore, audience reception to their performances was lukewarm.

The group had been trained in classical music and conventional Protestant hymns and anthems, and these were the pieces that constituted the bulk of their concert repertoire. But at the end of the day, the group would find solace by singing spirituals together in their rooms. White was familiar with these spirituals and knew that his singers sang them on their own without his conducting, so in an inspired move at a performance they were giving for a convention of Congregational Church ministers in Oberlin, Ohio, on November 15, he decided to include a spiritual toward the end of the program.

The group sang "Steal Away" and the response was so overwhelmingly positive that White decided to shift the programs of later performances to emphasize spirituals and to change the name of the group to "The Jubilee Singers." One of the members of the Oberlin Theological seminary agreed to serve as an advance agent for the next few months and help White, who was getting exhausted from managing so many aspects of the tour and acting as "musical director, advertising agent, ticket seller, and porter."[17]

By mid-December, the group had made it to New York City and their five-week stay there became another important turning point. Officials of the American Missionary Association took care of their needs while in the city, found endorsements, and helped them to plan their future performances. By January, they were nearly free from debt and, from its rocky beginnings, the tour emerged as an artistic and financial success. The group was generally enthusiastically received for the remainder of their tour, which included a performance for President Ulysses S. Grant in Washington, DC. They brought back more than $20,000 that was used to buy the land that is the present site of Fisk University.

The Fisk Jubilee Singers continued to perform and to tour, even to Europe in 1873 to play before Queen Victoria. At the close of this tour, the group brought back $150,000. This money was used to fund the building of Jubilee Hall, the first permanent building erected in the United States for the education of black students. The original group disbanded in Hamburg in 1878 after seven years' work. But their performances inspired other schools to establish choirs that sang spirituals, including Hampton Institute in Virginia and Booker T. Washington's Tuskegee Institute in Alabama. Thus, the group's performances not only saved their school and provided the funds for the school to expand to become Fisk University but also introduced the United States and Europe to African-American spirituals.

The Europeanization and Dissemination of the Spirituals

As the success of the Fisk Jubilee Singers inspired other institutions to form choirs that toured and performed spirituals, another process was taking place that both helped expose American society to the black spirituals and slowly transformed these spirituals. This was the process of creating arrangements of spirituals into four-part quartets and solo art songs for the concert stage. An early contributor was Hampton College choir director Thomas P. Fenner (1829–1912), who in his arrangements attempted to retain the spirituals' original character and "rude simplicity" while also trying to "develop" them musically."[18] He added classical European vocal harmonies, straightened out the tempos and meters, and "cleaned up" the patois of illiterate slaves by changing the words to ones that could be more clearly enunciated and more readily understood by white audiences. A second important early composer was Harry Thacker Burleigh (1866–1949), considered to be the first black man to acquire a national reputation as a composer, arranger, and singer. He is best known for his solo arrangement of "Deep River" in 1916.

[17] Silveri, Louis, "The Singing Tours of the Fisk Jubilee Singers: 1871–1874." In *Feel the Spirit: Studies in Nineteenth Century African-American Music.* George R. Kick and Sherill V. Martin Editors. New York: Green Wood Press, 1988, p. 108.

[18] Bekker, p. 32.

Break-Out Four

PROFILE *Huddie Ledbetter "Leadbelly"*

Huddie Ledbetter was born around 1885 in Mooringsport, Louisiana, and raised on a farm in the Caddo Lake district. Although the Civil War had ended twenty years earlier, most African Americans continued to live in a state of deep poverty and racism not unlike their years of slavery. Leadbelly learned the work songs, spirituals, lullabies, and hymns of his community from his elders, and played an accordion given to him by his uncle when he was ten years old. His father later gave him a guitar, and when Leadbelly was sixteen, he left home with the instrument strapped to his back to begin a life of traveling.

Leadbelly, the most famous African-American songster. *Source: Photo by Bernard Hoffman. Getty Images/Time Life Pictures.*

He worked in a variety of jobs, including as a fieldhand, a trainer of unbroken horses, a mule and oxen driver, and a ranch hand, using his free time to frequent bars and pool houses. In 1918, he met Blind Lemon Jefferson, a young blues singer. For a while, the two traveled and worked together. But soon after he was convicted of assault, given a thirty-year term, and sent to a prison in Texas. He remained in prison for over six years, continuing to learn new songs and musical styles, including the work song–derived chain-gang chants of his fellow prisoners. He was released in 1925 after performing his music for the governor of Texas.

Over the years, academic choirs and artists such as Roland Hayes, Paul Robeson, and Marian Anderson included spirituals in their concerts, helping raise the stature of spirituals in the repertoire of solo song and choral works. Because of both the proliferation of choirs specializing in the singing of spirituals and the solo and choir arrangements that were made of spirituals, the black spiritual became fairly well known throughout the United States by the end of the nineteenth century. Today, spirituals—both as solos and in choir arrangements—continue to be frequent additions to concert repertoire.

CONCLUSION

These three vocal traditions—work songs, hollers, and spirituals—are the earliest examples of African-American music that represent the fusion of both African and European elements. All three have clear cultural roots in African traditions, including free rhythm, ornamented melody, call-and-response structure, and the tonal language that became the defining "blue" notes so common to African-American music. They also reflect European influence in their use of increasingly metrical rhythm, major and minor harmonic language, homophonic texture,

He spent the next five years traveling, singing and accompanying himself with his twelve-string guitar until 1930, when he was convicted of murder and imprisoned again, this time in Angola, Louisiana. It was here that John and Alan Lomax "discovered" him in 1934 during their travels in the South to collect the folk songs of African Americans. With the help of the Lomaxes, Leadbelly was again given a governor's pardon, this time on the basis that he had been "broken" and reformed, and was safe now to be freed. He traveled to New York with the Lomaxes, who arranged for him to participate in their tours of college campuses where they were providing performances of folk music.

On January 21, 1935, he married Martha Promise, and two years later began recording for the American Record Company (later Columbia Records). Although the Lomaxes continued to be tremendously helpful, they also treated him in the paternalistic manner typical of the time, using him as a chauffeur when they would go on journeys to collect songs in the South and later employing him and his wife as domestic servants.

In 1940, Leadbelly participated in the "Grapes of Wrath" benefit in New York City along with Woody Guthrie, Pete Seeger, Burl Ives, and other prominent folksingers. Pete Seeger recalls how he and Woody used to visit Leadbelly and his wife at their apartment in New York's lower East Side, and how the four of them would make music together until the neighbors complained. He also recalls that one year Leadbelly started to use a cane and that his hands appeared to be stiffer and less certain on the guitar, the first hint of the disease that would eventually claim his life. In 1944, Leadbelly left New York for Hollywood and worked as a musician in a variety of capacities. In 1949, he embarked on a European concert tour.

Following his European tour, he returned to New York, quickly becoming seriously ill with amyotrophic lateral sclerosis, commonly known as "Lou Gehrig's Disease," a rare but fatal disease that causes the muscles to atrophy. He died on December 6, 1949, having never achieved commercial success and leaving Martha nearly penniless. But only six months after his death, a recording of his song "Good Night, Irene" by the folk song group known as "The Weavers" sold over two million copies.

Moe Asch, of Folkways Records, had recorded over nine hundred songs by Leadbelly and these recordings (along with those Leadbelly made for other labels) are considered priceless treasures of American folk music. Many of his songs, including "Good Night, Irene," "Old Cotton Fields at Home," and "Midnight Special," have become standards in the American folk music repertory.

transmission through notation, and performance on the concert stage. All three developed out of the slaves' experience in the United States. Furthermore, although work songs, hollers, and spirituals may have arisen as specific expressions of African-American culture at an earlier time in American history, they have played a seminal role in influencing and shaping later African-American musics and the musical traditions of America as a whole.

Bibliography

Abrahams, Roger D. and George Foss. *Anglo-American Folksong Style.* Englewood Cliffs, NJ: Prentice Hall, 1958.

Brooks, Tilford. *America's Black Musical Heritage.* Englewood Cliffs, NJ: Prentice Hall, 1984.

Chase, Gilbert. *America's Music: From the Pilgrims to the Present.* Third Edition. Urbana and Chicago: University of Illinois Press, 1987.

Courlander, Harold. *Negro Folk Music, USA.* New York: Columbia University Press, 1963.

Fischer, Mark Miles. *Negro Slave Songs in the United States.* New York: Citadel Press, 1990.

Hamm, Charles. *Music in the New World.* New York: W.W. Norton and Company, 1983.

Haydon, Geoffrey, and Dennis Marks. *Repercussions: A Celebration of African American Music.* London: Century Publishers, 1985.

Kick, George R. and Sherrill V. Martin, Editors. *Feel the Spirit: Studies in Nineteenth Century Afro-American Music.* New York: Greenwood Press, 1988.

Kingman, Daniel. *American Music: A Panorama.* New York: Schirmer Books, 1979.

"Ledbetter, Huddie," in *Dictionary of American Biography, Supplement 4: 1946–1950.* American Council of Learned Societies, 1974. Reprinted in *Biography Resource Center.* Farmington Hills, MI: The Gale Group, 2001. http://www.galenet.com/servlet/BioRC (Accessed 07-21-01).

Maultsby, Portia K. *Afro-American Religious Music: A Study in Musical Diversity.* New York: Wittenberg University, 1986.

Oliver, Paul and Max Harison, William Bolcom. *The New Grove Gospel, Blues and Jazz with Spirituals and Ragtime.* London: Macmillan London Limited, 1986.

Reagon, Bernice Johnson, ed. *We'll Understand It Better By and By.* Washington, DC: Smithsonian Institution Press, 1992.

Roberts, John Storm. *Black Music of Two Worlds.* New York: Praeger Publishers, 1972.

Roach, Hildred. *Black American Music: Past and Present.* Malabar, FL: Robert E. Krieger Publishing Company, Inc., 1985.

Silveri, Louis. "The Singing Tours of the Fisk Jubilee Singers: 1871–1874." In *Feel the Spirit: Studies in Nineteenth Century Afro-American Music.* George R. Kick and Sherrill V. Martin (Editors). New York: Greenwood Press, 1988.

Southern, Eileen. *The Music of Black Americans: A History.* New York: W.W. Norton, 1982.

———. "The 25 Most Important Events in Black Music History." Chicago, IL: *Ebony*, Vol. 55, Number 8; 06-01-2000, p. 140.

Whitsell, Shawn. "Let us not forget the music of African Americans". Tennessee: University Wire, 2-22-2001. http://www.elibrary.com/s/edumark/getdo. . . rn:bigchalk.com:US;EL&dtype=0~0&dinst=0(Accessed 05-05-01).

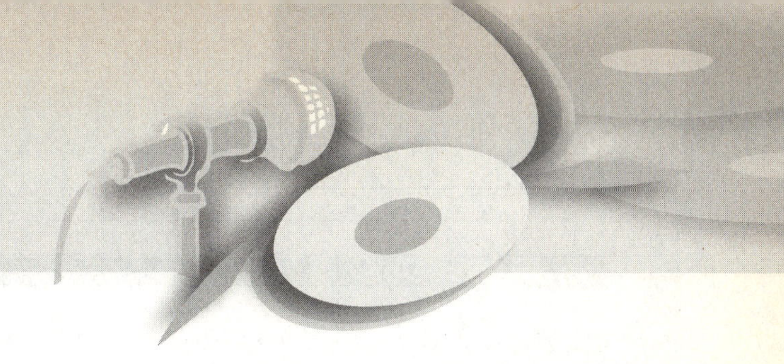

Chapter Five

The Roots of Latin American Music

Latin American music has become an increasingly substantial segment of the current music industry. Although there have been various Latin music categories within the regular Grammy Awards for decades, the National Academy of Recording and Arts Sciences (NARAS) launched a separate Latin Grammy Awards in 2000 because styles within this category now constitute such a large percentage of record sales. For similar reasons, Billboard—the organization that monitors sales and radio airplay data to create weekly charts—hosts an annual event titled Latin Music and Awards. Many of today's most prominent stars, including Jennifer Lopez, Mark Anthony, Carlos Santana, Christina Aguilera, Ricky Martin, Shakira, Enrique Iglesias, Gloria Estefan, Thalia, and Chayanne, have varying degrees of Latin American heritage.

This trend in music mirrors demographic changes in the United States. Citizens of Hispanic origin now constitute the largest ethnic minority. Increasing by 58 percent in the last census, they accounted for 12.5 percent of the resident population as compared with 12.1 percent blacks.[1] The term "Hispanic" designates a broad ethnic category, and not a racial category, as is the case with "whites," "blacks," and "Asians." Hispanics share Spanish language and culture. This group, therefore, includes people from North, Central, and South America as well as the Caribbean. "Latin music" reflects this diversity.

But the majority of "Hispanics" in the United States trace their ethnic roots to Mexico. Within the Hispanic population, 26.6 million are from Mexico, whereas the next largest group (Puerto Ricans) accounts for 3.4 million.[2] Because they constitute the majority of Hispanics in the United States, we will begin our exploration of Latin American music by looking at the roots of Mexican-American music.

The First Mexican Americans

The large percentage of Mexican-American Hispanics exists partly because most of what is now the southwestern United States was part of Mexico until the mid-nineteenth century. In 1848,

[1] Garcia, Edwin, Anne Martinez, and Jessie Mangaliman, "Numbers Show a Country in Racial Transformation." *San Jose Mercury News,* March 13, 2001, Front Page. Even as recently as 1995, blacks were still the largest, with 31,514 thousand as compared to 26,402 thousand Hispanics. In the 2000 census, there were 33,947,837 thousand blacks and 35,305,818 thousand Hispanics.

[2] Cuban Americans are 1.2 million; Dominican Republic are 764,945; El Salvador are 655,165; and Colombia are 470,684. *San Jose News,* May 10, 2000.

Break-Out One

INSIGHT *What's In a Name? The Challenge of Categories*

Citizens of "Hispanic" origin constitute the largest minority in the United States. They also present some of the greatest challenges as a category. First, rather than a racial category, the term "Hispanic" is a broad ethnic category, referring to those whose Spanish language and culture includes the peoples of Mexico, South and Central America, several islands such as Cuba and Puerto Rico, and, technically, people from Spain and Portugal, the countries that initially colonized these areas. Second, there is also considerable dissatisfaction with the term "Hispanic." It is a term that began to be used in this country by the U.S. Census Bureau in the 1960s to categorize Spanish-speaking peoples in the United States, and there is resentment against the fact that this classification and term were government-imposed. Additionally, the term stresses the colonial Spanish influence and does not acknowledge the considerable contributions of the indigenous peoples. It therefore reinforces the racist hierarchy of "white" Mexicans (of dominant Spanish descent) as being superior to "dark" Mexicans (of dominant indigenous descent). By contrast, proponents of the term "Hispanic" point out that "Hispano" comes from a mythological character whose father was Hispalo, one of Hercules' companions who is said to have founded the city of Hispalis, which later became Seville. Thus, the term "Hispanic" has a much older history that predates both Spain and its use by the U.S. census. They believe that "Hispanic" is the best term for one whose language and culture is predominantly Spanish.[3]

Because of problems with the term "Hispanic," some people prefer the name Latino/Latina, the male/female terms indicating people of Latin cultural descent. But others feel that in a manner similar to "Hispanic," this term's origin continues to place too much emphasis on European contributions. In fact, the term "Latin America" and "Latino" were created by the French when Napoleon III made Maximilian Emperor of Mexico (1863–1867) during a period in which France was pursuing an ambitious, imperialistic desire to increase its power in North America. To do so, France was trying to erase the presence of Spain and, by extension, the idea of "Hispanic America." Abandoning the proposed name of "Franco America" out of fear that there would be too much of a reaction against it, they adopted "Latin America" because they felt that because both Spanish and French language and culture are derived from the Latin language and Roman culture, this term was inclusive of both the Spanish and the French

[3] Pedro de Mesones. p. 15.

under the terms of a treaty following the U.S. defeat of Mexico in the Mexican-American war along with an additional purchase in 1853, former Mexican territories were acquired by the United States and became the states of Texas, California, and Utah, and parts of the states of Nevada, New Mexico, Colorado, Wyoming, and Arizona. The residents were given the choice of returning over what was now the new border of Mexico or becoming U.S. citizens. The 80 percent who chose to stay were the first official Mexican Americans. New immigrants from Mexico have continually augmented these initial Mexican Americans, and today there are more people immigrating into the United States from Mexico than from any other single country in the world. Mexican Americans bring to American culture a rich, complex blend of Indian, European, and African traditions.

influences. But Paris was the center of their concept of Latin America, and hence those who are opposed to "Latino/Latina" state that the term is consequently even more imperialistic and colonial in its origin. Furthermore, people don't come from a country named "Latin" and do not currently speak Latin. Nevertheless, it appears to be the more acceptable broad-category term for the groups of people who speak Spanish in North, Central, and South America. Both the terms "Hispanic" and "Latino/Latina" are used to describe citizens with a wide range of separate national origins, but the great majority of Hispanics and Latino/Latinas in the United States trace their ethnic background to Mexico.

Some citizens of Mexican heritage (including those born in the United States as well as those who immigrated) prefer the term "Chicano," derived from the Aztec word *Mexica*, which gave rise to the word *Mexicano*. In the Aztec language of Nahuatl, the *x* is pronounced *sh*. When the word is shortened to *xicano*, it is pronounced *shicano* in Nahuatl. Because the *sh* sound does not exist in Spanish, the *sh* is changed to *ch*. It is also recorded in history that the Nahuatl-Aztecs adopted the name *Mexica* during their migration from the mythical Aztlán to Mexico, and that the children of Mexitli transformed the name into Mexicatl by decree of their favorite god. Hence, rather than using "Hispanic," which is affiliated with the brutal Spanish conquistadors, the Chicanos stress their affinity with the Aztecs and other Indians of the Southwest.

For others, the term "Chicano" has negative connotations. First, the term was apparently originally used as a disparaging term by Mexicans to describe U.S. Mexicans who they believed were living a false life, having abandoned their cultural roots. In fact, the only early dictionary that includes and defines the word *chicano* is *Diccionario Enciclopédico de la Lengua Castellana* by Vastus, published in Buenos Aires in 1941, in which *chicano* is defined as "liar."[4] When young Mexican Americans identified themselves as Chicanos in the 1960s and 1970s, they were consciously challenging and diffusing this negative and hurtful association (in a manner similar to the gay population's appropriation of the term "queer") and proudly proclaiming their cultural ties to Mexico. By contrast, some older, conservative Mexican Americans connect the term "Chicano" with what they consider to be a disruptive, "trouble-making" activist movement. They therefore disapprove of the movement and the term "Chicano" in the same way some African Americans disapprove of "Black Panthers." And to some the term "Chicano" describes the less educated working-class Mexican Americans, and does not include or reflect the achievements of the many professional and highly educated Mexican Americans.

There are several other terms and still more issues related to the terms, but this is sufficient to demonstrate that clearly no single term is generally acceptable, and one must be sensitive to and respectful of the right of individuals to describe themselves as they prefer.

[4] Campa, L. Arthur, *Hispanic Culture in the Southwest*. Norman: University of Oklahoma Press, 1979, p. 7.

Pre-Conquest and Arrival of the Europeans

The Earliest Peoples in Mexico

Mexico was the site of some of the earliest and most advanced civilizations in the Western Hemisphere. There is evidence of people who lived in hunting societies at least as early as 21,000 B.C.E. and of crop-cultivating societies around 8,000 B.C.E. The first major civilization, the Olmecs, flourished between about 1500 and 200 B.C.E. This was followed by the Mayan culture, which attained its greatest development about the sixth century C.E. In the tenth century, the Toltec migrated from the north and established an empire, founding the cities of Tula and Tulacingo (north of present-day Mexico City). In the eleventh century, the Toltecs were vanquished and dispersed by the Chichimeca.

THE ARRIVAL OF THE AZTECS

In the twelfth century, seven allied tribes entered the valley from the north, probably from areas now in New Mexico and Arizona. In 1325, the leading tribe of these seven allied tribes, known as the Aztec—or Mexica—founded a settlement named Tenochtitlán. Under the leadership of the first Aztec emperor Itzcoatal, the Aztecs extended their influence throughout the entire Valley of Mexico, building great cities and becoming the preeminent power in central and southern Mexico by the fifteenth century. Aztec society was agriculture-based and built on the earlier civilizations of the Toltec and Chichimeca. It was highly developed both artistically and intellectually, and as Aztec power and influence grew, the Aztecs developed a complex and intricate social, political, and religious organization.

THE ARRIVAL OF THE SPANISH

When the Spanish initially came to the area of Mexico beginning in 1517, the native peoples consisted of those in the domains of the Aztec Empire, those of several other kingdoms,[5] the

This illustration of maize cultivation was created by an Aztec artist for the Florentine Codex, a book prepared to document Aztec culture after the Spanish conquest. 1739(3)-Codice Florentino-*Cultivating Corn*. Illustration from Florentine Codex, 1739, by Grunzinski. *Source: American Museum of Natural History. Image # 1739-3. Courtesy the Library, American Museum of Natural History.*

[5] Mixtec in Puebla State, Tarascan in Michoacan State, Zapotec in Oaxaca, Tlaxcalan in Tlaxcala, Otomí in Hidalgo, and Totonac in Veracruz.

surviving tribes of the Mayan culture (primarily in Yucatan), and many independent groups in the "frontier" regions of the north and south. In 1518, a second European explorer, Juan de Grijalva, explored the eastern coast of Mexico and brought back to the Spanish colony in Cuba the first reports of the rich Aztec Empire. The governor of Cuba was so enthralled with Grijalva's reports of Aztec wealth that he dispatched a large force in 1519 under the leadership of a Spanish nobleman, Hernan Cortés.

Cortés arrived at present-day San Juan de Ulloa on the north coast in April 1519, and by August commanded a force of four hundred infantry, sixteen horses, six cannon, and fifteen hundred Indian allies. These Indian allies came from the tribes that had been subservient to the Aztecs, and they saw in Cortés an ally who might help them in their battle against the rule of the Aztecs. Cortés' force reached the capital city of Tenochtitlán in November. The Aztecs fell relatively easily, for they were fighting with simpler weapons and they did not want to attack horses, strange beasts they had never seen before. Furthermore, there was a prediction in Aztec cosmology that a messiah-like god figure who was white and had iron skin—Quetzalcóatl, "Plumed Serpent"—would one day return and his return would signal the end of the current civilization. The Aztec ruler, Montecuhzouma, believed that Cortés, who had fair skin and wore the metal military garb of helmet and breastplate, was the incarnation of Quetzalcóatl.

A week after Cortés arrived, he was able to seize Montecuhzouma and overthrow the sacred idols in the temple. In June of the following year, Montecuhzouma was slain after vainly trying to quiet his people, and the next day Cortés and his men were forced to flee. Cortés and his forces fled the city of Tenochtitlán on June 30, 1520, but they returned with additional soldiers and by August 13 of the following year, the city surrendered. Cortés continued to conquer surrounding areas and in the process, thousands of Indians were killed. By 1535, the indigenous people were thoroughly decimated and the survivors vanquished.

Overview of the Music of the Aztecs and Other Indigenous Peoples

Challenges and Changes in Studying Indigenous Music of Mexico

Just as there were challenges to studying the indigenous music of Indians in northern areas of the American continent, there are also difficulties studying the indigenous music of Mexico. This is primarily because of the condescending and hostile attitude toward this music that prevailed up until the 1920s. Much of the perceptions of indigenous music were influenced by the writings of sixteenth-century observers such as the Bernal Díaz del Castillo.

Bernal Díaz del Castillo was a soldier in Cortés's force, and he provided vivid accounts of the music played and sung by the Aztecs. Díaz was writing at a time when he was unable to provide an objective and sympathetic account of the music. Not only was he writing when Europeans were generally very patronizing and condescending toward "primitive" cultures, but he was also describing music that was performed in conjunction with battles or was accompanying the ritual execution of his comrades-in-arms who had been taken prisoner by the Aztecs. Nevertheless, his descriptions do demonstrate the power of Aztec music:

> As we were retreating we heard the sound of the trumpets from the great Cue, which from its heights dominates the whole city *(the great Cue was the principal sacrificial temple, and stood on the exact spot where now rises the Cathedral of Mexico City)*. We heard also a drum, a most dismal sound indeed it was . . . as it resounded so that one could hear it two leagues off, and with it many small tambourines and shell trumpets, horns and whistles. At that moment . . . they were offering the hearts of ten of our comrades and much blood to the idols that I have mentioned. . . . The Mexicans offered great sacrifice and celebrated festivals every night and sounded their cursed drum, trumpets, kettle drums and shells, and uttered

Break-Out Two

IN-DEPTH FOCUS *Friars Toribo de Motolinía and Pedro de Gante*

Not all of the Europeans who came to Mexico with the Spanish Conquistadors were intent on subjugating and exploiting the indigenous peoples. Although the relationship was still colonial, the missionaries came with sincere beliefs that they were saving the natives from eternal damnation by converting them to Catholicism. Several missionaries attempted to protect the Indians from the worst brutalities of the conquistadors and to conduct the conversion in a benevolent way. One of the earliest was Father Toribo de Motolinía (1490–1569) who came with the original twelve missionaries who accompanied Cortés. Motolinía's name was the Indian word for "poor," a term they used to describe him because he walked barefoot and wore such a tattered habit. Motolinía hated the Spanish conquistadors and overlords and was even formally accused of petitioning for their expulsion. Motolinía also was appreciative of and nonjudgmental about indigenous music, and modern scholarship owes much to his careful and thorough descriptions of what he saw and heard because it balanced the hostile perceptions of other sixteenth-century writers.

Another of the early missionaries was Pedro de Gante (Peter of Ghent) who was born and raised in Ghent, Flanders (now northeastern Belgium). In Flanders he had grown up in an atmosphere of high Renaissance culture, and he had been familiar with the music of some of the great Flemish composers such as Johannes Ockeghem, Jacob Obrecht, and of the Frenchman Josquin des Prez. He was an aristocrat who was related to Charles V, one of the greatest of the kings of Spain and the Holy Roman Emperor from 1519 to 1556. In fact, Pedro was over forty years old and in Charles's employ

> yells and howls. Then they sacrificed our comrades . . . [6]

This treatment of the Spanish prisoners-of-war was not a new practice. Legend has it that when the Aztecs consecrated the Cue, twenty thousand captives had their chests cut open by priests wielding sharp obsidian blades amidst musicians performing on various percussion instruments.

In his *Historia verdadera,* Díaz provides a number of music references, but these references typically reflect the perspective typical of the time. The negative attitude represented in the writings of Díaz continued throughout the Colonial period and up through the early twentieth century. For example, in 1917, a faculty member of the National Conservatory of Music, Alba Herrera y Ogazón, published under the official auspices of the *Dirección General de las Bellas Artes* a treatise in which she vigorously condemned Aztec music as "barbarous and harsh."[7]

Beginning in the 1920s, following the surge of nationalism after the Mexican Revolution and when "authentic primitivism" and "barbarism" became valued characteristics by European artists (as seen, for example, in Stravinsky's music, Picasso's art, and Martha Graham's dance), people became more interested in indigenous music. The same qualities that were earlier found to be defects were now found to be merits. Leading this

[6] Stevenson, Robert, *Music in Mexico: A Historical Survey.* New York: Thomas Y. Crowell Company, 1971, p. 8.

[7] Ibid., p. 5.

when he converted to Catholicism, joined the Franciscans, and requested that Charles give him permission to go as a pioneer and missionary to the New World.

When Friar Pedro arrived in the summer of 1523, just two years after the fall of Tenochtitlán to the Spanish conquistadors, he set as his first task the learning of Nahuatl, the language of the Aztecs. He then founded a school, and this school is now considered to be the first school in the Americas for teaching European subjects. Although music was only one of several subjects taught at the school, it is clear from surviving letters and portraits of Friar Pedro that it was a subject that was very important to him.

Friar Pedro's teaching was very successful. Much of the credit must go to his students, for it was clear that the Indians had remarkable aptitude for music. But it was also partly because of attributes of Friar Pedro himself. He was apparently a very kind and caring teacher who was known for his gentleness and kindness. He insisted on teaching only the children of the Indians, and refused to work with the children of the Spaniards so that there would be no hint of racism entering his classrooms. And he treated his students respectfully, using his own advanced students as teachers of other students. He was very proud of their accomplishments. Just nine years after his arrival, he wrote to Charles V:

> I can tell Your Majesty without exaggeration that there are already Indians here who are fully capable of preaching, teaching, and writing. And with the utmost sincerity I can affirm that there are now trained singers who if they were to sing in your majesty's Chapel at the moment would do so well that perhaps you would have to see them actually sing in order to believe it possible.[8]

Friar Pedro's teaching was so effective that subsequent missionaries from other orders, as well as the secular clergy who came later, adopted his educational methods for many years.

[8] Stevenson, Robert, *Music in Mexico,* p. 54.

movement was Carlos Chávez who looked to pre-Conquest musical ideals as expressing "what is profoundest and deepest in the Mexican soul" and who observed that "the musical life of the aborigines constitutes the most important stage in the history of Mexican music."[9] This led a whole new generation of scholars to attempt to learn more about pre-Conquest music through the systematic study of (1) surviving musical instruments that peoples such as the Aztecs, Mayas, and Tarascans were known to have used; (2) descriptions of music by sixteenth-century authors who were friendly to Indian culture as well as opposed to it; (3) the study of Indian languages; and (4) the collection of melodies from contemporary but remote Indian groups that appear to have preserved in their music some of the elements and characteristics of pre-Conquest styles. These various sources of information have helped scholars deduce a number of important conclusions regarding Aztec and indigenous music.

Commonalities of Aztec and Other Indigenous Music

Music Was Functional

As with the indigenous music of the northern parts of the American continent, indigenous music in the southern areas was highly functional. Most of the instruments were inscribed with carvings that told

[9] Ibid., p. 6.

symbolically their purpose. This strong connection between music and function is also evident in that every piece of music appears to have been composed for a certain time, a certain place, and a certain occasion. As circumstances changed calling for something new, musicians were required to compose appropriate music, but they were also required to learn and remember all of the old songs. Music did not have a separate life as "entertainment," although music played an important role in conjunction with the numerous festivals that were coordinated with the 260-day religious calendar.

Music Was Based on Oral Tradition and Was Communal

There was no music notation, and scholars have concluded that the music was passed on through oral traditions. Only individual composers of royal blood are known. For example, the texts of approximately sixty songs are known of the Aztec King Nezahualcóyotl ("hungry coyote") who reigned from 1428 to 1472, but individuals of non-royal blood who composed music are unknown, for music was regarded as essentially a means of communal rather than of individual expression.

Music Was Very Precise

Because of the important role of music in sacred functions and rituals, music was in the hands of a professionalized caste that was rigorously trained to enable them to give absolutely perfect performances. Imperfect performances were considered to be offensive to the gods. Consequently, musicians who made errors (such as missing drum beats) were executed.

Musicians Held High Status

In Aztec society, the nobles and the temple personnel maintained professional performers. Officials organized rituals for each month, with hundreds of richly costumed, carefully rehearsed dancers and musicians. Musicians were drawn from the nobility and upper classes and trained thoroughly. Because of the importance of their work, musicians held high status in the society.

Structural Characteristics of Aztec and Other Indigenous Music

Because there are no examples of Aztec music, there are no clear conclusions regarding the music's structural characteristics. It is probably safe to say, however, that there were many similarities with the indigenous music of the peoples of the northern areas of the continent. But the Aztec civilization was also very complex, and this complexity was most likely also evident in the music.

Rhythm, Melody, and Harmony

Rhythm was primarily additive, although there is some evidence that suggests some of the music was metrical and that there was the use of combinations of meters. There was a great variety of melodies, and these melodies apparently were based on complex scales and were supported by the use of chords. Many were based on five-note pentatonic scales. This has been determined largely based on surviving pitched instruments such as the flutes. Written accounts also suggest that the musicians had an acute sense of pitch, and that great care was taken to ensure that their instruments were tuned correctly.

Texture, Form, and Instrumentation

The form and texture of the music were shaped by the function the music accompanied. For example, the rituals often involved a leader with a group, and hence the music associated with the ritual was responsorial singing. Another type of a ritual that was typical at pre-Conquest festivities was a dance in which the Indians would form concentric circles around the drums that were placed on a grass mat in the center of the dancing area. Indians of royal blood danced in the inner circles. Dancers synchronized their steps so that all circles completed each revolution at the same time. This required that the inner circles move at a slower pace than the outer circles. The movements of the dancers' arms and feet were coordinated to rise and fall with the beat and the melodic shape.

There was a similar group of instruments that were used among many different native groups. These instruments had a long history and had remained consistent over time. Pictures demonstrate that the same instruments that were used in the eighth century were still being used in the sixteenth century. All of the instruments were aerophones, idiophones, or membranophones; there were no cordophones.

An important aerophone was the *tepuzquizuiztli,* a conch shell trumpet and clay replicas reproduced in exact detail both internally and externally. There also were many types of flutes made of clay, bone, metal, and reeds. Two important kinds of flutes were the triple and quadruple flutes, which were tuned to play triads. There also was a double flute (with two cylinders), with similar placement of finger holes on both tubes, which was apparently intended to produce a beating effect between the near-unison pitches and which was capable of producing a tremendous amount of sound.

There also was a variety of percussion instruments. Membranophones included the *huehuetl,* an upright drum constructed from a hollowed tree trunk on which would be stretched a jaguar or deer skin that could be tightened or loosened to raise or lower the pitch and that was played with the fingers rather than mallets. Idiophones included the *ayotl* (a rasp made from the shell of a turtle in which the player would scrape the serrated shell with a two-pronged stag's antler); the *omitzicahuastli* (a different kind of a rasp made out of a notched human or animal bone); and the *ayacachtli* (a rattle made from a gourd filled with seeds or a clay container filled with pebbles to which a handle was attached that resembles the maracas used in modern bands).

One of the most impressive drums was the *teponaztli,* made of a section of tree trunk, as thick as the body of a man and about three feet long, in which an H-shaped incision was made on one of the closed ends. The two tongues created by the incision provided two different pitches, usually at an interval of a third or a second.[10] The blood of sacrificed victims was poured into the *teponaztli* during rituals. According to sixteenth-century authors, the sound of this drum was very mournful and could be heard over great distances.

Although instrumental music was important, it appears to have been always used in conjunction with singing. One sixteenth-century Spaniard described how the vocal quality of the Indians when singing was amusing, sounding out of tune and thin. The "out of tune" character would have been due to different pitch systems, and analysis of Indian musical terminology suggests that the falsetto and thinness was a preferred quality, associated with gold—the metal of the sun god, the principal Indian deity—and the roar of the jaguar.[11]

Mexican-American Music in a Historical and Social Context

The Spanish Colonial Period

Once the indigenous people were conquered, the Spanish established a form of colonial government and appointed the first Spanish viceroy, Antonio de Mendoza. The Spanish Colonial Period lasted until 1821. During that time, sixty-one different viceroys governed Mexico, directing a series of military and exploratory expeditions that eventually added present-day Texas, New Mexico, California, and other areas of what is now the southwestern parts of the United States as the northern provinces of "New Spain." There were three essential components of the colonial system that also had influence on the developing Mexican music: the Roman Catholic Church, the *repartimiento* policy along with the importation of African slaves, and the rigid racial and social hierarchy.

[10] Stevenson, Robert, *Music in Mexico: A Historical Survey.* New York: Thomas Y. Crowell Company, 1971, p. 9. Stevenson also explains that these instruments have different names in different cultures, but that they are the same instruments and that given here are the Aztec names.

[11] Behague, Gerard and E. Thomas Stanford, *The New Grove Dictionary of Music and Musicians.* Stanley Sadie (Editor). Vol. 12. New York: Macmillan Publishers, Limited, 1980, p. 230.

Roman Catholic missionaries accompanied the Spanish conquistadors, and the church became very influential in shaping Mexican culture. Exterior of Santa Barbara Mission, surrounded by Bougainvillea and trees, Santa Barbara, CA.
Source: Photo by Jonathan Nourok. PhotoEdit.

INFLUENCE OF ROMAN CATHOLIC CHURCH

Missionaries from the Franciscan order of the Roman Catholic Church had accompanied the Spanish conquistadors as early as 1523, and missionaries soon followed them from the Augustinian, Dominican, and Jesuit orders. The church was enormously influential in the shaping of the emerging Mexican culture and society. The church required the Indians to build and move into special villages called *congregaciones* that were formed around the new missions, to wear European clothing, and to convert to the Roman Catholic faith. They also educated the Indians in everything from the Spanish language to European music. In the process, the church became so powerful that by the time its holdings were nationalized between 1856 and 1859, it owned one third of all Mexican property and land.

REPARTIMIENTO AND THE IMPORTATION OF AFRICAN SLAVES

The second essential component of the colonial system was a practice known as *repartimiento*, a policy by which Spain encouraged colonization through granting to Spanish nobles, priests, and soldiers large tracts of land and jurisdiction over all the Indian peoples who resided on these lands. Although these Indians were supposed to be free and entitled to wages, in actuality they were treated little better than slaves. On several occasions, the missionaries and the Spanish government attempted to curtail mistreatment and exploitation of the Indians as laborers on the farms and in the mines, but their reforms were not effective primarily because of the difficulty of enforcement.

Hard labor combined with war and disease had a disastrous effect on the native population and millions of Indians died. In the densely inhabited central valley of Mexico, an estimated 90 percent of the population died before the end of the sixteenth century. In the Nueva Galicia area in the eastern part of Mexico, approximately two thirds of the population died within the brief thirty-year period of 1520 to 1550. On the northern frontiers of New Spain, approximately half the population had died by 1550 and then another half again by 1600.[12] These percentages indicate a very large absolute number, as scholars have estimated that there may have been as many as twenty million indigenous peoples living in this part of the Americas at the time of the Spanish conquest.

In an effort to save the Indian population from complete annihilation as well as to maintain labor productivity, the Spanish started bringing in slaves from Africa in the mid-sixteenth century.

[12] Tanner, Helen Hornbeck, Ed., *The Settling of North America: The Atlas of the Great Migrations into North America from the Ice Age to the Present.* New York: Macmillan, 1995, p. 34 and pp. 42–43.

Break-Out Three

LISTENING GUIDE *"La Llorona"*

Performing Artist: Suni Paz

La Llorona, "The Weeping Woman," is a famous figure in Mexican and Mexican American folk traditions and some scholars say the origins are in Aztec mythology. There are many different versions of the tale, but a common one is that a beautiful young woman has a relationship with a man of higher social status and together they have two children. When the man eventually abandons her (in some versions because he has grown tired of her or because he has met someone else, and in others because his parents forced him to marry someone of his own social class), she drowns the children out of grief and rage in the nearby river. Her weeping spirit continues to haunt the area and children are warned to be good or La Llorona might steal them or drown them. This version of the folk song does not tell the story of La Llorona, but rather describes the emotions of the man who loves her.

Rhythm	Triple
Melody	Clear contour
Harmony	minor
Texture	Homophonic
Form	Strophic, organized into aabb
Instrumentation	Solo female voice accompanied by guitar; later vocal harmony provided by male voice.

By 1580, there were slightly fewer than 15,000 Spaniards in New Spain but over 18,500 Africans.[13]

The Rigid Social/Racial Class Hierarchy

The highest class was the white Mexicans, who themselves were divided into two groups. At the top were the *peninsulares,* who were born in Spain and sent to Mexico to hold the most powerful offices in both the government and church administrations. These were followed by *criollas* who were persons of pure European descent who had been born and raised in New Spain. These *criollas* were discriminated against and usually denied the higher civic and church administrative positions. It was accumulated *criolla* resentment that helped foster Mexican rebellion beginning early in the nineteenth century. Next was a steadily increasing population of people with mixed Spanish, Indian, and later African blood called *mestizos.* At a social rank below *mestizos* were the freed blacks, and at the bottom of the colonial caste system were the Indians and the black slaves.

Influence of Colonial System on Mexican Music

The Roman Catholic Church and the Transplanting of European Music

To assist in the assimilation of the Roman Catholic faith, priests built churches on the ruins of temples and instituted Christian celebrations on what had been pre-Conquest holy days. Although Díaz's observations demonstrate the connection of music with what the missionaries would have seen as pagan rituals, the church did not actively try to eliminate indigenous music. In fact, one of the very effective early missionary techniques was to set instructional words of the Roman Catholic faith to native melodies, not only because the natives

[13] Stevenson, *Music in Mexico: A Historical Survey.* New York: Thomas Y. Crowell Company, 1971, p. 96.

Mestizo is the term applied to people of mixed racial relationships. In this eighteenth-century painting by a Mexican artist, the title "Espanol, con India, Mestizo" shows a Spanish father, an Indian mother, and their mestizo child. Copyright Schalkwijk/Art Resource, N.Y.
Source: Anonymous, 18th century. Human Races (Las Castas). Oil on Canvas, 1.04 × 1.48 cm. Museo Nacional del Virreinato, Tepotzotlan, Mexico. Copyright Schalkwijk/Art Resource, N.Y.

appeared to learn quickly through this process but also because missionaries were encouraged to leave to the Indians their original customs as long as these customs did not directly conflict with Christianity.[14]

The first Bishop of Mexico, Juan de Zumárraga, instructed the missionaries to use and teach music as "an indispensable aid in the process of conversion" of the Indians.[15] One of the earliest missionaries, Pedro de Gante (1480–1572), opened the first school where Indians were taught plainchant and instrument making. Gante's pupils were then instructed to spread this Spanish style throughout the colony. As early as 1539, the first of a series of highly influential music masters and composers (*maestros de capilla*) was appointed to the new Mexico City Cathedral that had been established on the former site of the great Cue described by Díaz. Sixteenth-century missionary and church chronicles constantly refer to the Indians' "admirable aptitude and talent" in learning the European musical system.

Indian choirs were taught to sing complex liturgical music in the Spanish Renaissance polyphonic style, as well as nonliturgical songs. The works of Spanish composers were sent to New Spain soon after publication and Indians were quickly put to work copying these and earlier music brought from Europe, producing thirteen liturgical books with music during the sixteenth century. Indians also manufactured their own European-style instruments. Early in the Colonial period it was said that there appeared "to be more flutes, sackbuts, trumpets and drums in Mexico than in all the rest of Christendom."[16]

Throughout the sixteenth century, Indian music changed rapidly as natives absorbed European music traditions and adjusted their use of music to conform to Roman Catholic dogma. During the seventeenth and eighteenth centuries, the Indians and the emerging *mestizo* population produced many outstanding musicians. There were several renowned composers, such as Juan Gutiérrez de Padilla (Puebla Cathedral's *maestro de capilla,* 1629–1664) and Antonio de Salazar (Mexico City Cathedral's *maestro de capilla,* 1688–1714), although the composers with the highest positions were usually brought in from Europe. Mirroring developments in Europe, music expanded in the eighteenth century beyond sacred music to secular music, including the production of operas.

Mexican music was, thus, primarily European in style, although it did retain some of its native identity. Many of the native melodies that were used as the basis for teaching the Roman

[14] Ibid., p. 33.
[15] Behague, Gerard and E. Thomas Stanford. "Mexico." *The New Grove Dictionary of Music and Musicians*, p. 226.
[16] Ibid., p. 231.

Catholic faith must have been retained in folk music in one form or another. For example, the folk song and legend of *La Llorona* is said to have Aztec roots. Certain indigenous elements also survived and were reminders of the indigenous music traditions that had flourished prior to the Spanish conquest. These included the predominance of flutes and drums; the use of rattles made from materials such as seashells, gourds, and cocoons; rhythmic complexity; and the practice of singing in a high-pitched falsetto when performing ceremonial songs. Even today, several of these characteristics can be heard in contemporary Mexican and Mexican-American music.

The Influence of the Repartimiento System and the Importation of African Slaves

One of the consequences of the *repartimiento* system and the Spanish importation of African slaves was the influence of African music traditions on Mexican music, for just as the African traditions blended with the dominant European traditions in the United States, so did African traditions blend with the traditions in Mexico. Africans brought to Mexico their own styles of dance and dance rhythms. These African rhythms, and the hybridized rhythms that came from the blend of African and Cuban traditions, later became popular dances such as the habanera, the danzón, rumba, and bolero. Africans also brought their tradition of accompanying dances with songs, and these songs contained words that were frequently hostile toward the colonial government. This tradition of rebellious songs had a direct influence on the development of the music of the Mexican revolution.

The Africans also contributed the marimba, an instrument that resembles a xylophone with tuned keys of cupapé wood that are arranged like the keys of a piano and struck by rubber-covered hammers. Various kinds of xylophones made of different materials were popular melodic percussion instruments in eastern and southern Africa. The term itself comes from the Bantu dialect, in which the prefix *ma* indicates many and *rimba* means notes. Marimbas and marimba ensembles became popular in Mexico as well as many other Latin American countries.

The Influence of the Rigid Social/Racial Class Hierarchy

The rigid social and racial hierarchy in colonial Mexico resulted in different groups being exposed to different kinds of music. The upper classes tended to maintain strict European musical traditions. For example, in the seventeenth century, choirs in the main cathedrals were performing polychoral masses and contrapuntal motets by both European composers and European composers who resided in Mexico. In the eighteenth century, the upper classes began to attend European-style operas. In fact, a native-born Mexican, Manuel Zumaya, composed the second opera known to have been produced in the Americas, *La Parténope* (1711).

Mexican Independence

Colonial Revolt and Mexican Independence from Spain

During the early nineteenth century, much of Europe was preoccupied with defending their countries from invasion by Napoleon. When Napoleon succeeded in occupying Spain, the link between Spain and Mexico was greatly weakened. The colonial government in Mexico was already not very strong. Political corruption had always been a problem. Furthermore, the *criollas,* who were now primarily *mestizos,* resented the way the white *peninsulares* treated them. Finally, the revolutions that were leading to colonial independence in other parts of the world laid the foundation for Mexico's fight for independence.

In 1808 the viceroy, under pressure from influential *criollas,* permitted some *criollas* to participate in administration. The *peninsular* officials objected and expelled the viceroy. Amidst these factional struggles, the Mexican people began a political rebellion. In 1810, Hidalgo—a village priest—demanded the abolition of Indian serfdom and caste distinctions. This revolt was initially successful but it was short-lived, and Hidalgo was captured and shot by royalist forces in 1811. In 1814, a second priest proclaimed a Republic of Mexico, independent of Spain. He, too, was defeated, but the struggle continued. In 1820, the Spanish revolution further weakened the link between colonial Mexico and the colonizing country and, in 1821, the last viceroy of New Spain arrived in Mexico and was forced to accept the Treaty of Cordobá, marking the formal beginning of Mexican independence. A turbulent period ensued comprised of a series of revolts until Santa Anna was elected president in 1833, installing a conservative government composed of church leaders, rich landowners, *criollas,* and army officials.

Mexico's Efforts to Strengthen the Northern Territories

Shortly after gaining independence from Spain in 1821, Mexico attempted to strengthen its northern territories by launching a program to encourage immigration into Texas. The program consisted of offering large land grants to contractors known as *empresarios,* who agreed to develop the land and to bring in a certain number of families to colonize their assigned areas. *Empresarios* such as Stephen Austin participated in this program and established colonies by bringing in immigrants from the United States and from Europe, particularly Ireland. But few *empresarios* were able to attract very many colonists and the result was that over half of what is now Texas was carved up into these land grants, but the numbers of inhabitants remained few.

By 1830, the Mexican government was unhappy with the results of their immigration program and particularly angry that the *empresarios* insisted on keeping slaves. They abandoned the program and closed Texas to Anglo-American colonization. But now, rather than a loyal population that would strengthen Mexican rule in Texas, the province was populated with Americans who wished to break away from Mexico.

The Texas Rebellion

In 1836, the residents of Texas rebelled, angered by the government's insistence that they abolish slavery and by President Santa Anna's plan to centralize the government. When the Mexican government sent soldiers to retake Texas, the rebels rallied around the Alamo mission in a small force. The Mexican troops attacked the Alamo, killing the two hundred Texans barricaded behind its walls. The battle at Alamo has become part of popular U.S. cultural history partially because at this battle, the frontier hero Davey Crockett was killed. When the troops retreated in victory, they were caught and defeated by the American forces of General Sam Houston.

The Texans proclaimed their victory and established the Texas Republic (1836–1845), with Sam Houston as president. The new republic immediately embarked on its own program to promote immigration. The main country that was targeted was Germany, and through Texas's "Society for the Protection of German Immigrants in Texas," thousands of German immigrants were recruited, many of whom settled in the Texas hill country.

Mexican Northern Provinces Become Part of the United States

The Mexican-American War and the First Mexican Americans

Mexico never recognized Texan independence, and it refused to acknowledge its American statehood. In 1846, Americans in the California province also rebelled against Mexico. This, combined with friction between U.S. citizens and Mexicans and a dispute over the western boundary of Texas, led to war between the Mexicans and the Americans. Within a year the Mexican forces were defeated. Under the terms of a treaty signed in 1848 and an additional purchase in 1853, the Rio Grande was fixed as the boundary of Texas, and the territory that now forms the states of Texas, California, and Utah and parts of the states of Nevada, New Mexico, Colorado, Wyoming, and

Arizona became part of the United States. Hence, the Mexican-American saying, "Some of us crossed over the border and, for others, the border crossed over us."

MEXICAN AMERICANS RELEGATED TO SECOND-CLASS CITIZEN STATUS

Although *mestizos* still outnumbered whites throughout the Southwest, the white minority gained control by discriminating against them. The derogatory stereotypes that were created about Mexican-Americans that became a staple of both popular thought and expansionist ideology made it inevitable that with the winning of the Mexican-American War, Spanish-speaking *mestizos* would be relegated to second-class status. Anglos took land from *mestizos,* limited their political power, and lowered their social position. Although Mexican Americans suffered from discrimination, the booming American economy continued to tempt thousands of poor Mexicans to cross the border. The Mexicans who had remained in the Southwest after transfer of the land to the United States grew to 75,000 by 1890, but then the Mexican-American population exploded to 562,000 by 1900.

Against this backdrop of political change, *mestizos* enjoyed a rich musical tradition, including the genres of the *son, canciones,* and *corridos.* These *mestizo* musics were the first music traditions of the earliest Mexican Americans.

MESTIZO MUSIC TRADITIONS

Structural Characteristics

RHYTHM, MELODY, AND HARMONY

The rhythm of most *mestizo* music is divisive and clearly metrical. The melodies tend to be European in style, based on major and minor scales with simple chords providing harmony. Sometimes the major and minor tonalities alternate within the same piece. The melodies are often in a limited range, with harmonizing melodies paralleling the primary melody at intervals of thirds or sixths, emphasizing the European-derived harmony. Melodies are frequently sung in a high-pitched falsetto, which is a vocal style that was retained from indigenous traditions.

TEXTURE, FORM, AND INSTRUMENTATION

Mestizo music is typically in heterophonic and homophonic texture. The call-and-response technique is manifested as a verse and refrain form, in which the verse, with constantly changing words, is sung by a soloist (the call) and the group sings a refrain (the response). Many of the indigenous aerophones have been replaced with the European version of the same basic instrument, such as the brass trumpet replacing the conch trumpet. Percussion instruments of the idiophone or membranophone category build on the indigenous forms (such as rattles) and add instruments of African origin, such as marimbas. Perhaps the most significant change was the addition of a variety of stringed instruments, including violins, harps, the *vihuela* (a small five-string guitar), *jarana* (a slightly larger five-string guitar), and *guitarrones* (large bass guitars).

Popular *Mestizo* Music Styles

SONES

The generic term for peasant or rural music is the *son,* which originated in the Spanish dance songs that were brought to Mexico by the Spaniards. The term *son* is used to describe a broad category of music that includes instruments, song, and dance. One of the unifying characteristics is its rhythmic vitality of duple meter alternating with triple meter. The two meters might also be used simultaneously, such that one instrument plays music in duple meter, while another plays in triple meter. Another common characteristic is that *sones* frequently incorporate *zapateado,* rapid movement of the feet against the ground to produce a percussive accompaniment.

Musicians perform Hispanic folk music in a public square in Guatamala, singing and playing the stringed instruments (such as the guitar) that were brought over by the Spanish. *Source: Photo by Robert Freck. Odyssey Production, Inc.*

The instrumental *son* ensemble varies regionally, but it is essentially a string band. A typical group would include two violins, a *vihuela,* a *jarana,* and a harp. The song texts are always in couplets of two phrases and are typically clever lyrics about love and women. The dance is performed by independent couples and is characterized by sections accompanied by music that alternates an instrumental section with a sung part. *Son* dances often imitate animals and human stereotypes, a practice that is reflected in their titles (e.g., "El burro" and "El distinguido," meaning the burro and the distinguished one, respectively). *Sones* are found throughout Mexico in both uniform national styles and in distinct regional styles (e.g., *son veracruzano* or *sones jaliscienses*). The international hit, "La Bamba," was originally a regional *son* from Veracruz, whereas *sones* from Jalisco are the basis for the popular style of music known as *mariachi.*[17]

MARIACHI

Mariachi is the most familiar genre of Mexican and Mexican-American music.

There is debate on the origins of the word "mariachi." An early popular explanation was that *mariachi* is the Spanish rendering of the French *marriage.* During the short reign of the French Emperor Maximilian (1863–1865) and the subsequent influence of French culture over Mexico, the name *mariachi* was given to the folk ensembles that went from wedding to wedding to play, and the musicians who played this important role supplementing the marriage ceremonies were called *mariacheros.* Another explanation is that the word originated in the language of the Coca Indians at the time of the Spanish conquest. It meant simply "musician" and was used to mean any person that engaged in musical activities.

A type of *son,* the original *mariachi* was comprised of a small ensemble of string instruments, typically two violins, a *vihuela,* a harp (later replaced by guitar), and a *jarana.* Sometimes referred to as "folk" mariachi bands, these ensembles still perform in the countryside of central Mexico. The more common contemporary *mariachi* consists of one to three trumpets, two to three violins, guitar, and *guitarrón* (the large bass guitar) with the guitarists also performing as vocalists singing a variety of *corridos* and *rancheras.*

Although the folk mariachis were popular in the country for centuries, they did not come to Mexico City until the 1920s, when Mexican

[17] Farquharson, Mary. "Much More Than Mariachi," in *World of Music: The Rough Guide,* vol. 2. Simon Broughton and Mark Ellingham (Editors). London: Rough Guides Ltd., 2000, pp. 464–465.

nationalism inspired great interest in "authentic Mexican" music. The contemporary commercial and most familiar kind of *mariachi* was not formed until the 1930s. One explanation is that Emilio Azcárraga Vidaurreta, the main director of radio station XEW that opened in Mexico City in 1930, wanted to play some authentic folk mariachi music but thought that the string ensemble sound was too soft and thin for reproduction by radio. He suggested replacing the harp with a trumpet. This was such an immediate success that it was quickly imitated and soon became Mexico's unofficial national ensemble. Mariachi music became extremely popular in the 1950s, when musicians played *ranchera* music to accompany Hollywood films.

CANCIONES AND CORRIDOS

The term *canción* is a very broad, general category designating any type of song as opposed to an instrumental piece. But when it is connected with another modifying word, such as *canciones ranchera,* it identifies a specific type of song. For example, *canciones ranchera,* sometimes just referred to as *rancheras,* are songs about life on the ranch.

Corridos were originally a literary genre, but because they have often been set to music, they are now typically defined as a genre blending text and music. The *corrido* has a very long history in Mexico, and there are basically two types. The *romance corrido* has its roots in Spanish folklore. Similar to the Anglo ballad, it tells an epic or love story, usually through the means of dialogue. *Romance corridos* were popular throughout the colonial period and reflect the strong connection between colonial Mexico and Spain.

The *corrido mexicano* developed out of the Spanish *romance corrido* during the late seventeenth and the eighteenth centuries. Instead of dialogue, the stories are narrated through the first or third person, with the singer acting as the observer of the event he or she is describing. *Corridos* frequently begin with an opening salutation and end with a farewell. The Mexican *corrido* has historically been connected with rebellion against the Spanish rulers, a characteristic that may reflect the influence of the dance-song texts of the African slaves. Inquisition records from the eighteenth century include many early forms of *corridos* ridiculing the Spanish viceroys.

Corridos have retained their strongly nationalistic and rebellious nature. During the political upheavals following the war for independence, and especially later during the Revolution, the Mexican *corrido* became very important. The history of Mexico from around 1845 to the present can be traced just by reading *corrido* texts. Later *corridos* conveyed information about murders, accidents of various kinds, the exploits of local heroes, and national and regional political events. Around the border area between Mexico and the United States, many of the *corridos* talk about smuggling and trying to escape over the border. Traditional *corridistas* accompanied themselves on a harp or guitar, but now vocalists in *norteño* and *mariachi* ensembles also sing *corridos.* Professional *corridistas* work throughout Mexico and the American Southwest and some, such as Lydia Mendoza, are nationally famous.

CONCLUSION

Mexican Americans possess a rich musical tradition derived from European religious, classical, and popular music, and the Mexican genres of the *sones* (including *mariachi*), *canciones*, and *corridos.* The Mexican genres, particularly, continue to be important to Mexican Americans as they strive to retain their cultural heritage. *Mariachi* is now an emblem of identity for both Mexicans and Mexican Americans, and mariachi bands provide entertainment for community gatherings ranging from park picnics to wedding celebrations. Linda Ronstadt, a popular music superstar of Mexican-American heritage, brought these music genres to mainstream attention when she recorded her *Canciones de Mi Padre* in 1988. This, and a follow-up album, consisted of a variety of *ranchera* and *corrido* classics with *mariachi* accompaniment. *Mariachi* has

Break-Out Four

PROFILE *Linda Ronstadt*

Linda Maria Ronstadt was born in 1946 in Tucson, Arizona, to a Mexican-American father and a German-American mother. She was raised on a ranch, and her first singing experience was with her sisters in a group they called "The Three Ronstadts." At Arizona State University, she met guitarist Bob Kimmel and together they moved to Los Angeles and joined up with the songwriter Kenny Edwards. The group sang in an urban folk style, took the name of the Stone Poneys (from a blues song), and recorded their first hit, "Different Drum," in 1967. In 1968, she embarked on a solo career. Over the subsequent decades, she became hugely popular and successful, recording and performing in a great many musical styles. With her voice, which has been described as "the most versatile, strongest and most alluring vocal sound in pop music",[18] she has been successful in performing country rock, country, rock 'n' roll, Latin, jazz standards, opera, light opera, and white soul. In 1987 she recorded *Canciones de Mi Padre* (Songs of My Father) and in 1991 *Mas Canciones.* These recordings brought *rancheras, corridos,* and other Mexican-American song styles to mainstream attention. For her work she has received two American Music awards, eight Grammy awards, and two Country Music Awards.

Linda Ronstadt. *Source: Photo by Barry Rankin.*

[18] Decurtis, Anthony et al., *Rolling Stone: Illustrated History of Rock and Roll.* New York: Random House, 1992, p. 544.

been one of the most modernized of all popular Mexican styles.[19] In the late nineteenth and early twentieth centuries, Mexicans and Mexican Americans incorporated into their music the music characteristics of the large number of German, Pole, and Czech immigrants who had moved into the Southwest, particularly Texas. These various traditions combined to form the unique *norteño* and Tex Mex styles of the early twentieth century. Although the style developed in the border areas, it became extremely popular throughout Mexico and the United States. These styles, and other forms of contemporary Mexican-American music that developed in the twentieth century, will be covered in a subsequent chapter.

[19] The phenomenal success of Luis Miguel and Alejandro Fernandez is based on their modernized *mariachi* music. In fact, Luis Miguel's "Romance," a multiplatinum-selling album, features *mariachi* songs from 1944 to 1986.

BIBLIOGRAPHY

Behague, Gerard. "Folk and Traditional Music of Latin America: General Prospects and Research Problems," *The World of Music* 25/2 (1982).

Behague, Gerard and E. Thomas Stanford. "Mexico." *The New Grove Dictionary of Music and Musicians,* vol. 12. Stanley Sadie (Editor). New York: Macmillan Publishers, Limited, 1980.

Campa, L. Arthur. *Hispanic Culture in the Southwest.* Norman: University of Oklahoma Press, 1979.

Caso, Alfonso. *The Aztecs: People of the Sun.* Translated by Lowell Dunham. Norman: University of Oklahoma Press, 1970.

Farquharson, Mary. "Much More Than Mariachi," in *World of Music: The Rough Guide,* vol. 2. Simon Broughton and Mark Ellingham (Editors). London: Rough Guides Ltd., 2000, pp. 464–465.

Garcia, Edwin, Anne Martinez and Jessie Mangaliman. "Numbers Show a Country in Racial Transformation." *San Jose Mercury News,* March 13, 2001, front page.

Geijerstam, Claesaf. *Popular Music in Mexico.* Albuquerque: University of New Mexico Press, 1976.

Goldfield, David et al. *The American Journey: A History of the United States.* Upper Saddle River, NJ: Prentice Hall, 2001.

Guzman, Isaac. "The Battlin' Latin Music Awards: 'Premio' vs. Grammys." *Knight-Ridder/Tribune News Service,* 2-3-2001. http://www.elibrary.com/s/edumark/getdoc.cgi?id=19596813x1. . . :US;EL&dtype-0~0&dinst= (Accessed 05–14–01).

Hispanic-American Almanac [The]: A Reference Work on Hispanics in the United States. Detroit, MI: Gale Research Inc., 1993.

Kirsch, Jonathan. "Chicano Power." *New West* (September 11, 1978), pp. 35–40.

Latino Encyclopedia, [The]. Richard Chabran and Rafael Chabran (Editors) vol. 5, Peyote—Spanish Americans. New York: Marshall Cavendish Corp., 1996.

"Latino Population soars in U.S.", *San Francisco Chronicle.* May 10, 2001, p. A3.

Mesones, Dr. Pedro de. "We Are Hispanics not Latinos!" Guest Editorial by Mesones, President of the Advancement of Hispanic Americans. *National Hispanic Reporter.* November 1990, p. 15.

Music in Latin American Culture: Regional Traditions. John M. Schechter (General Editor). New York: Schirmer Books, 1999.

Nettl, Bruno. *Folk and Traditional Music of the Western Continents.* Englewood Cliffs, NJ: Prentice Hall, 1965.

Olsen, Dale A. "Folk Music of South America: A Musical Mosaic," in *Musics of Many Cultures: An Introduction.* Elizabeth May (Editor). Berkeley: University of California Press, 1980.

Paredes, Americo. *A Texas-Mexican Cancionero: Folksongs of the Lower Border.* Urbana: University of Illinois Press. 1979.

Robb, John Donald. *Hispanic Folk Music of New Mexico and the Southwest: A Self-Portrait of a People.* Norman: University of Oklahoma Press, 1980.

Stevenson, Robert. *Spanish Music in the Age of Columbus.* The Hague, Netherlands: Martinus Nijhoff, 1960.

Stevenson, Robert. *Music in Aztec and Inca Territory.* Berkeley: 1968.

Stevenson, Robert. *Music in Mexico: A Historical Survey.* New York: Thomas Y. Crowell Company, 1971.

Stevenson, Robert. "The Afro-American Musical Legacy to 1800." *Musical Quarterly* 54 (October 1968).

Tanner, Helen Hornbeck, ed. *The Settling of North America: The Atlas of the Great Migrations into North America from the Ice Age to the Present.* New York: Macmillan, 1995.

Tenenbaum, Barbara A., editor-in-chief. *Encyclopedia of Latin American History and Culture.* New York: Simon & Schuster Macmillan, 1996.

Terrazas, Beatriz/staff writer, Rolling with the Rockeros Rock en espanol speaks to young immigrants with culture-changing power. *The Dallas Morning News,* 10-22-2000, p. 1F. http://www.elibrary.com/s/edumark/getdo. . . rn:bigchalk.com:US;EL&dtype=0~0&dinst=0 (Accessed 05-03-01).

Turino, Thomas. "Music in Latin America." *Excursions in World Music.* Bruno Nettl et al. (Editors). New York: Prentice Hall, 1992.

Webb, Karyn. "Don't Cry for Me, La Llorona: An Analysis of Llorona Myths and Their Effect on Gender-Based Identiy Issues of Hispanic Women." Unpublished paper. May 15, 2000.

Chapter Six

The Blues

Concert venues such as *The House of Blues,* organizations such as *The Blues Foundation,* PBS's film series titled *The Blues,* and extensive online sites such as *The Blue Highway* attest to the growing national recognition of one of America's greatest musical treasures. The blues are the basis for many of the most widely recognized American music forms, including jazz, rock 'n' roll, R & B, and hip hop. In the words of the African-American blues artist Willie Dixon, "The blues are the roots, everything else is the fruits." Many of the first recordings of rock 'n' roll, such as Bill Haley and the Comets' *Shake, Rattle, and Roll,* the Crew Cuts' *Sh-Boom* and Elvis Presley's *You Ain't Nothin' But a Hound Dog,* were covers of blues songs recorded previously by black artists. Most of the musicians in the big British groups, including members of the Beatles, the Rolling Stones, the Animals, Them, the Yardbirds, Cream, and Led Zeppelin began their musical careers performing blues and several of their biggest hits were their versions of traditional blues songs. The early music of the San Francisco acid rock groups such as Janis Joplin, the Grateful Dead, Jimi Hendrix, and Country Joe and the Fish were heavily amplified versions of the blues. The blues continues to be a vital music tradition in contemporary popular music. Musicians of many ethnicities record contemporary versions of the blues. It is this blues tradition, from its origins in the field hollers, spirituals, and work songs of African-American slaves, to its pervasive influence on twentieth-century rock 'n' roll, that is the subject of this chapter.

Overview of the Music Tradition of the Blues

Origin of the Term "The Blues"

"The blues" refers both to a melancholy emotional state and to a specific type of music. Use of the term to describe an emotional state has a long history, apparently beginning in Europe at least as early as the seventeenth century, when "the blue devils" meant a condition of sadness and depression. The term "the blues" was used off and on throughout the subsequent centuries. For example, Washington Irving, the nineteenth-century American author of *The Legend of Sleepy Hollow,* wrote in 1807 that he was experiencing a "fit of the blues."[1] However, despite scattered early use of the term, "the blues" to describe loneliness and sadness did not come into general usage in the United States until close to the end of the century. It was about this same time that the term "blues" was applied to a musical form. The blues as a distinct musical form appears to have developed after the Civil War and the emancipation of the slaves, growing out of a fusion of several musical influences, most notably African-American work songs, spirituals, and field hollers.

Stylistic Categories

From its origins in the rural South, the blues developed in several geographic areas and into several broad categories.

Country or Rural Blues

These terms refer to the style of blues that arose in the earliest phase of blues development, beginning after the Civil War and continuing into the first quarter of the twentieth century. Country blues are more directly the result of personal expression, and are therefore sung solo. Solo singing frees up the singer to be more expressive, so nonstandardized forms, both in the lyric pattern and in the harmonic progression, characterize these blues. The singer sometimes introduces and ends his performance with spoken words, and in the singing uses a great variety of vocal techniques, for example rough, growling tones contrasted with high falsetto. Country blues are accompanied by acoustic guitar, which is sometimes played using items such as a knife, tube, or bottleneck as a barre. Barres allow for both open tuning (in which the guitar strings are tuned to a chord and the barre is slid down the neck to change the chords) and they enable the performer to produce different kinds of sounds such as train whistles. There is also occasional addition of the harmonica. Examples of musicians singing in the country blues style include Charlie Patton, Blind Lemon Jefferson, and Son House.

City or Classic Blues

These terms refer to the style of blues singing which came into existence during the 1920s and which dominated to the mid-1930s. They are a by-product of the great migration of blacks out of the rural South into the cities, and were initially used as a form of entertainment in the minstrel and vaudeville shows. In this style, two or more instruments accompany the blues singer and the emphasis moves from unaccompanied guitar to piano. In order to coordinate the efforts of the ensemble of musicians, these blues use the standardized twelve-bar form and harmonic progression. Female singers dominate this style, and examples of musicians singing in the classic blues style include Ma Rainey, Bessie Smith, and Edith Johnson.

Piano Blues

Although the blues guitarists have received more attention, an important tradition of blues pianists also developed during the 1920s. Piano blues use the twelve-bar formal and harmonic pattern of classic blues but adds characteristics idiomatic to the piano. For example, to achieve the "blue notes" on the piano, pianists "crush" or "press" the keys (striking two or more keys not quite simultaneously). Several specific bass patterns developed in conjunction with piano blues under the general categories of boogie-woogie and barrelhouse. Examples of blues pianists include Eurreal "Little Brother" Montgomery, Roosevelt Sykes, and "Georgia" or "Barrelhouse" Tom Dorsey.

Urban, Modern, or Contemporary Blues

These terms refer to the style of blues singing that developed following the influence of jazz and the rise of the nightclub, in which entertainment served as a backdrop to conversation and drinking. To project over the noise, the vocal lines were sung in a shouting style and new and often

[1] Springer, Robert. *Authentic Blues: Its History and Its Themes.* Lewiston, NY: Edwin Mellen Press, 1995, p. 28.

amplified instruments were added to the accompaniment, including electric guitar, percussion and saxophone. Like city blues, these blues used the standardized twelve-bar form and harmonic progression. Within the accompaniment, there is frequent use of a "riff," a short melodic phrase that is coordinated with the blues progression and that is repeated in an ostinato. Furthermore, the music is sometimes notated and arranged. Examples of musicians singing in the contemporary blues style include Joe Turner, T-Bone Walker, and B. B. King and, more recently, The Kinsey Report and Vasti Jackson.

Rhythm 'n' Blues

This term refers to the transformation in the late 1940s and 1950s of the earlier blues forms into music that was primarily used for dancing. This form of blues served as the foundation for the development of rock 'n' roll. Defining characteristics include the addition of several electric and amplified instruments, including guitar, organ, and bass. Rhythm 'n' blues was primarily music for dancing, so although it included a vocal line, the words used were often employed for their rhythmic properties rather than their meaning. In the accompaniment, various patterns that had developed out of blues piano were used and the rhythmic structure emphasized the offbeat stress on the "weak beats" (two and four in a quadruple meter) that characterized contemporary jazz. Examples of early musicians singing in the rhythm-and-blues style are John Lee Hooker, Chuck Berry, "Little Richard" Peniman, and Fats Domino. It was "covers" of rhythm and blues recordings by white artists that launched rock 'n' roll.

The Structural Characteristics of the Blues

Rhythm, Melody, and Harmony

The blues is generally characterized by a steady, even, and percussive rhythm in the accompanying instrument(s) with a fluid rhythmic melody above. The meter is most frequently quadruple. Blues melodies usually have an underlying call-and-response structure: within each four-measure phrase, the sung melody typically takes up only two measures, leaving the remaining two for an improvised answer in the accompaniment. The melodies emphasize the notes of the chords that provide the harmony, but they also incorporate notes that are microtonally lower. These notes are typically the third, seventh, and sometimes fifth of the scale. Called the "blue notes," these lowered tones have their origins in African tonal practices and are found in all forms of African-American music. Blues singers also use the wide range of vocal techniques that are indigenous to Africa, including ornamentation, falsetto, and nonmelodic techniques such as moaning and groaning.

In the early stages of the blues, singers used whichever chords they wished to provide accompaniment. Later blues use a very regular harmonic progression derived from a key's "primary chords." Primary chords are the chords built upon the first, fourth, and fifth tones of the scale. In music theory, roman numerals are used to identify the chord's ordinal position in the scale, such that the chord built on the fifth tone of the scale is referred to as the "V" chord. In blues chords, an additional note that is an interval of a seventh away from the fundamental base note of the chord is also used, indicated by adding an Arabic number 7 on top, such as "V^7." The chords are also given names. Using all these identification systems, the primary chords of any key with their added seventh tone are identified as the tonic (I^7), subdominant (IV^7), and dominant (V^7). Although there can be slight variations, below is the most common form of the standard twelve-bar blues harmonic progression that underlies the majority of blues.

The Standard 12-Bar Blues Progression

Vocal "Call"		Instrumental "Response"	
I^7	I^7	I^7	I^7
IV^7	IV^7	I^7	I^7
V^7	IV^7	I^7	I^7

It is not clear precisely how these chords became so standard, but it probably began as the result of exposure to European popular songs and Protestant hymns, both of which rely heavily on these three chords. Then, when blues began being sung by groups, the series of chords became fixed so that all players could start and stop together and so that all players had a solid, predictable harmonic foundation over which they could improvise as soloists.

Texture, Instrumentation, and Form

The blues are sung in a homophonic texture, with the primary melody accompanied by guitar or, in later versions of the blues, by an instrumental ensemble. There is also a built-in performance texture of "call-and-response" between the voice and instruments. The early blues singers accompanied themselves on the banjo, which was a direct descendant of the African *bania* or *moanza.* But by the end of the nineteenth century, most singers were accompanying themselves on the guitar. The reasons were varied. First, the short, staccato notes of the banjo were not as appropriate as the warmer, more sonorous and resonant notes of the guitar to establish the mood of the blues. Second, the guitar was more flexible and could provide a more sensitive accompaniment. For example, strings could be "bent" more easily to produce the microtones for blue notes; and a knife, bottle top, and so on could be more readily played across the neck to achieve new timbres simulating such sounds as whining and train whistles. The second stage of blues development, called "classic" or "city" blues, used an ensemble such as piano and guitar to accompany the singer. In contemporary blues and rhythm and blues, this ensemble used electric guitars and additional instruments of percussion, brass, and woodwinds.

In the early years of its development, the blues structure was extremely varied, with different lengths and different patterns used to convey the particular thoughts and feelings of an individual. Later the blues became more stabilized and fixed most commonly into twelve bars with a specific lyric pattern of AAB in three lines, each four measures in length. This lyric pattern of a repeated phrase followed by an answering phrase is another example of the influence of call and response. A verse from the famous "Crossroads Blues" shows this typical lyric pattern:

Call

Line 1 (A)	I went down to the cross roads, got down on my knees.
Line 2 (A Repeated)	Yes I went down to the cross roads, got down on my knees.

Response

Line 3 (B)	I begged the Lord for mercy, if you please.

Sometimes this form is contracted into eight bars and sometimes it is expanded into sixteen bars, but the twelve-bar blues is the form that is heard most frequently.

The Blues in a Historical and Social Context

The Civil War and Reconstruction

When the Civil War broke out in 1861, the elimination of slavery was not President Abraham Lincoln's foremost intent. Although he was morally opposed to slavery, he hoped to preserve the Union without having to abolish slavery or northern discrimination against blacks. But black abolitionists fought for black inclusion in the military services on the Union side with the goal that the war would result in the elimination of slavery. At first, few blacks were allowed to join the military, but as casualties mounted in 1862, northern military commanders needed to augment their forces and one way they did this was with black recruits. Later that year, Lincoln signed his "Emancipation Proclamation" freeing all slaves held by southerners who were still rebelling as of January 1, 1863.

When the war ended in 1865 and the United States entered the period known as "The Reconstruction," the two main questions pressing the nation were what to do with the Confederate

Break-Out One

LISTENING GUIDE *"Cross Road Blues"*

Performing Artist: Robert Johnson

The enigmatic Robert Johnson (1911–1938) has been extraordinarily influential on modern music despite the fact that he recorded his music only twice, once in San Antonio, Texas, in 1936 and then again in Dallas, Texas, in 1937. "Cross Road Blues" is one of his most famous songs, perhaps because of the "crossroads" legend associated with Johnson. Johnson reportedly went down to the "crossroads" at midnight to make a deal with the Devil, exchanging his soul for the ability to be a phenomenal guitarist. He was later poisoned to death after drinking whiskey that had been laced with strychnine by the jealous husband of a woman Johnson was seeing. No doctors would help him, and he died in agony.

Rhythm	Loose quadruple
Melody	Blues form of AA melody with B in both melody and lyrics.
Harmony	Blues scale
Texture	Homophonic, with call-and-response between voice and guitar
Form	AAB of early blues; early twelve-bar form
Instrumentation	Male voice with guitar; guitar also played with slide and as rhythm instrument.

states and what to do with the four million slaves who were now "freedmen." Regarding the ex-slaves, the Freedmen's Bureau was set up to bring such things as food, shelter, and schools to assist blacks. In terms of the Confederate states, although Lincoln and his successor, Andrew Johnson, wanted to establish a lenient policy with as little recrimination as possible, many northern citizens wanted the states to be punished. This attitude strongly contributed to the bitterness felt by southern whites after the war. The bitterness fueled antiblack sentiment, and many whites joined forces to ensure that former slaves would be confined to a lower social status.

Confining the former slaves to a lower social status was done through the legal process in a series of laws stripping blacks of their new rights. These "Jim Crow" laws (named after a black cartoon character) culminated in the Supreme Court's *Plessy v. Ferguson* decision of 1896 in which blacks were required to use separate public facilities. It also was achieved through sheer terror by the intimidation strategies of secret terrorist organizations such as the Ku Klux Klan (founded in 1866) and the Knights of the White Camellia, who kidnapped, beat, whipped, and lynched "uppity" blacks. It was in this historical context that the blues was born.

Origins of the Blues to 1900

Although some scholars theorize that the blues existed before the Civil War, the preponderance of current evidence suggests that the blues as a distinct musical style developed after the Civil War when the southern slaves were freed. The large plantation system was no longer economically viable, and the huge tracts of land were broken up and parceled into small farms. Because most blacks could not afford to purchase a farm, they elected instead to work a "share" of the farm in exchange for the use of a mule, farming equipment, a simple cabin, and basic food. Typically half of the produce they farmed would go to the farm owner, and the other half would be used to pay off the debt they accrued for the things that they had borrowed. Hence, a new system called sharecropping peonage developed. Although the group labor of the plantations was thus replaced by individual work, the methods of sowing, weeding, and harvesting the crops remained.

Change and Continuity in Music Traditions

While the farmer worked in the field, he might sing to the rhythmic strikes of the hoe for his own amusement or sing to communicate with the members of his family who were also working in the field. Hence the cries, calls, and hollers that had existed on the plantations continued to exist to some extent on the small sharecropping farms. Work songs, with their strong call-and-response characteristics, had served an important function in a variety of venues on the plantations ensuring that the work progressed evenly, coordinating movements (and hence preventing injury), and generally motivating the workers by fostering a sense of community. For the most part, work songs disappeared on the small farms, but they were taken over by the penitentiary system and used to coordinate the efforts of the chain gangs. Spirituals continued to be sung both in religious services and as a kind of folk song that communicated the joys and sorrows of everyday life. These three musical traditions had been in existence before the Civil War. Emancipation brought about several changes that helped these established musical traditions develop into the blues.

Banjo Lesson: This painting by Henry Ossawa Tanner from 1893 shows an African-American man teaching a child how to play the banjo. The banjo evolved out of the African instrument called the *mbanza*. *Source: Henry Ossawa Tanner,* The Banjo Lesson, *1893. Oil on canvas. Hampton University, Hampton, Virginia.*

Changes in the Social Context That Allowed for Development of the Blues

Perhaps the most important change after the Civil War was that in addition to freeing the slaves physically, emancipation freed the slaves emotionally, intellectually, and spiritually. Freed from bondage, African Americans could now celebrate both their humanity and their individuality. No longer were they technically just chattel—property owned by others in the same manner as livestock or equipment. No longer were they herded into groups both in living arrangements and out on the fields. They had time to be alone, and the personal freedom to conduct their lives the way that they saw fit. As LeRoi Jones says,

> The emancipation of the slaves proposed for them a normal human existence, a humanity impossible under slavery. Of course, even after slavery the average Negro's life in America was, using the more ebullient standards of the average American white man, a shabby, barren existence. But still this was the black man's first experience of time when he could be alone. . . . (And) the small farms and

> sharecroppers' plots produced not only what I think must have been a less self-conscious work song but a form of song or shout that did not necessarily have to be concerned with or inspired by, *labor.* Each man had his own voice and his own way of shouting—his own life to sing about.[2]

The intensely personal style of early blues conveys this celebration of individuality and humanity that was so severely curtailed when African Americans were slaves.

Second, emancipation brought about more leisure time. Farming was hard work, and at the height of the cotton-picking season at the end of the summer, everyone labored from early morning to late at night. But during the rest of the year, especially in the interlude between when the cotton was planted and when it was harvested, there was some respite at night and at the end of the week, when Saturday night became a traditional entertainment night in southern rural communities. Folks would gather at a central location, perhaps a "juke joint" (a term for a road house developed out of the West African Bambara word *dzugu*) and drink, dance, and listen to the more talented individuals sing a wide variety of songs. These individuals were called "songsters."

MUSIC OF THE SONGSTERS

Songsters accompanied themselves on the banjo or guitar and were found in rural communities all over the South. Huddie Ledbetter, known as Leadbelly (born in 1885), Charlie Patton (born in 1891), and Mississippi John Hurt (born in 1895) are examples of the last generation of these songsters. Their songs drew from the various slave musical traditions and the popular songs and ballads of the day that had filtered down into the rural communities. The ballads of Anglo folk song tradition, brought to this country and retained by European Americans, were a particularly important genre. But because songs of the Elfin King and Barbara Allen meant little to the African-American community, blacks adapted the concept to convey their own legends and immortalize their own heroes. In this manner, some of the great ballads developed about events in the lives of black people, or about events with which they could relate. The ballads *John Henry, Stack o Lee (Stagger Lee), Joe Turner,* and *Railroad Bill* are examples.

THE MERGING OF EUROPEAN AND AFRICAN TRADITIONS

The blues developed through the songsters from the cross influences of African-American hollers, work songs, and spirituals and the European popular songs and ballads. Essentially, the African traditions contributed the tonal characteristics, free rhythm, call-and-response style, and sense of personal expression and the European traditions contributed the structured regularity and harmonic characteristics. The earliest documented blues reflect these various links of slave musical traditions and European ballads. For example, in the mid-1890s, Buddy Bolden is credited with improvising "a blues" on the cornet, which was described as a "field holler that was played instrumentally."[3] And the ballad of Joe Turner, a work song ballad about a "long-chain man" who would bring prisoners from Memphis to the Nashville jail in the 1890s, became the very popular *Joe Turner Blues.*

THE "BIRTH" OF THE BLUES

The precise time when these various traditions fused into what we now call country, rural, or archaic blues has been a subject of considerable scholarly debate and will probably remain obscure for two main reasons. First, transmitted in an oral tradition by largely illiterate people, there is no written documentation of these early blues. And, second, the fusion occurred probably before the result was actually called "the blues." This is reinforced by the recollections of the oldest blues singers such as Fred McDowell: "Sure, we used to

[2] Jones, LeRoi. *Blues People: Negro Music in White America.* New York: William Morrow and Company, 1963, p. 61.

[3] Oliver, Paul, *Story of the Blues*, p. 16.

play a lot of what they call blues now, only then we played it they didn't call it the blues—they called it the 'reel.'"[4] McDowell's statement has been corroborated by others, and suggests that in its early forms, blues may have even been sung and played at a faster tempo to accompany dancing.

Since many of the sharecropping farms were located in a region known as the Mississippi Delta—a fertile area bordered by the Mississippi River on the west and the Yazoo River on the east, and extending northward and southward from Vicksburg to Memphis—and some of the most important early blues musicians such as Charlie Patton and Son House—came from this area, and the Mississippi Delta has been designated as the area that gave birth to the blues. But very close in time (if not simultaneously), blues were being sung all over the South, including in Texas with Blind Lemon Jefferson and Leadbelly (Huddie Ledbetter).

Spread of the Blues from 1900 to 1920

There were three main influences that helped spread the blues and fostered its transition from the country/rural blues to the classic city blues: urban migration, medicine/minstrel/vaudeville shows, and the published blues of W. C. Handy.

Urban Migration

The great migration of blacks from the rural South into the cities and the North began soon after emancipation and gained momentum through the turn of the century. Several factors contributed to this migration: the intense racism that had resulted as a white backlash to having lost the war; the extreme poverty in which the sharecropping farmers had to live; the destruction of crops by the cotton boll weevil, which first appeared in Texas in the 1890s and infested Mississippi by 1905; and the simple desire to enjoy the new freedom of movement to explore new lands. Country singers brought the blues with them to the cities, putting out their hat or tin cup, singing along places such as the railroad tracks, and encouraging passersby to contribute nickels and dimes. To the multitudes of people who had left their farms looking for a better life in the city, these singers recalled for them their earlier lives and sang about their current predicament in language and a style they understood.

Medicine, Circus, and Minstrel Shows

Throughout the South, a frequent site in vacant lots was the medicine show. Traveling by wagon, a "typical Southern gentleman doctor" would set up a rough stage and introduce various performers to provide entertainment and help attract a crowd. These performers might include dancers, a jug band, or a songster or blues singer. When enough people had gathered, "The Doctor" would produce a bottle of miracle tonic, show its effectiveness by trying it out on one of the performers, and then start trying to sell bottles of medicine.[5] Several blues singers and songsters spent their active performing years working these shows, including Jim Jackson, Walter "Furry" Lewis, Tommy Johnson, and Robert Wilkins.

Additionally, many blues singers made their performance debuts through sideshows to the "second" companies of the big circuses. These second companies played for black audiences only, and included sideshows, medicine shows, and general entertainment in which blues singers could perform. Sometimes these companies followed the main circus, and sometimes they made a separate tour. Eventually, these trailer shows became independent shows themselves.

The American minstrel show had already crystallized as a form of popular entertainment in the early 1840s. These shows used white comedians with faces blackened by burned cork in a series of songs and skits portraying black characters

[4] Springer, p. 29.

[5] Although the doctors were frequently totally unqualified and their tonics worthless, these medicine shows were considered an important and reasonable means for providing medicine to African Americans. The South, there were only a handful of legitimate clinics and just a few thousand hospital beds to serve several million black people.

Break-Out Two

INSIGHT *The Blues as the Devil's Music*

The blues have had a long tradition of being associated with the devil. The term "the blues" itself seems to have had this connection, as when the term "the blues" first started being documented in Europe in the early seventeenth century as a condition of sadness and depression, it was because someone had been the victim of "the blue devils." One of the earliest blues singers from the Mississippi Delta was Son House, who learned to play the blues directly from the "Father of the Blues," Charlie Patton, and recorded with him in 1930. Up until about two years before that recording date, Son House had been a preacher, but the lure of the sound of the blues played with a slide guitar caused him to give up his preaching career in exchange for one as a bluesman. In an interview shortly before his death, Son House stated,

> I played the blues and I played gospel some too, but you can't take God and the devil on together, cause these two fellows, they don't communicate so well together. They don't get along so well together. The Devil, he believes in one thing and God, well he believes in another, and you've got to separate the two guys. How you going to do it? You've got to follow one or the other.[6]

Perhaps the connection between the blues and the devil was simply because of the blues' development in the juke joints. Juke joints were the simple shacks in which blacks would gather, especially on Saturday night, to drink, dance, and be entertained by musicians, and it is believed that the blues originated there in a fusion of various African-American musical traditions. To devoutly religious people, the cavorting at these juke joints may have been sinful and, hence, the music that accompanied it was sinful as well. And there is no question that some of the most influential and famous blues singers lived "sinful" lives characterized by hard drinking, womanizing, and violence.

But the music historian Robert Palmer suggests the connection goes deeper:

> The whole idea of the blues as being the devil's own music seems to have been an old story in black folklore in the South,

[6] Son House, in video documentary *Bluesland.*

in a sentimental and patronizing manner.[7] Minstrel shows performed by blacks began in 1855 and, before the end of Reconstruction, one of the first black minstrel companies had been formed. These minstrel shows featured a variety of acts, including wrestlers, comics, jugglers, and vaudeville teams, but they also contained a number of blues singers.

Most of the "Classic" blues singers, including Ida Cox, Ma Rainey, and Bessie Smith, began their performing careers with circus or minstrel shows. They had heard the country/rural blues when they were growing up and modified them to appeal to audiences by using a pianist and a backup band as accompanists. Rather than moving around all of the time, these shows eventually became stationery. As early as 1907, a small number of southern theatres for blacks were founded, culminating in the Theatre Owner's Booking Agency established in 1909 (T.O.B.A., sometimes referred to as "Tough On Black Artists") that coordinated performances at approximately forty theatres in

[7] Hitchcock, H. Wiley. *Music in the United States: A Historical Introduction.* Third Edition. Englewood Cliffs, NJ: Prentice Hall, 1988, p. 113.

probably older than blues, actually. The first sort of famous instance of it is Tommy Johnson[8] who grew up in Southern Mississippi and went up to Dockery's Plantation around 1912, 1915 and learned music from Charlie Patton and also picked up all this sort of flashy devil lore. When he came back from Dockery's, he told his brother that he had gone to a crossroads at midnight and sat there playing a tune and this big black form walks up and takes the guitar and tunes it and plays something and hands it back to him and then he could play anything he wanted.[9]

Whatever its origins, the blues have continued to be associated with the devil. Sometimes this is indicated in the lyrics, such as in this example from *Preachin' the Blues* by Son House:

Oh, in my room I bowed down to pray.
Oh, in my room I bowed down to pray.
But the blues came along, and they drove my spirit away.
I met the blues this morning walking just like a man,
Oooh, walking just like a man.
I said, "Good morning, blues, now give me your right hand."[10]

Sometimes it is in the titles of the songs as well, such as in Robert Johnson's *Me and the Devil Blues.* And sometimes the connection was emphasized by the blues singers themselves, as in the example of Peetie (William Bunch) Wheatstraw who billed himself officially on his record labels alternately as "The Devil's Son-in-Law" or "The High Sheriff From Hell."

Interestingly, this association was carried over to rhythm and blues. As Barry Pearson points out, in the great R & B decade from about 1945 to 1955, most African Americans did not think positively about rhythm and blues. The middle class considered it vulgar, the intelligentsia preferred the more cerebral forms of jazz and considered it simplistic and commercial, and the many, many blacks who were religious and churchgoing condemned it in the same way they had condemned the earlier forms of blues for to them it remained, "the devil's music."[11]

[8] Some people have attributed this story to Robert Johnson; the most apparently knowledgeable sources, however, attribute it to Tommy Johnson.

[9] Robert Palmer, in video documentary *Bluesland.*

[10] Printed in Cohn, p. 47.

[11] Pearson, "Jump Steady: The Roots of R & B" in Cohn, et al., pp. 338–339.

places such as New Orleans, Cincinnati, Detroit, and Chicago.[12]

The Composed and Published Blues of W. C. Handy

William Christopher Handy (1873–1958) was the son of a minister and born in Florence, Alabama. He had had organ lessons as a boy, played cornet with the local brass band, and sang in neighborhood quartets. He went on to have a varied career in music, teaching school, and working as an itinerant musician. In 1903, Handy heard the blues for the first time. As he explains,

> One night at Tutweiler, as I nodded in the railroad station while waiting for a train that had been delayed nine hours, life suddenly took me by the shoulder and wakened me with a start. As (a ragged, lean guitarist) played, he pressed a knife on the strings of the guitar in a manner popularized by Hawaiian guitarists who used steel bars. The effect was unforgettable. His song, too, struck

[12] Oliver, p. 69.

Break-Out Three

IN-DEPTH FOCUS *Dockery Farms and Charlie Patton*

The first blues singer to become famous was Charlie Patton, and the name for his collected recordings, *Charlie Patton: Founder of the Delta Blues,* emphasizes his seminal influence on the blues. Patton was born in 1891, one of twelve children, in the hill country between Jackson and Vicksburg, Mississippi. In 1905, his father moved his family to the Dockery plantation right in the heart of the Delta near Tutweiler (where W. C. Handy first heard the blues in 1903) to join some of their old neighbors who had settled there. Dockery plantation was a huge track of cotton land that had opened in 1895 and functioned using hired hands, one of several farms trying to provide an alternative to the sharecropping system. When Patton moved to Dockery's, he was already a young teenager and he remained there until he was thirty-four.

He was highly influenced by an older songster who sang at Dockery's, Henry Sloan, and learned some of Sloan's repertoire including *Spoonful* and the *Ballad of the Boll Weevil,* which Patton later called *Mississippi Bo Weevil Blues.* Although Patton sang a variety of song styles in the older, songster tradition, by the time Patton was beginning to record, his songs were mostly blues.[13]

Many blues singers were either taught directly by Patton or were influenced by him, including Willie Brown, Son House, Bukka White, and Howlin' Wolf. Soon the Dockery plantation became known all over Mississippi as the place to go if you wanted to learn to play the blues. And even blues artists who were working other parts of the Delta, such as Tommy Johnson, Dick Bankston, and Mott Willis who came from Crystal Springs, south of Jackson and out of the Delta region, are known to have visited the musicians at Dockery's plantation. Consequently within the state, especially the Delta region, a web of cross influences developed.

Patton wanted more freedom and adventure than was available at Dockery's, so although he kept the plantation as his home base, he left in his early twenties to begin a new life as an itinerant musician. He continued to roam for twenty years and there is hardly a town in Mississippi that he did not visit and impress with his highly personal blues style. Dave Evans summarizes Patton's style:

> Patton's style practically epitomizes the Delta blues while at the same time displaying distinctiveness no other musician ever came close to capturing. His voice was tough and raw, suggesting a rough-and-tumble life and a barely suppressed rage. Though he had a superb touch on the guitar and mastery of the subtleties of tone and timing, he often liked to snap and bend the strings and slide a knife over them to produce percussive and whining effects. These techniques were supplemented by other special effects, such as playing the guitar behind his head or between his legs. He often accented normally weak syllables and words of secondary importance for the song's meaning in order to give full weight to every part of his performance. He delivered a spoken commentary on many of his songs, seeming to create his own audience and context even in the recording studio.[14]

Beginning in 1929 and continuing until his death in 1934, he recorded over fifty songs. Through these recordings, as well as his direct teaching of musicians such as Son House, Bukka White, Willie Brown, and Howlin' Wolf and his widespread influence as a traveling musician, Charlie Patton holds the unique distinction of being the earliest and most important singer of the blues. Hence, the Mississippi Delta, with its Dockery Farms and Charlie Patton, is now commonly cited as the birthplace of the blues.

[13] Oliver, p. 31.

[14] Evans, "Goin up the Country: Blues in Texas and the Deep South" in Cohn, et al., p. 43.

> me instantly. Goin' where the southern cross the Dog. The singer repeated the line three times, accompanying himself on the guitar with the weirdest music I had heard.

At Tutweiler, the Southern Railroad crosses the Yazoo-Delta Railroad on the Illinois Central line, popularly called "the Yellow Dog." This is one of the earliest references to a specific blues, and it became the basis for W. C. Handy's "Yellow Dog Blues." In 1907, W. C. Handy established a music publishing company and in 1909, wrote and published his first blues composition. The song, *Mr. Crump,* was written for Edward H. Crump, who was a mayoral candidate running on the reform ticket. Handy wrote the song as a campaign song, writing in a style that he hoped would appeal to other blacks. It was an instant success, and in 1912, Handy rewrote it as a piano piece, renaming it as *The Memphis Blues.* In 1914, he wrote the *St. Louis Blues,* in 1915 *Joe Turner Blues,* and in 1925, he published *The Blues: An Anthology.* Although Handy's blues were significantly different from what would be later called the blues (incorporating characteristics of the currently popular tango and ragtime), he did initiate a whole industry of commercial, composed, and published blues.

The 1920s and Initial Expansion of Blues Styles

The First Recordings of the Blues

It was not the rural/country blues of the songsters and early blues singers but, rather, the urbanized blues sung by the mostly female blues singers coming out of the circus/minstrel show traditions that were first recorded. Instead of accompanying themselves on guitar, these singers were accompanied by bands and instead of playing for passersby out by the railroad tracks, they performed for audiences in theatres. In 1920, the African-American composer Perry Bradford persuaded the General Phonograph Company to use the black singer Mamie Smith, instead of the popular white entertainer Sophie Tucker, to record his song "Crazy Blues." This recording, released in August 1920, sold phenomenally, and it brought this popularized form of the composed blues to a much wider audience. Smith's recording set the pattern for a series of recordings by similar "Classic" blues singers, including Edith Wilson, Sara Martin, Clara Smith, Ida Cox, Ma Rainey, and Bessie Smith. It was in these blues that the text typically based on AAB form and the standard succession of harmonies was crystallized.

In 1924, the first country style blues was recorded with Papa Charlie Jackson's *Papa's Lawdy Lawdy Blues,* in which he sang in the older songster style and accompanied himself in the older style with a banjo. But soon other recordings followed, such as Blind Lemon Jefferson's *Long Lonesome Blues* in 1926. Recording companies

Bessie Smith was known as the Empress of the Blues, and was a critically important female blues singer in the classic blues style. *Source: Getty Images, Inc. Hulton Archive Photos. Frank Driggs Collection/Hulton Archive by Getty Images.*

such as Columbia, Victor, and Okeh set up talent centers in Dallas, Texas, Jackson, Mississippi; and Memphis, Tennessee, and used mobile recording units to record the singers. Through these recordings, blues in both the Classic and the rural style soon became well known.[15]

large influx of immigrants needing somewhere to live forced up rents. Blues pianists were popular features at "rent parties," where it was hoped that their lively performances would motivate party attendees to contribute money for the residents' rent.

Blues on the Harmonica and the Piano

Although the blues singers and guitarists have received the most attention, there also developed during this time important traditions of blues harmonica players and blues pianists. Harmonica playing came from an older tradition of playing "the quills"—a panpipe made of usually three cut canes.[16] Harmonicas, or "French harps" as the blues singers called it, replaced the quills because they had more volume, were more versatile, and came ready-made. Blues singers would enhance their singing by playing harmonicas imitating trains, fox hunts, and so on. DeFord Bailey from Nashville, Tennessee; George "Bullet" Williams, from Selma, Alabama; and Burl "Jaybird" Coleman, from Gainseville, Alabama, were some of the early accomplished harmonica players.

Two important centers for piano blues were Chicago and Detroit, both of which had become target locations in the great migration of southern blacks to the North. The population shifts in Detroit illustrate: in 1910, there were 5,471 African-American residents; by 1918, that number had grown to over 35,000 and, by 1926, 80,000, most of whom had migrated from the South. Similar trends occurred in Gary, Indiana, St. Louis, Louisville, Indianapolis, Cincinnati, and Cleveland, Ohio. The numerous nightclubs and theatres that had been established all over these cities gave performance venues to professional blues and jazz singers. Additionally, the

Boogie-Woogie and Barrelhouse Blues

Boogie-woogie was a term coined by one of the early blues pianists, Pine Top Smith, in his piece *Pine Top's Boogie Woogie* (recorded 1928). This style was favored by blues pianists playing in the city bars and for rent parties, and is characterized by a fast tempo, and a percussive, forceful, repetitive left-hand figure. Characteristic early recordings of boogie-woogie blues pianists include Charles Avery's *Dearborn Street Breakdown* (1929) and Romeo Nelson's *Head Rag Hop* (1929).

But although a great number of blues pianists had moved to the north, there also was another large group that played in the "barrelhouse jukes" of the levee, mining, turpentine, and sawmill camps on the southeast circuit. These pianists contributed to the development of a blues piano style called "Barrelhouse Blues" because this style originated in the "Barrelhouse Jukes" of the camps (so called because the simplest version of these juke joints consisted of a plank placed over two barrels over which liquor would be served). Barrelhouse blues were characterized by a regular quadruple meter with the left-hand playing a pattern called "stomping," similar to ragtime. Sometimes this was varied by using a steady "walking bass" of broken or spread octaves moving through the blues harmonic progression. The bass lines provided a strong rhythmic and harmonic foundation, and over them the right hand would play a highly syncopated melody. Characteristic early recordings include *Barrel*

[15] Although these mobile recording units provided an adequate flow of talent from the companies' perspective, it left large areas of the rural south, especially in Arkansas, Florida, and Alabama, unrepresented. But they also helped foster the development of different "schools" of blues playing. As one example, in Atlanta, Georgia, a "school" of blues singers who accompanied themselves on twelve-string guitars was recorded, including Barbecue Bob, Charlie Lincoln, Curlie Weaver, Peg Leg Howell, and Blind Willie McTell. Several of these artists used the barreing technique in which a knife or bottleneck was pressed against the strings on the fret. With the guitar tuned to a chord (rather than the traditional fourths of E–A–D–G–B–E), the guitarist could slide the barre down the neck to produce different chords as well as to imitate human cries and the wails of trains.

[16] Oliver, p. 48.

House Man (1927) by Will Ezel and *The Dirty Dozen* (1929) by Speckled Red.

Ensemble Blues

In addition to working solo, blues pianists often teamed up with other musicians. Sometimes, these ensembles would be purely instrumental (such as the pianist Leroy Carr's association with the guitarist Scrapper Blackwell), and sometimes they would play with other instrumentalists to provide accompaniment to singers, such as Georgia Tom Dorsey's joining with the guitarist Tampa Red to accompany Ma Rainey. Many of these blues pianists went on to influence the development of other styles (such as Tom Dorsey's influence on Gospel and Ferdinand "Jelly Roll" Morton's on jazz) but these contributions are detailed in other chapters.

Through a combination of live entertainment and numerous recordings, the blues in a variety of forms had become a popular and well-known musical style by the end of the 1920s. But when the stock market crashed in 1929, most blues recording stopped, and even the most famous classic blues artists such as Ma Rainey had difficulty sustaining their careers. For the most part, it was the jazz-blues singers who were able to survive the Depression.

The 1930s and the Development of Urban Blues

In the early part of the decade, the most popular blues artists were the piano and guitar duo Leroy Carr and Scrapper Blackwell.[17] They made their first recording in 1928, but stopped along with so many other musicians at the onset of

Gertrude Ma Rainey, another classic female blues singer, poses here with the band that accompanied her during the 1920s and 1930s. *Source: Photo by Frank Driggs. Getty Images, Inc. Hulton Archieve Photos.*

[17] Francis Hillman Blackwell was born in 1906 to a musical family with sixteen children and as a child he made his first guitar out of a mandolin neck and a cigar box. In the 1920s, he had a flourishing business making moonshine and only reluctantly agreed to make a recording with a new company that had been established in Indianapolis. It was here that he met the pianist Leroy Carr. Carr was a few years younger than Scrapper, had spent part of his youth traveling with a circus, and one year in the state penitentiary for bootlegging. The two struck up a solid friendship and began recording as a duo in 1928. Carr died in 1935 at a party from an acute reaction to too much alcohol. Starr never recovered from the loss and his work as a musician was virtually over. He was murdered in an Indianapolis side-street almost thirty years later.

the Depression. When money started flowing back, they were among the first to resume recording, with a classic version of *Midnight Hour Blues* issued in 1932. Their music was characterized by soft, mellow, rolling piano playing contrasted with a guitar style that alternated chord sequences with single-line finger picking. Their lyrics were reflective and their singing style cooler and more introspective, with the lyrics delivered less passionately than the previous generation of blues singers. The cynical, disappointed character of Blackwell and Carr's blues reflected the general mood of the decade and the duo had considerable influence on other blues artists, including Bumble Bee Slim (Amos Eastman) and Walter Davis.

In Chicago, however, the tough urban conditions inspired a more aggressive and extroverted musical style. Tampa Red (Hudson Whittaker), a guitarist who had worked with "Georgia" Tom Dorsey to accompany Ma Rainey and in fact had accompanied her on her last recording in 1928, recorded two hundred titles during the 1930s, typically augmenting his guitar playing with the heavier sound of the Chicago Five band. This band included Blind Bob Davis or Black Bob on piano, and a variety of other musicians playing percussion and brass instruments such as trumpet and tenor saxophone. This style of heavier, ensemble blues became a well-established and highly influential style. One of the most important to follow Tampa's lead was Big Bill Broonzy, who was frequently joined by harmonica virtuoso Sonny Boy Williamson.

Toward the end of the decade, there was a resurgence of interest in the rural style of blues and a new generation of blues singers from Mississippi, maintaining the tradition of Charlie Patton and Son

McKinley Morganfield, known as Muddy Waters, playing the guitar and singing the blues in a recording session. *Source: Michael Ochs Archives Ltd.* MICHAELOCHSARCHIVES.com

House, began to record. Most famous and influential of this group was Bukka White and Robert Johnson. Also during the 1930s, pianists became more prominent, especially Roosevelt Sykes and Little Brother Montgomery.

The 1940s and Three Important Bluesmen

Muddy Waters

In 1941, the highly influential folk collector Alan Lomax came with John Work to Mississippi to look for Robert Johnson, not being aware that by that time, Johnson was already dead. They were directed instead to a sharecropper who played in a manner that was very similar to Johnson's because he had copied the style off of Johnson's records. The sharecropper's name was McKinley Morganfield, but everyone knew him as Muddy Waters. Lomax recorded a few of Waters's blues for the Library of Congress and, after Lomax left, Waters became restless and joined a band on tour, eventually moving up to Chicago. Muddy Waters's early work was highly influenced by Robert Johnson, but he soon added harmonica, piano, and additional guitar and drums to fill out the sound in the manner of the Chicago groups.

Howlin' Wolf

Another important blues artist of the 1940s was Chester Burnett. Burnett was born in Aberdeen and had been a student of Charlie Patton's. He played guitar and sang in the fierce style of Patton but because he could not sing in the falsetto style that was popular with the older blues singers, he developed a sort of cry instead, which earned him the nickname Howlin' Wolf. When Patton died, Wolf went to work on a plantation near Memphis and after serving in the army in World War II, returned to Memphis to continue working there. In the late 1940s, he formed a band fusing his powerful country blues style with the heavier band style that had developed in Chicago. With Wolf's harsh vocals, the band rapidly drew attention and Wolf was offered a job as a disc jockey on a West Memphis station that prominently featured the blues. Ike Turner arranged for Wolf to record for Bihari's RPM label with himself playing piano and through this Wolf began his commercial recording career.

T-Bone Walker

Out in California, having migrated from Texas where he was born in 1913, a virtuosic guitarist named Aaron "T-Bone" Walker had been working professionally for years, having recorded when he was only sixteen under the name of "Oak-Cliff T-Bone" and having worked in bands which had accompanied the great blues singers Ma Rainey and Ida Cox. Walker's music was characterized by brilliant scale passages and flamboyant arpeggios ideally suited for the new electric guitar. The first experiments with electric guitars had taken place in the 1930s, and Leo Fender created the first production model in 1936–7. Eddie Durham, the guitarist for Count Basie, pioneered the new electric guitar in jazz, but T-Bone is generally credited with being the first blues guitarist to use an electric guitar and his influence on subsequent musicians was tremendous. Incorporating amplification, Wolf and T-Bone and many of the other blues singers of their generation began focusing on projection and increasing the volume and performing in a fierce style. This shift reflects a change in the relationship of the blues singer to the audience: rather than the very personalized, intimate expression of its early development, blues singing became a performance, and the lyrics became more standard, stereotyped, and audience-driven.

Important Developments in the 1950s

Although musicians such as T-Bone and Howlin' Wolf continued to be popular, there were two new developments in the 1950s that proved to be highly influential. The first was the development of rhythm 'n' blues, and the second was the influence of the blues in Europe. We will look first at the development of rhythm 'n' blues.

Rhythm 'n' Blues

Ever since the blues were first recorded in the 1920s, a few large companies such as Okeh and Columbia controlled the recordings. The recordings were segregated, and classified and marketed as "race" records. After World War II, resistance to this segregated recording tradition laid the foundation for the development of the term "rhythm and blues." Although this term was free of racial connotations, the musical style was still aimed at segregated black audiences. This term was used to categorize a broad variety of musical styles, including not only the works of older artists such as Howlin Wolf and T-Bone Walker but also the new, younger artists such as Chuck Berry and Bo Diddley.

Rhythm and blues used the harmonic scheme and the traditional formal pattern of the blues with its 12 bars divided into three four-bar phrases (although later this pattern was frequently replaced by the AABA or ABAB form that had been so popular with Tin Pan Alley). Accompanying the solo singer was an instrumental ensemble including electric piano or organ, electric bass, drums, and occasionally additional instruments from the jazz influence like saxophones or trumpets. The singers sang in the throaty and hoarse style of the blues singers (as opposed to the smooth and cultivated tradition that had dominated popular music in the Tin-Pan Alley style) and there was considerable use of ornamentation. Additionally, although the instruments maintained a steady quadruple beat, the singers would use a more flexible approach, often singing slightly ahead of or slightly behind the beat. And although traditional blues had been sung to a slow tempo, the new rhythm and blues used a faster tempo with a heavy downbeat.

Exportation of Blues to Europe

A major development in the 1950s was the influence of the blues in Europe. Leadbelly, who was more a songster than a blues singer, had toured Europe in the 1940s. But Big Bill Broonzy went to Europe in the early 1950s and soon after his death in 1958, the team of Brownie McGhee and Sonny Terry went to Europe. This was the beginning of a succession of blues artists who toured Great Britain and the Continent, many of whom decided to stay, including the pianists Memphis Slim, Eddie Boyd, and Champion Jack Dupree. These blues artists were enormously successful in Europe and they played to large and enthusiastic audiences.

One by-product of these early tours was the development of "skiffle," a term which had originally referred to the entertainment at rent parties during the 1930s. At folk music coffee houses and clubs in Great Britain and Germany, white performers created skiffle bands copying the music that they heard from recordings of black performers in a quasi-country-blues band style. The bands typically included acoustic guitar, harmonica, kazoo, jug, washtub bass, washboard, and drums. Most of the British musicians who became famous in the "British Invasion" of the 1960s began their musical careers as blues skiffle players. For example, before the Beatles, John Lennon's first group, The Quarreymen, was a blues skiffle group. The Scotsman Lonnie Donegan, modeling his music after the music of Leadbelly, made the most famous skiffle recording in the late 1950s.

The success of skiffle bands initiated the first serious studies of the blues, beginning in 1959, and led to strenuous efforts, mostly by Europeans, to find and record early blues singers. Some singers were discovered and recorded for the first time, including Mance Lipscomb and Robert Pete Williams. Others, such as Mississippi John Hurt, Bukka White, and Son House were "rediscovered."

The 1960s and British Blues

Building on the 1950s success of skiffle and on the growing number of European blues fans, the decade of the 1960s witnessed a great resurgence of interest in the blues. Part of this was fueled by the new popularity of folk music. Blues were seen as the powerfully honest and direct folk music of African Americans, and it was often linked up with Anglo folk music. In 1962, the first American Folk Blues Festival, featuring (among others) T-Bone Walker, Sonny Terry, John Lee Hooker, and Brownie McGhee made an enormously successful European tour. Although European audiences generally were enthusiastic about the performances, the greatest response came in Great Britain. When the festival was presented in London, sitting in the audience were several blues fans (including members of the Rolling Stones) who became influential in ultimately revitalizing American interest in the blues.

These British blues fans were almost fanatical in their interest and devotion to authentic American blues. For example, Eric Burdon of the Animals described the importance of blues in his life: "I remember slashing my hand and writing 'Blues Forever' in my blood."[18] Keith Richards of the Rolling Stones recalled meeting Mick Jagger for the first time at a train station, stopping him after noticing that Jagger had the blues album *Best of Muddy Waters* under his arm.[19] In fact, the Stones were formed as a blues group: when Brian Jones was attempting to give the group exposure by getting the BBC to invite the Stones to perform on television, he wrote, "The band's policy is to play authentic Chicago rhythm and blues music, using outstanding exponents of the music by people such as Howlin Wolf, Muddy Waters, Bo Diddley, Jimmy Reed, etc."[20] Muddy Waters's manager, Bob Messinger, recalled, "One of the first things the Beatles said when they got here (on their first tour of the United States) was that they wanted to go see Muddy Waters and Bo Didley."[21]

In London, clubs were founded to provide a venue for young white British musicians to play the blues. Frequent visitors to the most influential of these clubs included John Mayall (later of John Mayall and the Bluesbreakers), Keith Richards, Mick Jagger, and Brian Jones (later of the Rolling Stones), and Jeff Beck (later of the Yardbirds). Others, such as Van Morrison (of Them) and Eric Burdon (of the Animals) learned much of their blues style by listening to recordings. Although initially these recordings were difficult to acquire, they soon became more readily available through such labels as PIE (which was the European distributor for Chess Records) and Origin Jazz Library.

BRITISH BLUES IMPORTED TO AMERICA

By the mid-1960s, the blues had completed its transatlantic cycle by returning to the United States through these blues-based English groups such as the Rolling Stones, the Yardbirds, Cream, Fleetwood Mac, and Jimi Hendrix (an American brought back to the United States as an imported act). In their interviews, members of the groups openly avowed their debt to the African-American blues artists that they were emulating, and they also brought attention to these blues artists through the songwriters' credits on their albums. American groups, particularly those coming out of the San Francisco acid rock scene such as The Grateful Dead and Janis Joplin with Big Brother and the Holding Company, continued the tradition by creating their highly amplified versions of both traditional blues and rhythm 'n' blues. As a result, there were more blues records in the pop music charts and on pop radio in the 1960s than in any decade before or since.[22]

Through this process, thousands of European and American rock fans were exposed to both authentic blues and rhythm and blues and the new version of the blues as created by British and American rock 'n' roll groups. By the end of the decade, the blues were an acknowledged and respected distinct musical tradition, a fact that was

[18] Episode Five, The Crossroads, in *The History of Rock and Roll.*

[19] Episode Five, The Crossroads, in *The History of Rock and Roll.*

[20] Episode Five, The Crossroads, in *The History of Rock and Roll.*

[21] Apparently, a reporter replied, "Where's that?"

[22] Cohn, Lawrence, Mary Katherine Aldin, Bruce Bastin, Samuel Charters, John H. Cowley, David Evans, Mark A. Humphrey, Jim O'Neal, Barry Pearson, Richard K. Spottswood, and Charles Wolfe. *Nothing But the Blues: The Music and the Musicians.* New York: Abbeville Press, 1993, p. 394.

Break-Out Four

PROFILE *B. B. King*

B. B. King is the most famous and influential late-twentieth-century blues artist. Born Riley B. King on a plantation near Itta Bena, Mississippi, in 1925, he sang in Gospel quartets as a child and began playing the blues when he was about twenty, singing on the streets of various Mississippi towns. He knew many of the important blues singers of the day: he was the younger cousin of Bukka White, he learned much of his guitar style from Robert Jr. Lockwood, the stepson of the legendary Robert Johnson, and it was Sonny Boy Wiliamson who helped him launch his career by getting him started in Memphis, Tennessee. In was in Memphis that King got his name and his early fame as a disc jockey/blues singer for the radio station WDIA. As the first major radio station in the South that was operated and owned by African Americans, it was an extraordinarily important station, and King worked there from 1948 to 1952 as "Beale Street Blues Boy," later shortened to B. B.

Constantly trying to improve himself, he consciously sought out a wide variety of musical styles, including jazz, gospel, and country music. He personally credits Django Reinhardt and Charlie Christian as key influences, along with

B.B. King *Source: The Jazz Image. Lee Tanner/The Jazz Image.*

Lowell Fulsom, Elmo James, Johnny Moore, and T-Bone Walker. The style that he evolved, in which he would accompany his rich tenor singing with extensive single string runs on his electric guitar, "Lucille," all supported by a thick, bluesy band, has become one of the most universally recognized form of contemporary blues.

King began recording in 1949, and his first big hit came in 1951 with his recording of *Three O'Clock Blues* by Lowell Fulsom, the success of which allowed him to quit his radio job and concentrate full-time on performing. This phase of

reflected in both the growing literature and research on the blues and in the 1969 three-day Michigan Ann Arbor Blues Festival, generally regarded as the first major national all-blues festival.

The 1970s to the Present

American interest in the blues has continued to flourish. Following the 1969 Ann Arbor Blues Festival, a series of pure blues festivals was established in cities across the country, attracting larger and larger audiences. For example, in 1973, the San Francisco Blues Festival was founded and it attracted about two thousand attendees; by 1991, the festival drew twenty-two thousand people. The largest blues festival in the United States, the Chicago Blues Festival, drew seven hundred thousand people in 1990.[23] This shift from the intimate settings that had characterized earlier blues performances to huge stadium performances with multiple play-

[23] Cohn, p. 392.

his career was similar to most of the other black blues singers of the time: for very little money, singers would arrange their own transportation (usually on the Greyhound bus) to a series of one-night stands in joints all through the South, which they would have scheduled previously directly with the club owner. In this manner, King was kept very busy, performing 342 engagements in 1956 alone. But toward the later part of the 1950s, his popularity began to wane, as the early commercial success of black rhythm and blues artists was taken over by white musicians who "covered" their recordings for the emerging rock 'n' roll industry.

In 1966, King's career took an important turn as he was "discovered" by the white rock audience through the British blues-based rock groups. Eric Clapton (originally with the Yardbirds and later with Cream and Derek and the Dominoes) and Mike Bloomfield (of the Butterfield Blues Band) stated bluntly that "B. B. King was the master," and soon King was in constant demand, booked at places such as San Francisco's Fillmore Auditorium and the Monterey Jazz Festival. He also was frequently scheduled on American television and on European tours. By the end of the decade he had had twenty-seven blues songs on the Billboard Charts and his recording *The Thrill is Gone,* released in late 1969, went on to become a national pop hit.

In the 1970s, the "blues revival" gave way to interest in other musical genres, but the blues themselves have continued to flourish and today, King is considered something of an institution. His influence has been many faceted. Through his lead-guitar-dominated electric blues bands, he is responsible for having "fathered" a whole generation of rock guitarists (including, in addition to Bloomfield and Clapton, Jimi Hendrix, Jimmy Page, and Alvin Lee). He also was instrumental in bringing respect to the blues tradition both to middle-class blacks (who had generally rejected the blues as being of lower class) and white audiences. He is still an active performer. And he contributes his time and money to a variety of causes to help others, particularly aspiring musicians. For example, King serves on the foundation for the Lucille Award (named after his legendary guitar) and each year, would-be artists from all over the country travel to Memphis to compete for this honor. As he has written recently, "I've made lots and lots of records, had—like everyone else—high points and low points, but what has always stayed the same has been the blues. The thrill may be gone for other things, but not for the blues."[24] And through his recordings, performances, and many other activities, he continues to be the most famous and influential blues singer of our time.

[24] Cohn, Foreword, p. 9.

ers mirrors changes that affected most popular music performances in the United States in the 1980s and 1990s. But it is only the first example of many similar changes that have affected the blues.

A second important change has occurred in the recording of the blues. In the early stages of blues recordings, talent scouts would bring a blues singer to a recording studio in the city. Alternately, noncommercial recordings were made by researchers "in the field" using portable equipment. The formal studio recordings often produced a rather stilted, uncomfortable performance because the blues artist found himself in such an artificial environment, while the field recordings, although more natural, had poorer sound quality. The influence of technology has created vastly improved recordings. By contrast, it has substantially increased production costs and because of the expense, the resultant recordings are slicker and more polished because producers require that the music be well rehearsed before using up valuable studio time. Additionally, recording companies must favor those blues artists that they know will have commercial success because they need to justify the cost of recording.

Conclusion

A legacy of the interest in the blues by white British rockers has led to a whole generation of white blues bands and singers. Although it is easy to condemn these singers as yet another example of white mainstream appropriation of African-American musical traditions, it is hard to dismiss the inherent musical quality of their work. In the words of blues scholar Lawrence Cohn, "Eric Clapton, Johnny Winter, Stevie Ray Vaughan, Paul Butterfield, Charlie Musselwhite, and Bonnie Raitt (who learned to play slide from Mississippi Fred McDowell) . . . have gone on to surprise us all."[25]

These various influences have contributed to a thriving contemporary blues scene, but it is

Break-Out Five

PROFILE *Susan Tedeschi*

Susan Tedeschi is a guitarist, singer, and songwriter who is part of the younger generation of blues musicians that keeps the genre fresh and contemporary. Born in 1970, Tedeschi grew up in a Boston suburb listening to her father's blues and folk records. She began playing in bands and writing songs when she was thirteen, and formed her own group at eighteen. After graduating from Boston's Berklee School of Music in 1991, she started playing at local blues clubs. In 1995, she scraped together enough money to record and release an independent album and, that same year, was named the "Best R & B Act" by Boston magazine. Her first national CD, *Just Won't Burn,* included covers of earlier blues songs as well as her own original blues-based songs, which she explains were inspired by situations and events in her own life. This album earned her two prestigious W. C. Handy Blues Awards. In 2002, she released her second album, *Wait for Me,* and, in 2004, *Live from Austin, Texas.* She tours extensively, appearing in major blues festivals as well as at concerts in other music styles (for example, she was the opening act for the Rolling Stones tour). When asked about black versus white blues players, she says, "White people always ask me if I've been harassed. But African-Americans have always taken me in."[26]

Singer Susan Tedeschi, nominated for a 2000 Grammy award as "Best New Artist" smiles as she sings the National Anthem at the Boston Red Sox home opener against the Tampa Bay Devil Rays, April 6, 2001, at Fenway Park in Boston. *Source: Corbis-NY. Photo by Jim Bourg . © Bourg/CORBIS. All Rights Reserved.*

[26] Freydkin, Donna. Reporting for CNN News. "Another Lady Sings the Blues," http://www.cnn.com/SHOWBIZ/Music/9908/11/tedeschi/ (accessed 2-5-05).

[25] Cohn, p. 397.

a blues scene that is significantly different from the original blues of the Mississippi Delta. Attendance at huge stadium performances in which the blues singer is frequently at binocular distance has irrevocably altered the urgent, intimate communication characterized by the traditional blues performance. Reengineered and reissued CD recordings of early blues singers as well as the polished recordings of contemporary, highly rehearsed blues bands also have replaced the raw immediacy of live performance. White guitar virtuosos such as Johnny Winter, Eric Clapton, and Stevie Ray Vaughn have set a new and different standard for blues guitar playing.

Clearly the conditions that produced the original blues singers have dramatically changed. But the blues, like other musical traditions, would not have survived if it had been preserved only as artifacts in a kind of living museum. In order to continue to be a viable musical tradition, the blues have had to adapt so that they can still speak for and to people living in today's world. The new blues singers have adopted a more contemporary urban style because they have grown up in urban settings in the highly technological society of the late 20th century. Although the work of today's singers such as Susan Tedeschi, Barbara Carr, Robert Cray, Kenny Neal, and Joe Louis Walker is significantly different from the blues of first generation singers such as Charlie Patton and Robert Johnson, it is still the blues.

In addition to the festivals, the higher profile of the blues in the media, and the many new singers who are singing blues, there are other indications that the blues are flourishing. The national Blues Foundation, established in the 1980s, presently has over fifteen hundred members, a thirty-member board of directors, and a fifteen-member advisory board. The magazine *Living Blues,* founded in 1970, had a circulation of fifteen thousand in 1991 and its subscriber base is still growing. A complete set of reissued Robert Johnson recordings went to number eighty on the Billboard pop charts and sold over half a million copies by 1992. Also in 1992, Eric Clapton's album *Clapton Unplugged,* containing both newly composed blues and traditional blues by Big Bill Broonzy, Robert Johnson, and Leadbelly, became a national bestseller. As the new millennium begins, it appears that the blues may be enjoying more mainstream popularity than at any other time in their history. There is every reason to believe that the blues will continue to thrive. It may be in new forms and styles, but it will still be "the blues," forever building on the musical legacy left by African Americans in the South more than a century ago.

Bibliography

Bluesland. New York: Dutton, 1991.

Brooks, Tilford. *America's Black Musical Heritage.* Englewood Cliffs, NJ: Prentice Hall, 1984.

Charters, Samuel B. *The Bluesmen.* New York: Oak Publications, 1967.

———.*The Country Blues.* New York and Toronto: Rinehardt Co., 1959.

———.*The Legacy of the Blues.* New York: Da Capo Press, 1975.

Chase, Gilbert. *America's Music: From the Pilgrims to the Present.* Third Edition. Chicago: University of Illinois Press, 1987.

Cohn, Lawrence, Mary Katherine Aldin, Bruce Bastin, Samuel Charters, John H. Cowley, David Evans, Mark A. Humphrey, Jim O'Neal, Barry Pearson, Richard K. Spottswood, and Charles Wolfe. *Nothing But the Blues: The Music and the Musicians.* New York: Abbeville Press, 1993.

Cook, Bruce. *Listen to the Blues.* New York: Charles Scribner's Sons, 1973.

Davis, Angela Y. *Blues Legacies and Black Feminism: Gertrude "Ma" Rainey, Bessie Smith, and Billie Holiday.* New York: Pantheon Books, 1998.

Ellison, Mary. *Extensions of the Blues.* New York: John Calder Riverrun Press, 1989.

Escott, Colin with Marin Hawkins. *Good Rockin' Tonight: Sun Records and the Birth of Rock 'n' Roll.* New York: St. Martin's Press, 1991.

Ferris, William R. *Blues from the Delta.* New York: Oak Publications, 1970.

Finn, Julio. *The Bluesmen: The Musical Heritage of Black Men and Women in the Americas.* New York: Quartet Books, 1986.

Finn, Timothy. "A Little Blues, a Little Cajun, a Lot of Zydeco." *Knight-Ridder/Tribune News Service,* 2-27-2001. http://www.elibrary.com/s/edumark/getdo. . . rn:bigchalk.com:US;EL&dtype=0~0&dinst=0 (Accessed 05-05-01).

Freydkin, Donna. "Another Lady Sings the Blues." http://www.cnn.com/SHOWBIZ/Music/9908/11/tedeschi/ (Accessed 2-5-05).

Groom, Bob. *The Blues Revival.* London: Studio Vista, 1971.

Hamm, Charles. *Music in the New World.* New York: W.W. Norton and Company, 1983.

Haralambos, Michael. *Right On: From Blues to Soul in Black America.* New York: Drake Publishers, 1975.

Harris, Sheldon. *Blues Who's Who: A Biographical Dictionary of Blues Singers.* New Rochelle, NY: Arlington House, 1979.

Harrison, Daphne Duval. *Black Pearls: Blues Queens of the 1920's.* London: Rutgers University Press, 1988.

Herzhaft, Gerard. *Encyclopedia of the Blues.* Fayettsville: University of Arkansas Press, 1992.

Hitchcock, H. Wiley. *Music in the United States: A Historical Introduction.* Third Edition. Englewood Cliffs, NJ: Prentice Hall, 1988.

Hochman, Steve. "Mississippi Blues and Beyond Color the Allstars' Tapestry." *Los Angeles Times,* August 16, 2000, p. F-2. http://web1.infotrac.galegroup.com/itw/. . . xrn_19_0_CJ64255992?sw_aep=santacc_main (Accessed 05-05-01).

"Howlin' Wolf," in *Contemporary Black Biography,* vol. 9. Gale Research, 1995. Reproduced in *Biography Resource Center,* Gale Group, 2001. http://galenet.com/servlet/BioRC (Accessed 05-21-01).

Jones, LeRoi. *Blues People: Negro Music in White America.* New York: William Morrow and Company, 1963.

Kava, Brad. "John Lee Hooker, 1920–2001: Legendary Bluesman Dies at 80." *San Jose Mercury,* June 22, 2001, front page.

Keil, Charles. *Urban Blues.* Chicago: University of Chicago Press, 1966.

"King, B. B." in *Contemporary Musicians,* vol. 24. Gale Group, 1999. Reproduced in *Biography Resource Center,* Gale Group, 2001. http://galenet.com/servlet/BioRC (Accessed 05-21-01).

Kingman, Daniel. *American Music: A Panorama.* New York: Schirmer Books, 1979.

Middleton, Richard. *Pop Music and the Blues.* London: Golancz, 1972.

Oliver, Paul. "The Blues." *The New Grove Dictionary of Music and Musicians.* Stanley Sadie (Editor). New York: Macmillan Publishers, Limited, 1994.

———.*Blues Fell This Morning: Meaning of the Blues.* New York: Cambridge University Press, 1990.

Oliver, Paul and Barry Kernfield. "The Blues," in *The New Grove Dictionary of Jazz.* Barry D. Kernfield (Editor). London: Macmillan Press Limited, 1988.

Oliver, Paul. *Blues Off the Record: Thirty Years of Blues Commentary.* New York: Hippocrene Books, Inc., 1987.

———. *The Story of the Blues.* New York: Chilton Book Company, 1969.

Patterson, Raymond R. *Elemental Blues.* Merrick, NY: Cross-Cultural Communications, 1989.

Shaw, Arnold. "The Blues." *Dictionary of American Pop/Rock.* New York: Schirmer, 1982.

Skelly, Richard. "Susan Tedeschi." http://launch.yahoo.com/ar-273050-bio—Susan-Tedeschi (Accessed 02-05-05).

Sonnier, Austin M. *A Guide to the Blues.* Westport, CT: Greenwood Press, 1994.

Springer, Robert. *Authentic Blues: Its History and Its Themes.* Lewiston, NY: Edwin Mellen Press, 1995.

"Walker, T-Bone," in *Contemporary Musicians*. Vol. 5, Gale Research, 1991. Reproduced in *Biography Resource Center,* Gale Group, 2001. http://galenet.com/servlet/BioRC (Accessed 05-21-01).

Walton, Ortiz M. *Music: Black, White, and Blue—A Sociological Survey of the Use and Misuses of Afro-American Music.* New York: William Morrow and Company, Inc., 1972.

Waters, Muddy in *Notable Black American Men*. Gale Research, 1998. Reproduced in *Biography Resource Center,* Gale Group. 2001. http://galenet.com/servlet/BioRC (Accessed 05-24-01).

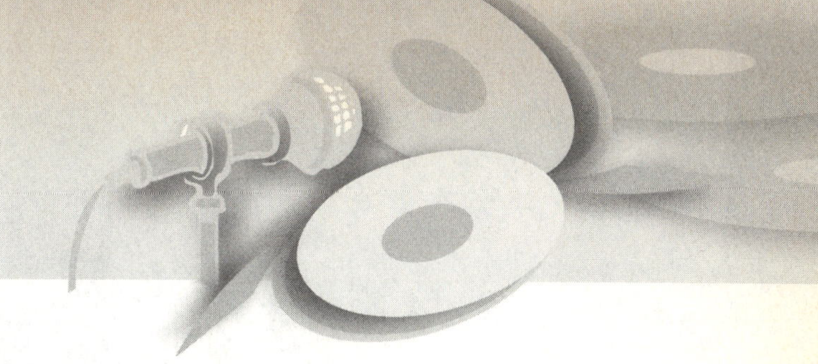

Chapter Seven

Jazz

When the Original Dixieland Jazz Band released the first recording of jazz in 1917, it created a sensation both in the United States and in Europe. The music was new and exciting, and it was quickly imitated. Almost ninety years later, when people are asked what they believe is the quintessential "American" music, many would respond "*jazz.*" Jazz is a uniquely American phenomenon, developing in this country as the music traditions of European Americans blended with those of African Americans. From these beginnings, jazz went on to become a major influence in twentieth-century music. European classical composers such as Maurice Ravel, Erik Satie, and Igor Stravinsky and American classical composers such as George Gershwin, Aaron Copland, and Leonard Bernstein have all embraced jazz musical idioms in their compositions. Enormously popular rock groups of the 1960s and 1970s such as Chicago, Blood, Sweat and Tears, and Steely Dan fused elements of jazz to rock. More recently, groups such as OutKast and The Bad Plus have incorporated jazz into their fusions with hip-hop and other contemporary styles. And, of course, the great jazz musicians, ranging in style from Duke Ellington to Thelonius Monk and Miles Davis to Wynton Marsalis are virtually household names. It is this African American tradition of jazz that is the focus of this chapter.

Jazz: Primarily African American or European American?

That jazz *is* an African-American tradition has been challenged by people who say that it is at least as strongly European American in origin. This challenge is based on the fact that jazz utilizes European harmonic materials, that the important instruments of jazz (saxophone, trumpet, trombone, piano, string bass) are European in origin, that there are strong cross-influences between jazz and European-based classical, and that there are a large number of Europeans and European Americans who play jazz. European-American jazz musicians such as Bix Beirderbecke, Tommy Dorsey, Benny Goodman, Lennie Tristano, Stan Getz, Dave Brubeck, John McLaughlin, Chuck Mangione, Keith Jarrett, Diana Krall, and European musicians such as the Belgian-born Gypsy Django Reinhardt, the Algerian-born Frenchman Martial Solal, and the Englishman John Surman have all made important contributions to jazz. In fact, the Original Dixieland Jazz Band, which introduced the broad public to jazz in the first place through their 1917 recording of *Livery Stable Blues*, consisted of European-American musicians. They even stated on the record cover that they were the *creators* of jazz. Furthermore, it was the white groups, led by bandleaders such as Tommy Dorsey and Benny Goodman, who brought jazz to

The Original Dixieland Jazz Band was a white band that made the first recording of jazz. *Source: Courtesy of the Hogan Jazz Archive, Tulane University.*

mainstream America in the first radio and television broadcasts of jazz ensembles.

Although there is truth to these various events, connections, and shared attributes, it is a gross distortion of history to deny that jazz has anything but clear African-American origins. The term "jazz" itself was a slang word for sexual intercourse, which has been traced back to the coast of West Africa.[1] The music that began to be called "jazz" sometime after the turn of the century was developed by African Americans following emancipation, drawing most strongly on the slave musical traditions that had evolved into the styles of ragtime and the blues. The incorporation of European harmonic materials came through the influence of the New Orleans Creoles of Color, individuals of shared African and European lineage. Hence, even the European harmonic practices came to jazz through "black" musicians. Although the ex-slaves played European instruments, they played them in a highly Africanized manner.

Even more important, the music itself had (and has retained) a clear link to African music traditions in that jazz is at its essence *improvised.* The earliest documented jazz style, New Orleans jazz, was collective improvisation. This emphasis on improvisation has remained throughout all of the subsequent stages of jazz development. As we have seen in previous chapters on African-American music, improvisation (the spontaneous creation of music rather than the performance of music that is recreated from directions provided by music notation) is one of the most important characteristics of African and African-American music. European and European-American music is based on the entirely different values inherent in the tradition of composition.[2]

The fact that it was white groups imitating the black jazz groups that first introduced mainstream culture to jazz and became commercially successful is merely the predictable result of the social conditions that prevented black groups from being offered recording or television

[1] *The Oxford English Dictionary* (vol. VIII, 1989) says that the first reference to the word was in 1909, and in 1917 it was found that the word was African in origin and common on the Gold Coast of Africa. A later reference, in 1937, suggested that the word was from "Negro patois" meaning to excite in an erotic way, and in 1950, it was traced again to the West Coast of Africa where it meant to "hurry up." An alternative suggestion from 1925 stated that the word had originated as a shortened version of the name of an African-American itinerant musician called Jasbo Brown.

[2] It is true that at different times in European classical music there has been improvisation, and some of the greatest composers such as J. S. Bach and W. A. Mozart were well respected for their ability to improvise. And there are isolated examples of improvisation within Classical forms, such as the ornaments in Baroque music and the cadenzas in Classical concertos. But this improvisation was fundamentally different from African-based improvisation. The improvisations of European composers and musicians were solo-based (African improvisation is more typically community-based); improvised ornaments were just a few notes around the notated score using a prescribed vocabulary such as trills or mordents (African improvisation constituted the entire musical performance); European improvisation was in recognized classical forms and was often designed to demonstrate the virtuosity of the musician, and so on.

contracts in the first place. Even here, however, the white groups would frequently hire African-American arrangers (such as Benny Goodman's hiring of the brothers Fletcher and Horace Henderson, as well as Jimmy Mundy, Edgar Sampson, and Benny Carter) and a few would hire black musicians who helped their bands acquire a true "jazz" sound. Although white musicians who play jazz are numerous and often truly excellent musicians, every major stage of jazz stylistic evolution has been initiated by the innovations of African-American musicians, often as a result of trying to reclaim as their own a style which they felt had been appropriated by white mainstream culture.

A list of African-American jazz musicians includes Jelly Roll Morton, Scott Joplin, James P. Johnson, Earl "Fatha" Hines, Fats Waller, Billie Holiday, Ella Fitzgerald, Sarah Vaughan, Art Tatum, King Oliver, Louis Armstrong, Count Basie, Cab Calloway, Fletcher Henderson, Duke Ellington, Charlie Parker, Dizzy Gillespie, Thelonius Monk, Charles Mingus, Sonny Rollins, Miles Davis, Ornette Coleman, Cecil Taylor, John Coltrane, Herbie Hancock, Wynton Marsalis, and Cassandra Wilson. When one further understands how several of these individuals have done the essential shaping of jazz in all stages of its development, there can be no honest dispute that jazz is fundamentally an African-American musical tradition.

At the same time, it is evident that since its inception, jazz has gone on to become a global phenomenon. American jazz groups were playing in Europe by the end of World War I, and by 1920, European musicians had assimilated enough jazz ideas to be able to perform jazz themselves. In a similar manner, jazz-influenced dance bands in South America were popular in the large capitals such as Buenos Aires and Caracas by the late 1920s. Africa and Japan have also produced a number of fine jazz musicians. But because of the ethnic focus of this book and the fundamental role African Americans have played in the origin and development of jazz, it is primarily the contributions of African-American jazz musicians that we will look at in this chapter.

Overview of the Music Tradition of Jazz

Stylistic Categories

Since its origins in the late nineteenth century, jazz has had a rich stylistic evolution such that now there are so many different kinds of music that we call jazz, no single description can be accurate and encompass all its various styles. The following describes the most influential of the styles.

Ragtime

This term generally refers to a style of piano playing that emerged in the 1880s that achieved great popularity from about 1895 to 1917. It grew out of the slave tradition of "ragging" a European melody to give it the more complex rhythmic characteristics slaves valued from their African music traditions. The basic rhythmic pattern ("rag time") was a regular, metrical rhythm in the bass over which a syncopated melody was played. Although "ragging" was done with songs and on a variety of instruments (such as the banjo), by the late 1800s its most popular instrument was the piano, and piano rags became the most successful form of published ragtime. As published piano rags became more and more commercially successful, the earlier complex rhythms gave way to easier rhythms simply because the average, moderately trained pianist could not play the more difficult rhythms. The African-American composer Scott Joplin is the most famous composer of ragtime music.

New Orleans Style Jazz, Hot Jazz, and Dixieland

This term refers to the earliest fully documented jazz style that emerged centered in New Orleans, Louisiana, at the turn of the century. Bands playing in this style consisted of six instruments: a trio of cornet or trumpet, clarinet, and trombone accompanied by a rhythm section of a tuba or string bass, banjo, and drums. The cornet or trumpet played the melody, the clarinet a counter-melody, and the trombone played rhythmic slide and sounded the root notes of the chords that provided the harmony. The tuba or string bass provided the bass line, a banjo filled in the harmonies, and the drums further enhanced the rhythmic accompaniment. Exuberance and volume were highly valued, and the entire ensemble improvised simultaneously within the confines of their specific roles. Early musicians and groups include Buddy Bolden, Jelly Roll Morton, and King Oliver's Creole Jazz Band (with Louis Armstrong on second trumpet).

In the mid-1920s, Louis Armstrong recorded the first of his "Hot Five" and "Hot Seven" records. "Hot" referred to the energetic quality of the improvised solos and the way the recording grew in intensity and volume to a climax. Larger bands soon imitated Armstrong's style and the emerging recording industry helped spread the sound across the country.

The term "Dixieland" has come to refer to the earliest style of jazz in the New Orleans style as played by white musicians. The term originated from a band of white New Orleans musicians who made the first jazz band record in 1917, and called themselves The Original Dixieland Jazz Band. This recording created a sensation both in Europe and in the United States and soon many recordings were made by both white and black bands.

Big Band/Swing, Kansas City Style, and Gypsy Jazz

Derived from the New Orleans style, "Swing" and "Big Band" developed during the 1930s, when large groups of jazz musicians began to play together, especially to provide the music for the new jitterbug style of dancing. These "big bands" became so popular in the 1930s and early 1940s, that that period is sometimes known as the Big Band Era, or the Swing Era, because these bands developed extensive use of swing rhythms. This rhythmic change into swing was the result of bands smoothing the two-beat rhythms of the earlier New Orleans style into a more flowing four beats appropriate for dancing. Big Bands also developed a call-and-response performance style using short melodic patterns called "riffs." To facilitate this call and response style, ensembles were subdivided into instrumental sections (e.g., saxophones, trumpets, and trombones), each with their own riffs and each given opportunities for one of their musicians to improvise as a soloist. The most influential Big Band leaders were Duke Ellington and Fletcher Henderson (with his arranger Don Redman). In order to achieve a cohesive performance, particularly as Big Band music became more commercially successful, arrangers began writing down the music to be played—even the soloist's "improvisation."

A different style of Big Band music developed in Kansas City in the 1930s, led by Count Basie. Kansas City style reflected more emphasis on improvisation, relying either on memory for the basic melody and harmonic progressions, or providing just a rough sketch in a notated score. The Kansas City Style also possessed a more "bluesy" feeling and it emphasized extended solo improvisations and a strong rhythmic interplay in the riffs.

During the 1930s, the French Gypsy guitarist Django Reinhardt merged Eastern European folk music, French dance hall music, and Swing to create a style known as Gypsy Jazz. Rather than the brass instruments of traditional Swing, Gypsy Jazz uses primarily nylon stringed guitars (sometimes as many as six) along with violins and bass violin. While one guitarist improvises solos, the other guitars play backup rhythm. Gypsy Jazz is still heard in European bars and small venues, and is appreciated all over the world. Furthermore, in mid-1990s, Swing music was revived (although typically with smaller ensembles) as young people in America and Europe were introduced to retro dance styles.

Bebop ("Bop")

This style emerged in New York in the early 1940s as a reaction to what had become the polished, accomplished, commercialized styles of Big Band music. Younger musicians, most noticeably Charlie Parker and John Birks "Dizzie" Gillespie, wanted to reclaim the energy that had characterized earlier jazz. Bebop's principal characteristics include (1) improvisations derived from the harmonic structure rather than improvisations based on the melody; (2) more complex harmonies including ninth, eleventh, and thirteenth chords with all their enharmonic versions and emphasis on the upper thirds of these chords; (3) freer harmonic progressions, such as half-step chord shifts and "implied" chords, and release from the traditional rules requiring resolution of sevenths and ninths at the end of a phrase; (4) looser rhythm, with accented second and fourth beats as opposed to the accented first and third beats of swing; (5) smaller ensembles (frequently a quintet of piano, bass, drums, reed instrument and trumpet) and a more melodic rhythm section; and (6) the use of new formal approaches, most noticeably a regular progression through statement of the theme followed by solo improvisations in a standard sequence of reed solo, trumpet solo, piano solo, and bass or drum solo.

Cool Jazz and Bossa Nova (Brazilian Jazz)

This is a variation of Bebop (sometimes called "soft" Bop) that emerged in the late 1940s and early 1950s and was centered in California. The attribute of "cool" was achieved in a variety of ways. In an ensemble formed by trumpeter Miles Davis that recorded in 1949 and 1950, cool was achieved through Davis's absence of vibrato and the ensemble's light, sparse, and lyrical sound as opposed to the dense, hot sound of Bop. In the music of white musicians such as Lennie Tristano, Gerry Mulligan, and Dave Brubeck, cool was achieved through the incorporation of European classical techniques (such as the formal organization of the music into fugues and rondos) that provided a kind of academic and intellectual calm. In the music of the Modern Jazz Quartet, "cool" was achieved not only through lighter textures and academic techniques but also through timbre, such as their use of the vibraphone with its diffused tonal qualities. Finally, Cool Jazz shifted its emphasis from improvisation to the written score and often used a relaxed tempo that consciously avoided a "swinging" beat.

Brazilian musicians such as Joao Gilberto and Antonio Carlos Jobim blended West Coast Cool with Latin rhythms, subtly accentuated by acoustic guitar riffs, and lyrics sung in Portuguese and English. This style came to the United States in the early 1960s, with "Girl from Ipanema" achieving great mainstream popularity.

Hard Bop, Soul Jazz, and Groove

An extension of Bebop, Hard Bop emerged on the East Coast in the mid-1950s as a reaction against the West Coast Cool Jazz. Founded by pianist and composer Horace Silver, and including musicians such as Art Blakey, Les McCann, and Julian "Cannonball" Adderley, it attempted to bring back the emotional element and vitality that had been conscientiously subdued in Cool Jazz. It expanded the traditional two-bar riff into an eight-bar theme, and incorporated an instrumentation technique in which the horns played riff patterns and rhythms as accompaniment material. Perhaps most important, it reclaimed African American elements of the blues and gospel music. The Hammond organ was also used, and keyboardists (particularly Horace Silver) infused funky, Gospel-based vamps. Because of these characteristics, it was sometimes referred to as "Soul Jazz" in its later variations, and Soul Jazz became one of the most popular jazz styles of the 1960s. Emerging out of the Soul Jazz style, Groove focuses on a "funky" rhythmic pattern or "hook" that dominates and is played continuously.

Afro-Cuban or Latin Jazz

Ry Cooder's 1997 CD *The Buena Vista Social Club* followed by Wim Wender's identically titled 1999 documentary film on the making of the CD, brought mainstream popularity to a style of jazz that fused elements of jazz from North, South, and Central America. The Cuban musicians in this particular project, such as Compay Segundo, Ibrahim Ferrer, and Elides Ochoa, were now in their sixties and seventies and were recalling the music they heard and performed many decades earlier. This style had roots in Bebop. In general, Afro-Cuban or Latin jazz is distinguished by its use of complex, dance-based Latin rhythms (see Chapters 14 and 15), Spanish-language lyrics, and a driving, intense rhythm section. In particular, Latin percussion instruments such as the conga, timbale, bongo, vibes (a percussion instrument evolving out of the African-based marimba that added electrically driven resonators beneath a set of metal bars that are struck with small mallets) characterize this style. Representative artists include Arturo Sandoval, Tito Puente, Mongo Santamaria, Pancho Sanchez, Chucho Valdes, and Pete Escovedo.

The Avant-Garde, Free Jazz, and Modal Jazz

Beginning in the late 1950s and lasting through most of the 1960s, this movement was initiated by Ornette Colman and was expanded by the musicians Sonny Rollins, Miles Davis, and John Coltrane. It emphasized freedom from limitations, including those imposed by the traditional treatment of key, harmonic progressions, form, rhythm, and even the European sense of absolute pitch. It also challenged and abandoned the standard practice of using a melodic or harmonic basis for improvisation and even the ensemble arrangement structure.

As jazz musicians searched for new ways to create fresh sounds, they moved beyond the major and minor harmonic systems by drawing from European medieval church modes. These modes, identified by names such as Dorian, Mixolydian, and Phrygian, had different interval patterns and allowed soloists an expanded repertoire of tones and an alternative organizational context from which to improvise.

Fusion, Acid Jazz, European/House Jazz

"Fusion" refers to a new style of jazz that emerged in the mid-1960s and gained momentum in the 1970s as the result of fusing elements of rock with jazz. Rock elements included amplified, electronic instruments, rock rhythms, and a heavy rock beat. Begun by Miles Davis with younger musicians including Herbie Hancock and Wayne Shorter, the concept was expanded by groups such as Weather Report, Donald Byrd and the Blackbirds, Chicago, Blood, Sweat and Tears, and Steely Dan. In the 1980s, musicians such as Sting and Joni Mitchell continued to fuse jazz elements into their own music styles. More recently, contemporary artists such as Outkast have sampled jazz recordings to provide beats for new works. These recordings have become popular with audiences that do not otherwise listen to jazz. This "crossing over" of a jazz-based style (or any musical style) into several different audience markets is referred to as "crossover."

In the late 1980s, the term "Acid Jazz" was used to categorize a variety of fusion efforts evolving out of the British dance scene. Musicians fused sampled jazz recordings with funk, hip-hop, soul, Latin, and other music styles to create new, electronic compositions.

Several European musicians have extended this approach, combining fragments of various musical styles along with acoustic renditions that are then manipulated electronically. Nicknamed "the European " style, this approach includes the work of Norwegian pianist Bugge Wesseltoft, trumpeter Nils Petter Molvaer, and French saxophonist Julien Lourau along with pianists Marial Solal and Laurent de Wilde. Because the final result is a technology-based collection of many different musical parts that do not always include live musicians or improvisation, this style provokes questions as to what is really 'jazz.'

Smooth Jazz

Smooth Jazz is a type of fusion that is one of the most commercially successful forms of jazz in the first decade of the twenty-first century. Musicians typically combine layered synthesizer and rhythm tracks with "live" performance of instruments such as soprano sax, electric keyboards, percussion, and guitar into a highly polished recording. The total "ensemble" sound is more important than the individual parts, and improvisation is minimal. Because the resulting sound flows steadily with minimal contrasts (such as change in dynamics), it is unobtrusive and similar to New Age music, and is hence sometimes described as "aural wallpaper." Very successful musicians in this category include Kenny G, Marc Antoine, David Sanborn, Bob James, Dave Koz, and Keiko Matsui.

Structural Characteristics

Jazz is comprised of many different styles, each with unique characteristics. Furthermore, many of the styles developed as a reaction against a prior style, such as the creation of Bebop to bring back the energy musicians felt had been lost in the last stages of the Big Band/Swing style. To be effectively different, the new style consciously attempted to incorporate alternative musical characteristics. Therefore, it is particularly difficult to generalize musical characteristics in the jazz idiom. Recognizing that jazz is very diverse, the following musical characteristics are only generally applicable.

Rhythm, Melody, and Harmony

Rhythm is the foundation of virtually all styles of jazz and it is complex, clearly reflecting the influences of African rhythmic traditions. Generally performers create rhythms that are constantly syncopated, with the accents occurring on the beats that Western music traditions consider the weak beats. For example, instead of **1** 2 **3** 4 **1** 2 **3** 4, a very popular style of jazz would be felt 1 **2** 3 **4** 1 **2** 3 **4.** Additionally, particularly in the earlier styles, there is the use of "swing," in which the note on the second part of the beat is slightly delayed, giving a sense of pulling back.

Jazz is based on the principle that melodies should be constantly varied, and that an infinite number of melodies can be created to fit the established chord progression. In many jazz styles, the harmonic progression is repeated over and over while different soloists are featured improvising their unique version of the melody that fits the progression. Additionally, jazz melodies incorporate the African traditions of "colorization," in which the melody is ornamented with a variety of techniques such as glissandi and slides, nuances of pitch in which there are microtones used within the basic twelve-tone Western system, and tonal effects such as growls and wails.

Jazz harmony is complex and most jazz musicians (even more so than "classical" musicians) are very knowledgeable about the theoretical structure and principles that guide their particular style. Jazz harmony uses chords that consist of several thirds stacked on top of the basic triad. So, for example, where folk music, rock and roll, and early Classical music rely primarily on the triad, jazz uses sevenths, ninths, elevenths, and thirteenths as part of its standard harmonic vocabulary. Additionally, jazz musicians have brought back their own form of the earlier ecclesiastical modes (e.g., Dorian, Phyrgian, etc.) to serve as the basis from which many improvised melodies are derived.

Texture, Instrumentation, and Form

Jazz uses both polyphonic and homophonic textures. In the earliest stage of jazz, New Orleans Style jazz, all the musicians improvised melodies simultaneously, creating a polyphonic texture. More typically, however, jazz will feature the ensemble or a soloist playing the principal melody, while the remaining instruments provide harmonic accompaniment in a predominantly homophonic texture.

The foundation of the jazz ensemble is the rhythm section, which is a subgroup of the main ensemble. The rhythm section consists of piano, string bass, drums, and optional guitar and it provides the rhythmic and harmonic foundation over which the melodic voices improvise. Beyond the rhythm section, the instrumentation varies with the style. Big Band music uses a large ensemble comprised of many different instrumental sections, whereas Bebop favors a smaller ensemble, such as a quintet of piano, bass, drums, reed instrument, and trumpet.

Jazz uses a variety of formal patterns, but there are two forms that are the most common. The first is the form that is used in most popular-song choruses, and consists of thirty-two bars (measures) in duple meter in an AABA form.

A 8 Measures

A Repeat of the eight measures

B The "Bridge" consisting of eight measures often in a different key

A Return to the original eight measures

These thirty-two bars may follow any harmonic progression. The second popular jazz form is the blues form of twelve bars following the I–I–I–I/IV–IV–I–I/V–IV–I–I. A typical jazz style will then take either of these basic forms and then repeat them giving various solo instruments opportunities to improvise. In the Free Form style that emerged as part of the Avant-Garde in the 1960s, musicians consciously avoided the restrictions of form.

Improvisation

One of the most consistent characteristics of jazz is its emphasis on improvisation. Improvisation refers to a performance style in which the music is spontaneously created as opposed to recreating music by following the directions provided by a composer on a notated score. As we have seen in previous chapters, improvisation is a strong characteristic of African music traditions and it continues to be one of the most distinguishing characteristics of African-American music traditions. At its earliest stage (the New Orleans style), jazz was collective improvisation. In some sense, as each new style became more mainstream (with increased influence from the European traditions), the emphasis on improvisation would give way to notation. But in the inevitable reaction, often as an attempt by African-American musicians to reclaim their own musical tradition, the new style would reassert an emphasis on improvisation.

Break-Out One

LISTENING GUIDE *"Take the A Train"*

Performing Artists: Duke Ellington and Ella Fitzgerald

Ella Fitzgerald has had one of the longest recording careers in jazz history. This recording of Billy Strayhorn's composition "Take the A Train" was recorded in 1957 for Fitzgerald's "Duke Ellington Songbook." The recording has become a classic, not only for its free flowing style but also because it includes Fitzgerald, Ellington, and Dizzy Gillespie, making it a "three-star" special.

Rhythm	Fast Quadruple
Melody	Challenging with skips and wide range.
Harmony	Complex jazz harmonies
Texture	Polyphonic, listen to call-and-response
Form	Standard thirty-two-measure AABA Form, followed by repeats with various improvisations.
	Introduction with scat and imitation of train whistle.
	Eight bars (A): You must take the A train . . .
	Eight bars (A): If you miss the A train . . .
	Eight bars (B—Break): Hurry get now its coming . . .
	Eight bars: Aw, boy, get on the A train . . .
Instrumentation	Swing orchestra with prominent brass instruments emphasizing trumpets and trombones, with Dizzy Gilliespie on trumpet. The rhythm section consists of Duke Ellington on piano, with Sam Woodyard on drums, and Jimmy Woode on bass.

Jazz in a Historical and Social Context

Precursors to Jazz: Ragging and Ragtime

From their earliest time in America, African Americans attempted to retain the musical traditions that had been such an important part of their African culture. As we saw earlier in this book, music was an essential and inseparable part of African society, thoroughly integrated into every aspect of life. Hence, when Africans were forcibly brought to the United States as slaves, they continued to use music to express the whole range of emotions and to enhance as much as possible their daily activities just as they had used music when they had not been slaves. Thus, using their African musical inheritance as the primary source, African Americans developed a rich new musical tradition with a variety of styles, including blues, spirituals, and folk song. These styles are all vocal music, but African Americans also developed traditions in instrumental music.

Ragging the Rhythm

Even before the Civil War, slaves had played instrumental music on either homemade instruments or on purchased instruments. Probably the earliest instruments to be played were variations of the guitar and the banjo, a descendent of a popular African instrument. There are eighteenth-century reports of groups of blacks playing various combinations of violin, fife, banjo, and percussion. One of the most popular practices was "ragging" Irish and Scottish folk dances and folk songs. In this technique, African Americans would achieve a version of the polyrhythmic complexity of West African musical traditions by overlaying the basic rhythm or melodies of European songs and dances with a simultaneous, syncopated cross-rhythm emphasizing off-beats. This was accomplished by two or more musicians, or by a single musician playing a separate pattern with different finger and thumb combinations.

"Ragtime" had thus been around for years. A *Pea Patch Rag* was published in an 1845 clarinet instructional book, and the American composer Louis Moreau Gottschalk approached the style as early as 1847 in his composition *La bamboula—Danse des negres,* which recalled the slave music he had observed as a child visiting Congo Square in New Orleans. But it became most popular after the Civil War, spreading rapidly with the urban migration as thousands of blacks fled the repressive post-war rural South looking for better lives in the cities up North. This new freedom also gave them access to different instruments, especially the piano, and soon the piano emerged as the instrument favored for ragging. African-American rag pianists played at parties and sometimes for dancing, and achieved their "rag time" effect by the combination of a syncopated right-hand melodic line juxtaposed over a very rhythmically straightforward left-hand bass.

Scott Joplin

One of the blacks who migrated to the North during the "Great Migration" was Scott Joplin, who had been born into a musical family in East Texas and moved to St. Louis, Missouri, while still a teenager. St. Louis was a thriving river port and railroad center with a prosperous red-light district that offered employment to black musicians who provided entertainment in the saloons, nightclubs, brothels, dance halls, and theatres.

Joplin found his first job there working as a pianist at "Honest" John Turpin's Silver Dollar Saloon. Here, and later at another place established by Turpin's son called the Rosebud Cafe, Joplin refined his ragging skills. In 1899, a white music publisher named John Stillwell Stark heard Joplin playing a rag at the Maple Leaf Club in Sedalia, Missouri. He liked it, bought if for $50 and royalties to the composer, and published it as the "Maple Leaf Rag," which quickly sold a million copies and ushered in an era of widely disseminated published rags. The "Maple Leaf Rag" has continued to be one of the most popular piano rags. Ragtime was given further exposure through a series of world fairs: the Trans-Mississippi Fair at Omaha in 1899; the Pan-American Fair at

Buffalo in 1901; and the Louisiana Purchase Fair at St. Louis in 1904. Soon ragtime became the rage of Broadway and Tin Pan Alley.

Ragtime Evolves into Different Styles, Including "Stride"

Over the years, ragtime went through different stages of development, each associated with a specific geographic locale. Joplin's St. Louis – based rags used a heavy march-style duple meter and were supposed to be played slowly. The New Orleans style, made famous by the pianist Jelly Roll Morton, had melodies that had a more romantic, lyrical quality derived from the influences of the French, Spanish, and Italian classical and folk music that were prevalent in that city. The rags also were livelier with a more complex texture. For example, in the accompaniment, there was more use of countermelodies, as opposed to the strict treble and accompanying bass of Joplin's rags. And in New York City's Harlem, ragtime evolved into a new style—stride. Stride retained the rhythmic syncopation of ragtime but replaced the marching, rhythmically regular and straightforward bass line with a bass line that incorporated complex rhythms. Furthermore, it was played brilliantly and fast. The "father" of stride piano was James P. Johnson, who had been influenced by Jelly Roll Morton and Eubie Blake. Johnson and his fellow New Yorker, Willie "The Lion" Smith, passed on the stride tradition to the next generation of pianists, particularly Thomas "Fats" Waller. At the same time, the boogie-woogie style that had developed from the blues was added to the jazz pianist's vocabulary.

Thus, by the end of the century, spread through the great urban migration of blacks out of the South following Emancipation, a variety of ragtime-based music traditions on solo instruments and in small ensembles were evident in many states in the Northeast, Midwest, and South. For example, the pianist Eubie Blake who was born in Baltimore, Maryland, in 1883, remembers playing ragtime there when he was just a teenager. And the bassist Pops Foster has noted, "What's called jazz today was called ragtime back then."[3] And the early jazz trumpeter Jabbo Smith has indicated that in Charleston, South Carolina, there was a thriving rag/jazz music scene early in the century. Acknowledging that no city can therefore claim that it was responsible for the birth of jazz, there *is* one city that did more than any other to fuse the various existing styles into a distinct and recognizable form. This city was New Orleans.

The "Birth of Jazz" in New Orleans: 1865–1917

New Orleans was founded about 1718 as a colony of France. In 1762, it was ceded to Spain. In 1800, it was ceded back again to France. Then in 1803, the French sold the Louisiana Territories (of which the city New Orleans was a part) to the United States. Hence, in less than a century, the city had shifted political allegiance four times. The multiple-ethnicity brought about by the political changes was further extended by a steady stream of immigrants from Italy and French-Canada (Cajuns), and by the development of a mixed-ethnic class of individuals known as Creoles.

Creoles of Color

"Creole" was the French version of the Spanish word *Criolla.* Originally, *Criollas* were the sons and daughters of Spanish natives who were born in the New World and *Creoles* were the sons and daughters of French natives who were born in the New World. Later the term was applied to the offspring of intermarriages between people of French and Spanish ancestry. Later still, the term was generalized to apply to persons of mixed race and ethnicity. Eventually an entire social class called "Creoles of Color" emerged, most typically individuals born from the liaisons of white men

[3] Rich, p. 5.

Break-Out Two

INSIGHT *The New Orleans Creoles of Color*

Jazz developed out of a fusion of African-American and European-American traditions. One of the most influential contributions from European Americans was the European harmonic language of chords and chord progressions. This contribution to the development of jazz came primarily through the New Orleans "Creoles of Color." In order to understand who these Creoles were, it is important to understand their historical background and the background of the term itself.

The term "Creole" is derived from the Spanish word, *criolla,* meaning "native to the place." It was used by the Spanish to signify a child born of Spanish parents in a foreign land, and was consistently applied to the offspring of Spaniards who were born in the foreign territories of the New World in which the Spanish settled, including South America, Central America, Mexico, the West Indies, and the United States. The French settlers of Louisiana substituted the term *Creole* for *criollo.* The first generations of French offspring in the New World were known as Creoles. And when there was intermarriage between the Spanish and French, their offspring were called Creoles. Still later, the offspring of liaisons between the French and Spanish with other Louisiana natives, predominantly individuals with African ancestry, were called Creoles. Specific names were developed to indicate the particular percentages of mixed blood: "octoroon" described an individual with seven parts white blood and one part black; a "quadroon" described an individual with three parts white and one part black; a "mulatto" was half white and half black; a "giffon" described an individual with three parts black blood and one part white; and a black Creole indicated a person who had seven parts black and one part white.[4]

Although these Creoles had enjoyed a reasonably high social status in the tolerant first century of New Orleans history and many had been trained in European musical traditions, in the post–Civil War Southern White backlash they were forced to accept a lower social position and "stay in their place" along with the freed black slaves. Denied musical opportunities in the European tradition, they began performing with the ex-slaves whose styles had retained more clearly their African roots. The Creole musicians read music, were trained on their instruments (as opposed to the ex-slaves, who were largely self-taught) and they understood the principles of European harmony. There were many Creole musicians who influenced jazz in its early stages, including Lorenzo Tio, Alphonse Picou, Edward "Kid" Ory, and Buddy and Joseph Petit. But the most influential was Ferdinand "Jelly Roll" Morton, an active ragtime pianist who incorporated the new jazz idioms and became jazz's first composer.

[4] Roach, Hildred, *Black American Music: Past and Present,* Volume 1. Malabar, FL: Robert E. Krieger Publishing Company, Inc., 1973, pp. 60-61.

with African-American women. Dating back to Louisiana's "Black Code" of 1724, which allowed for individual manumission (freeing) of slaves, the French and Spanish white men would sometimes provide for the emancipation of their African-American mistress in their will. Because children held the same status as their mother, any children resulting from this relationship would also be free. Creoles of Color enjoyed a higher social status than the black slaves. Many were sent to France for education, and many became wealthy landowners and prosperous businessmen.

New Orleans as a Multiethnic and Multiracial City

The shifting European allegiances, the steady influx of immigrants, and the development of a prosperous class of Creoles were both the result of, and a contributing factor to, the development of a cosmopolitan, multiethnic, and racially tolerant city culture that was very different from that of other American cities. It was also a very musical city, boasting one of the earliest opera houses and enjoying a variety of popular and folk musics. Even the black slaves were allowed to maintain their African music and dance traditions as well as the Caribbean traditions many African Americans had absorbed in their transitional stay in the West Indies. One example of this cultural tolerance was that African drums were permitted in New Orleans, although they were generally prohibited in other parts of the United States largely because of their communicative power. A very popular city custom was for people from all backgrounds to gather at a large open field at the junction of Rampart and Orleans Streets called Congo Square to share their various ethnic traditions.

Within this general cultural context, two specific influences contributed to the creation of early jazz: (1) the proliferation of instrumental bands and (2) the increased interaction of the Creoles of Color with the emancipated slaves following the Civil War. Let us first look at the proliferation of instrumental bands.

The Proliferation of Instrumental Bands

Military bands had become very popular in France during the rule of Napoleon. As a former colony of France, New Orleans excelled in this French band tradition. Bands were used to provide music for a variety of occasions, from picnics and parties to funeral processions and riverboat rides. These bands played music in the classical European manner and whether they were comprised of white, Creole, or free black musicians, the music had virtually no African influence. During the Civil War, military bands became an important component of both the Union and Confederate war effort. When the Civil War ended, most of the bands broke up. From a combination of surplused military instruments and instruments that had been pawned by former soldiers, brass instruments were now plentiful, cheap, and readily available. Large numbers of ex-slaves were able to acquire brass instruments and, following in the city's well-established band tradition, they formed their own street bands to play for their own functions. Their bands were smaller, less formal, and most of the musicians could not read music nor had they received any formal training on how to play their instruments. Although they played the march and popular tunes of the day as did the other bands, because these ex-slaves had not been formally trained and because they already possessed strong African-based and Caribbean-influenced musical traditions of their own, the music performed by these bands was considerably different.

Change in the Status of the Creoles of Color

Changes during the nineteenth century, particularly after the Civil War, had consequences for the Creoles. When New Orleans became part of the United States following the Louisiana Purchase in 1803, a steady stream of Southern whites moved to the city bringing with them very different attitudes about race and color than were held by the city's Spanish, French, Italian, Cajun, and Creole citizens. The tolerant culture that had characterized the city for almost a century began to give way to the racism typical of other American cities at the time, and this racism escalated in a racist backlash following the Civil War. In 1874, the White League was organized both to throw out the Yankee "carpetbaggers" and to keep blacks "in their place."

As segregation and prejudice grew, the Creoles found themselves increasingly pushed from the mid-level social status that they had enjoyed for generations to the lowest social status that had been forced upon the black slaves and was now held by ex-slaves. As the Creoles began to lose their position in New Orleans society, Creole musicians found themselves more frequently playing with the ex-slave musicians. It was through this merging of the European traditions of harmony and instrumental performance from the highly sophisticated, classically trained Creole musicians with the Caribbean influences and the African-based traditions of blues, field hollers, and work songs from the ex-slaves that jazz was born. Some of the important Creole musicians who helped shape the new jazz forms were Lorenzo Tio, Alphonse Picou, Edward "Kid" Ory, and Ferdinand "Jelly Roll" Morton.[5]

Street Bands, Funeral Processions, and Pianists for Storyville Entertainment

During this very early period, jazz was played mainly in the streets and used to accompany parades and funerals. For funerals, the band would play a slow, somber dirge following the hearse as it transported the coffin to the cemetery, and then switch to a lively, syncopated rendition of a song following the internment as the mourners left the cemetery. The city also valued pleasure and loose living, and there was a thriving brothel district called "Storyville" (named after Alderman Story who had tried to contain prostitution within one section of the city). Storyville businessmen hired pianists (who by the nature of their instrument could not join the mobile, outdoor street bands) to provide music primarily in the gambling houses and cabarets of the district. But in the bands outside and elsewhere in the city, the basic instrumentation of the jazz ensemble was getting established. The rhythm section was comprised of string bass (sometimes replaced by tuba, guitar, or banjo) and drums. To this was added the melodic section, which would include two brass instruments (cornet, trumpet, or trombone) and two reed instruments (earlier the clarinet, and later the saxophone). By the turn of the century, there were several outstanding bands playing in this new style. One of the best of these early bands was Charles "Buddy" Bolden's Ragtime Band. Although not yet called "jazz," the music that these musicians were playing was different from what had been before. It was freer, fiercer, and more informal, and before long, it would be called "jazz."

The 1920s: The Migration of Jazz Out of New Orleans

New Orleans was a seaport and, in 1917, the Secretary of the Navy decided that it was unsafe, unhealthy, and immoral for his sailors to frequent the brothels in Storyville. He succeeded in obtaining a government order to close all the brothels. Although popular jazz history claims that it was this closing that forced all of the jazz musicians to move to other cities to find work, the reality is that the vast majority of musicians were not working in Storyville (which hired primarily the pianists) and the expansion of jazz to various other cities had already begun, spread through the great migration that affected Blacks in all professions. For example, Jelly Roll Morton had begun his travels in 1904, using his skills as a ragtime pianist to escape the intense Creole prejudice that by now existed in New Orleans.

Jazz in Chicago

One of the major targets of migration out of the South was Chicago, and the jazz historian Frederick Ramsey Jr. estimates that, by 1920, there were more than forty top New Orleans jazz musicians who had moved there. Thus, Chicago began to replace New Orleans as the nation's jazz center.[6] Included in this group were Joseph "King" Oliver, Johnny Dodds, and the New Orleans Rhythm Kings. King Oliver's Creole Jazz Band became the most popular of these bands and represented the culmination of the New Orleans style. In this band was Louis Armstrong, who had come to Chicago in 1922. Performing in the New Orleans style, Oliver and Armstrong played duet

[5] Brooks, Tilford. *America's Black Musical Heritage.* Englewood Cliffs, NJ: Prentice Hall, 1984, p. 86.

[6] Rich, p. 14.

breaks on their cornets, improvising in a fast, technically impressive, very exciting style. The popularity of their duets contributed to interest in solo improvisations and led to the general move away from the collective improvisation of the New Orleans style to the solo improvisation of later styles.

New York and the Harlem Renaissance

The second most important magnet in the move out of New Orleans (and from other places in the South) was New York, especially a section of the city known as Harlem. Harlem had become the base for a new cultural movement among blacks known as "The Harlem Renaissance" that fostered artistic achievement in literature, poetry, and the visual arts as well as in music. In music, its most influential musicians at this time were Fletcher Henderson and a few years later "Duke" Ellington. Henderson had moved to New York from Atlanta, Georgia in 1920 to further his studies in chemistry. He soon abandoned his academic work to work as a blues pianist, accompanying several of the classic blues singers such as Bessie Smith, Ma Rainey, and Ida Cox. In 1923, he formed his own band, playing blues and pop songs, eventually moving into jazz. This band contained two more musicians (saxophonists) than the eight musicians of the New Orleans-style. But more important than the larger number, Henderson organized the musicians in a new way. By adding the two saxophonists and replacing one of the cornettists with another saxophonist, the band now had a "reed" section. When he later added an additional trumpetist and trombonist to the brass section and increased the rhythm section to four players, he had replaced the earlier small band with a "big" band.

Duke Ellington had come to New York from Washington, DC, where he had played professionally as a ragtime pianist. In late 1927, King Oliver declined an invitation to play at a nightclub called the Cotton Club and Ellington's orchestra got the job instead. The Cotton Club catered to white audiences, and staged elaborate dances (frequently set in a jungle scene) for which Ellington provided the music. His band became very popular, and helped in the spread of jazz to the white community. In addition to using his many talented musicians to contribute musical ideas, he brought his pianistic style to orchestration (for example, using the parallel blocks of sound that he played on the piano and voicing them for his instruments) and he expanded the formal structures beyond the commonly used thirty-two-bar song form or the various blues forms.

New York also became the center for developments in jazz piano. Earl "Fatha" Hines, a pianist who had been strongly influenced by "Fats" Waller, took the ragtime and stride traditions and the various blues and boogie-woogie patterns that now existed, and used them as the foundation for developing a freer piano style. Using a variety of left-hand bass patterns, he placed his emphasis on right-hand virtuosity displayed in fast, running scale passages. The Hines style was very influential and one of the last great jazz pianists still playing in this tradition was Art Tatum, a pianist who further transformed basic stride into virtuoso jazz performances with elaborate melodic improvisations, complex chord changes, and brilliant playing.

Jazz in Kansas City

One last geographical region developed a unique style that strongly influenced the development of jazz: Kansas City and the Southwest. Interest in jazz began later there than in Chicago and New York, primarily because this area had such a strong tradition of ragtime that it continued playing ragtime even when Chicago and New York had already made the transition from ragtime to jazz. The African-American Bennie Moten led one of the most popular bands and it was centered in Kansas City. The band played primarily ragtime. But then in 1920, the Okeh Record Company hired Moten's band to record a variety of blues material in an effort to fill the demand for new blues recordings the company had initiated the year before with their recording of Mamie Smith's *Crazy Blues*. Thus, when Moten's band shifted to jazz later in the decade, it incorporated these blues idioms it had developed recording for Okeh Records. One of the most important of these blues idioms was a brass and reed riff chorus based on the twelve-bar blues structure. These blues riffs became a fundamental jazz orchestral technique in the emerging jazz style. After Moten died in 1935, his band became the nucleus for the band led by William "Count" Basie, which moved to New York in 1937.

While Chicago and New York remained two of the largest centers for jazz, jazz also had spread to many other cities and towns. As it spread and its popularity increased, many different styles began to emerge and cross-influence each other. The African-American roots of jazz—ragtime (with its derivative style of stride) and blues—continued to thrive. More "raw," blues-rich riff bands coexisted with the development of more refined, concert bands in the big cities. Small, regional styles met with the large cosmopolitan styles. These various styles all cross-influenced each other and somewhere in this mix, a style known as "swing" was born.

The 1930s and 1940s: The Swing Era

Understanding the Term "Swing"

The ragtime/early jazz pianist Jelly Roll Morton was the first musician to use the term "swing" on a recording. Jelly Roll had formed a band called the Red Hot Peppers and they released a recording titled *Georgia Swing* in 1928. The term "swing" fundamentally refers to the rhythmic treatment of a piece. This treatment is difficult to define precisely, but there are certain qualities that can be described generally and certain qualities that apply to jazz specifically. Generally, music that "swings" is music that makes you want to dance, clap your hands, or tap your feet. One important contributor to this feeling is constant tempo and a strong beat. In "Classical" music, the tempo is always subtly adjusted so that the musician or musicians can convey the artistic subtleties of the phrase. They might slightly accelerate toward a climactic note and then slow down ("ritard") as they move toward the end of a phrase. This rhythmic treatment is called "rubato." In rock and roll, country, and most jazz styles, the rhythmic treatment is quite different in that the tempo is held constant and a steady beat is maintained. A second important contributor to a general swinging sense is that the music has a certain buoyancy, a rhythmic lilt that is impossible to define but is probably achieved when the musicians involved have enough technical competence and mastery of the music that they can relax and have fun.

Swing as applied to jazz has all of these general qualities, but it also has some very specific attributes. The most important is a kind of syncopation in which the notes are not played precisely on the beat, but just slightly before or after the beat. This rhythmic flexibility is a direct descendent of the West African rhythm traditions. The second attribute is an elusive combination of slight rhythmic hesitation with a suggestion of acceleration in a way that is impossible to notate. When jazz performers see notation of jazz music in "straight" rhythmic notation, they instinctively modify the rhythm to reflect the swing style. But the specifics can't be notated, and of course if these characteristics could be precisely notated, the music would lose the magical, improvisatory feeling of "swinging."

The First "Big Bands"

Although there were some exceptions, swing was "big band" music. In the early years of jazz, a typical jazz band would have had perhaps five instruments and a "big band" would have consisted of eight or nine instruments. By the late 1920s, largely because of the influence of Fletcher Henderson in New York, the bands had expanded to thirteen to sixteen pieces and the instrumentation placed new emphasis on saxophones. Available in different ranges (e.g., soprano, alto, tenor, bass), composers and arrangers would form three-, four-, or five-instrument sections within the larger ensemble. These larger ensembles created a sense of strong rhythmic propulsion and provided the flexibility to mix what had become the two prevalent jazz styles: "hot" jazz (with its blistering, shouting soloists) and "sweet" jazz (with the mellow sounds of the reed instruments or muted brass).

Examples of the early big swing bands were those led by Luis Russell and Earl Hines and somewhat later by Woody Herman, Lionel Hampton, and Count Basie. Swing music became enormously popular with the younger generation and was heard at dances and at all of the "hot" parties.

As more whites were exposed to jazz, they began to form their own bands in imitation. One of the early white musicians was Bix Beiderbecke who had begun playing in the early 1920s with a suave, white jazz/dance band called the Wolverines, modeled after another white band called The New Orleans Rhythm Kings. He later worked with Paul Whiteman's orchestra, an orchestra that played a jazz-flavored symphonic sound and which premiered Gershwin's *Rhapsody in Blue* in 1924. Another important white band was led by Benny Goodman, born and raised in Chicago. Following a career as a freelance musician that had begun when he was only thirteen years old, he formed his first big band in 1934. This orchestra was featured on a program of the National Broadcasting Company called "Let's Dance" and it was an instant success. Goodman would hire black arrangers such as the brothers Horace and Fletcher Henderson, Benny Carter, and Jimmy Mundy who would create for him arrangements that would be a combination of written-out orchestrations for the full ensemble with some room for solos.

In addition to Benny Goodman's band, other white groups such as those led by Artie Shaw and Tommy Dorsey became extraordinarily popular. These groups achieved huge financial success: Benny Goodman's orchestra earned $350,000 in 1937, with each band member receiving about $10,000).[7] But with the exception of the Count Basie and Duke Ellington bands, most black bands made very little money and found it difficult to survive. These bands, such as those led by Earl Hines, Don Redman, and Chick Webb were not nearly as famous as the white bands, but they contributed much to the aesthetic development of jazz. In contrast, the white bands were enormously successful, and although they played an important role encouraging mainstream acceptance of jazz and they created many outstanding recordings, they actually had little direct influence on jazz's stylistic development.

Vocal Jazz

Although big bands dominated the swing era, another performance medium emerged in the late 1920s, and that was the tradition of jazz singing. Jazz singing by its very nature developed separate musical practices than instrumental jazz. One reason is that singing is linked to words, and these words are the lyrics that comprise the verses and chorus of a song. In a "good" song, the words and music are so inextricably linked that they are virtually inseparable, and a "good" singer is one who powerfully conveys the meaning of the words as well as delivers the melody in an aesthetically pleasing vocal style. Progressing through the verses and choruses of a song does not lend itself to the succession of improvised variations on a melody that is the standard for jazz instrumental playing. The alternative is to use the voice purely as a tone source. This is done in many non-Western cultures and in Africa there was a strong tradition of using the voice in many different ways beyond just conveying the words of a song. These techniques were used in jazz in the development of scat singing (discussed later) but in the early years, jazz singers developed out of the blues singers, and hence the emotional power of the words was considered to be very important.

The First Jazz Singers

The first jazz singers were the legendary blues singers such as Ma Rainey and Bessie Smith, who toward the late 1920s began incorporating a certain "jazz" sense to their blues singing. Rather than improvising on a theme, these singers would improvise on every word of the song, subtly infusing it with a personal style that shaped both the music and the sense of the word in something

[7] Brooks, Tilford, *America's Black Musical Heritage*. Englewood Cliffs, NJ: Prentice Hall, 1984, p. 106.

Billie Holiday, known as "Lady Day," helped define the vocal jazz style, and is shown here performing in the early 1930s. USA. *The Sounds of Jazz.* CBS. TV programme. December 1957. *Source: Frank Driggs Collection. Getty Images, Inc. Liaison. © Frank Driggs Collection/Getty Images.*

which came to be known as jazz phrasing. These primarily female blues singers laid the foundations for the development of the jazz phrasing that came to characterize the jazz vocal style.

Billie Holiday

The greatest and most influential of the new jazz singers was Billie Holiday. Born Eleanor Fagan, she was the illegitimate daughter of Clarence Holiday (who played with several important bands, including those led by Fletcher Henderson and Don Redman) and she was nicknamed "Billie" after the actress Billie Dove. Holiday had begun singing in the late 1920s in New York and, in 1933, the legendary producer John Hammond heard her and arranged for her to record with Benny Goodman. Throughout the 1930s and 1940s, she continued to record and perform, and her conception of jazz phrasing and her ability to affect audiences influenced a large number of jazz and pop singers.

Other Jazz Singers

Most of these jazz singers became famous in conjunction with big bands. Ella Fitzgerald first achieved prominence singing with Chick Webb's band in the 1930s, and her first record, "Love and Kisses" was recorded with Webb and released in 1935. Sarah Vaughan began working with Earl Hine's band as a "second" vocalist and then went on to record in 1944 with a band organized by Billy Eckstein (the first of the big-voiced male band singers to achieve wide popularity). Although most of the singers were female, there were male singers as well, many also coming out of the blues tradition as "blues shouters"—named for their firm, full-voiced singing style that contrasted with the quieter, often rougher sound of the traditional blues performers. Some of the best-known male singers were Big Joe Turner who achieved wide popularity working with the boogie-woogie pianist Pete Johnson in the 1930s, and Jimmy Rushing, who sang with Bennie Moten's Orchestra in the 1920s and with Count Basie beginning in 1935.

The 1940s and 1950s: Bebop

Search for a New Style

As the 1930s progressed, the emphasis in swing shifted more and more away from the intrinsic artistic worth of the music itself to the entertainment function of providing appropriate accompaniment to dancing. The rhythm became predictable, the performances became very polished, the bands got larger, and in order to coordinate everyone's playing, the music was often precisely arranged and notated. Furthermore, there was a sense that what had been primarily black music had now been appropriated by white, mainstream culture.

> There was resentment among many Black musicians because of the way White musicians in the thirties had "stolen" their music. There was also dissatisfaction with the static condition of jazz at the end of the swing era as exemplified by White bands. . . In the opinion of Blacks, an inertness had pervaded swing as a result of commercialism and the distorting effect of Tin Pan Alley. When the swing movement was in the hands of Black musicians, it was comparatively safe from commercial dilution because of the color bar and the prevalent attitude of White society toward Black performers . . . Because the swing movement had degenerated, it became obvious that jazz must either seek a revolutionary solution or struggle vainly against Tin Pan Alley.[8]

Several of the more creative and restless musicians, particularly Charlie Christian, a guitarist in the Benny Goodman orchestra, inspired a younger generation of musicians to search for new harmonies and different ways to play their instruments. The most important and first truly influential of these young musicians was the saxophonist Charlie Parker.

Charlie Parker and "Dizzy" Gillespie

In the 1930s, working in Kansas City playing with a big band led by Jay McShann, Parker had achieved some fame for the unique, rounded and precise tone he was able to produce on his alto saxophone. In 1939, Parker moved to New York and began to hang around the local nightclubs and bars listening to and playing music. He recalls how at one of these clubs he was inspired to combine his ability to produce a clear and precise tone with a new harmonic concept:

> by using the higher intervals of a chord as a melody line and backing them with appropriately related changes I could play the thing I'd been hearing. I came alive.[9]

This represented a fundamental shift away from improvising around a given tune to improvising a melody out of the notes of the harmony. There were other musicians who shared Parker's innovative vision. One of these was a young trumpeter named John Birks "Dizzy" Gillespie and another was the drummer Kenny Clarke.

Minton's Playhouse and the New Style of "Bebop"

In 1940, a former swing bandleader named Teddy Hill became the manager of a Harlem club called Minton's Playhouse. Harry Minton, a former saxophonist and the first black to be accepted into the local branch of the musicians union, the American Federation of Musicians, had opened Minton's Playhouse in the Hotel Cecil. With his club, he wanted to provide a place where all musicians could expand their musical potential without fear of restrictions and without having to please an audience. Hence, the club became an important place for musicians to experiment. Minton's new manager, Teddy Hill, began his assignment by asking his former drummer, Kenny Clarke, to form a house band. Clarke hired the pianist Thelonius Monk, the bass player Nick Fenton, and the trumpeter Joe Guy to work with him and together they made Minton's a popular site for jam sessions, particularly for musicians with the innovative style that would become known as bebop or bop.

[8] Books, Tilford, *America's Black Musical Heritage*. Englewood Cliffs, NJ: Prentice Hall, 1984, pp. 114-150.

[9] Shapiro, Nat and Nat Hentoff, *Hear Me Talkin' to Ya.* New York: Dover Publications, 1966.

Soon other clubs also were playing the new style, including Monroe's, the Onyx, the Three Deuces, the Spotlight, the Hickory House, and Birdland, all of which became popular "bop" clubs in the early 1940s. In 1944, a twelve-piece bop-influenced swing band led by Coleman Hawkins that featured "Dizzy" Gillespie made the first bop records. The new music was given a name apparently derived from a feature of the new solos which was to end a phrase with two short notes on the downbeat, which, expressed in words, sounded like "be-bop."[10] Charlie Parker made his first real bop records in 1945. At first, the new style was not accepted either by the general public or by many musicians. But by 1950, the intellectually and artistically challenging bop style had become the new force in jazz, and attracted several other musicians, including the pianists Bud Powell and Thelonius Monk, Miles Davis, and later Charles Mingus.

Music Characteristics of Bebop or Bop

There were several changes in the musical structure that characterized the shift from swing to bop. First, with the break from needing to accompany dancing, the rhythm became much freer and more complex, with one of the clearest shifts being a move away from accents on the first and third beats (the "normal" rhythmic pattern in Western music and important beat guideposts for dance music) to accents on the traditionally weaker second and fourth beats. Second, the harmonic language was vastly expanded to include eleventh and thirteenth chords and the old rules for how to treat the chords no longer seemed to apply. For example, a new harmonic progression was achieved by a half-tone shift such as from F to F#, a progression that would have not been accepted in the earlier jazz styles. Additionally, whereas swing would have required the seventh and ninths of a chord to resolve according to strict harmonic rules, bop did not require these resolutions. Third, the musical texture was much denser, with all of the musicians playing many more notes. Fourth, the band size was reduced from the large swing band groups to smaller ensembles, especially a quintet of piano, bass, drums, reed instrument, and trumpet (occasionally expanded to include a trombone or second reed instrument and a guitar in the rhythm section). Fifth, it incorporated new roles for the musicians. For example, the bass instrument assumed

In this 1950 photograph, bebop pioneers Charlie Parker (saxophone) and Dizzie Gillespie (trumpet) perform with Tommy Potter (bass) and John Coltrane (tenor saxophone).
Source: Corbis/Bettmann.

[10] Brooks, Tilford, *America's Black Musical Heritage*. Englewood Cliffs, NJ: Prentice Hall, 1984, p. 124.

more of the responsibility for maintaining the beat while also playing more melodic lines. The piano became less of a rhythmic instrument and played lighter, sparser lines. Sixth, there developed a standard format in which the song's melody was first stated, followed by improvisations on the harmonic structure that underlied that melody in a relatively prescribed order of reed solo, trumpet solo, piano solo, bass or drum solo, and then concluding with a restatement of the melody. Sometimes a technique called "trading fours" was incorporated, in which the instruments would alternate four measures of improvisation. Finally, a technique called "quoting" was used extensively, in which musicians would insert brief passages from easily recognizable tunes into their improvisations.

Vocal Jazz: Scat and Vocalese

Along with this shift from the large, big bands of swing to the small combos of bop came two new styles of vocal jazz: scat and vocalese. Scat uses the voice as an instrument to produce sounds rather than to sing words. Using nonsense syllables such as "scop-bop-a-de-bop," scatting is usually done in a fast, playful manner. Scatting was done earlier in jazz as a novelty device in swing—apparently invented by Louis Armstrong, who said that he started to scat one night when he was singing a song and forgot the words. The basic concept of using the voice to create sounds that contribute to the overall musical and rhythmic texture was a common African tradition. But during the bop era, musicians such as Babs Gonzales, Joe Carroll, Melvin Moore, and Dizzie Gillespie used scat extensively, bringing an energetic humor to bop.

Vocalese combined the instrumental style of scat with words. Singers took a melody and a good jazz instrumentalist's improvisation on that melody and then they would write stream-of-consciousness words to it. Although this approach appears to have been created by Leo Watson, it was the singer/dancer Eddie Jefferson who first began to really develop it with songs such as "Moody's Mood for Love," based on a James Moody solo on "I'm in the Mood for Love." Another singer, King Pleasure (Clarence Beeks) made the song very popular and also went on to write similar vocalese. The style was further expanded by the group Lambert, Hendricks and Ross. Other singers associated with bop (although they did not sing exclusively with either scat or vocalese) were Billy Eckstine, Jackie Paris, and Abbey Lincoln.

Bop never became the incredibly popular style of music that swing did, partially because it wasn't recorded much (there were recording bans from 1942–44 and again in 1948) but primarily because it wasn't very accessible music. Bop was music for musicians rather than for dancing or entertainment. It was intellectually and artistically sophisticated, and it did not provide the steady rhythm and recognizable melody music requires to appeal to a general audience. After Charlie Parker died in 1955, it faded as the predominant new style and gave way to variations that became the "modern" jazz of the 1950s and 1960s. Two of the most important variations were cool jazz and hard bop.

The 1950s and 1960s: Cool Jazz and Hard Bop

The main person responsible for developing "cool" jazz was one of the bop players, the trumpeter Miles Davis. Davis formed a unique ensemble in 1948 (reformed for recording sessions in 1949 and 1950) that augmented the traditional basic rhythm section of piano, bass, and drums with trumpet, trombone, French horn, tuba, and alto and baritone saxophones. Rather than improvising, the ensemble played music that was carefully written out to produce a very light, lyrical, sparse, and texturally delicate "cool" style of music. In 1949, they recorded an album *Birth of the Cool,* which prophesied the development of a new kind of music. Although not generally popular, this music was widely listened to by other musicians. Several white musicians expanded the "cool" style. For example, the pianist Lennie Tristano along with saxophonists Lee Konitz and Wayne Marsh played music that was "cool" by being emotionally detached, intellectual, and precise. Davis and Tristano influenced other cool jazz musicians, especially in California, which became a center for this style with musicians such as Gerry Mulligan and pianist Dave Brubeck. Brubeck had studied with the French classical composer Darius Milhaud, and he incorporated classical formal structures such as fugues, rondos, and variations that contributed a high art, academic quality to cool jazz.

"Hard" bop developed as a reaction to "cool" jazz. Although many people were drawn to the more accessible, lyrical, Europeanized cool jazz, others felt jazz had lost its "soul," and they wanted to revitalize it and give it the hot and hard edge it had had in its early years. The style that they developed was called "hard bop" and, like the earlier bop, it emerged in New York. Its two strongest proponents were the drummer Art Blakey and the pianist Horace Silver. In 1955, Blakey formed a group called The Jazz Messengers with Silver and others whose music was characterized by strong, solid percussion and impressive, virtuosic solo work. The group has had a long performing and recording career, and has been the training ground for many later musicians, including the white musicians Woody Shaw, Chuck Mangione, and Keith Jarrett (many people believe Jarrett is African American, but his actual ethnic heritage is Hungarian).

In a similarly intense manner were groups such as the Horace Silver Quintet, Cannonball Adderly, the Ramsey Lewis Trio, the Jazz Crusaders, and Ray Charles, each of whom infused the hard bop style with their own unique emphases, such as the Silver Quintet's reliance on blues and Ray Charles's incorporation of rhythm and blues and gospel. In the area of vocal jazz, there were few singers associated with the hard bop style. But there were several singers who sang either in their own jazz style or in a jazz-influenced style that "crossed-over" into the popular arena. These include Nat "King" Cole (also a fine jazz pianist in the Earl Hines tradition), Mel Torme, and Tony Bennett (who had worked with Count Basie and Duke Ellington). By the early 1960s, bop, cool jazz, and hard bop had given way to new trends in jazz, but they have continued to exert a strong influence on contemporary jazz and their styles constitute the kind of music most people today recognize as "jazz."

The 1960s and 1970s: The Avant-Garde, Free Jazz, and Fusion

Miles Davis and Kind of Blue

In the mid-1950s, Miles Davis (who had earlier worked with the bebop groups led by Charlie Parker and had later initiated the cool jazz stage) formed his own quintet and, in 1959, this group recorded one of the landmark albums in jazz history, *Kind of Blue.* One of the revolutionary characteristics of this recording was that Davis selected tunes that at some points remained as many as sixteen measures on a single chord. This was radically different from the bebop style of using complex chords and substitute chords to achieve a fast-moving harmonic rhythm. To provide the basic context of improvisation, Davis used modes over the chord, thus shifting the emphasis away from the harmonic context (which had become standard in bebop) to a melodic context. This shift laid the foundation for Coltrane's emphasis on melody and also paved the way for the extreme melody-based improvisations in free jazz.

Ornette Coleman, Don Cherry, and Free Jazz

The saxophonist Ornette Coleman and the trumpeter Don Cherry initiated free jazz at the end of the decade. The two musicians met in Los Angeles and discovered that they had similar ideas about music. These ideas represented a radical break from all that had been before it: an expanded sense of form replaced the traditional, basic song forms; free, meter-less rhythm replaced the strong rhythmic sense of preceding jazz styles; atonality (systematic avoidance of a tonal center and a harmonic framework) and use of nonconventional scales replaced the sophisticated and highly structured harmonic language of chords; and improvisations based on emotional impulses or spiritual inspirations replaced improvisation on a conventional melody. This new approach sometimes referred to as "free jazz" or "the new music" represents the avant-garde.

Break-Out Three

PROFILE *Miles Davis*

The most influential jazz musician of the last half of the twentieth century was Miles Davis, who single-handedly issued in several distinct styles of jazz, including cool jazz and rock jazz-fusion. A brilliantly capable trumpeter, Davis was at least as highly regarded for the integrity and artistic content of his work as for his technical ability. He also was an outstanding leader, with an unshakable

Miles Davis (1926–1991) was one of the most influential jazz musicians, and was a catalyst for the development of several jazz styles. A Jazz trumpeter, he is shown here on May 3, 1960.
Source: UP1/ Bettmann. Corbis/ Bettmann. © Bettmann/ CORBIS.

Coleman and Cherry released their celebrated album, *Free Jazz,* in 1960. This album was a 36.5-minute uninterrupted recording of two completely independent jazz quartets playing simultaneously against each other in a complex polyphonic texture. Although Coleman decided to retire about a year after the album was released, the two musicians had opened the door for a flourishing

commitment to excellence and innovation and who also was a generous mentor to many other musicians, including John Coltrane, Sonny Rollins, Herbie Hancock, Wayne Shorter, John McLaughlin, Chick Corea, among many others.

Miles Davis was born in Alton, Illinois, in 1926 to a reasonably affluent dentist and brought up in East St. Louis, Missouri. He began studying trumpet with a well-known local music teacher who not only taught him music theory but also introduced him to the work of a variety of outstanding jazz trumpeters. While a teenager, Davis played in a local group and while he was in this band, he heard Billy Eckstine's bop band when it passed through on tour. He asked if he could have the opportunity to sit in and play with the group at one point, and although nobody was apparently particularly impressed with his performance, he did meet Charlie Parker and Dizzy Gillespie. When he reached college age, his father sent him to New York City to study music at the nationally recognized music conservatory, Julliard. He later related how he spent his first month's allowance looking for Charlie Parker and soon was working with Parker, Coleman Hawkins, Benny Carter, and Eddie "Lockjaw" Davis. In 1945, he made some records with Parker but, by 1949, decided to break out on his own. He formed a nine-piece group which recorded two albums, including *Birth of the Cool,* which became highly influential in issuing in the new style of cool jazz.

One of the remarkable things about Miles Davis is that he has never been satisfied with maintaining the status quo, and as soon as he had been the catalyst in the development of cool jazz, he went on to explore new territory. Unfortunately he also became addicted to heroin, and his playing became uneven and the next five years were ones of relative obscurity. In 1954, through great effort, he was able to kick his addiction to heroin and then his playing became uniformly strong.

In 1955, he appeared at the Newport Jazz Festival with a new quintet (including John Coltrane and later adding Cannonball Adderly), which played so brilliantly that he became an immediate star and was offered a recording contract by Columbia Records. In 1959, he recorded an album titled *Kind of Blue,* which was one of the most provocative recordings in jazz in over a decade. One of the revolutionary aspects of the album was that in order to ensure the improvisations were fresh and not worked out ahead of time, most of the tunes were given to the musicians only when they arrived at the recording studio. A second characteristic was that most of the improvisation was done using modes such as Dorian, Phyrgian, and Mixolydian. This basing improvisation on modes virtually reversed the course of modern jazz that had, since the bebop era, based improvisations on harmonic content. By shifting the improvisation context to modes, Davis returned jazz improvisation to being based on melodies. This in turn laid the foundation for the work of John Coltrane and also to some extent the extreme melodic improvisation of Ornette Coleman and the Free Jazz era.

In the 1960s, Davis ushered in yet another jazz style with a group of younger musicians including Wayne Shorter, Herbie Hancock, and Ron Carter (the last two later replaced by Chick Corea and Dave Holland). This group eventually defined the first stages of rock/jazz fusion with the albums *Filles de Kilamanjaro, In a Silent Way,* and *Bitches' Brew.* Davis continued to experiment, and in the 1970s began incorporating Brazilian and Indian percussionist and Indian classical musicians into his groups. Then he experimented with rhythm and blues and began playing keyboard instruments. In 1972, he had a serious automobile accident that continued to cause him considerable pain, a situation that resulted in his being hospitalized again in 1975, after which he took a break from his public career. In the late 1980s, he began developing a more rock style and in 1987, recorded a video entitled "Miles Davis and Group," which was a somewhat mocking version of a pop-rock show. Miles Davis died in 1991, after exerting enormous influence on several generations of jazz musicians.

avant-garde musical scene, particularly in Chicago and New York. Other musicians continued in the avant-garde, including the pianists Cecil Taylor (highly influenced by the atonal writing of European "classical" music composers) and the saxophonist John Coltrane.

As the 1960s progressed, the avant-garde movement in jazz became strongly linked to the situation of blacks in general. Jazz was conscientiously reclaimed by blacks and became both highly political and highly emotional. It was seen as an expression of uniquely black feeling, especially intense anger, which white players could imitate or augment, but not honestly create. This new jazz was consequently not easy to listen to: it was challenging musically and emotionally, and it demanded a level of concentration and attention from its audience that was far removed from the earlier, easy entertainment of swing bands. Four of the most influential musicians in this style were the reed players Eric Dolphy, Archie Shepp, Albert Ayler, and Pharoh Sanders. By the late 1970s, the avant-garde had given way to music that was more accessible and philosophical, but its core characteristics—freedom from the strictures of traditional form, harmony, and rhythm along with intense emotion—continued to influence more mainstream jazz.

FUSION

Whereas the avant-garde was esoteric and appealed primarily to a small group of jazz aficionados, another movement was bringing jazz to larger audiences. This was the movement of jazz and rock fusion, a term that was applied in the late 1960s to a new kind of music that integrated elements of jazz with elements of rhythm-and-blues and rock music. In 1964, Miles Davis formed a new group with younger musicians that included drummer Tony Williams, bassist Ron Carter, the pianist Herbie Hancock, and saxophonist Wayne Shorter. In 1968, they recorded two albums, *Miles in the Sky* and *Filles de Kilmanjaro,* which had elements of rock. In the first album, Herbie Hancock played electric piano and in the second, there was the use of rock rhythms and a heavy beat. In 1969, the Davis group released *In a Silent Way,* an album that used a number of electric instruments and in 1970, they released the highly influential *Bitches Brew.* These albums demonstrated that it was possible to use rock musical idioms in a way that was more sensitive and complex. Consequently, other groups also began to incorporate rock elements into a jazz ensemble, or jazz elements into a rock ensemble. The first fusion group to achieve significant popular success was the group Blood, Sweat, and Tears (BS & T), formed in 1968. BS & T consisted of a strong vocalist, David Clayton-Thomas, who sang with an ensemble of a typical rock band augmented by a jazz-oriented horn section. The success of BS & T inspired other fusion groups, including Tower of Power, Chicago (originally Chicago Transit Authority), Weather Report, and the Mahavishnu Orchestra.

Along with these groups, two keyboardists were also important to fusion. The first of these, Chick Corea, had worked with Latin-flavored jazz bands led by Mongo Santamaria in the early 1960s. He made his debut album as a bandleader in 1968 and then proceeded through a variety of styles, including working on and off with Miles Davis. He also performed with a trio formed in 1970 known as Circle that had strong avant-garde influences. In 1972, he formed a group Return to Forever, which became one of the most exciting fusion groups. The second keyboardist was Herbie Hancock, who had had a successful hard bop group in the early 1960s (at which time he wrote *Watermelon Man,* a song that became a popular hit for the group Mongo Santamaria) before he began working with Miles Davis. In 1973, he formed a fusion group called The Headhunters, a group that was to become one of the most commercially successful fusion groups. Various fusion efforts continued into the 1980s by musicians such as Sting, Joni Mitchell, and Pat Metheney.

In addition to fusion derived primarily from incorporating rock elements, there were also fusion efforts incorporating other stylistic traditions. One of the most popular trends merged jazz idioms with Classical music characteristics. The connection between Classical music and jazz was, of course, not new. For example, as early as 1934, Duke Ellington had created his *Ebony Rhapsody* on a piece by Liszt, and later composed entire suites on the music of Grieg and Tchaikovsky. But in the 1970s, this kind of stylistic collaboration found renewed popularity. One example was Eumir Deodato, who arranged

Richard Strauss's tone poem, *Also Sprach Zarathustra* using jazz idioms. Another was the Frenchman Claude Bolling's very popular *Suite for Jazz Flute and Piano* released in 1975. Other musicians used classical attributes rather than classical pieces themselves, such as Keith Jarrett's use of classical composition techniques and Chuck Mangione's integration of a large orchestra playing in a jazz style.

The 1980s and 1990s: Classicism, Smooth or Contemporary Jazz, and Acid Jazz

During the 1980s, there appeared to be a rejection of the loud, amplified fusion efforts and the esoteric complexity of avant-garde styles in favor of a return to earlier jazz styles. One example of this renewed interest in the past was Natalie Cole's enormously popular album *Unforgettable,* released in 1991, in which she sang the jazz standards made famous decades earlier by her father, Nat King Cole. On a more general basis, classicism manifested itself in a revival of swing music and bop (sometimes described as "Post Bop" or "Bop Revival"). Younger musicians, such as the trumpeter Wynton Marsalis, attempted to recapture the clean harmonies and crisp technique of prior jazz greats. This new veneration for the past also provided the means for older musicians who had been working for decades in relative obscurity to become the 'new' jazz stars. For example, the pianist and vocalist Shirley Horn was fifty-three when her career finally took off with the 1987 recording of a live performance at Hollywood's Vine Street Bar and Grill, even though she had counted among her fans influential jazz musicians such as Miles Davis twenty-five years earlier. The vocalist Abbey Lincoln also had been working for more than three decades before becoming a star in the early 1990s. The saxophonist Joe Henderson had first established himself in the 1960s but remained relatively unknown until his 1992 release of *Lush Life,* which garnered him not only a Grammy award but *Down Beat* magazine's Jazz Artist of the Year Award.

A second trend was a fusion of pop and jazz that was eventually called "smooth jazz." There are conflicting accounts of the origins of this style. One explanation is that it emerged in the Boston area as the successor to the "Beautiful Music" or 'easy listening' format (such as Musak) that served primarily as background music for

Wynton Marsalis is one of the most important contemporary jazz artists. Here he is in concert at Lincoln Center, New York City, 1991. *Source: Jack Vartoogian.*

the workforce.[11] Another account is that in the early 1980s, a disc jockey for KIFM in San Diego by the name of Art Good began concentrating on contemporary instrumental jazz, especially by artists such as Chuck Mangione, and Spyro Gyra. This format was adopted a few years later by KTWV ("The Wave") in Los Angeles, with the modification of alternating contemporary jazz tracks with pop vocals. First called "Quiet Storm," the station changed the format name to "Smooth Jazz" in the late 1980s. KTWV was owned by Clear Channel Communications. CCC created the smooth jazz play list, and then transmitted it electronically to its owned affiliates who added in regional names, events, and themes to make the station feel local. Because CCC was one of the world's largest syndicated music programmers and owned approximately thirteen hundred stations, the "Smooth Jazz" format and term became well known.[12]

Many jazz-trained and popular musicians created music to meet the growing demand, and by 2005, "Smooth Jazz" had become one of the most commercially successful forms of jazz. Smooth Jazz musicians concentrate on producing polished, unobtrusive recordings that combine, in various degrees, technology with live performance. Individual parts are less important than an ensemble blend that can be described by smooth jazz buzzwords such as silky, seductive, and sultry. Some of the best smooth jazz musicians also perform live in concerts, especially in venues such as wine festivals.

Closely related to "Smooth Jazz" is a genre called "Contemporary Jazz." In fact, there is much debate as to what distinguishes the two. Fans suggest the following criteria: when there is extensive use of electronics such as synthesizers and drum machines, along with a degree of "sameness," the music tends to be placed in the "smooth" category; when there is more variety and a significant amount of improvisation and interaction between live musicians, the music tends to be placed in the "contemporary" category. Boney James, Rick Braun, Kenny G, Keiko Matsui, Steve Cole, and Norma Brown are considered "smooth jazz" artists. Eric Marienthal, the Rippingtons, Spyro Gyra, Acoustic Alchemy, and the Pat Metheny Group are considered "Contemporary Jazz" artists.

In the late 1980s, a style broadly referred to as "Acid Jazz" emerged in European clubs, with musicians combining samples of jazz recordings with a variety of other music genres such as funk, soul, and hip-hop. The goal was to use jazz tracks as the basis to create dance music. Essential to the development of Acid Jazz was Chris Bangs, who both created and produced other artists. His first releases appeared under the name of "Quiet Boys," and included "Can't Hold the Vibe," (1992), "Bosh" (1995), and "Dazzle—Ultra Edition" (1998). In 1999, he released The Chris Bangs Project. Other musicians include Gilles Peterson, Charles Kynard, Johnny Hammond, and groups such as Us3 and Funk Inc. Struggling to find new names for later developments, similar music has been called Nu Jazz, New Groove, Urban Groove, New Jazz Spectrum, and, sometimes simply, "the European style." Thus, musicians continue to integrate jazz samples with a variety of acoustic and electronic tracks to create new compositions, but with the "distribution" outlet shifting from clubs to radio.

Conclusion

Both fusion and classicism continue to dominate the jazz scene today. In terms of fusion, for example, an acoustic trio called "The Bad Plus" has received critical acclaim for its blend of jazz, pop and rock. But "Classicism" is perhaps more widespread. Ken Burns's ten-episode documentary on jazz (2001) was very popular and exposed the general public to jazz's history and various styles. In 2002, the Smithsonian launched its annual "Jazz Appreciation Month" to pay tribute to jazz as both an historic and living art form. In 2003, President George W. Bush signed Public Law 108–72, which urges "musicians, schools, colleges, libraries, concert halls, museums, radio and television stations, and other organizations . . . (to) . . . develop

[11] West, Shannon, "Smooth Jazz Radio," http://www.smooth-jazz.de/Essays/shannon.htm (accessed 2-9-05).
[12] Rodger, "A Small Piece of Smooth Jazz Historical Trivia" http://www.smooth-

programs to explore, perpetuate, and honor Jazz as a national and world treasure." In 2005, the National Endowment for the Arts created "Jazz in the Schools," an educational resource for high school teachers to help them create curriculum for students to explore jazz as an indigenous American art form and as a means to understand American history.[13]

As a consequence of these efforts and the renewed interest in jazz, every earlier jazz style continues to exist. Whole "revival" and "preservation" musical organizations have been founded to maintain New Orleans style jazz. High schools and colleges across the country continue to maintain jazz bands and combos playing predominantly swing and bebop-style jazz. Many professional and amateur musicians still form smaller jazz combos that play bop, cool jazz, and hard bop as well as the new fusion styles. It is clear that we are not only drawing upon a century's worth of jazz styles founded in African-American traditions, but also that we will continue to enjoy various fusions as musicians integrate jazz with the musical traditions of a wide range of ethnic heritages. As such, jazz remains one of America's greatest cultural achievements and contributions to the world community.

BIBLIOGRAPHY

Berlin, Edward A. *Ragtime: A Musical and Cultural History.* Berkeley: University of California Press, 1980.

Brooks, Tilford. *America's Black Musical Heritage.* Englewood Cliffs, NJ: Prentice Hall, 1984.

Dexter Jr., Dave. *The Jazz Story from the 90s to the 60s.* Englewood Cliffs, NJ: Prentice-Hall, Inc., 1964.

Dow Dell, D. C. Author of Web site: *A Passion for Jazz: Music History and Education.* http://www.apassion4jazz.net

Gitler, Ira. *Swing to Bop: An Oral History of the Transition in Jazz in the 1940s.* New York: Oxford University Press, 1985.

Gridley, Mark. *Jazz Style: History and Analysis.* Fifth Edition. Upper Saddle River, NJ: Prentice Hall, 1994.

Hennessey, Thomas J. *From Jazz to Swing: African American Jazz Musicians and Their Music, 1890–1935.* Detroit: Wayne State University Press, 1994.

Jones, Morley. Alan Rich, Editor. *The Simon and Schuster Listener's Guide to Jazz.* New York: Simon and Schuster, 1980.

Levine, Mark. *The Jazz Piano Book.* Petaluma, CA: Sher Music Company, 1989.

Megill, Donald D. and Richard S. DeMory. *Introduction to Jazz History.* Englewood Cliffs, NJ: Prentice Hall, 1989.

Morgan, Thomas L. and William Barlow. *Cakewalks to Concert Halls: An Illustrated History of African American Popular Music from 1895 to 1930.* Washington, DC: Elliott and Clark Publishing, 1992.

Oxford English Dictionary, Volume VIII. "Jazz." 1989.

Roach, Hildred. *Black American Music: Past and Present,* Volume 1. Malabar, FL: Robert E. Krieger Publishing Company, Inc., 1973 and reprinted 1985.

Rodger, "A Small Piece of Smooth Jazz Historical Trivia." From website "Smooth & Soul: Your Guide to the World of Smooth Jazz." http:/ /www.smooth-jazz.de/Essays/shannon.htm (Accessed 02-09-05).

Schuller, Gunther. *Early Jazz: Its Roots and Musical Development.* New York: Oxford University Press, 1968.

Shapiro, Nat and Nat Hentoff. *Hear Me Talkin' to Ya.* New York: Dover Publications, 1966.

Tirro, Frank. *Jazz: A History.* New York: W.W. Norton and Company, 1977, 1993.

Walton, Ortiz M. *Music: Black, White, and Blue—A Sociological Survey of the Use and Misuses of Afro-American Music.* New York: William Morrow and Company, Inc. 1972.

West, Shannon, "Smooth Jazz Radio." From Web site "Smooth & Soul: Your Guide to the World of Smooth Jazz." http://www.smooth-jazz.de/Essays/shannon.htm (Accessed 2-9-05).

Williams, Martin. *Jazz Changes.* New York: Oxford University Press, 1992.

[13] Dow Dell, D.C. "Jazz Milestones." On Web site, *A Passion for Jazz: Music History and Education.* http://www.apassion4jazz.net (Accessed 2-9-05).

Chapter Eight

Gospel

Gospel music is perhaps the most joyous and exuberant of all African-American music traditions. When listening to it, it is almost impossible not to smile and feel uplifted. Like blues and jazz, Gospel has played an extensive and seminal role in influencing contemporary American music. Furthermore, all three are deeply rooted in black culture and possess similar music structural characteristics. But Gospel music is also fundamentally different from blues and jazz. Although blues and jazz are forms of secular music that have risen to prominence in their role as entertainment, Gospel is sacred music that is created as an integral component of worship in church. Blues and jazz serve primarily as vehicles for personal expression; Gospel serves as a vehicle for community cohesion and collective expression. The lyrics of blues and jazz address problems of everyday life; Gospel aims through Christianity to provide a solution to the challenge of human existence not only in this life but also for eternity. Furthermore, although blues and jazz tend to be performed by trained musicians, Gospel is largely sung by thousands of nonmusicians in congregations across the country every Sunday in church.[1] Finally, in the commercial music industry, blues and jazz are readily appealing to many different kinds of people; Gospel as religious music has tended historically to be most appealing to people who share Christian beliefs. This is changing, however, and Gospel music is becoming increasingly popular outside of the church. Kirk Franklin's "Why We Sing" from his 1993 debut album not only spent one hundred weeks on the Billboard Gospel charts but also crossed over to R & B and became the first Gospel album to go platinum (selling over one million copies). William Becton and Yolanda Adams are other Gospel artists who have enjoyed tremendous success beyond the traditional Gospel music market. In many ways, Gospel music has transcended its historical definition as religious music to become an important force more generally in American music and popular culture.

Overview of Gospel Music

Distinguishing Gospel from Spirituals

One of the first questions many people ask about Gospel music is, how is it different from spirituals? Although both are forms of religious music, they emerged at different times and out of different social contexts. The spiritual emerged in rural communities, specifically the large agricultural

[1] Crawford, Richard. *America's Musical Life: A History.* New York: W. W. Norton & Company, Inc., 2001, p. 749.

plantations of the pre–Civil War South. During the years of slavery, spirituals increased in number and style in the independent black churches, segregated camp and bush meetings, and in what are called the "invisible churches" on the plantations. (The churches were "invisible" because they were maintained without physical structures, as the religious gatherings of slaves often had to be kept hidden from the surveillance of whites.) Whether spirituals should be sung in the formal worship service of an established church was controversial, as many of the Protestant clergymen wanted the congregations to sing the hymns and psalms of the white church.[2]

Gospel music, by contrast, evolved in urban settings in the twentieth century and reflects the influence of emancipation. After the Civil War, new religious denominations began to develop founded by individuals who had left the traditional churches. These new denominations fell into two categories: those that followed the conventions and procedures of the European-based "mother" churches, and those that struck out in new directions that emphasized African traditions. These later churches included various holiness and sanctified sects. In these churches, the African-based musical practices of the earlier slave "invisible churches" were maintained. These musical practices included hand clapping, foot stomping, call-and-response performance, rhythmic complexity, melodic improvisation, heterophonic textures, and percussive accompaniment.[3] It was within the services of these churches that Gospel music was born. Further differences between spirituals and Gospel music can be seen in their structural characteristics.

Structural Characteristics

Melody, Rhythm, and Harmony

Melodies in Gospel music incorporate many of the "bent notes" and "blue notes" (lowered thirds and sevenths) associated with the blues. Spirituals, by contrast, only occasionally use these notes. Gospel music is rhythmically intense, with strong emphasis on the second and fourth beats (the beats that tend to be deemphasized and considered "weak" in European-based music). Often the rhythm is further characterized by syncopation and enhanced by percussion instruments and by the playing of other instruments in a percussive manner. Spirituals, by contrast, are often in a free, rhapsodic rhythm or, in their concert versions, in a style more closely associated with the nonsyncopated and metrical rhythm of European classical music.

Texture, Instrumentation, and Form

Gospel songs are sung in a homophonic texture, with a great deal of emphasis on call-and-response performance style. The early spirituals, by contrast, were sung in a monophonic or heterophonic texture and in a direct performance style. Concert versions of spirituals are homophonic, but still in direct performance style. Gospel songs are accompanied by instruments such as the piano, organ, and drums and this instrumental accompaniment is considered integral to the performance. Spirituals, by contrast, are sung without accompaniment (*a capella*) or with simple, understated accompaniment. Gospel is sung by an ensemble; spirituals (except in concert arrangements for choirs) are sung by soloists. In terms of form, Gospel typically uses strophic forms, with verses and refrains. The songs tend to be organized in eight-bar phrases, grouped together in units of sixteen measures or thirty-two measures. Spirituals often are organized into single melodies that are repeated, represented by the letters a, a, a, or sometimes a b.

Texts of Spirituals and Gospel

An additional important distinction is in the texts. The lyrics to Gospel songs are poems that concentrate on a single theme such as conversion, salvation, and yearning for spirituality. This theme is stressed

[2] Other ministers were more lenient and even encouraging of blacks to sing their own religious songs.

[3] Southern, Eileen. *The Music of Black Americans*, pp. 452–453.

Break-Out One

IN-DEPTH FOCUS *Camp Meetings, Bush Meetings, and "Shouts"*

Throughout the nineteenth century, black and white churches, especially those affiliated with the Methodist and Baptist denominations, sponsored "camp meetings." Advertisements for meetings were printed in newspapers that would inform people of the date, time, and place of the meetings, and sponsoring or supporting organizations would provide transportation from the cities to the wooded sites out of town where the meetings were held. As many as five thousand people would attend one of these gatherings, and the events could last from a couple of days to a week. People would assemble under large tents and listen to preachers, sing songs, and generally participate in spiritual renewal. Although the white and black camp meetings were segregated, in the separate black church gatherings, some whites attended both as participants and as guest preachers. Bush meetings were similar, but they were smaller and conducted out in the open, not under tents.

Much of our knowledge of these camp meetings comes from Daniel Alexander Payne (1811–1893), who recalled his experiences attending these meetings in *Recollections of Seventy Years* (1888) and *History of the African Methodist Episcopal Church* (1891). In *Recollections*, he describes his horror observing a bush meeting:

> After the sermon, they formed a ring, and with coats off sung, clapped their hands and stamped their feet in a most ridiculous and heathenish way. I requested the pastor to go and stop their dancing. At his request they stopped their dancing and clapping of hands, but remained singing and rocking their bodies to and fro. . . . After the sermon in the afternoon, having another opportunity of speaking alone to this young leader of the singing and clapping ring, he said: "Sinners won't get converted unless there is a ring. . . . The Spirit of God works upon people in different ways. At camp meeting there must be a ring here, a ring there, a ring over yonder, or sinners will not get converted."[4]

These ring dances were direct descendants of African traditions. In West Africa, a popular activity was to gather to watch dancers who were dancing in a ring and participate by joining in the song refrains, clapping hands, tapping feet, or even entering the dance ring on occasion. The tradition encouraged them to shout words of encouragement or disapproval to the performers. These ring dances survived as the "shout spirituals" throughout the nineteenth century.

For these shout spirituals, people would gather into two groups called the shouters (who were the dancers) and the singers. The singers would stand in one place and the shouters would move around in a circle for as long as four and five successive hours. The spiritual would be repeated over and over, taking on the character of a chant. Although the ring moved slowly at first, gradually the pace would quicken until the religious fervor of the participants and the loud and incessant music of the singers combined to produce a state of ecstasy in all present. Shouters often fell to the ground completely exhausted but, when they did, new dancers would take their place.

Although white observers found the shouts or ring spirituals fascinating, they also often disapproved of it, regarding the dance as barbaric. As Southern points out, knowing nothing of African traditions, they often failed to recognize that (1) shouters used dance in the same manner as song and prayer to communicate with God; and (2) a shouter reached his or her deepest connection with God when the Spirit entered his body to take possession of his soul.[5]

[4] Quoted in Southern, Eileen, p. 130, from *Recollections*, p. 69.

[5] Southern, p. 13, and pp. 182–183.

In the early 1900s, African Americans in New York City gather together for a religious meeting and sing the spirituals and hymns that laid the foundation for the development of Gospel. *Source: Brown Brothers.*

through the repetition of phrases. Gospel texts are subjective and tend to exhort the singers to be good and to do right. Spiritual texts are group-oriented and tend to tell stories about biblical events.[6]

Gospel Music in a Historical and Social Context

The Foundation for the Development of Gospel Music

Three influences at the turn of the century contributed to the development of Gospel music: jubilee quartets, the tabernacle songs of Reverend C. Albert Tindley, and the Pentecostal Revival. Let us look first at the jubilee quartets.

Jubilee Quartets

Jubilee quartets were based in a community. They took advantage of the many arrangements of spirituals that had been published in the later part of the nineteenth century that were now available in notated scores of music. The quartets sang these and contemporary songs in the same manner as university choirs only with the addition of dramatic vocal solos. The Tidewater, Virginia area (with the Hampton Institute located nearby) and Jefferson County, Alabama (the location of Tuskegee Institute) were both fertile areas for the development of jubilee quartet singing. Quartet singing became so popular that one Gospel historian, Lynn Abbot, states, "the pervasiveness of quartet singing during the 1890's and early 1900's . . . was nothing less than a national pastime."[7]

[6] Southern, pp. 459–460.
[7] Lornell, p. 9.

The Tabernacle Songs of Reverend C. Albert Tindley

The Methodist minister, the Reverend C. Albert Tindley (1851 or 1859–1933) was a highly influential composer who helped launch the development of Gospel music through his writing of tabernacle songs—songs to be sung in the tabernacle (the place of worship) focusing on a single theme and featuring a call-and-response performance style. Tindley was born to a slave and a free black woman on a farm in Maryland and he wrote these tabernacle songs to supplement his powerful sermons. He relied heavily on spirituals (and in fact in some popular songbooks his compositions are classified as spirituals). He is credited with publishing the first Gospel songs that included both words and music in 1899. Although not prolific, many of Tindley's songs continue to be popular, including "I'll Overcome Some Day" (written in 1901 and the source for the Civil Rights anthem, "We Shall Overcome"), "Stand By Me" (1905) and "We'll Understand it Better By and By" (1905).[8]

Split Between Orthodox and the New "Holiness" and "Sanctified" Churches

The third and most important influence on the development of Gospel music was the split that occurred within African-American churches at the end of the nineteenth century. This split was between the established and traditional orthodox churches and the new "Holiness" or "Sanctified" groups. The earliest "Holiness" churches were founded by dissatisfied Baptist preachers, and include the Reverend C. P. Jones, who formed Church of Christ Holiness in Selma, Alabama, in 1894 and Reverend William Christian, who founded the Church of the Living God in Wrightsville, Arkansas.[9] These new groups were referred to as "holiness" or "sanctified" groups because they stressed living a perfectly holy and sanctified life free from sin. They incorporated healing, prophesy, and speaking in unknown tongues. Worshipers were encouraged to abandon themselves to the spirit, to let Christ take possession of their bodies.

This engraving from 1874 shows the First African Baptist Church in Richmond, Virginia. In the South particularly, black churches such as these were the center of African-American life in the years following the Civil War. *Source: The Granger Collection.*

[8] The standard practice of the time for publishing black spiritual songs was to write only the words while the melodies had to be passed on through oral tradition. In a manner similar to the Anglo ballads, a singer needed to learn the melody from another singer or to have learned it as part of a community's musical traditions. Part of the reason the Gospel composer Thomas Dorsey achieved such influence and success was that he changed this practice to publishing both words and music on single sheets, which could then be purchased for 15¢.

[9] *The New Grove Dictionary of Music and Musicians*, p. 196.

Services in these churches included "shout" songs and "witness" rituals, with great emphasis on freedom of expression and rhythm. Eventually, churches added musical instruments such as drums, tambourines, triangles, pianos, and guitars, a change regarded by orthodox black churches as a sinful attempt to bring ragtime and blues into the church. The Holiness churches used Tindley's songs as the models for songs to be used in their services, and modified them to include opportunities for the congregation to improvise free interpolations (such as "Hallelujah") and to use instrumental accompaniment. The combination of the popular quartet singing, the tabernacle compositions of Reverend Tindley, and the worship practices of the Holiness churches laid the foundation for the development of a repertoire of music and a performance style known as "Gospel."

The Work of Thomas Dorsey in the 1920s

The individual who had the greatest influence on the development of Gospel was Thomas "Georgia Tom" or "Barrelhouse Tom" Dorsey (1899–1993). Dorsey was a multifaceted musician who had been involved with Gospel music in Chicago when he joined the Pilgrim Baptist Church in 1921. Dorsey had begun his musical career much earlier. He had worked as part of a blues ensemble with "Tampa Red" (Hudson Whittaker) and as a member of a band called The Whispering Syncopators. He also served as a barrelhouse blues pianist, an arranger, and as an accompanist and composer for "'Ma" Rainey and Bessie Smith (the foremost female blues singers of their era). In 1926, he wrote one of the masterpieces of Gospel, "If You See My Savior." By 1928, he was incorporating more rhythmic emphasis and blues riffs into his Gospel music and also providing opportunities for the soloist and the accompanist to improvise and personalize the interpretation. But even as Gospel music continued to rise in popularity, the orthodox black churches continued to disapprove of it, banning it from their services. The fundamental reason for the disapproval was Gospel's connection with the sanctified and holiness churches. Many black leaders resisted these churches and the Gospel music that evolved in these churches because they felt the services and music too strongly emphasized African cultural roots. "Progressive blacks" were trying to help their people by encouraging them to try to assimilate into the European-based white culture of mainstream America represented in the orthodox churches.

Thomas Dorsey was not supportive of the undisciplined and raucous nature of much of the singing that was occurring in the holiness churches. He criticized choirs for taking "too many embellishments that may be mistaken for spirit" and condemned the "loud vociferous singing, uninspired gesticulations, or self-incurred spasms of the body."[10] But he did consciously attempt to bring emotional fervor to his music. This contrasted with the staid and disciplined music of the orthodox churches, and he was often rebuked. As Dorsey himself stated,

> This thing of gospel, it was something new; they didn't take to it well. Preacher don't want you singing no gospel. The preacher'd get up there and say, "You can't sing no gospel, only preach the gospel." I've been thrown out of some of the best churches in the country for that.[11]

The resistance of the orthodox churches motivated Dorsey. He later recalled, "When I realized how hard some people were fighting the gospel idea, I was determined to carry the banner. . . . I borrowed five dollars and sent out 500 copies of my song, "If You See My Savior," to churches throughout the country. . . . It was three years before I got a single order. I felt like going back to the blues."[12]

Despite the resistance of the orthodox churches to Gospel music, it continued to flourish. One old-time choir director, James Mundy, explained that Gospel music's success was because of its strong roots in African tradition—the very

[10] Bekker, p. 44.

[11] Harris, pp. 182–183.

[12] Petrie, Phil. "The History of Gospel." On the Web site "Black Gospel Music: Presented by Smith/McIver," http://afgen.com/gospel.html (Accessed 02-11-05).

reason orthodox churches had resisted it. He explains the attraction allegorically:

> The Negro people liked Gospel 'cause it goes back to Africa. That's why it got hold of them. It's indigenous. An eagle laid an egg among chickens and when it hatched, it went along with the chickens because it didn't know the difference. But then one day it heard an eagle cry, it wasn't a chicken anymore but flew up to its mother. . . . So that's the way it is with the American Negroes; there's an awakening. This mother is Africa. They were sort of going along with the chickens and they heard that cry. Eagles running with chickens. But this scream had something innate within it; (the eaglet) went up to its mother where it belonged.[13]

During this decade, two Gospel traditions were established that have been retained and that distinguish it from other forms of black music. First was its clear function as liturgical music intended to be performed in the church. Second was the practice of having it performed by members of the church, for even though guest artists might be invited to enhance the performance by singing solos or entire choirs might visit as part of a church-concert tour, the music was primarily created by the members of the congregation. Two distinct forms of Gospel groups also emerged: "quartet singing" and "gospel choir singing." The Gospel quartet consisted of four or five male singers dressed in business suits who sang without instrumental accompaniment in a barbershop "harmonizing" style. The singers would enhance the rhythmic aspect of their music by snapping their fingers and slapping their thighs. The Gospel chorus was a group of females who wore choir robes. They were accompanied by the piano and enhanced the rhythm of their performance by clapping their hands.[14]

The "Birth" of Gospel in Chicago and the 1930s and 1940s

The year 1930 is often cited as Gospel's official moment of birth. It was in this year that Thomas Dorsey, at the Jubilee Meeting of the National Baptist Convention in Chicago, performed "If You See My Savior." The performance created a sensation and the traditional, conservative convention officially endorsed Gospel music. In an effort to give Gospel music further respect, Dorsey founded the National Convention of Gospel Choirs and Choruses, Inc. in Chicago in 1932, an organization that exists today. That same year, he composed one of the most famous Gospel pieces, "Precious Lord, Take My Hand," in the days following the death in childbirth of his wife and newborn child. Dorsey went on to achieve great fame and success as a composer, writing over five hundred songs, some of which have been published in twenty-six languages, and performed both by black and white musicians, including Mahalia Jackson, Clara Ward, Sallie Martin, Tennessee Ernie Ford, and Elvis Presley.

In 1933, John Hammond (1910–1987)—a legendary and highly influential record producer, talent scout, and jazz critic—organized a show called "From Spirituals to Swing" at Carnegie Hall in New York City. He hired Mitchell's Christian Singers to perform the spirituals and Sister Rosetta Tharpe (1915–1973) to perform Gospel songs. The entire show was so well received that Hammond organized a second show the following year and also began nightclub tours, which contributed to moving the religious-based music out of the churches and into secular arenas.

The decade of the 1930s also witnessed other changes in the Gospel tradition. The first was apparently initiated by Dorsey, who in 1936 promoted a "battle of song" between Roberta and Sallie Martin at Chicago's DuSable High School. He charged 15¢ admission, the first time anyone had apparently charged for entry into a sacred-music concert. The concert's success created a vogue for Gospel-music concerts with paid admission, a tradition that has lasted to the present time. It also led to the development of paid, professional Gospel singers who record and who receive pay for their singing.[15]

[13] Harris, Michael W. *The Rise of Gospel Blues: The Music of Thomas Dorsey in the Urban Chruch,* New York: Oxford University Press, 1992. p. 180.

[14] Southern, Eileen. *The Music of Black Americans: A History.* New York: W. W. Norton, 1982, p. 464.

[15] Ibid.

In the 1940s, particularly after World War II, the commercial success of a multitude of vocal groups such as the Soul Stirrers, the Swan Silvertones, the Dixie Hummingbirds, the Fairfield Four, the Sensational Nightingales, and the Pilgrim Travelers ushered in an era known as "sweet-gospel." Important milestones included the founding of the radio program "Gospel Train" in 1940 by Joe Bostic (1909–1988) for station WLIB in New York, and "Sister" Rosetta Tharpe's performance in 1943 at the Apollo Theatre in Harlem. The radio show and the proliferation of groups and secular performances in the 1940s led to a commercial boom for Gospel music in the following decade.

The Recording and Popularizing of Gospel in the 1950s

The 1950s began with the first all-Gospel concert in history: the Negro Gospel and Religious Music Festival at Carnegie Hall in New York. The concert was produced by Joe Bostic and featured Mahalia Jackson (1911–1972), who went on to become one of the most influential and successful Gospel singers of all time. Additionally during the 1950s, radio shifted from live entertainment to records, and several recording labels were founded giving performers an opportunity to start earning big money. This era of "hard Gospel" brought fame to groups such as the Original Five Blind Boys of Alabama and the Gospel "divas and dons" Mahalia Jackson, Clara Ward, Marion Williams, James Cleveland, Roberta Martin, and Della Reese. Although most of these artists had begun their careers in churches, they were now on heavy tour schedules, performing in auditoriums, stadiums, and concert halls and some even in nightclubs and theatres.

In 1958, the Recording Industry Association of America (RIAA), an organization that monitors record sales, began to award "gold" and "platinum" record awards. Gold records are awarded when a recording has sold one million copies of a single or five hundred thousand of an album. In 1958, the RIAA awarded a gold record to Laurie London for her Gospel rendition of "He's Got the Whole World (in His Hands)." Some of the Gospel singers, such as Mahalia Jackson and James Cleveland, managed to maintain their spiritual focus, whereas others, such as Della Reese, did not apologize nor hesitate to perform for commercial gain.

Break-Out Two

LISTENING GUIDE *"How I Got Over," composed by Clara Ward*

Performing Artist: Mahalia Jackson

"How I Got Over" was written by Clara Ward (c. 1922–1973). Like most of her contemporaries, Clara's earliest musical experiences were singing in church. As Gospel music began to achieve a wider audience and commercial success, she formed a group, the Clara Ward Singers, that featured other outstanding Gospel singers such as Marion Williams. The group became enormously popular with both sacred and secular audiences, achieving its greatest popularity in the 1950s.

Rhythm	Quadruple
Melody	Clearly contoured
Harmony	Essentially E^b major, with reasonably complex chords
Instrumentation	Vocal with piano

The 1950s also witnessed the fusion of Gospel with rhythm and blues and the creation of "soul" music. One of the most important links between Gospel and soul was Sam Cooke, who began singing with the Gospel group the Soul Stirrers in 1951. The leader of the Soul Stirrers, Rebert H. Harris, developed an improvisatory vocal style of repeating sounds, which he trained Sam Cooke to do. This was a major departure from the barbershop style singing. As Cooke experimented with bridging the musical style and intensity of Gospel with the emerging rhythm and blues style, he recorded under the name of "Dale" Cook so as not to alienate his religious audience. In 1957, he became the first major Gospel star to cross over with the hit "You Send Me." In 1955–1957, Ray Charles horrified Christian traditionalists by taking Gospel tunes and rewriting them into popular hits such as "I've Got a Woman," "This Little Girl of Mine," and "Hallelujah, I Love Her So." In 1959, the Isley Brothers' "Shout" and Ray Charles's "What'd I Say," both using the intensity and call-and-response stylistic characteristics of Gospel, became two big "soul" hits.

Gospel in the Last Half of the Twentieth Century

As Gospel music moved out of the churches and became more popular in the secular world, it underwent several important stylistic changes.

Changes in Instrumentation

In the early years, Gospel quartets sang without accompaniment, whereas Gospel choirs were accompanied by piano and possibly small percussion instruments such as tambourines. During the 1950s, this changed. The Gospel quartet began to add guitars and occasionally a bass and piano. The Gospel choir added male voices to what had been a totally female group, and the instrumental accompaniment was expanded to include electric organ, amplified guitars, and drums. By the 1970s, this was further expanded to include strings, brass instruments, and additional percussion instruments including bongo and congo drums. For big concerts in really large performance halls, the accompaniment might be a full orchestra along with synthesizers and electronic instruments.[16]

Changes in Keyboard Style

Early Gospel pianists played in a relatively simple style, concentrating on blues-style chords performed in a fairly straightforward manner with little ornamentation and embellishment. During the last half of the century, this style changed significantly. More complex chords and complex progressions replaced the simpler blues harmonies. Furthermore, the playing style was brilliant and flashy, stressing the pianist's ability to improvise in technically demanding ways.

Contemporary Gospel singers in Church, reinforcing the rhythmic quality of their singing with handclapping.
Source: Photo by Zigy Kaluzny, Getty Images, Inc. Stone Allstock.

[16] Southern, pp. 475–476.

THE PROLIFERATION OF INDIVIDUAL STYLES

Gospel soloists also began to develop unique, personal styles that distinguished them as professional performing artists. One approach was to sing in a way that incorporated extensive kinds of embellishments in terms of pitch, rhythm, and text. The singers also included a wide range of vocal qualities, from falsetto (especially for men) to full-throated singing in low registers (especially for women). Another way to demonstrate individuality was through the use of improvisation, an enduring value in black music.

Break-Out Three

INSIGHT *White Gospel*

Members of the white church of the rural South were exposed to many of the music traditions of their African-American counterparts. Often these poor whites could relate to the poverty and desire for a better life expressed in black spirituals, hymns, and Gospel music. As a consequence, these rural white churches developed their own version of Gospel music, referred to as "white Gospel" or "southern Gospel." Many white country musicians and early rock 'n' roll musicians were raised on white Gospel music. Because white rural Baptists and Pentacostalists viewed much of the nonchurch music as "the Devil's music," many white country boys and girls had to depend on the church as their means to learn music. By the 1930s, white choirs were touring white church halls and performing for radio stations their versions of black Gospel. Prominent white musicians such as Hank Williams, the Carter Family, Boz Scaggs, Tennessee Ernie Ford, Elvis Presley, and Jerry Lee Lewis all have performed and recorded white Gospel. Today, southern (white) Gospel is a fully developed subgenre within country music, with its own charts to track the progress of recordings and its own award ceremonies.[17]

Doyle Lawson and Quicksilver feature Gospel songs done bluegrass style with three- and four-part harmonies. *Source: Photo by Marc D. Marquette. Doyle W. Lawson.*

[17] Broughton, Viv and James Attlee. *Gospel: Devil Stole the Beat. World Music: The Rough Guide*, Vol. 2. Simon Broughton and Mark Ellingham (eds.). London: 2000, pp. 568–580.

Break-Out Four

PROFILE *Kirk Franklin*

Kirk Franklin was born and raised in Fort Worth, Texas. Abandoned in infancy by his mother, and never knowing his father, he was raised by his aunt. A strict churchgoing Baptist, Kirk's aunt made sure her charge was raised in the Christian faith and nourished in a strong church environment. He displayed musical talent at a very young age, and to help foster his musical gifts, Franklin's aunt collected and resold aluminum cans to pay for piano lessons when he was only four years old. By the age of eleven, he was equally adept at by-ear playing and notation-reading. As a young teenager, Franklin rebelled against the strong religious upbringing and turned to a life of "violence, intimidation, and larceny." When his close friend died of gunshot wounds, Franklin decided to return to the church and began composing songs and recording demo tapes. Having absorbed a variety of secular music influences along with Gospel, he formed a seventeen-member vocal ensemble of neighborhood friends and associates, dubbed "The Family," in the early 1990s. When president and CEO of Gospo Centric Records Vicki Mack-Lataillade heard the demo tape, she signed him to a recording contract. Following his record-breaking debut album, *Kirk Franklin and the Family*, he created another record-breaking album in 1998 titled *Nu Nation Project* and, in 2002, a solo album titled *The Rebirth of Kirk Franklin.* Celebrated for his weaving together disparate musical influences—R & B, modern rock, hip-hop, pop, jazz—into his foundation of traditional Gospel, he has created a sound that transcends boundaries of genre, race, denomination, or societal background and has since enjoyed some of the greatest commercial success ever seen in Gospel music. In Franklin's own words,

Kirk Franklin (right) at the Essence Awards evening in New York, April 30, 1999.
Source: Corbis/Sygma. Photo by Pace Gregory.

"It's taken me these ten years, and longer to fully realize that keeping everything we do focused on the love of God is what music, and life, is all about . . . and it's kind of ironic to be this many years into the pilgrimage only to realize that's the way it was at the start, still is, and always will be. I can look over my life and career now and see both seasons of success as well as struggles and pitfalls, and God has allowed it all. It's all done with the purpose of the Lord drawing you closer to Him—getting you closer to where He wants you to be."[18]

[18] Kirk Franklin Biography. http://www.nunation.com/main.html (Accessed 02-11-05).

During the 1950s, several different record labels such as Sar, Stax, Scepter, and Chess were founded, and distributed recordings of Gospel and soul music among other styles. But the first widely distributed label, which also achieved a distinctive sound, was established by Berry Gordy with his Tamla Motown (for Motor Town) company in Detroit in 1959. By 1961, it had achieved million-sellers with Smokey Robinson and the Miracles' "Shop Around" and the Marvelettes, "Please, Mr. Postman." Gordy went on to achieve tremendous success with other soul artists such as the Supremes, Stevie Wonder, Marvin Gaye, Mary Wells, Martha and the Vandellas, and the Temptations. His contributions will be discussed more fully in Chapter 13. In terms of "straight" Gospel, the Edwin Hawkins Singers achieved a hit "Oh Happy Day" that reached number four on the Billboard chart in 1969. In 1971, Aretha Franklin was awarded a gold record for her rendition of "Amazing Grace," a recording that remains on the "Top Ten Gospel Music Albums" of all time.

By the 1980s, large Gospel choirs had replaced quartets in terms of general popularity. One of the most popular choirs was the Mississippi Mass Choir, founded in 1988 by a former Gospel quartet singer, Franklin Williams (1947–1993). The choir's first recording was an immediate success, and named number one spiritual album of the year by both *Billboard* and *Score* magazines. There are many large contemporary choir groups that continue to demonstrate standards of excellence. One of the more radical of the contemporary choirs is the Sounds of Blackness from Minnesota. Winning three Grammys and an additional five Grammy nominations since their 1991 debut album, *The Evolution of Gospel*, they combine multiple African-American music genres into their repertoire.

Conclusion

The traditions of black spirituals and Gospel music have each had a period in American history when they were one of the strongest musical expressions of African-American culture. Even after their particular era of dominance had passed, they continued to influence all subsequent music. Spirituals, both as solos and in choir arrangements, are frequent additions concert repertoire. Gospel music still plays a vital role in worship services for both African American and white churches and is crossing over into the secular arena.

Gospel singers Kirk Franklin's music has been embraced by the same fans that listen to many other kinds of contemporary music, and he describes his own music as "just chillin' with the Lord." Franklin also sang on the soundtrack of Spike Lee's movie, *Get on the Bus*, and his fourth album *The Nu Nation Project*, entered the Billboard album chart at No. 7 on its release in November 1998. Yolanda Adams received a Grammy award for her 1993 gospel album, *Save the World*, and one-quarter of her tours are bookings by secular promoters at theme parks, universities, and city-owned venues. Gospel continues to influence other forms. For example, many rappers style their cadences after the rhythmic patterns in Gospel music and the percussive preaching style of Black ministers. Joseph Simmons, better known as "Run" of Run-D.M.C., contends that the Gospel sound is just beginning to reach its secular audience potential. His rap duo's gospel-inspired version of "Down with the King" (1993) sold a million copies as a single, with the album selling in excess of 500,000 copies.

Gospel music is now firmly established as a musical tradition throughout the United States and has also become popular internationally. In addition to serving a vital function in the liturgical services of churches of all denominations, Gospel choirs are also becoming increasingly popular additions to the performing ensembles on college campuses. In Chicago, around 70,000 Gospel fans gather every year for the Chicago Gospel Festival where acts range from traditional choirs and quartets to contemporary sounds and fusions. Church conventions in which Gospel music plays an important role, such as the annual COGIC (Church of God in Christ) Convention in Memphis, Tennessee, hosts delegations from as far away as Africa, Haiti, and London. The Gospel-music performing United Choir at this convention frequently consists of several thousand singers. The recording industry is also producing Gospel music recordings of both famous and not famous musicians. Hence, although Gospel music may have arisen as a specific expression of African American culture at an earlier time in American history, it continues to be tremendously popular as it also influences and shapes the musical traditions of America as a whole.

Bibliography

Allen, Ray. *Singing in the Spirit: African-American Sacred Quartets in New York City.* Philadelphia: University of Pennsylvania Press, 1991.

Blackwell, Lois. *Wings of the Dove: The Story of Gospel Music in America.* Norfolk, WV: Donning Publishers, 1978.

Brooks, Tilford. *America's Black Musical Heritage.* Englewood Cliffs, NJ: Prentice Hall, 1984.

Broughton, Viv. *Black Gospel: An Illustrated History of the Gospel Sound.* London: Blandford Press, 1985.

Broughton, Viv and James Attlee. "Gospel: Devil Stole the Beat." *World Music: The Rough Guide,* vol. 2. Simon Broughton and Mark Ellingham (Editors). London: 2000. pp. 568–580.

Chase, Gilbert. *America's Music: From the Pilgrims to the Present.* Third Edition. Urbana and Chicago: University of Illinois Press, 1987.

Courlander, Harold. *Negro Folk Music, USA.* New York: Columbia University Press, 1963.

Crawford, Richard. *America's Musical Life: A History.* New York: W. W. Norton & Company, Inc., 2001.

Fischer, Mark Miles. *Negro Slave Songs in the United States.* New York: Citadel Press, 1990.

Gersten, Russell. "Aretha Franklin," in *The Rolling Stone Illustrated History of Rock and Roll.* New York: Random House, 1980.

Hamm, Charles. *Music in the New World.* New York: W.W. Norton and Company, 1983.

Harris, Michael W. *The Rise of Gospel Blues: The Music of Thomas Dorsey in the Urban Church.* New York: Oxford University Press, 1992.

Haydon, Geoffrey and Dennis Marks. *Repercussions: A Celebration of African American Music.* London: Century Publishers, 1985.

Heilbut, Anthony. *The Gospel Sound.* New York: Anchor Press/Doubleday, 1985.

Jackson, Jesse. *Make a Joyful Noise Unto the Lord!* Boston: G.K. Hall & Co., 1974.

Jasen, David A. and Gene Jones. *Spreadin' Rhythm Around: Black Popular Songwriters, 1880–1930.* New York: Schirmer Books, 1998.

Jones, Ralph H. *Charles Albert Tindley: Prince of Preachers.* Nashville: Abingdon Press, 1982.

Kick, George R. and Sherrill V. Martin, Editors. *Feel the Spirit: Studies in Nineteenth Century Afro-American Music.* New York: Greenwood Press, 1988.

Kingman, Daniel. *American Music: A Panorama.* New York: Schirmer Books, 1979.

Kirk Franklin Biography. http://www.nunation.com/main.html (Accessed 02-11-05).

Lornell, Kip. *Happy in the Service of the Lord: African American Sacred Vocal Quartets in Memphis.* Second Edition. Knoxville: University of Tennessee Press, 1995.

Maultsby, Portia K. *Afro-American Religious Music: A Study in Musical Diversity.* New York: Wittenberg University, 1986.

Morse, Jenifer Corr. *Book of World Records.* New York: Georgian Bay Associates, LLC for Scholastic, Inc. 2001.

Oliver, Paul and Max Harison, William Bolcom. *The New Grove Gospel, Blues and Jazz with Spirituals and Ragtime.* London: Macmillan London Limited, 1986.

Palmer, Robert. *Rock and Roll: An Unruly History. The Companion Volume to the PBS Television Series.* New York: Harmony Books, 1995.

Petrie, Phil. "The History of Gospel." On the Web site "Black Gospel Music: Presented by Smith/McIver," http://afgen.com/gospel.html (Accessed 02-11-05).

Perry, Claudia. "Gospel Breaks Out: The Music and the Message Crosses Over and Beyond Church Walls." *San Jose Mercury News Supplement, Eye,* November 24, 1995, pp. 19–21.

Reagon, Bernice Johnson, ed. *We'll Understand It Better By and By.* Washington, DC: Smithsonian Institution Press, 1992.

Roberts, John Storm. *Black Music of Two Worlds.* New York: Praeger Publishers, 1972.

Roach, Hildred. *Black American Music: Past and Present.* Malabar, FL: Robert E. Krieger Publishing Company, Inc., 1985.

Silveri, Louis. "The Singing Tours of the Fisk Jubilee Singers: 1871–1874," in *Feel the Spirit: Studies in Nineteenth Century Afro-American Music.* George R. Kick and Sherrill V. Martin (Editors). New York: Greenwood Press, 1988.

Southern, Eileen. *The Music of Black Americans: A History.* New York: W.W. Norton, 1982.

Szatmary, David P. *Rockin' in Time: A Social History of Rock and Roll.* Englewood Cliffs, NJ: Prentice Hall, Inc., 1987.

Chapter Nine

Cajun and Zydeco

Cajun and Zydeco are excellent examples of music that developed "at the crossroads." Cajun music is the music of the white French-speaking families who are the descendants of exiles from the seventeenth-century French colony of Acadia (*Acadie* in French). This colony was located primarily in present-day Nova Scotia, Canada. The Acadians were forced into exile by the British in the mid-eighteenth century and about four thousand of these refugees eventually settled in southwest Louisiana. The term "Cajun" is derived from the term "Acadian". As French-speaking Roman Catholics, Cajuns were culturally separate from the English-speaking Protestants that dominated colonial America and the early United States. Yet, despite long periods of repression, Cajun culture survived. Cajun musicians performed at the Newport Folk Festival in 1964 and helped launch a "renaissance" in Cajun culture. By the 1980s, Cajun music was enjoying a worldwide boom in popularity that continues to this day.

Zydeco is the music of the French-speaking black people of the same region in Louisiana, who also initially came to the area in the eighteenth century. These blacks came both as free persons of color and as slaves from the South and the Caribbean. The term "zydeco" is believed to have been derived from the phrase "*Les haricots* sont pas salés" (the snap beans aren't salty), in which the first two words are pronounced in the Cajun dialect as zydeco. This phrase is a metaphor for hard times. (In good times, Creoles seasoned their food with salted meat; during hard times, there wasn't sufficient salted meat to flavor foods such as beans.) The phrase occurs in several Creole songs and is the basis for the title of a popular zydeco recording titled "Zydeco est pas sale." "Zydeco" is also used to refer to a party or the event in which zydeco music is played. But zydeco now generally means a style of music that emerged from the black cultures of the Louisiana bayou region. It is related to Cajun music, but it carries the unique stamp of having been created by and for "Creoles."

The term "Creole," as was discussed in Chapter 7, has had several different meanings over time and has consequently led to lots of confusion. Many people believe Creoles and Cajuns are the same, but they are not. In fact, blacks define themselves as separate from Cajun culture by identifying themselves as "Creole." Originally, Creole was the French version of "criolla," the Spanish word used to designate members of European descent who had been born in the New World. Later it was applied to the offspring of mixed race relationships. "Creole" is also the term for the French dialect spoken by blacks in the former French colony of Haiti. Blacks in the Louisiana area also currently use the term to acknowledge and celebrate their mixed ancestry. Some of their forebears were slaves brought directly from Africa or through the

Caribbean. Others were free blacks and *gens libres de couleur*—free persons of color—who had moved to the area after the Haitian revolution of 1791. Regardless of their origins, over the years these people intermarried or had relationships with whites, resulting in mixed race children. Thus, modern Creoles share an ethnic and racial heritage of a combination of diverse black groups with American Indians and Europeans (especially the French and Spanish). Zydeco is the music tradition that has emerged out of this complex Creole heritage.

Overview of Cajun and Zydeco Music Traditions

Little was known of Cajun music before a few recordings that appeared in the mid-1920s. But based on these early recordings, and the assumption that because Cajuns had remained more isolated than other groups, scholars surmise that these recordings may accurately reflect very old traditions. Cajun music is fundamentally instrumental music for dancing. A communal dance—called the *fais dodo*—was, and continues to be, an important Cajun family recreation. Zydeco is a later style, created essentially out of the cross-fertilization of Cajun and African-American styles such as blues, rhythm 'n' blues, and jazz. Both Cajun and zydeco share basic music characteristics because they came from the same geographical area. With a long history of interaction between the white and black peoples of the region, they share a common repertoire of songs and dances. Also, the words to songs were historically sung in the French-derived dialects. When these dialects were forbidden in schools beginning in 1916, English started to be used with more frequency. Today, Cajun and zydeco songs are sung in the French dialects, in English, or sometimes in both.

Structural Characteristics

Melody, Rhythm, and Harmony

The melody in Cajun music is very important, and it is clearly phrased and easily remembered. The melody is typically either sung or played by the fiddle or accordion. An early recording of "*Mon Cherie Bebe Creolo*" alternates vocal and instrumental verses of the same melody. Cajun music is dancing music, and the rhythm is consequently emphasized and is very metrical. The two most common dances now are "two-steps," which require music in duple (or quadruple) meter, and waltzes, which require music in triple meter. The harmonies in Cajun music are generally simple triads, emphasizing the primary chords and created from the basic major and minor European scales.

Zydeco music uses the same basic stylistic characteristics of Cajun music but incorporates the characteristics of African-American music. Hence, zydeco tends to be faster with more complex rhythms and rhythmic syncopation, and it integrates harmonic and melodic aspects of African-American music such as the "blue notes," seventh chords, and the melodic ornamentation found in such genres as blues, rhythm 'n' blues, soul, and funk.

Texture, Instrumentation, and Form

Cajun music is typically played with a small ensemble in which the fiddle is the dominant instrument. In early Cajun music, two fiddlers played simultaneously, with one playing the melody and the other alternating between doubling the melody and playing a rhythmic accompaniment pattern. At some point (probably during and after the 1840s when German immigrants began to move into the area) the concertino began to be used in Cajun music. A concertino is like a small accordion, producing its sound through bellows held between two casings. Each bellow has a small button keyboard that activates a mechanism that allows the air to flow through one of the reeds to create a specific pitch. The country musicians play a concertino with one row of buttons; the urban players play an instrument with two or even three rows of buttons. In addition to the fiddle and concertino, the ensemble frequently includes a guitar, a percussion idiophone instrument called a triangle (*tit-fer*), and sometimes a steel guitar, bass, and drums.

One of the characteristic instruments that zydeco adds to the Cajun ensemble is a *frottoir*, a

Cajun musicians gather together to practice in Louisiana. The gentleman on the far right is playing the concertino, and the other musicians play fiddle or guitar. Cajun musicians at Savoy Music Center, Eunice, LA. Jam sessions occur in the accordion factory of Marc Savoy on Saturday mornings. *Source: Jack Vartoogian.*

corrugated steel rubboard worn like a vest that was derived from the old laundry washboards. The *frottoir* is rubbed or "scrubbed" with spoons or bottle openers. Additional zydeco instruments are electric guitars, keyboards, and brass instruments incorporated through the influence of jazz and rhythm 'n' blues. Finally, zydeco accordion players such as C. J. Chenier and Queen Ida prefer the larger keyboard accordion (as opposed to the button concertino) because it allows for more complex, blues-derived harmonies.

Cajun and Zydeco Music in a Social and Historical Context

The Roots of Cajun Music

The roots of Cajun music go back to northwest France, from which a large number of families emigrated in the early 1600s to found a colony in "New France" (the present-day Canadian territories of New Brunswick, Nova Scotia, and Prince Edward Island). These immigrants brought with them to the colonies their old-world European music traditions. They also continued to be affected by developments in their home countries.

Impact on Acadia of Political Developments in France and England

Back in Europe, the Roman Catholic King of England, James II, was overthrown in 1688 and the throne was assumed by his daughter Mary and her Dutch Protestant husband William III. William had been invited to invade England by an alliance of Protestant English noblemen who had feared two things. First, they feared that the Catholic King James would ally himself to the powerful Catholic French King, Louis XIV, which would put them in political, economic, religious, and physical danger. Second, they feared that James would favor his Catholic subjects and provoke the now dominant Protestant majority in England to start a civil war, weakening England and thus jeopardizing her power in Europe. In addition to reestablishing a Protestant monarchy, the accession of William and Mary also led to the countries of Scotland and Wales becoming politically united with England to form the Protestant "Great Britain." The power of this unification was a threat to Catholic France both in Europe and to her colonial presence in North America.

Exile of the Acadians and Settling in Louisiana

Conflict between France and England resulted in Great Britain acquiring some of the colonial territories of New France, including Acadia, in 1713. Hostilities continued, and a large-scale expression of the tensions erupted in what is now called the French and Indian War (1754–1763) in which the British and the French fought each other in North America, each with their respective Indian allies. In the autumn of 1755, the Acadians numbered about thirteen thousand in what was now British territory, and the British commander feared that they would be an internal threat in the war with France. The Acadians refused to swear full allegiance to the British crown. Full allegiance meant that they would be willing to fight as soldiers against the French, which they refused to do. The British commander ordered troops to deport them by force. Expelled from their colony, some of the Acadians returned to France and some went to the French Caribbean. A much larger number of Acadians journeyed south looking for refuge, stopping at several places along the Atlantic coast. They ultimately ended up in the Louisiana area, another area that was French territory. The French had founded the city of New Orleans in 1718, and had largely restricted their settlement to the city, but they were happy enough to allow the Acadian refugees to settle in the rural areas outside of town. The Acadians added new songs to the existing repertoire chronicling their journeys and the hardships of their lives.

Integration of Spanish and Blacks

Fifteen years later, the Acadians who had been allowed to remain in Acadia or who had hidden in other areas of New France, such as on the remote islands of St. Pierre and Miquelon off present-day New Foundland, also were deported when France declared its support for the American Revolution. Following the Revolutionary War, many Acadians made their way back to the northeastern coastal areas of present-day Canada, but few were able to recover their former homes. Thus, in 1785, another sixteen hundred sailed to Louisiana. By this time the French had ceded Louisiana to the Spanish (they had relinquished it in 1762 after the French and Indian War) but the Spanish maintained the French policies and allowed Acadians to continue to settle in the rural hinterlands and along the banks and bayou lands of the Mississippi River. The Spanish attempted to restrict the increasing French population and strengthen the Spanish presence, but eventually they were absorbed in the dominant French culture themselves, and they ceded Louisiana back to France in 1800.

Over the subsequent decades, particularly after the new U.S. government acquired these areas in the Louisiana Purchase of 1803, diverse groups of people came to settle in Louisiana. Many of these were the French-speaking people of African descent who were *gens libres de couleur* (free persons of color) and others were slaves or escaped slaves from the South. They brought with them music traditions that included Afro-Caribbean rhythmic complexity and syncopation, the practices of improvisational singing, a call-and-response chanting style called *jure*, and African-style percussion instruments (of which the rubboard is a descendant). They also brought music such as the field hollers and the tradition of accompanying their singing with handclapping and foot-stomping.

As these new settlers arrived, many Acadian farmers began to sell their lands and retreat into the less desirable swamp and prairie lands that were still unclaimed. Settlement of the swamps required new ways of making a living, and the Acadians gradually abandoned their farming ways in favor of fishing. By the middle of the century, the Acadians had slowly mixed with their neighbors of African and Indian ancestry and with other whites that moved into the area. In the process, they became known as Cajuns. But even with this degree of mixing, they still remained relatively isolated from mainstream British-Protestant American life. They continued to practice the Roman Catholic religion and they retained a distinctive dialect now called "Cajun" that was a combination of archaic French (the language they had spoken in Acadia) with the addition of words taken from Spanish, English, German, and the languages of the Africans and Native Americans.

Cajun and Creole Music Early in the Twentieth Century

Cajuns and Creoles shared many cultural links, including the French language, the Catholic religion, and the various festivals that came out of both ethnic and religious contexts. They also shared a love of music and dancing, with a dance on Saturday night being the high point of the week. These Cajun dances were called *bals de maison* (house parties) or *fais do-dos* ("go to sleep"—a term derived from putting the children to bed so that the adults could party in the next room). The Creole equivalent was called a *la-la*, hence the term "la-la music" for old-fashioned Creole music. Up until 1900, the parties were held in local homes. They were accompanied by lots of drinking and eating as people danced a wide variety of "Old World" dances, including mazurkas, polkas, and waltzes to the music created by local musicians. Eventually, community dance halls replaced the house parties. Musicians learned to perform at a loud enough dynamic level to project above the partying crowd. This is one of the reasons for the Cajun use of the concertino (which is louder than the traditional fiddle) and for the characteristic high intense singing style. The wide variety of dances eventually shrunk down to the two that are most common today, the two-step and the waltz.

First Recordings of Cajuns and Creoles

In the late 1920s, the same recording companies (RCA Victor and Columbia) that had searched for Anglo folk traditions in the Appalachians also began to make field recordings of Cajun and Creole music. The first Cajun recording was made of Joseph and Cleoma Breux Falcon performing a song called "Allons a Lafayette" ("Let's Go to Lafayette," which was a prominent Cajun city). Joseph and Cleoma were brother and sister, and played accordion and guitar. Although it was unusual for women to have been so prominent in Cajun music at this time, as cultural restrictions discouraged females from performing publicly, Cleoma recorded and apparently composed the most famous of all Cajun songs, "Ma Blonde Est Partie" ("The Blonde Is Pretty"), also known as "Jolie Blond" ("Pretty Blonde").

Black Creole musicians were also prominent in the late 1920s. The most famous and perhaps most tragic was the accordionist Amedee Ardoin, who began recording in 1929 with his friend and partner, a white fiddler named Dennis McGee. Their collaboration laid the foundation for what has become the style and repertoire of contemporary Cajun music.

Amedee Ardoin and Dennis McGee

Amedee was born in 1896 to a sharecropping family in L'Anse Rougeau, near Basile. When still young, he met white Cajun fiddler Dennis McGee, who also was working as a sharecropper on a nearby farm. The farmer encouraged Dennis and Amedee to play together for the Cajun house parties in the local neighborhood. Their fame spread and they continued to travel, perform, and record together.

Amedee, particularly, was very active in both black and white groups. Often he would perform in a band for a white dance and then when that was finished, go to a Creole party where he would sing and play blues and Creole music for the black audiences. Ardoin also crossed the race barrier to become one of the most popular early black "French" recording stars. He had a powerful, high-pitched voice that could be heard above the party noise, and that style of vocal production became the standard for Cajun-style singing. He also was able to sing very emotionally and sensitively, and he knew a wide repertoire of traditional French, Creole, and African songs.

Although Amedee had been successful generally crossing racial lines, eventually two white men felt he had gone too far. In the mid-1930s he was performing at a white dance party and he accepted a white woman's handkerchief to wipe his face, which was perspiring from the heat on a hot summer's night. Two white men took him out after the dance, beat him savagely, and left him for dead. Locals insist that the men came from out of the area, as they all knew and liked Amedee and would not have hurt him. Ardoin never recovered from the beating, especially mentally as a result of blows to his head. He was eventually committed to the Louisiana State Institution for the Mentally Ill where he died in 1941.

Called the "Dean of Cajun Eiddlers," Dennis McGee performed and taught fiddle until his death in 1989 at age ninety-six. Here he is at age 93 at the Savoy Music Center, June 9, 1988. *Source: Jack Vartoogian. © 1988 Jack Vartoogian.*

Dennis McGee was born in 1893 in Bayou Marron to a father of Irish descent and a mother who was half-French and half-Seminole Indian. His mother died when he was two years old, and Dennis was left on the farm in the care of his eight-year-old brother. Later he was sent to live with his grandmother, and here he heard his father first play the fiddle. When he was ten years old, he was sent to live with an older cousin who was a farmer. He lived and worked on the farm until he was fourteen, when he went to live with another cousin, Theodore McGee. Theodore bought Dennis a fiddle and, in six months, Dennis was playing for house dances. When Dennis met his younger neighbor, Sady Courville, he learned the old, traditional fiddle songs from Sady's father and uncle, who were popular twin fiddlers. Thus, McGee became a link to the Acadian culture's pre-accordion past. Dennis partnered together with Sady as he had also partnered with Ardoin, and the two recorded in 1928. By 1934, McGee had recorded fifty-three times, half on his own and half in partnership with other musicians.

Working as a musician was not sufficient to earn a living, and by the 1950s, he was residing in Eunice and working on the farm of Louis Savoy, the grandfather of contemporary accordionist Marc Savoy. McGee gave up playing music because he feared it was bringing bad luck to his family, but he started to play again in 1970 when interest in Cajun music resumed. This late-in-life career (he was in his eighties by this time) included national tours and also teaching, including teaching Michael Doucet. He continued to play and perform until his death in 1989 at the age of ninety-six, and is known as the "Dean of Cajun Fiddlers."

Despite the racial separation in the community that was expressed so violently in the beating of Ardoin, there was still considerable interaction between black Creole and white Cajun musicians. Cajuns borrowed the blues sounds and some of the rhythmic vitality of the music of the Creoles; Creoles adapted many of the songs and dance melodies of the Cajuns. Both styles also incorporated elements of other music traditions. For example, in Ardoin and McGee's music, musicologists have heard influences from the old Acadian colony in Canada, of France, Ireland, Africa, the Caribbean, Spain, England, Germany, and Native Americans.

Cajun Music in the Middle of the Twentieth Century

In the 1930s, the discovery of oil in the area, along with the later expansion of the federal and state highway systems, reduced the isolation of the Cajun and Creole communities. Furthermore, the radio broadcasting that was exposing other cultural groups to Cajun music also brought to the Cajuns and Creoles the sounds of other styles, including jazz and eventually country and rock 'n' roll. The fiddle also made a comeback once electronic amplification was introduced. Furthermore, the ensemble was augmented with pedal steel guitar, bass, and drums. Sometimes, the only "Cajun" or "Creole" aspect that remained in the music was the Cajun dialect French language.

During the 1940s, the accordion was brought back into Cajun music, because returning World War II vets yearned for the distinctive styles of their youth. Older accordionists who had been out of vogue, such as Lawrence Walker and Aldus Roger, were once again in demand. Harry Choates became an extremely popular player who blended Cajun styles with Western swing and sang Texas style songs. In 1946, he recorded a western swing version of "Jole Blon" (his version of the famous Cajun song "Pretty Blonde"), which became a regional hit and the Cajun "national anthem."

Swamp Pop

In the early 1950s, the accordionist Ivy LeJeune, an almost-blind son of a tenant farmer, helped usher in a brief revival of the traditional style Cajun music. By the mid-1950s, however, record companies were once again abandoning this style in favor of a rock 'n' roll influenced Cajun style called "swamp pop." Although the actual term "swamp pop" was not coined until around 1970,[1] the style became extremely popular in the 1960s, outselling both Cajun and zydeco recordings. Swamp pop consisted of covers of popular rock 'n' roll hits, but reshaped to incorporate Cajun and zydeco sounds, especially the use of the accordion. Floyd Soileau described Swamp Pop as, "Sometimes its bluesy, sometimes it's country and sometimes it has a heavy Cajun accent. It's that gumbo, that mixture of all those influences. When you hear something that was cut from down here, you'll be able to say 'Aha, that was cut in south Louisiana!'"[2] Classics of the genre include Dale and Grace's "I'm Leaving It Up to You," Johnny Preston's "Running Bear," Freddy Fender's "Before the Next Teardrop Falls," Phil Phillips's "Sea of Love," and Jimmy Clanton's "Just a Dream," all of which became top ten national hits. The Swamp Pop "anthem" is a cover of Chuck Berry's song "Promised Land" by Johnnie Allan. (Contrary to popular belief, Creedence Clearwater Revival is not an example of this genre.) Swamp Pop is still being played in south Louisiana and east Texas clubs and at regional festivals. There also are occasional recordings that achieve some level of mainstream popularity, such as Charles Mann's version of Dire Straits' "Walk of Life" in the 1990s. In addition to swamp pop, Cajun recording stars such as Doug Kershaw, Vin Bruce, and Belton Richard borrowed from various popular styles, adding them to a traditional Cajun base.

Cajun music was also of interest to researchers such as Alan Lomax (who had recorded Cajun and Creole music in the 1930s for the Library of Congress) and to musicians who were interested in various folk musics. In the first Newport Folk Festival in 1964, the fiddler Dewey Balfa was a tremendous success and helped initiate a new era of interest in traditional Cajun music. Michael Doucet and the accordionist Marc Savoy contributed their skills to launching a renaissance in Cajun music that has continued to the present. These musicians attempt to retain their traditional Cajun roots, while incorporating into their music elements of rock, jazz, and other styles. In 1984, the Cajun French Music Association was founded in Basile, Louisiana, to promote and preserve Cajun music as well as various aspects of the Acadian heritage. One of their activities is to sponsor the

[1] "Cajun Music." The Encyclopedia of Cajun Culture. http://www. cajunculture.com (Accessed 02-10-05).

[2] Broughton, Simon and Jeff Kaliss, "Cajun and Zydeco: Music Is the Glue," in *Music, The Rough Guide*, p. 558.

Break-Out One

PROFILE *Michael Doucet*

Michael Doucet is considered one of the founders of the Cajun renaissance that began in the 1970s. Born in 1951 in Scott, near the important Cajun city of Lafayette, Michael grew up in a musical, middle-class family. His mother played clarinet, an uncle played Cajun fiddle, and several aunts sang traditional ballads. When Michael was six, he started to play banjo, an instrument that had been given to him by his uncle. He later learned how to play guitar and trumpet. Although his family spoke English, Michael picked up the Cajun dialect at family gatherings. During the 1960s, Cajun music was at a low, overshadowed by swamp pop. But interest in folk music in general (evident in the Urban Folk Revival) started to generate interest in Cajun music. Michael's sister, Pauline, was interested in folk music and this also inspired Michael to begin to pursue his own ethnic roots.

When Michael went to Louisiana State University, he enrolled in a course on folk music and this began his lifelong study of Cajun traditions. When he graduated from the university in 1973, he accepted an invitation to play at a folk festival in France. Here he and his friend and distant relative Zachary Richard heard French folk bands playing Cajun songs. Returning to Louisiana, he and Zachary formed the Bayou Drifter Band. The band lasted less than a year, and Doucet and Richard split up, with Richard going up to Canada to become famous as a Cajun player there. Michael searched out the old fiddle master Dennis McGee (as well as Dewey Balfa and Canray Fontenot) and took fiddling lessons from them. He also found other young musicians who shared his interest, and in 1975, he and Dewey Balfa helped to found what has become the annual *Festivals Acadiens* to showcase Cajun musicians.

Michael Doucet playing the fiddle and leading the Cajun Band Beausoleil at B.B. King's Blues Club in New York City on February 13, 2001. *Source: Jack Vartoogian © 2001 Jack Vartoogian.*

By 1975, Doucet founded Beausoleil (with Bessyl Duhon on accordion and Kenneth Richard on mandolin). Beausoleil became very popular with the college and folk festival crowd, and the band expanded. On a cultural exchange trip to France in 1976, the band recorded their first album, *The Spirit of Cajun Music.* By 1986, the fame and success of Beausoleil was sufficient to allow Doucet to concentrate full time on performing and promoting Cajun music.

"Le Cajun" Festival, a three-day event that includes Grammy-style awards for the best in Cajun music and includes a two-day dance festival. This event honors and recognizes contemporary Cajun musicians such as Ray Abshire, Kevin Naquin and the Ossun Playboys, and Ashley Hayes.

Zydeco

Out of the Creole music traditions emerged "Zydeco." The earliest Creole music was purely vocal and created in the fields by the blacks who were working as sharecropping farmers. Less melodic than Cajun music, this early rural Creole tradition was called "la-la" music. Eventually instruments were added, including the concertino and fiddle from the neighboring Cajun style and the washboard or rubboard from African traditions. By the 1940s, Creoles were listening to rhythm 'n' blues and jazz on the radio and in clubs, and musicians such as Clifton Chenier and BooZoo Chavis were beginning to add to their la-la music the urban characteristics of these other traditions. During the 1950s, the Creole accordionist Clifton Chenier appeared on the scene and virtually invented the official genre of "zydeco" by blending his Creole la-la music with the blues and rhythm 'n' blues styles.

CLIFTON CHENIER

Clifton Chenier was born in 1925 to poor sharecroppers near Opelousas, and he grew up working in fields planting and harvesting cotton, rice, sugar, and corn. His father played the button accordion and he heard this music at home and also the French songs, southern blues, and the recordings of Amedee Ardoin. Rather than play button accordion, Chenier decided to play the larger "piano" accordion with the full keyboard so that he could better recreate the harmonies and sounds of the blues. His older brother, Cleveland, accompanied him on their mother's washboard, which eventually was modified by Clifton to be worn as a vest and which has become a fixture of zydeco bands ever since. In the late 1940s, the brothers were still working in the oil companies during the day and playing at local dances at night.

In 1954, the talent scout J. R. Fulbright discovered Clifton and his brother playing in the middle of a road surrounded by a crowd outside Lafayette. He arranged for the brothers to be recorded and their recording of "Ay-Tete-Fee" ("Little Girl") became a nationwide hit. He also popularized an old Creole song "Les Haricots Sont Pas Sale"—heard and titled by Chenier as "Zydeco Sont Pas Sale" ("The Beans Are Not Salted," which is a reference to hard times)—thus creating the zydeco name.

Break-Out Two

LISTENING GUIDE *Zydeco*

Performing Artist: Queen Ida

Queen Ida (Ida Lewis) was born in 1930 to a musically talented family in Lake Charles, Louisiana. She learned to play accordion from her mother. Her family moved to Texas when she was ten and then to San Francisco, where she married and raised a family. In the early 1970s she began performing with local bands, and eventually founded her own band, the Bon Temps Zydeco Band. This song is from her eighth album and reflects the Cajun and zydeco music characteristics in the lyrics and in the instrumentation.

Rhythm	Duple
Melody	Clearly contoured
Harmony	E^b Major with primary trends
Texture	Homophonic
Form	Strophic with one line chorus
Instrumentation	Female voice with background vocals, prominent fiddle, drums, washboard, accordion, slide guitar, guitar, and less prominent horns and keyboard

Break-Out Three

PROFILE *Queen Ida and Buckwheat Zydeco*

Born Ida Lewis in 1930, Ida Guillory came from a musical family in the Lake Charles area of Louisiana. Her mother, as well as a couple of her uncles, played accordion. After World War II, the family moved to the San Francisco Bay area and she abandoned playing the accordion. She picked it back up two decades later when she was in her forties and practiced during her off-times from driving a school bus. Eventually she teamed up with her older brother, Wilbert Lewis, and the two started to play at local parties. Her big break came at a Mardi Gras zydeco party and her performance was such a success that it was covered in the newspaper, the *San Francisco Chronicle*, where the reporter named her "Queen Ida." From there she went on to play for larger venues, including the San Francisco Blues Festival. Starting in 1976, she began recording albums and has put out nine albums to date. For her work in this area, she has received several Grammy nominations, wining a Grammy for her 1982 album *Queen Ida and the Bon Temps Zydeco Band on Tour.*

The Ritz, New York City. Queen Ida (Guillory) leading her Bon Temps Zydeco Band on May 4, 1988.
Source: Jack Vartoogian. © 1988 Jack Vartoogian.

Stanley Dural Jr. was given the nickname "Buckwheat" when he was growing up because his braided hair reminded his friends of the character with the same name in the television program, *The Little Rascals.* Raised in a two-room house in Layfayette, Buckwheat grew up in a musical family that included eleven siblings. At the age of nine, he joined an R & B and soul band called Sam and the Untouchables, and later formed his own group called Buckwheat and the Hitchhikers. In 1996, Buckwheat was seen by more than three billion viewers who watched the closing ceremonies of the Summer Olympics in Atlanta, where he played "Jambalaya," a song that has been part of zydeco ever since Clifton Chenier performed it in 1975. In 1997, he opened and closed President Clinton's inaugural ceremonies. During his international career, he has received four Grammy nominations, and performed as the opening act for musicians such as Eric Clapton, U2, Robert Cray, and Los Lobos. He has collaborated with many musicians, including Keith Richards of the Rolling Stones, and has performed in many films and commercials. In 1999, Buckwheat Zydeco celebrated the twentieth anniversary with the LP *Trouble.*

By the 1970s, Chenier was performing with his Red Hot Louisiana Band, and for the next two decades, the band toured nationally and in Europe. Wearing a jeweled crown, he was now titled "The King of Zydeco." In the late 1970s, Chenier won Grammy awards and a National Heritage Fellowship that enabled him to play at the White House for President Ronald Reagan. In 1984, he won another Grammy. In 1979, he started to suffer more severely from diabetes, which eventually led to his death in 1987. When he died, his son, C. J. Chenier, continued his legacy with the Red Hot Louisiana Band.

Various zydeco musicians and bands continue to record and to perform today, now drawing on contemporary pop music sources like reggae, rap, and hip-hop. It also is increasingly performed with English (as opposed to Creole) lyrics and has attracted a loyal fan base outside of Louisiana. Some of the most famous stars include Queen Ida, Rockin' Sidney, Nathan Williams, Zydeco Cha Chas, and Buckwheat Zydeco. Contemporary musicians in zydeco strive to maintain their musical roots while still experimenting with sounds and styles of more currently popular music, including hip-hop and rap. In the words of Chenier's son, C. J., "Even when you listen to Clifton, he doesn't limit himself to zydeco, he's blues and boogie. It's a different age now, and even if I play his song, it's gonna sound different."[3] Partially because of its "party" flavor, association with dancing, and the fact that it stays sounding "current" by absorbing other musical influences, zydeco appears frequently in movies, TV programs, and commercials, and is popular worldwide. Younger zydeco musicians, such as Corey Arceneaux and the Zydeco Hot Peppers, T-Broussard and the Zydeco Steppers, and Terry and the Zydeco Bad Boys, ensure that zydeco stays fresh and contemporary, while still retaining its role as an important expression of Creole culture.

Conclusion

Much has changed in the century following the work of musicians such as Amedee Ardoin, Dennis McGee, and Clifton Chenier. The geographical area of the Southwest was officially named Acadiana by the Louisiana state legislature, and younger Cajuns and Creoles are proudly studying and reviving their ethnic culture. Most now speak English as their primary language and need to study the French dialects that are now offered in schools after having been banned for decades. Musicians from both groups continue to lead the way for crossing the color line that still exists in much of the South. For example, in 1997, an "outside" man tried to open up a dance club and hire both Cajun and zydeco bands until some young local whites told him that if he wanted to have a zydeco band playing in the same place, he "might be returning in sheets."[4]

Despite this enduring challenge of "meeting at the crossroads," most young musicians share the views of the Cajun bandleader Christine Balfa, who expressed in a letter to the local newspaper, "White and black musicians playing together is nothing new. One can look back to Amedee Ardoin and Dennis McGee, some of the first to record 'French Music' from the area. Have you ever heard old 'Acadian' music and compared it to 'Cajun' music? I can tell you, a large part of what we consider Cajun music came from the influence of the Creoles. It is something we should be proud of."[5] Although there is not a counting of the number of individuals who claim "Creole" heritage, more than 750,000 American citizens can now trace their ethnic origins to the approximate 4,000 Acadian refugees who settled in the Louisiana area in the eighteenth century. Cajun music and culture, and the zydeco music of their Creole neighbors, have not only endured but are currently thriving.

[3] Ibid., p. 562.

[4] Tisserand, Michael, *The Kingdom of Zydeco.* p. 7.

[5] Quoted in Tisserand, p. 7.

BIBLIOGRAPHY

Allan, Jonnie. *Memories: A Pictorial History of South Louisiana Music, 1910s–1900s.* Lafayette, LA: Johnnie Allan/Jadfel Publishing, 1995.

Ancelet, Barry Jean. *Cajun Music: Its Origins and Development.* Lafayette: Center for Louisiana Studies, University of Southwestern Louisiana, 1989.

Ancelet, Barry Jean (photographs by Elemore Morgan Jr.). *The Makers of Cajun Music.* Austin: University of Texas Press, 1984.

Ancelet, Barry Jean, Jay Edwards, and Glen Pitre. *Cajun Country.* Jackson: University Press of Mississippi, 1991.

Broven, John. *South to Louisiana: The Music of the Cajun Bayous.* Gretna, LA: Pelican, 1983.

Broughton, Simon and Jeff Kaliss. "Cajun and Zydeco: Music Is the Glue," in *World of Music, The Rough Guide*, vol. 2. Simon Broughton and Mark Ellingham (Editors). London: Rough Guides Ltd., 2000, pp. 552–567.

Buckwheat Zydeco Online. http://www.buckwheatzydeco.com/index.html (Accessed 2-10-05).

Cajun French Music Association. http://www.cajunfrenchmusic.org/ (Accessed 2-10-05).

Doucet, Michael in *Contemporary Musicians*, Vol. 8. Gale Research, 1992. Reproduced in *Biography Resource Center*, Gale Group, 2001. http://www.galenet.com/servlet/BioRC (Accessed 07-28-01).

Encyclopedia of Cajun Culture. http://www.cajunculture.com/ (Accessed 02-10-05).

Finn, Timothy. "A Little Blues, a Little Cajun, a lot of Zydeco." *Knight-Ridder/Tribune News Service.* http://urn:bigchalk.comUS;EL&dtype=0~0&dinst=0 (Accessed 05-08-01).

Kaganoff, Penny. "Cookin' with Queen Ida: Bon Temps Creole Recipes (and stories) from the Queen of Zydeco Music (book reviews)." *Publisher's Weekly*, November 16, 1990 v237 n 46 p51(2). Reproduced in *Biography Resource Center.* Gale Group, 2001—article #A9112346. http://www.galenet.com/servlet/BioRC (Accessed 07-28-01).

Lichtenstein, Grace, and Laura Dankner. *Musical Gumbo: The Music of New Orleans.* New York: W.W. Norton, 1993.

Nyhan, Pat and Brian Rollins, David Babb. *Let the Good Times Roll: A Guide to Cajun and Zydeco Music.* Maine: Upbeat Books, 1997.

"*Queen Ida*" in AMG All Music Guide—AMG Biography. Netscape Internet Resource. http://allmusic.com/cg/x.dll?p=amg&sql=B89074 (Accessed 07-28-01).

Skorburg, John W. "Allons au Zydeco: Southwest Louisiana's Creole Music: Four Keys to Success." *The World & I*, vol. 14. http://urn:bigchalk.com:US;EL&dtype=0~0&dinst=0 (Accessed 05-08-01).

Tisserand, Michael. *The Kingdom of Zydeco.* New York: Arcade Publishing, 1998.

"Visual Zydeco Portrays Images of Creole, Cajun Culture," Noah Adams, host. *All Things Considered (NPR).* http://urn:bigchalk.com:US;EL&dtype=0~0&dinst=0 (Accessed 05-08-01).

Chapter Ten

Country Music

Country music has become one of today's most popular and profitable music genres. Since 2000, even when other areas of the music industry struggled, numbers of fans and sales of country music recordings increased. On the touring front, for example, more tickets were sold in 2004 for concerts by the country stars Kenny Chesney and Shania Twain than for all other genres of music. During that same time period, several country musicians crossed over to film and television. Reba McEntire starred in her own hit sitcom, *Reba*; Tim McGraw debuted in the film *Friday Night Lights;* and Faith Hill appeared in the remake of *The Stepford Wives.*

Country music has its roots in the folk music traditions brought to the United States by European immigrants. In the eighteenth century, the folk music of the British immigrants dominated, because it was immigrants from these areas who constituted the majority of people who came and settled the "New England" colonies. As industrialism in the nineteenth century helped move the United States from a primarily rural nation to an urban one, traditional folk music was retained in the backwoods sections of the Southeast. Here, in an area ranging as far north as the Ohio River and as far west as Texas, but especially in the Appalachian mountains of Virginia, West Virginia, Kentucky, Tennessee, and North Carolina, the old music traditions were preserved. In these remote and generally impoverished areas, people continued to live without electricity, without indoor plumbing, and without the conveniences of the "modern" world. Despite their poverty, their lives were rich with music, as each successive generation passed down the songs and instrumental music that they had learned from the previous generation. Music was used to accompany work, worship, social gatherings, celebrations, and simply to "while away the hours" with family members and neighbors on the porch at the end of a hot summer day.

Because of their simple country ways, these poor white folks were derisively called "hillbillies" when they came into town to look for work or buy supplies. "Billy" is a name for a male goat, and "hill" reflected these people's homes in the more remote areas of the mountains. "Hillbilly" was also the term that was used to describe this old-time mountain music, and the term first appeared in print in the *New York Journal* on April 23, 1900.[1] It is from this music that "country" emerged as a music industry genre in the 1920s. After hitting a low point in the 1980s, country music "rebounded" in the 1990s and achieved an unprecedented level of commercial success. By 1996, country music had become the

[1] Oermann, Robert K. *A Century of Country: An Illustrated History of Country Music*. New York: TV Books, L.L.C., 1999, p. 11.

In the late nineteenth century, poor white sharecroppers in North Carolina experienced much of the same harsh farming life as did blacks. It was on porches such as this that many of the old Anglo folk songs were preserved. *Source: North Carolina Division of Archives and History. Courtesy of the North Carolina Division of Archives and History.*

dominant radio format in the United States, with a total of 43 percent of all radio listeners.[2] Over the years, country music evolved into different styles and enjoyed (or suffered through) various levels of popularity. Country music, from its origins in hillbilly music to its present status as a major American music genre, is the focus of this chapter.

Overview of Country Music

The hillbilly music that was the foundation for the development of country music came from several different sources. One major source was the ballads, lyric songs, and lullabies of the folk song tradition that had been brought over by British immigrants. At first this music was simply transplanted onto American soil. But as the years went by, the music became "Americanized" as the words, melodies, and performance style were changed gradually over time either unintentionally because of error in oral transmission, or intentionally to reflect more local interests and needs. Another source was the instrumental music that was used to accompany group activities from barn raisings and hog slaughterings to weddings and harvest celebrations. This instrumental music was performed by small string bands, usually some combination of fiddles, guitar, dulcimer, banjo, and autoharp.

A third source was the religious music of the churches. Most of these rural people were Protestants, especially Old Regular Baptists. Church leaders in this denomination strongly disapproved of music instruments in worship services. They believed that instrumental music in church was distracting, reminiscent of the practices of the Roman Catholic Church (from which the Protestants had rebelled centuries earlier), and could even be tools of the Devil. Therefore, in the worship services of these Baptists, the congregation sang unaccompanied and unharmonized (monophonic) psalms and hymns. Many whites in

[2] Feiler, Bruce. "Gone Country: The Voice of Suburban America." *The New Republic*. 02-05-1996, p. 19(5).

As pioneers moved out into the backcountry, they built rough structures such as this log cabin, homes that could be built in a day with the help of neighbors. Callot, Georges-Henri-Victor. Paris, 1826. pl. 16, *An American Log House.*
Source: The New York Public Library/Art Resource.

this area also were followers of the Holiness Pentecostal churches that began to appear in the mid-nineteenth century. In these churches, instruments (especially banjos and guitars) and rhythmic clapping were welcomed. It was in these churches that black (and white) Gospel music was created. Emerging from a blend of these traditions of the British settlers in the Southern backcountry, country added influences from other immigrant traditions such as those of the Cajuns and African Americans, and developed into several specific musical styles over the subsequent decades.

Stylistic Categories

Old-Time Country

This term is now used for the string band and "hillbilly" music that constitutes the earliest country music genre. The most popular instruments were the fiddle, banjo, and guitar, but after 1900, other instruments were added such as the mandolin, string bass, and Hawaiian steel guitar. Old-time music was disseminated across the country in the first recordings and radio broadcasts from the 1920s and 1930s. Some of the famous early musicians and bands were Jimmie Rodgers, the Carter Family, Gid Tanner and the Skillet Lickers, Charlie Poole and the North Carolina Ramblers, and prominent fiddlers included Uncle Jimmy Thompson, Blind Joe Mangrum, and Uncle Am Stuart. Later musicians, such as Roy Acuff, Doc Watson, Uncle Dave Macon, and the Red Clay Ramblers maintained that style.

Cowboy Songs

An immensely popular derivative of country in the 1930s, this included romantic, composed songs about the prairie and the Old West, sung by cowboys and cowgirls dressed in fringed, rhinestone-studded clothes and wearing Stetson hats. This style of music corresponded with the rage in "Westerns," films romanticizing life in America's "Wild, Wild West." Popular musicians in this genre included Gene Autry, Roy Rogers, Patsy Montana, Tex Ritter, Sons of the Pioneers, and Riders in the Sky.

Western Swing

This is a category of music that developed in the late 1930s in the Southwest. Traditional string ensembles incorporated characteristics from other music genres, especially jazz, into a big-band sound that accompanied dancing. In Western swing bands, instrumentation was expanded to include drums, pianos, and electric guitars. One of the leaders of this style was Bob Wills with the Texas Playboys.

Bluegrass

Although closely related to old-time hillbilly music, bluegrass developed as a distinct style in the 1940s. Led by the mandolin player Bill Monroe, the band called themselves The Blue Grass Boys after the famous bluegrass of their home state, Kentucky. Bluegrass music's chief characteristic was a return to a purely acoustic instrumental ensemble that typically included some combination of fiddle, banjo, mandolin, guitars, and string bass to accompany high-range solo singing. Furthermore, it incorporated solo improvisation at a fast, virtuosic pace. Other artists include Lester Flatt and Earl Scruggs, the Stanley Brothers, and the Osborne Brothers. Bluegrass remains a vital, contemporary music tradition. Musicians such as Alison Krauss and Union Station create a fresh, "popier" style of bluegrass that became very popular because of films such as "O Brother, Where Art Thou." Other musicians, such as David Grisman, Bela Fleck, and the New Grass Revival, are creating bluegrass with a jazzy twist, a genre that is sometimes referred to as "New Grass."

Honky Tonk

Honky tonk music embodied the spirit of living hard—dancing, drinking, violence—that thrived in the dance halls of the same name. These "honky tonk" dance halls had sprung up in the 1930s throughout the Southwest, especially in Alabama and Texas. Working-class white folks gathered there to relax after a long, hard day. The honky tonk music that evolved in the 1940s out of this context was most closely related to the old-time string bands, but with a harder, rhythm-based edge appropriate for dancing and drinking, and the angst and Depression-imbued lyrics of losing loved ones, often due to affairs. Although the most famous of honky tonk singers was Hank Williams, other important artists include Floyd Tillman, Ernest Tubb, Al Dexter, Hank Thompson, Ray Price, Kitty Wells, Webb Pierce, and Carl Smith.

The Nashville Sound and Country Pop

In the 1950s, 1960s, and 1970s, Nashville became the acknowledged center of country music. Recording artists attempted to create music that reflected folk origins, while absorbing elements from the broader popular culture. The band was sometimes expanded to an entire orchestra, performing music in pop-style arrangements designed to appeal to both country and pop audiences. In any particular recording, the pop elements or the traditional elements might be more or less emphasized. Examples of musicians who have recorded in this style include Jim Reeves, Patsy Cline, Eddie Arnold, Loretta Lynn, Tammy Wynette, Kenny Rogers, the Mandrell Sisters, Crystal Gayle, Glen Campbell, and Dolly Parton.

The Outlaws (The Texas Sound)

During the 1960s and 1970s, primarily as a reaction against the dominance of Nashville and the popular music industry, various styles of country emerged in other parts of the country. Bakersfield, California, was home to musicians such as Buck Owens and Merle Haggard. In Austin, Texas, the thriving club scene generated "rebel" country musicians including Willie Nelson, Waylon Jennings, and Lyle Lovett. These musicians were called "outlaws" because of their rejection of the mainstream country music industry. By the end of the 1990s, another related genre of country music emerged in which the musicians were referred to as "The Hats," because one of their signature looks was their cowboy hats. Musicians such as George

Strait, Garth Brooks, and Lyle Lovett—important "Hat" acts—sing in a traditional style as well as a style that has been influenced by rock 'n' roll.

Contemporary Country (New Country, Young Country)

"Contemporary Country" (sometimes termed "New Country" or "Young Country") refers to the highly produced, pop-oriented country that is heard on most commercial radio stations. The music is marked by a youthful and fresh energy, incorporating characteristics of different musical styles (particularly pop and rock 'n' roll) or a singer's own artistic innovations into country-based music. Beginning with groups such as Alabama in the 1980s, this genre encompasses performers such as Randy Travis, Trisha Yearwood, LeaAnn Rimes, Garth Brooks, Alan Jackson, George Strait, Travis Tritt, and Kenny Chesney. Many country musicians have moved out of the confines of the "country" labels altogether and are marketed to broader audiences. Examples of musicians who began in country but have had broad crossover appeal or have eventually shifted into other music styles are Wynonna Judd, Shania Twain, The Dixie Chicks, and Faith Hill.

Traditional and Alternative Country

"Traditional" is used to refer to any of the older styles as well as to describe younger country musicians who record in these styles. These musicians purposefully strive to retain the simpler, acoustic roots of traditional country music. "Alternative" is similar, describing country music that is made and distributed outside of the mainstream Nashville music industry and that does not typically get airplay on commercial radio. Musicians in this category include k.d. lang, the Palace, Jeffrey Jeff Walker, and Robert Earl Keen. Often the music is eclectic, pulling from a variety of styles, even to create new fusions with names such as "Cow Punk"—a fusion of country and punk, created by groups such as The Beat Farmers, Mojo Nixon, and Dash Rip Rock.

Structural Characteristics

Melody, Rhythm, and Harmony

Melodies in country music are constructed in clear, regular phrases, frequently organized into "parallel" construction emulating speech patterns of question and answer. They are generally simple and designed to be easily remembered, often with a "hook" that captures people's attention. The rhythmic organization is divisive, with strong, steady metrical organization, most frequently in duple and quadruple meters. The melodies and the supporting harmonies are in European tonal systems, with major mode predominating. In most of the styles, the accompanying chords stress the primary triads of I, IV, and V.

Instrumentation, Texture, and Form

Textures are homophonic, and the performance style is direct. The formal structure is typically strophic, with repeated verses of text set to the same music or they are strophic with a refrain. In terms of instrumentation, early songs were sung with simple accompaniment that emphasized strings, such as the fiddle, guitar, banjo, string bass, dulcimer, and autoharp. Later instrumentation varies with the particular style. For example, "bluegrass" is a style that is characterized by a small acoustic ensemble while the "Nashville Sound" of the 1950s and 1960s augmented a basic string group with an entire orchestra and "Contemporary Country" can add electric guitars, drums, and synthesizer.

The Steel or "Pedal" Guitar. One instrument that has become strongly associated with country music is the "steel" or "pedal" guitar. These guitars originated in an instrument called the "Hawaiian" guitar, which was introduced to people in the South early in the century and again after World War I. Hawaiian guitars were laid flat across the player's knees or were placed on a stand. The guitar had metal strings that were raised away from the neck and body of the guitar so high that the strings had to be stopped by a steel bar held in the player's hands. (Conventional guitars have the strings depressed by the fingers of the guitarist's left hand.) The guitarist slides the steel bar across the strings, which are tuned to a single chord, and the steel bar changes the pitch of the chord by its location on the strings. The sliding of the bar gives the guitar a distinctive wavering timbre. Eventually, pedals and knee levers were added that gave the guitarist a means of changing the tuning of the strings as one plays. Many modern pedal or steel guitars are now electric, and they have one to four knee levers and up to eight floor pedals.

Country Music in a Historical and Social Context

The 1920s and the Beginnings of "Country" Music

The 1920s was a glitzy decade in which the United States thrived in the post–World War I economy and extravagant lifestyle known as "the Roaring Twenties." Excitement was generated by experiments in new technologies, and foremost among these were the technologies of recording and radio broadcasting.

Developments in Electrical Recording

The first practical phonograph had been built by the American inventor Thomas Edison in 1877. Edison, however, had intended the phonograph to be used as a dictating machine in business offices. It was not until the invention of the flat-disk phonograph in 1887 by another American inventor, Emile Berliner, that there was a machine used to record music. These early phonographs had several limitations, however, and it took until 1920 for the old mechanical recording process to be replaced by electrical recording. This method also was finally able to produce records that were of high enough quality to make it a truly practical commercial product.

Radio Broadcasting

Along with the development of recording there was the development of the radio. The first transmission of a human voice over "radio" waves occurred in 1906, but the idea of using radio for broadcasting to mass audiences was not formulated for another decade. At that time, David Sarnoff, an executive of the American Marconi Company, suggested to his bosses that radio could become a household utility in which audiences could enjoy programs such as lectures and music recitals. The idea was essentially ignored, and it was not until four years later that the American engineer Frank Conrad attracted attention by broadcasting records to local audiences. The concept gained support, and Conrad was asked to build a more powerful transmitter. On November 2, 1920, Conrad made the first news broadcast announcement to about one thousand people that Warren G. Harding had been elected president. To stimulate the sale of radio sets, equipment manufacturers provided transmitting facilities to a variety of individuals and groups, but programming was difficult to come by, as the recording industry was new too, and there were few records available.

The New Radio Programs

One idea for programming that began at WLS in Chicago was to broadcast amateur musicians in a "Barn Dance of the Air." This broadcast was so immediately popular that soon "barn dances" and "hayrides" could be heard on several radio stations at all hours of the day and night. The program was renamed *The National Barn Dance*, and a newspaperman from Indiana named George D. Hay was hired as the "master of ceremonies." Assuming the folksy persona of the "Solemn Judge" (drawn from a minstrel character of a white judge presiding over a black defendant), George D. Hay broadcast string bands, square-dance callers, and fiddlers. The radio and recording programs called this "hillbilly" music. In 1925, the National Life and Accident Insurance Company lured George D. Hay to Nashville where he began to emcee a new program titled "The WSM Barn Dance" on their radio station, WSM.

WSM carried a number of different programs, including a broadcast of classical music from New York City that sometimes preceded the Barn Dance program. Apparently, one night Hay opened his show with, "Folks, you've been up in the clouds with grand opera . . . now get down to earth with us . . . in a shindig of Grand Ole Opry!" Whatever the case may be, by 1926, the WSM show title was changed to *Grand Ole Opry.*

The Bristol Recording Sessions

Both radio executives and recording executives were constantly looking for new talent, and in 1927, a New York Victor Records executive named Ralph Peer went on a talent hunt in the rural South. Setting up a mobile recording studio in a warehouse in Bristol, Tennessee, he advertised for folk musicians, offering $50 per song. During this particular search, Peer located The Carter Family and Jimmie Rodgers.

The Carter Family. The Carter family had its musical roots with the singing of Alvin Pleasant (A. P.) Delaney Carter, born in 1891 in nearby Maces Springs in the mountain areas of western Virginia. One of nine children, A. P. had been brought up in a musical family. In 1915, he married Sara Dougherty, and the couple settled down near Maces Springs. Sara had learned to play autoharp, banjo, and guitar, and would sing and accompany A. P.'s bass singing. The couple entertained neighbors with mostly traditional folk songs or folk song variations. Sara's cousin Maybelle married A. P.'s brother Ezra and the four of them formed the foundation from which would be several variations of a performing group known as "The Carter Family." The Carters, especially A. P., would search through the hills of Maces Springs (often accompanied by black guitarist Leslie Riddle) looking for musical material. Sara and Maybelle would then create the ensemble arrangements. (See "Profile" in Chapter 3 for more information on the Carter Family.)

Jimmie Rodgers. Jimmie Rodgers was born on September 8, 1897, in Meridian, Mississippi. He was the son of a railroad worker and, when he was a young teenager, he left school to work with his father on the railroad, laboring as a waterboy, callboy, and brakeman. As he traveled working for the Mobile and Ohio Lines, he heard a great variety of music and learned the basics of banjo and guitar from some of the black laborers to whom he brought water. Always sickly and slight, Rodgers was forced to quit working for the railroad in 1924. He then began to make money as a musician and was referred to as "The Singing Brakeman." Rodgers recorded approximately one hundred songs, and developed an eclectic style in which he infused the various styles he had heard while working on the railroad into his unique personal style, including his version of Swiss yodeling. Rodgers died of tuberculosis in 1933, soon after completing one of several recording sessions for Ralph Peer. When the Country Music Hall of Fame was created in 1961, Jimmie Rodgers was the first performer to be inducted.

Impact of the Depression

When the stock market crash of 1929 brought the "Roaring Twenties" to an end and issued in the Great Depression, the simplicity and sincerity of "hillbilly" music continued to attract large audiences. Recordings of the Carter Family and Jimmie Rodgers were broadcast over the radio in towns across the country, forming the source from which the several later forms of folk and country music flow. The Carter Family's traditional, conservative music became great inspirations to younger generations of "folk" musicians (in fact it was a Carter Family melody—"Darlin' Pal of Mine"—that became the melody to Woody Guthrie's famous "This Land Is Your Land.") Rodgers's eclectic style was inspiration for a whole range of country music genres such as cowboy, honky tonk, and outlaw country. Thus, although the Carter Family went on to become primarily an important influence on the urban folk revival, Jimmie Rodgers is credited with launching the "commercial school" of country music.

The 1930s and the Emergence of "Country Western"

In 1930, a singer named Gene Autry launched a new kind of country performing act called the "singing cowboy." Although from Tioga, Texas, Autry was not a cowboy. Yet he sang songs about the prairie, the range, and the "Wild, Wild West." He quickly became a national sensation, building on the general interest in cowboys created by the Hollywood "Westerns." The first cowboy to sing in a movie may have been John Wayne, who self-consciously sang a song in the film *Riders of Destiny* in 1933. But it was Gene Autry, who sang in the 1934 movie *In Old Santa Fe*, and who is generally credited with initiating this genre. Other "cowboy singers" followed in his "boot" steps, including Roy Rogers, Tex Ritter, and Monte Hale, as well as groups such as "The Songs of the Pioneers."

These singers did not sing the cowboy songs that had been sung by real cowboys around the campfire and in their bunkhouses in the late 1800s. Instead, their songs were professionally composed for commercial profit to enhance movie westerns, TV shows, and the careers of the singers themselves. The singing cowboy genre not only created great careers for men but for a few women as well, such as Dale Evans (who married Roy Rogers) and Patsy Montana, who became the first woman to sell one million records as a solo performer with "I Wanna Be a Cowboy's Sweetheart" in 1935. A related consequence of this popularity of westerns was that the terms "country" and "western" were put together to replace the less flattering descriptor "hillbilly" music.

It was also during the 1930s that a more sophisticated style of cowboy music developed known as "Western Swing." Led by fiddle player Bob Wills and his group "The Texas Playboys," Western Swing blended elements of blues, jazz, and mainstream popular music and instrumentation (notably saxophones and drums) with the traditional fiddle-based string bands to create a fast-paced dance-style music.

In the late 1930s, a series of new stars came to Nashville to perform at the Ole Opry. Many wore the cowboy costumes that had become so popular in the outfits of the Hollywood cowboys.

Bill Monroe was a virtuosic mandolin player and band leader who was instrumental in founding the style of country music known as "bluegrass." *Source: AP Wide World Photos.*

A mountain fiddler named Roy Acuff performed on the Grand Ole Opry stage in 1938, and his performance was so immediately popular that he was invited by George W. Hay to perform regularly. Acuff reigned as an Opry star until his death in 1992. In 1939, another flamboyant instrumentalist performed. This performer, the Kentuckian Bill Monroe, was an accomplished guitar and fiddle player, but his specialty was playing mandolin. Instrumental-based performances by groups such as Monroe's laid the foundation for what would evolve as "bluegrass" music in the next decade.

The 1940s with Honky Tonk and Bluegrass

One of the cowboy singers that arrived in Nashville was Ernest Tubb (1914–1984), who was a fan of Jimmie Rodgers. Tubb met and befriended Jimmy's widow, Carrie, who in turn introduced him to executives at Decca Records. In 1941, Decca released

"Walking the Floor Over You," a recording that propelled Tubbs into stardom. Tubb's use of an electric guitar and the addition of a drum set to his musical ensemble resulted in his being credited as the founder of "honky tonk."

Honky Tonk

"Honky tonks" were the name of cheap taverns and dance halls in the South, many of which were so rough they were called "blood buckets." Honky tonk musicians such as Ernest Tubb, Lefty Frizzell, and George Jones celebrated in their music the rough, shady, seedy side of life that was the reality for many of the people who drank at the honky tonks. The songs sung in Nashville had spoken of loyal sweethearts, good mothers, home, and the challenges of the workingman. Honky tonk songs sang about "cheatin', lyin', thievin,' and fightin'" and the lyrics engaged a different and rougher audience.

One of honky tonk's most famous heroes was Hank Williams (1923–1953), a singer who began work as a street musician, went on to perform on various radio programs, and who made his debut at the Grand Ole Opry in 1949. Almost immediately after his Opry performance, Hank Williams's career skyrocketed. Within a year he was country music's biggest star, even going over to Germany to entertain the U.S. troops that were engaged in World War II. Among his hits were "Your Cheatin' Heart" and "I'm So Lonesome I Could Cry." Williams died of heart failure (probably from extended alcohol and drug abuse) in 1953 on his way to a performance in Ohio. With Jimmie Rodgers, he was one of the first three people to be inducted into Country's Hall of Fame. Meantime, another subcategory of country music was developing—bluegrass.

Bluegrass

The person credited with founding bluegrass was the mandolinist Bill Monroe. Monroe had hired several different fiddle players over the years to perform with him at the Opry. These fiddlers helped establish the bluegrass fiddle sound, which was jazzier and faster than traditional old-time dance fiddling. In 1942, Monroe hired his first banjo player, a step that was critical in the development of bluegrass. By 1943, Monroe's band "The Blue Grass Boys" (named after his home state of Kentucky) was popular enough to have its own touring system and records.

In 1945, the new music was still not called "bluegrass," but that year the guitarist and lead singer Lester Flatt joined the band and created ending phrases to songs that have eventually helped to define bluegrass rhythm guitar. In 1945 Monroe also added a virtuosic banjo-picker named Earl Scruggs, who had the technical ability to hold his own against the high-speed mandolin, guitar, and fiddle playing of the rest of the Blue Grass Boys musicians. This style spawned a whole new genre. For example, Scruggs and Flatt departed Monroe's band and founded the Foggy Mountain Boys. Other groups such as the Stanley Brothers and the Osborne Brothers went on to promote the new sound. Somewhere around 1950 this sound was called "bluegrass," probably stemming from individuals calling radio stations asking for Monroe's "blue grass" records.

A musicians union strike in the mid-1940s also had the unintended effect of promoting the development of individual singers. Singers weren't part of the strike because they weren't allowed in the union, but they were allowed to keep recording with backup bands. This shift to interest in individual singers laid the foundation for developments in the 1950s.

The 1950s and the Creation of "The Nashville Sound"

The post–World War II boom years were good years for country music. Americans were happy that the war was over. They had money to spend, they were buying records, and they were going to concerts. The Grand Ole Opry was broadcast to millions of listeners every Saturday night on network radio, and television performances by country musicians were becoming more and more frequent. But this decade also saw the birth of a

Break-Out One

LISTENING GUIDE *"Rocky Top"*

Performing Artist: The Osborne Brothers

This is an example of a subgenre of country music known as "Bluegrass." Bluegrass came out of the old-time hillbilly string music, but developed as a distinct genre in the 1940s with the work of Bill Monroe and a band called the Blue Grass Boys. Bobby (b. 1931) and Sonny (b. 1937) Osborne were two brothers from Kentucky who had worked with bluegrass musician Bill Monroe in the 1950s, then teamed up with guitarist Jimmy Martin in 1954. This song is a classic and its lyrics talk about making moonshine and comparing living in the country with city life.

Rhythm	Quadruple or fast duple
Melody	Simple, memorable
Harmony	Major
Texture	Homophonic
Form	Verse with chorus
Instrumentation	Male voice (notice the high tessitura in the style of Bill Monroe), mandolin, banjo, acoustic bass, guitar

new form of music: "rhythm and blues." "Rhythm and blues" was the term record companies had come up with to replace the older category of "race records"—records made by and for black audiences. Covers (rerecordings) of these black records were made by white musicians and introduced onto the pop charts as "rock 'n' roll." This new sound became immensely popular with young audiences and, as more rock records were sold, radio programmers began switching their formats from country music to rock 'n' roll.

THE IMPACT OF ROCK 'N' ROLL

The success of these early rock 'n' roll musicians, such as the country boy Elvis Presley (who recorded in a style called "rockabilly"), combined with the success of new "urban" folksingers such as the Kingston Trio, put pressure on country musicians to update their sound. The resulting changes were known as the "Nashville Sound." Led by guitarist and record producer Chet Atkins and his colleague, producer Owen Bradley, the "Nashville Sound" focused on solo singers such as Jim Reeves, Patsy Cline, and Conway Twitty. Thick, complex arrangements of background vocals with classical-style string sections combined with steel guitars were created to accompany the singers. These arrangements paved the way for the country/pop "superstars" of the 1960s.

The 1960s and 1970s

THE IMPACT OF TELEVISION

As the 1950s blended into the 1960s and television became an important new broadcast medium, several new "country" programs such as ABC's *The Johnny Cash Show* and CBS's *Hee Haw* brought the Nashville Sound to mainstream audiences. This in turn spawned an era known as the "Country Pop Superstars," with the next generation of singers, such as Johnny Cash, Kenny Rogers, Glen Campbell, Roy Clark, Buck Owen, Loretta Lynn, and Tammy Wynette propelled to superstardom. As country music was adapted to reach even wider audiences, a style known as "crossover country" with musicians such as John

Denver, Dolly Parton, Barbara Mandrell, and Crystal Gayle developed that appealed to country and pop music audiences alike.

THE TEXAS SOUND

This heavily commercialized "Nashville" music in many ways helped to preserve country music through the rock 'n' roll era, but it also alienated younger talents who wished to return to country's simpler and less formulaic roots. These new talents avoided Nashville and went to other recording areas, noticeably Austin, Texas, to cultivate a new, less commercialized sound. Some of the musicians who fled to Austin from Nashville were Willie Nelson, Leon Russell, Kris Kristofferson, and Waylon Jennings. These musicians became known as the "outlaws" because of their contempt for Nashville commercialism. Although the style of these outlaws differed among each other, one characteristic was to eliminate the large instrumental arrangements that had come to characterize the

Break-Out Two

INSIGHT *Country Music's Inherent Traditionalism*

One of the characteristics that tends to distinguish country music from most other American musical genres is its persistent value of tradition, political conservatism, and its serving as a "voice" of the working class. This was demonstrated in its earliest commercial stages. For example, Nashville's founding radio personality George W. Hay coined the term "Grand Ole Opry" precisely to distinguish his program from the "stuck in the clouds" classical opera program being broadcast earlier in the morning from New York. Up until the 1970s, the audience for country music remained largely white, rural, and working class. Although both the "Urban Folk Revival" and "Country Music" come from the same roots, it is partly the politics and socioeconomic class of the performers and the audience that distinguishes the two. Urban folksingers were from the city, often college educated, and they were the sons and daughters of middle-class and professional parents. Urban folksingers also were more politically liberal. Country singers stress their rural, working-class origins, their commitment to "family values," but downplay (if they have one) their college educations.

At different times throughout country music's development, new styles may have emerged, but the traditional, older styles also were maintained. When new country music derivatives develop and stray too far from the traditional country styles, the older styles re-emerge. Country music stars of all styles and ages are typically quite vocal about their reverence for earlier country music singers, and of their commitment to honoring and preserving the country music traditions. It is this valuing of tradition that explains, to some extent, resistance by the established country music community to contemporary stars such as Shania Twain, who manifests in her lyrics and performance style a more liberal and urban tone.

Another expression of this commitment to preserve tradition is the founding of the "Country Legends Association" in 1997. This association is a national/international organization dedicated to assuring that country music preserves its traditions and its position in American history. The association is made up of "traditional country music" fans and performing artists who have well-established careers in traditional country music. Its official mission is to ensure that those individuals who laid the foundation for country music continue to be recognized, and to help direct the development of the future of country music so that it retains its strong ties to the past.

The Dixie Chicks' blend of musical skill, good looks, irreverent attitude, and progressive style has made them one of the most popular and award-winning contemporary country groups. *Source: Photo by Paul Skipper. Getty Images, Inc.-Hulton Archive Photos.*

Nashville sound. They also simplified their performance style, and refused to wear the costumes and surround themselves with the stage productions that had become associated with Nashville. Some musicians, such as Leon Russell and Charlie Daniels, incorporated a hard rock-style edge. In 1975, a public television station KLRU launched *Austin City Limits* to showcase the new talents, and this broadcast was soon picked up by PBS, which gave it national airing. Here the careers of new musicians such as Lyle Lovett, Joe Ely, and Townes van Zandt were launched.

The 1980s to the Present

The work in Texas laid the foundation for a rebounding of traditional country styles in the 1980s and 1990s. Musicians such as Randy Travis, Garth Brooks, Emmylou Harris, Reba McEntire, and the Judds initiated a return to the simpler values of early country. Their phenomenal popularity launched a new era in country music and great commercial success in the 1990s. As with so many other music forms, these musicians also began to experiment with a variety of styles as they attempted to develop their own artistry. Many of them created fusions (particularly with rock 'n' roll). They also infused their music with a youthful spirit and irreverence that helped label the music "Young Country" or "New Country." Throughout the 1990s, country music developed a huge international audience, with nations other than the United States (such as Australia and Czechoslovakia) generating their own, local "country" musicians. Today, multiple styles of country music exist simultaneously. A journalist describing the Forty-Seventh Annual Grammy awards wrote, "the many genres of popular music are more alike and intertwined than they are different and isolated."[3] Thus, traditional country artists such as Loretta Lynn and Earl Scruggs were honored along with musicians in other genres who were reaching into country, such as the rock group Los Lonely Boys.

[3] Flippo, Chet. "Grammy Report: Awards Were a Cross-Section of Pop Music," http://www.cmt.com/news/articles/1496954/20050214/lynn_loretta.jhtml?headlines=true (Accessed 02-16-05).

Break-Out Three

PROFILE *Shania Twain*

Shania Twain is one of the most well-known women in country music. Part of the reason for her commercial success is her "crossover" appeal, perhaps partly due to the sexy videos she made under the tutelage of her husband, writer/producer Mutt Lange. Mutt's experience was in the pop/rock genre, and he brought considerable expertise having worked with acts such as Def Leppard and Bryan Adams. Before Shania met Mutt, her debut on PolyGram records had only two charting singles, both which reached only number fifty-five on the charts. Mutt helped her become what is known as a "progressive" country singer, because (unlike "traditional country" singers) she records and performs songs that have fusion elements with other musical styles such as rock 'n' roll and pop. This has upset the more traditional country fans that have (apparently) denounced her for "tainting" "real" country music.

Shania Twain, performing on stage in black vinyl pants in 1999.
Source: Getty Images, Inc.-Hulton archive Photos.

Shania Twain was born in Windson and raised in Timmins, Ontario, in Canada. She was the second oldest of five children, born to a poor working-class family. To help the family earn more money, she began performing when she was only eight years old. Her parents actively promoted her performing career, pushing her to perform at convalescent homes and community centers as well as local TV and radio shows. When her parents died in a car accident when she was twenty-one years old, she was left with the responsibility of raising and providing for her younger siblings. To do this, she took a job singing at a resort. After three years, her younger brothers were able to take care of themselves and she was released to do what she wanted. She put together a demo record of music that she had written and signed a contract with Mercury/PolyGram in Nashville.

But the record company didn't like her name, Eileen Twain. When they suggested she drop the name "Twain," she resisted, as this was her stepfather's name and she had always seen him as her true father. As an alternative, she replaced her first name with "Shania," which is an Ojibway Indian name meaning "on my way." When the tabloid newspapers discovered that she was not a real Ojibway Indian, they criticized her, but she felt justified in taking the name because her stepfather Jerry had been an Ojibway Indian and had raised all the children to respect his heritage. She released her first album, which included both "The Woman in Me" and "Any Man of Mine," under this name. This album became extremely successful in the United States and in Europe. Since 1995, she has won over forty awards, including Grammy Awards, Country Music Awards, and American Music Awards. She continues to be a major country star, recently winning the "Favorite Country Female Singer" in the People's Choice Awards.

CONCLUSION

Country music emerged out of the rural American South as a derivative of the folk traditions of the British immigrants. From these "homespun" roots in American folk music, country was shaped and transformed over the years by the commercial entertainment industry into its contemporary status as a billion-dollar global product. Today, country music generates tremendous revenue in record sales and performances and is a dominant radio format. Country music industry executives have tried to make country music appealing to a national urban audience while still preserving an image of small-town, rural simplicity and informality. Once associated almost solely with white, Anglo-Saxon male Protestants, country music stars have gone on to include not only females but also occasionally African-American musicians (Charley Pride) and Latino musicians (Johnny Rodriguez).

At the beginning of the millennium, country music includes a vast array of styles, each with its own music industry "label." For example, in addition to older styles such as Western swing, honky tonk, bluegrass, and country pop, there are contemporary variations such as alternative country, new grass, or even "super grass" and "space grass." In each of these styles, musicians strive to preserve their music's rural heritage and folk origins, while searching for and absorbing elements from other musical styles that are satisfying on a personal artistic level and/or popular in mainstream American culture. In this way, country musicians continue to refresh and adapt their music for contemporary audiences, while preserving the essence of the traditional folk music brought over by the first European immigrants almost four centuries ago.

BIBLIOGRAPHY

Acuff, Roy in Newsmakers 1993, Issue 4. Gale Research, 1993. Reproduced in Biography Resource Center. Gale Group, 2001. http://www.galenet.com/servlet/BioRC (Accessed 05-24-01).

Acuff, Roy, and William Neely. *Roy Acuff's Nashville: The Life and Good Times of Country Music.* New York: The Putnam Berkeley Group Inc., 1983.

Bekker, Jr., Peter. O.E. *Country: The Life, Times and Music Series.* New York: Friedman/Fairfax Publishers, 1993.

Busnar, Gene. *Superstars of Country Music.* New York: J. Messner, 1984.

"Carter family." Excite Music; Netscape Internet Resources. http://music.excite.com/artist/biography/-193090 (Accessed 08-02-01).

Dellar, Fred. *The Illustrated Encyclopedia of Country Music.* New York: Harmony Books, 1977.

Emery, Ralph, with Patsi Bale Cox. *50 Years Down a Country Road.* New York: HarperCollins Publishers Inc., 2000.

Encyclopedia of Country Music: The Ultimate Guide to the Music. Paul Kingsbury, Laura Garrard, Daniel Cooper (editors). New York: Oxford University Press, 1998.

Feiler, Bruce. "Gone Country: The Voice of Suburban America. (Popularity of Country Music)". *The New Republic*, 02–05–1996, cover story, p. 19(5). http://www.elibrary.com/s/edumark/getdo . . . rn:bigchalk.com:US;EL&dtype=0~0&dinst=0 (Accessed 05-05-01).

———. "Home of the Silver Screen Cowboys: Sons of the Pioneers Page." Sons of the Pioneers. (Netscape Internet Resources). http://www.cowboypal.com/sons.html (Accessed 07-23-01).

Flippo, Chet. "Grammy Report: Awards Were a Cross-Section of Pop Music." http://www.cmt.com/news/articles/1496954/20050214/lynn_loretta.jhtml?headlines=true (Accessed 02-16-05).

"Jimmie Rodgers Biography." Netscape Internet Resources. http://www.jimmierodgers.com/Main/Biography/biography.html (Accessed 08-02-01).

Lewis, George H. "Everybody's Goin' Country," *The World & I*, 07-01-1996, p. 34. http://www.elibrary.com/s/edumark/getdo . . . rn:bigchalk.com:US;EL&dtype=0~0&dinst=0 (Accessed 05-05-01).

Malone, Bill C. *Country Music USA.* Revised. Austin: University of Texas Press, 1997.

Malone, Bill C. *Singing Cowboys and Musical Mountaineers: Southern Culture and the Roots of Country Music* (Lamar Memorial Lectures, No 34). Georgia: Georgia University Press, 1993.

Marschall, Rick. *The Encyclopedia of Country and Western Music.* New York: Exeter Books, 1985.

McCall, Michael, David Hoekstra, and Janet Williams. *Country Music Stars: The Legends and the New Breed.* Lincolnwold, IL: Publications International, 1992.

Oermann, Robert K. *A Century of Country: An Illustrated History of Country Music.* New York: TV Books, L.L.C., 1999.

Rodgers, Jimmie in Encyclopedia of World Biography Supplement, Vol. 19, Gale Group, 1999. Reproduced in *Biography Resource Center*, Gale Group, 2001. http://www.galenet.com/servlet/BioRC (Accessed 08-01-01).

Sachs, Howard L. "Creating Country Music." Chapel Hill, NC: University of North Carolina Press; *Social Forces*, Vol. 77, no 5, 03-01-1999. (Book review: *Fabricating Authenticity* by Richard A Peterson. University of Chicago Press, 1997.) http://www.elibrary.com/s/edumark/getdo . . . rn:bigchalk.com:US;EL&dtype=0~0&dinst=0 (Accessed 05-05-01).

Scott, Jeffry. "Country Isn't Cool Again: Industry Seeks to Boot Rustic Image." *The Atlanta Constitution*, 5-1-2001, p. A1. http://www.elibrary.com/s/edumark/getdo . . . rn:bigchalk.com:US;EL&dtype=0~0&dinst=0 (Accessed 05-05-01).

Selvin, Joel. "Living Large: Real Country Music May Be Dead, but Its Last True Cowboy, Merle Haggard, Carries on the Original Sound." *San Francisco Chronicle Magazine*, June 3, 2001, p. 8.

———. "Sons of the Pioneers: 1989 WMA Hall of Fame Member." Western Music Association. http://www.westernmusic.org/fame/SonsOfThePioneers.html (Accessed 07-23-01).

Stambler, Irwin and Grelun Landon. *The Encyclopedia of Folk, Country & Western Music.* Second Edition. New York: St. Martin's Press, 1983.

Steinberg, Brian. "Country Radio and Labels Are in Discord: As New Territory Is Charted, Some Seek a Return to Roots." *Wall Street Journal*, May 8, 2001, p. B11A(3).

Twain, Shania in Contemporary Musicians. Vol. 17. Gale Research, 1996. Reproduced in *Biography Resource Center*, Gale Group, 2001. http://www.galenet.com/servlet/BioRC (Accessed 08-01-01).

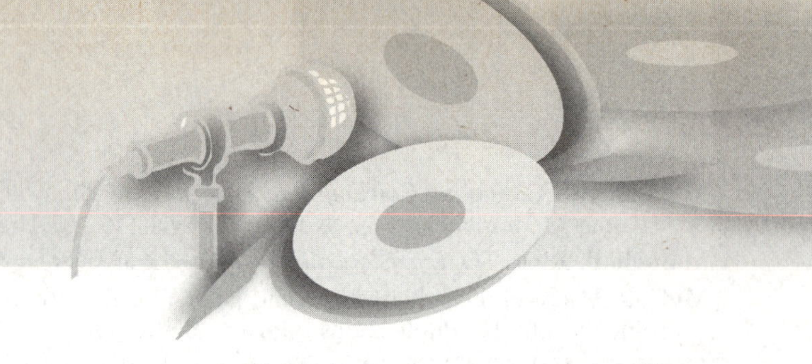

Chapter Eleven

The Urban Folk Revival

The Urban Folk Revival profoundly affected the evolution of American popular music. Although the connection is not always obvious, contemporary musicians such as John Mayer, Jack Johnson, Ben Harper, Tori Amos, and Norah Jones are direct musical descendents of the innovations in songwriting made by musicians who participated in the Urban Folk Revival. To better understand the influences, we must clarify the term. "Folk music" is broadly defined as music that is composed and performed by amateurs and passed down in an oral tradition to successive generations of musicians who have not had formal music training. Used in this way, the term could apply to a variety of music traditions, including African-American rural blues and Native American ritual songs. In the twentieth century in the United States, however, the definition was used almost solely to refer to the British folk traditions that had been maintained in backwoods rural communities. From this wellspring of "hillbilly" music, two main rivers eventually flowed. The first developed into what we call "country" music, a genre that was covered in Chapter 10. The second moved from the country into the city and also eventually included a shift from preexisting traditional songs to newly composed "folk" songs. This second stream is now referred to as the "Urban Folk Revival," and it is this genre that is the focus of this chapter.

Overview of the Music of the Urban Folk Revival

Renewed Interest in Traditional Music

Although British folk music was maintained in the remote areas of the Appalachian Mountains, by the end of the nineteenth century, scholars began to be concerned that folk music would disappear because of increased industrialism and urbanization. In 1898, the American Folk Song Society was created specifically for the purpose of preserving folk music. This new concern for folk music inspired several individuals to become folk song collectors and, starting at the turn of the century, these people gathered thousands of songs such as "Barbara Allen" and "On Top of Old Smokey" from different parts of the United States. The subsequent publication of collections and anthologies of folk music such as John Lomax's *Cowboy Songs and Other Frontier Ballads* (1910), Cecil Sharp's *English Folk Songs of the Southern Appalachians* (1917), and Carl Sandburg's *The American Songbag* (1927) fueled a resurgence of general appreciation for American folk music.

Break-Out One

INSIGHT *Joe Hill*

Joan Baez opened her set at the Woodstock Music Festival in 1969 with the song "Joe Hill," which she introduced as one of the favorite songs of her husband, David Harris. David was a prominent spokesperson against the Vietnam War, and was in jail at the time for resisting the draft. The song was based on a real character, Joe Hill, who had become an important symbol of political resistance in the United States. In fact, in *The Incomplete Folksinger*, Pete Seeger writes about the injustice with which he feels the legendary Joe Hill was treated.

Joe Hill was a Swedish immigrant who became a songwriter for a radical coalition of workers called the Industrial Workers of the World (IWW) at the turn of the century. In 1909, the IWW (popularly known as the Wobblies) distributed a book titled *I.W.W. Songs: Songs of the Workers to Fan the Flames of Discontent*, informally known as *The Little Red Song Book*. Salvation Army Bands would often try to overpower IWW street corner speakers, so many of Joe Hill's songs were parodies (new words to old songs) to Salvation Army Songs, like "Nearer My Job to Thee."

On November 19, 1915, Joe Hill was executed for murder in Salt Lake City by a Utah firing squad. Seeger, as well as many others, is convinced that Hill was framed. It is virtually impossible to prove one way or another now, because the complete court records of the trial disappeared from the county clerk's office and all the records in the office of the IWW were either seized by federal agents or burned in a fire that gutted the headquarters of the organization a few years later. Shortly before Joe Hill was executed, he sent a message to the IWW president urging him not to mourn his death but to continue the efforts to organize for workers' rights. His spirit of political activism inspired later folksingers such as Woody Guthrie and Pete Seeger as well as Joan Baez.

Dissemination and Popularization of Traditional Music

Radio programs such as Grand Ole Opry in Nashville and National Barn Dance in Chicago were founded in the mid-1920s and focused on live performances of folk songs. With the stock market crash of 1929 and the subsequent slowdown of the economy known as the Great Depression, the large commercial music industry suffered, but interest in traditional folk music continued to rise. Two major performers during the Depression were the Carter Family and Jimmie Rodgers, discovered by Victor Records representative Ralph Peer in 1927 during one of his talent scouting expeditions for new performers.

The Carter Family had been performing for years at local events in the Appalachian Mountains of Tennessee. After Peer's discovery and their subsequent recording debut, they went on to a fourteen-year recording career of over three hundred songs issued on several different labels, and achieved national fame for songs such as "The Wabash Cannonball" and "Will the Circle Be Unbroken." Jimmie Rodgers had spent years working on the railroad and was therefore known as the "Singing Brakeman." Although his recording career was relatively brief (he died of tuberculosis in 1933), he recorded over a hundred songs, achieving tremendous commercial success and going on to play an important role influencing country music.

Break-Out Two

IN-DEPTH FOCUS *Folk Song Collecting and John and Alan Lomax*

Collection of British folk songs began in the mid-nineteenth century with the pioneering work of the Harvard professor Francis James Child (1825–1896) and the publication of his 305 traditional ballads in the monumental five-volume work, *The English and Scottish Popular Ballads* (1882–1898). But Child had virtually no interest in the melodies to which these ballads were sung, and the task of collecting the tunes fell on the next generation of collectors, noticeably Cecil J. Sharp (1859–1924), who published the results of his work in *Folk Songs from Somerset* (1905–1909) and *English Folk Songs* (1920).

Sharp was an Englishman who became interested in American folk music primarily at the urging of an American collector, Mrs. Olive Dame Campbell, who assured him that in the rural areas of the United States, British folksinging was very much alive. Sharp came to the area in 1916 and spent forty-six weeks in North Carolina, Kentucky, Virginia, Tennessee, and West Virginia, recording 1,612 tunes. In 1917 he published 968 of these tunes in *English Folk Songs from the Southern Appalachians*. The work of Child and Sharp laid the groundwork for two of the most influential American collectors, John (1867–1948) and Alan (1915–2002) Lomax.

John Lomax describes his introduction to folk song collecting in the opening words to *American Ballads and Folk Songs:*

> When I went first to college in Texas I carried in my trunk, along with my pistol and other implements of personal warfare, a little manuscript roll of cowboy songs. My father's farm and small ranch was located on the Chisholm Trail, over which many thousand Longhorn cattle were driven to Dodge City, Kansas; sometimes on to Montana and the Dakotas. Especially at night when lying awake, I had heard the cowboys sing to the cattle "bedded down" near our home. These songs and others like them were also current among a number of neighbor boys, older than myself, who each spring witnessed the round-up and afterwards trailed a herd of cattle to a Northern market. They brought new songs back with them for the entertainment of their friends. On one occasion

The success of the Carter Family and Jimmie Rodgers helped members of the commercial music industry recognize the vast market potential for traditional music, and both new and existing recording companies began focusing on folk music. The Works Progress Administration (WPA), established by President Roosevelt in the 1930s as part of his New Deal to help move the United States out of the Great Depression, funded several projects including the Federal Music Project and the Archive of Folk Song. In 1934, the first National Folk Festival was initiated in St. Louis, Missouri, with several hundred participants from a dozen states. In 1939, Alan Lomax began producing *Wellsprings of America*, a weekly syndicated radio show on CBS radio's Columbia School of the Air. Through this radio program, Lomax introduced a number of important folk and blues musicians to the public, including Leadbelly, Muddy Waters, Son House, and Woody Guthrie. Although musicians such as Muddy Waters and Son House became important influences in the African-American development of the blues and subsequently rhythm 'n' blues and rock 'n' roll, Woody Guthrie exerted strong influence on the Urban Folk Revival.

I exhibited my store of cowboy songs to a somewhat startled Texas English professor. I was told politely that they had no value. So I put them away until I became, years afterwards, a student in Harvard.[1]

Encouraged by his Harvard professor, he applied for and received a Traveling Sheldon Fellowship to "investigate American folk songs" and by 1909, he appeared before the Modern Language Association to read an article entitled "Cowboy Songs of the Mexican Border," perhaps the first academic presentation of folk songs. In 1910, he published *Cowboy Songs and Other Frontier Ballads,* which included an endorsement from former president Theodore Roosevelt. Among the songs that Lomax collected were "Home on the Range," "The Streets of Laredo," "Sweet Betsy from Pike," and "The Ballad of Jessie James."

John Lomax continued to keep folk song collecting as an avocation, working as an associate professor of English from 1903 to 1910 at Texas A&M College and from 1910 to 1917 as secretary of the University of Texas in Austin. He was later involved in the banking business and when, in 1933, his bank failed during the Depression, he contacted a publisher in hopes of offsetting his monetary loss by producing another volume of songs. With his seventeen-year-old son Alan, he went to the South to collect the folk songs of African Americans, particularly convicts. In 1933, the Library of Congress supported his efforts by providing him with a 315-pound portable recording machine that he and Alan mounted in the back of their Ford sedan. In 1934, the results of their work were published as *American Ballads and Folk Songs* and, that same year, he became honorary consultant and head of the Archive of Folk Song.

Alan Lomax worked as an assistant archivist at the Library of Congress from 1937 to 1942, traveling extensively to collect material for the Archive of Folk Song. His work yielded three thousand twelve-inch records. In 1939, he initiated his radio program *Wellsprings of America* and introduced the American public to many important folksingers, including Woody Guthrie, Pete Seeger, and Leadbelly. Over the subsequent years, he has held numerous positions in the academic community, including work at Indiana University, the University of Chicago, and New York University. He became a research associate at the Department of Anthropology at Columbia University in 1961. Both in his original work with his father and in the work he has continued since his father's death in 1948, he has had an immeasurable influence on folk music and is considered America's most eminent folk song collector and scholar.

[1] Lomax, John and Alan Lomax. *American Ballads and Folk Songs.* New York: The Macmillan Company, 1934, p. xi.

Trends in Folk Music in the Mid-Twentieth Century

By the mid-1950s, two distinct trends emerged, which characterized what is now known as the Urban Folk Revival.

Solo Singer/Songwriter

One trend was to follow in Guthrie's footsteps and add to the traditional folk song repertoire by writing new songs that one would sing as a soloist, accompanying oneself on the guitar. These individuals also tended to emulate Guthrie's political activism and socially conscious left-wing orientation. The most famous of these individuals were Bob Dylan and Joan Baez, but the group also included people such as Ramblin' Jack Elliot, Paul Simon, Phil Ochs, Gordon Lightfoot, Tim Hardin, Tom Paxton, Buffy Sainte-Marie, and Joni Mitchell.

Folk Singing Ensembles

The second trend followed more in the footsteps of the Carter Family, where musicians took both traditional folk songs (such as the Child ballads) and the songs of the first group (such as those written by Bob Dylan) and arranged them for small singing ensembles who accompanied themselves on guitar and perhaps banjo and string bass. These groups tended to be less overtly political than the first group and assumed more the role of performing musicians (as opposed to the poet/artists of the first group). These groups included Peter, Paul, and Mary, along with the Kingston Trio, the New Christy Minstrels, the Limeliters, and the New Lost City Ramblers.

After 1965, the first "camp" of solo songwriters merged with rock 'n' roll, whereas the second camp continued to perform and maintain traditional music at folk festivals. The Urban Folk Revival never went through the stages of stylistic evolution that country did, and by the 1970s, the revival ended. Nevertheless, folk music has remained an important genre of American music enjoyed in small clubs and in countless folk festivals throughout the United States and Europe.

Structural Characteristics

Melody, Rhythm, and Harmony

Melodies are clearly structured and easily remembered. Rhythmic organization is divisive, with a readily apparent metrical beat. Most urban folk melodies have transformed the original modal melodies to major and minor scales. The harmonies that support the melodies are also derived from these scales, with emphasis on the basic I, IV, and V or V7 triads.

Texture, Instrumentation, and Form

Textures are primarily homophonic. In group performances, some of the more sophisticated arrangements also incorporate polyphonic textures. The formal structures are clearly articulated. There is a significant use of the strophic form and of the strophic form with refrain. The simplest and most common urban folk instrumentation is solo voice accompanied by guitar. In the ensembles, additional voices alternate singing the melody or providing harmony. The instruments are expanded to include a second guitar, string bass, and occasionally autoharp or banjo.

The Urban Folk Revival in a Social and Historical Context

1900–1940

In the first decades of the century, the renewed interest in folk music was reflected in the publications of anthologies of folk songs by collectors such as John Lomax, Cecil Sharp, and Carl Sandburg. Additionally, radio programs were established that broadcast live performances of folk music across the country. One of the major performing groups to be broadcast over the radio was the Carter Family, who sang traditional folk songs that the leader of the group, A. P., had collected in the rural Clinch Mountain area of West Virginia. Members of the Carter Family also wrote their own songs in the same folk style. One person who listened to the Carter Family on the radio and who became an important influence in his own right was Woody Guthrie.

Woody Guthrie

Woody Guthrie was born in the farming country of Oklahoma in 1912 to a family who had been among the pioneering settlers in the region. His family was marked by tragedy. By the time he was a young teenager, Woody's sister had perished in an accidental fire (as did his daughter Kathy, many years later), his father failed in his real estate business, and his mother was committed to a mental institution. But it was also a musical family. He learned many of his folk songs by copying recordings of the Carter Family songs he heard over the radio. Largely because of the problems at home, he was adopted by different families until finally these conditions, combined with his own

Woody Guthrie (1912–1967) hopped trains and hitchhiked across the country describing what he saw in almost one thousand songs. Many of his songs, such as "This Land Is Your Land," have been absorbed into the folk song repertoire.
Source: Getty Images, Inc., Hulton Archive Photos.

restless spirit, prompted him to drop out of school when he was sixteen and begin traveling.

Over the years, he rambled through nearly every state, laboring and singing with coal miners, loggers, migratory workers, farmers, longshoremen, ranch hands, factory workers, and union members. He chronicled much of his life in his singing and writings in large notebooks. Thus, using whatever writing implement was available, he wrote down his observations of the Depression, the Dust Bowl refugees, union organizing, and his love for his country. Over the years his fame increased and he was given the opportunity to share his thoughts and his music through recordings, co-hosting a radio program, maintaining his own newspaper column, and performing for both public and private audiences. By the time he was hospitalized in 1954 with Huntington's Disease (chorea), he had written nearly one thousand songs, many of which have become part of the standard folk song repertoire.

Break-Out Three

PROFILE *Pete Seeger*

Pete Seeger is perhaps the most important and quintessential urban folksinger of the twentieth century. Born in 1919 in New York, his father was the internationally famous and highly influential musicologist Charles Seeger. His mother, Constance, was an accomplished violinist. Pete learned to play banjo when he attended a private high school in New England. After graduation in 1936, he went to Harvard University, where he learned to play guitar and numerous other folk instruments. But he became bored with college and dropped out after two years.

Folksinger, Pete Seeger. *Source: The Library of Congress.*

It was through his father that he met Alan Lomax, who was at the time working at the Archive of Folk Song in Washington, DC. Alan invited Pete to be his assistant and also introduced him to several folksingers, including Leadbelly. In 1940, Pete met Woody Guthrie at the Grapes of Wrath benefit and, a few months later, Woody invited Pete to go with him on a cross-country trip through the United States. It was on this trip that Pete and Woody picked up the term "hootenanny" at a political event in Seattle, Washington.

When Pete returned to New York in late 1940, he met Lee Hays and the two of them founded the Almanac Singers, the first "urban" folk singing group, which included at various times Woody Guthrie, Cisco Houston, Brownie McGhee, and Sonny Terry.

Seeger was drafted into the army in mid-1942, and served in the South Pacific, where he met and later married Toshi Ohta. After the war, Seeger formed the organization People's Songs, Inc., to provide new or blacklisted singers with an alternative to the music industry establishment. People's Songs went bankrupt and folded in 1949, but one of their publications (*The Bulletin*) served as the forerunner of a folk song magazine called *Sing Out!*, which has been published since 1950.

While working at People's Songs, Seeger and Hays met other musicians and eventually formed the Weavers. As the United States became

The 1940s

THE MEETING OF PETE SEEGER AND WOODY GUTHRIE

On March 3, 1940, a year after Steinbeck's book *The Grapes of Wrath* was published, actor Will Greer organized a "Grapes of Wrath" benefit to raise funds and to help New Yorkers learn more about the plight of California migrant workers. The show featured artists such as Burl Ives, Leadbelly, and Woody Guthrie, and it was the concert debut for Pete Seeger. Seeger was very impressed with Guthrie, and Alan Lomax later described the meeting of these two as "the Renaissance of American folk song." Two months after their meeting, Woody

involved in Korea, anticommunist sentiment grew. The Weavers were kept under surveillance by the FBI and, in 1952, an informant who had an important position in People's Songs testified before the House Un-American Activities Committee that all four of the Weavers were, or had been, communists. The Weavers were blacklisted and disbanded after most of their recording and performance opportunities were canceled. (Incidentally, it also was around this time that Alan Lomax moved to Great Britain, not only to do research there but also to avoid the constant pressures and threat of the investigation.) The Weavers made a successful comeback in 1952, but Seeger left the group and decided to work as a solo artist.

In 1955, Seeger was summoned and asked to testify before the House Un-American Activities Committee and a year later he was cited for contempt of Congress. It took another year before he was indicted, and he was not tried until 1961. Seeger was found guilty of contempt of Congress (not of being a Communist) and sentenced to a year in jail. He was granted bail pending appeal and, a year later, three judges of the U.S. Court of Appeals reversed the decision. But, as Seeger says,

> Of course, acquittal in open court does not greatly impress the groups who share HUAC's view of "Americanism." I am far more lucky than most. The HUAC ruined the careers of many people. But my income comes from so many sources that they were not able to cut it off. From time to time, the hate groups do campaign to keep me out of an auditorium—sometimes successfully. But I have learned that many an American town has other citizens—whether liberals or authentic conservatives—who will indignantly insist on their right to think for themselves—to hear this music in person before judging how dangerous it might be.[2]

Pete Seeger has continued to be a strong advocate for his political views, and was a powerful musical force in the Civil Rights movement and later the Vietnam peace movement, performing at rallies and marches all over the country. He also has been an active songwriter, writing in the true folk song tradition in which several of his songs, such as "Where Have All the Flowers Gone," "If I Had a Hammer," and "Turn, Turn, Turn," have become such standards in the contemporary folk repertoire that few people even realize he wrote them.

He also continues to be an active performer, working with a variety of contemporary folksingers. In an interview in the late 1980s, he said,

> I wish I could learn to retire gracefully, but I don't know how. Every day a bushel of mail comes in and somebody says, "We are trying to raise some money here and it would help us so much if you came and performed." The next thing I know, I'm going through my calendar with my wife trying to find out if I can spare a few hours. There is a big, beautiful world that could be destroyed by selfishness and foolishness. We musicians have it within our power to help save it. In a small way, every single one of us counts.[3]

[2] Seeger, Pete. *The Incomplete Folksinger*, pp. 474–475. Jo Metcalf Schwartz (Editor). New York: Simon and Schastor, 1972.

[3] Hood (ed.), "Pete Seeger," by Mary Gallanter in *Artists of American Folk Music*, p. 35.

invited Pete to leave New York with him and go on a cross-country trip to explore the United States.

Founding of the Almanac Singers

When Seeger returned to New York in late 1940, he met a song leader named Lee Hays (1914–1981) and the two of them decided to form a group that they called the Almanac Singers. (Hays suggested the name, pointing out that most rural families had two books, the Bible and an Almanac, the one to guide them to the next world, and the other to guide them through this one.) Membership in the

Almanac Singers fluctuated, but at various times included Woody Guthrie, Cisco Houston (1918–1961), Sonny Terry (1911–1986), and Brownie McGhee (1915–1996). Many of the members of the group lived in a commune in Greenwich Village known as the Almanac House. On one of the tours of the Almanac Singers in the West Coast in 1941, Pete Seeger and Woody Guthrie performed at a political fund-raising event in Seattle that was advertised as a "Midsummer Hootenanny." When they returned to New York, they adopted the term "hootenanny" for their rent parties and for the Sunday afternoon basement concerts that they used to garner support for their leftist social and political goals.

Impact of World War II and Anticommunism

Beginning in 1941, national attention shifted to the war effort as the United States was drawn into World War II. With the war, the politics of the Almanac Singers shifted because of their strong opposition to fascism. At first, they achieved great success and were performing both on network radio and Office of War Information programs. But under the direction of J. Edgar Hoover, the FBI kept members of the Almanacs under surveillance and the Almanacs' success was soon undermined when the media began to attack them for their peace songs and their connections with the Communist Party. (When asked if he was a communist, Woody Guthrie used to say, "That ain't necessarily so, but it is true that I've been in the red all my life.") Blacklisted by the music industry, their performance and recording opportunities dissolved and the group disbanded. Woody Guthrie and his close friend Cisco Houston went into the Merchant Marines, and Pete Seeger was drafted into the army.

People's Songs, Inc.

In 1946, the founders of the Almanac Singers—Pete Seeger and Lee Hays—founded an organization called "People's Songs, Inc.," a type of songwriters' union established to provide an alternative to the existing music industry for aspiring or blacklisted musicians. When working with People's Songs, Pete Seeger and Lee Hays met many musicians. In 1949, they established a new group called "The Weavers," which was the title of a German play about a nineteenth-century strike by textile workers. Although the Weavers sang a variety of folk songs, with only a portion of them with political undertones, the members of the group continued to be involved in radical, socialist causes. As vocalist member Gilbert stated, "We felt that if we sang loud enough and strong enough and hopefully enough, somehow it would make a difference."

The 1950s

The House Un-American Activities Committee's Impact on Folk Music

As the United States became involved in the Korean War beginning in 1950, anticommunist sentiment grew. The FBI and the House Un-American Activities Committee (HUAC) had continued to scrutinize several folksingers and the People's Songs organization. In 1952, Harvey Matusow, an informant who had been in charge of People's Songs Music Center, testified in front of HUAC that all four of the Weavers were, or had been, members of the Communist Party. The Weavers were blacklisted and previous offers of a weekly television series on NBC, scheduled performances, and recording opportunities were canceled, despite the fact that their record sales were in the millions. The group disbanded at the end of 1952. This dichotomy between the popularity of folk music and folk music's association with the very unpopular communism strongly influenced folk music in the early 1950s. Many folk musicians were called to testify before HUAC. Those who were found guilty, such as Pete Seeger and Paul Robeson, were blacklisted. Those who were informants and those who willingly testified, such as Burl Ives and Josh White, continued to have successful careers.

Mid-Decade Interest in Folk Music

In 1955, the folk revival had a landmark year. The Weavers staged a successful comeback, abandoning their socialist orientation. The first coffee house opened in Philadelphia and sparked a national trend of establishing these venues to encourage artistic, informal performances of music and poetry for small, intellectual audiences. Guitar sales reached half a million, and interest in folk music, particularly on college campuses, soared. The popularity of folk music on college campuses was a result of several reasons. One was that it was participatory. With minimal musical skills, a student could learn to play a few chords on the guitar and if he or she had a reasonably pleasant voice, could both sing as a soloist and lead others in informal hootenannies. Another reason for its popularity was that it didn't require many resources: one didn't need to purchase expensive musical instruments or equipment, take lessons, buy music, or join with others in a band. Additionally, it provided a more intellectually satisfying alternative to the current "pop" and lightweight rock 'n' roll.

The Kingston Trio

In 1957, three students (one a graduate student at Stanford University) formed "The Kingston Trio." They had their first break when they substituted for the comedienne Phyllis Diller at a folk club in San Francisco. In 1958 they made their recording debut with an album that featured the song "Tom Dooley." The recording sold more than three and a half million copies as a single. The commercial and polished style of the Kingston Trio, along with their wholesome image (close-cropped hair and button-down shirts) and their apolitical songs, made them appealing to a wide audience and helped ensure their success. The Kingston Trio became very popular on college campuses and *Life* magazine did a cover story on the group in 1959. Their success paved the way for other respectable collegiate-looking groups such as the Brothers Four, the Chad Mitchell Trio, the Highwaymen, and the Limeliters. Success of groups such as these, along with the founding of the Newport Folk Festival in 1959 (which attracted an audience of thirteen thousand) are key markers of the "Urban folk Song Revival"—so named because this new interest in folk music had moved out of the country and into the city.

The 1960s

Joan Baez

One of the singers who made her professional debut at the first Newport Folk Festival was Joan Baez, and in 1960, she released her first record consisting primarily of traditional ballads. Born to a father who was from Mexico and a mother who was from Scotland, Baez spent part of her youth in Switzerland and in Iraq, where here father was a physicist working at the university of Baghdad. At the university, communists had been helpful to her family, so she was surprised at the strong anti-communist sentiment she found when her family returned to the United States. As a high school student in Palo Alto, California, Baez was deeply affected by a seminar she attended on world issues in which the young reverend Martin Luther King Jr. spoke. Baez bought a guitar and began imitating the recordings she heard of The Kingston Trio, Odetta, Harry Belafonte, and other folk musicians. When her father was offered a position at MIT in 1958, the family moved to Boston and she became a lead performer in the urban folk movement. As she became more involved in folk music, she adopted a more purist stance, critical of the "bastardized and unholy" commercial style of musicians such as The Kingston Trio.

Bob Dylan

Also in 1960, a young man named Robert Zimmerman entered the University of Minnesota where he was exposed to the music of Woody Guthrie and Guthrie's autobiography, *Bound for Glory*. Dylan dropped out of school, assumed and

The "Queen of Folk," Joan Baez, helped boost the career of Bob Dylan and has continued to contribute her time, energy, money, and musical talent to support political causes. *Source: Vanguard Records.*

legalized his new name, "Bob Dylan," and went to New York in late 1960 with a strong motivation to meet Woody Guthrie who was, by this time, spending most of his time as a patient at Greystone Hospital. He met Guthrie and other prominent folksingers, including Ramblin' Jack Elliott, Cisco Houston, Dave van Ronk, and Pete Seeger. Dylan began performing at local coffeehouses. In late fall of 1961, *The New York Times* critic Robert Shelton observed Dylan in performance and wrote a rave review, entitled "Bob Dylan: A Distinctive Folk-Song Stylist." Dylan was soon offered a contract with Columbia Records, becoming one of the first young folksingers to be signed by a major label. In February 1962, his debut album *Bob Dylan* was released. Many of Dylan's early songs retained the political orientation of his idols in the earlier Urban Folk tradition, including: "The Ballad of Hollis Brown" (an impoverished farmer who, in desperation, kills himself and his family), "The Lonesome Death of Hattie Carroll" (the murder of a black domestic by her white employer), "With God On Our Side" (a bitter chronicling of U.S. wars), and "Only a Pawn in Their Game" (about the murder of the black civil rights leader Medgar Evers).

Joan Baez, who had met Dylan in New York where he was "singing his 'Song to Woody'" at an important coffeehouse, gave Dylan's career a boost by singing several of his songs at her concerts and inviting him to participate with her at her performances. By this time she was considered the "Queen of Folk Music," had three albums on the charts, and was featured as the subject of a cover story by *Time Magazine.* Also in 1962, the trio Peter, Paul, and Mary, who had been playing in coffeehouses across the country, released their first album featuring the songs, "If I Had a Hammer" and "Lemon Tree," which became top commercial hits. Dylan, who had continued to record and to perform, was the

Break-Out Four

LISTENING GUIDE *"Barbara Allen"*

Performing Artist: Joan Baez

This is the complete version of the ballad introduced in the chapter on European roots, and therefore provides a useful comparison between traditional folk and the urban folk revival. Joan Baez, known as the "Queen of Folk Music" during the Urban Folk Revival, recorded this version. Baez was born in Staten Island, New York, in 1941. She quit her studies at Boston University to sing in coffeehouses, gaining more general fame after her performance at the Newport Folk Festival in 1959. The following year she recorded the first of her thirty-plus albums. During the 1960s, she actively protested the U.S. involvement in the Vietnam War, and was twice jailed for her participation in those protests. Famous for her clear and beautiful voice, Baez is among the most revered folksingers in America. She continues to have an active singing career, and has established organizations devoted to human rights and nonviolence.

Rhythm	Quadruple
Melody	Simple and memorable
Harmony	The melody utilizes a clear B major scale, and expands the tonal language by adding the vi chord to Seeger's recording, which used the basic primary chords.
Texture	Homophonic
Form	Strophic, ABCD
Instrumentation	Solo female voice with guitar

box-office attraction at the 1963 Newport Folk Festival, where he was named "The Crown-Prince of Folk Music."

THE HOOTENANNY SHOW

Also in 1963, ABC purchased the right to the concept and to the name "Hootenanny" from a club in New York called the Bitter End that had been holding weekly hootenannies. The ABC television network began a program in which a half-hour folk music show was taped on a different college campus each week. Many traditional folksingers were contemptuous of the program for its noncontroversial, apolitical style. And, of course, the show was contemptuous of many of the traditional folksingers, and did not, for example, invite folksingers such as Pete Seeger to perform on the program because he had been blacklisted during the McCarthy era. Many popular folksingers, including Joan Baez, Bob Dylan, Peter, Paul, and Mary, and The Kingston Trio, boycotted the show out of support for the older generation of folksingers and, although the program was quite popular for some time, it was canceled in 1964.

FOLKSINGERS AND THE CIVIL RIGHTS MOVEMENT

The Civil Rights movement, which had begun in the 1954 court decision to desegregate public schools, peaked during the spring of 1963 when federal troops were sent into Birmingham, Alabama, to quell racial violence. Joan Baez, Bob Dylan, and several other prominent folk artists showed their commitment to social and political activism by participating in various civil rights rallies. In the summer of 1963, Dylan and Baez joined Seeger, Peter, Paul, and Mary, and others in a powerful rendition of "We Shall Overcome" at

Break-Out Five

PROFILE *Bob Dylan*

The grandson of Jewish-Russian immigrants, Dylan was born Robert Allen Zimmerman on May 24, 1941, in Duluth, Minnesota. In 1947, Dylan's father moved the family to the small town of Hibbing, Minnesota. In the fall of 1959, Dylan moved to Minneapolis to enroll in the University of Minnesota. There he began to listen to the music of a wide variety of musicians, including Robert Johnson, Hank Williams, and Woody Guthrie. The next year he decided to drop out of college and travel to New York. He had two goals: to become a part of the burgeoning folk music scene in the Greenwich Village area of the city, and to meet Woody Guthrie. He achieved both goals, becoming a popular performer in the Village's folk clubs and coffeehouses and spending considerable time with Guthrie, who was by this time hospitalized in New Jersey with Huntington's disease, a disease that attacks the nervous system. Dylan began writing songs, including his tribute "Song to Woody." It also was around this time that he assumed the stage name Bob Dylan. It is presumed that he did this in honor of the late Welsh poet Dylan Thomas, but Dylan has denied this throughout his career.

Bob Dylan in 1978, after he had moved from the acoustic music of urban folk to playing electric guitar. Bob Dylan in concert at the Universal Amphitheater, June 1978. *Source: Photo by Joel Axelrad. Retna Ltd.*

In the fall of 1961, Robert Shelton, a critic with the *New York Times,* saw Dylan perform at Gerde's Folk City, and raved about Dylan's talent. A month later, legendary Columbia Records executive John Hammond signed him for a recording contract. Dylan cut his first album primarily of traditional folk songs and blues, and the album was released in 1962. In 1963, he released the album *The Freewheelin' Bob Dylan*, which contained his own songs, including two that would go on to become civil rights anthems: "Blowin' in the Wind" (covered by Peter, Paul, and Mary) and "A Hard Rain's A-Gonna Fall." His next album, *The Times They Are A'Changin'*, continued the protest style except for the last song, in which he concluded that he'd "bid farewell and not give a damn." In his next album, *Another Side of Bob Dylan*, his songs were not political but, rather, introspective and personally revealing.

It was after the release of this album that he became involved with Joan Baez, a relationship

the opening performance of the Newport Folk Festival. On August 28, 1963, Dylan, Baez, Peter, Paul, and Mary, Harry Belafonte, Mahalia Jackson, Odetta, and others performed at the March on Washington rally at which Martin Luther King, Jr. delivered his famous "I Have a Dream" speech.

THE "BRITISH INVASION" AND FOLK-ROCK

The year 1963 was the high-water mark for the folk music revival. Bob Dylan had become folk music's undisputed leader, contributing his powerful personality and musical style to galvanize

that helped them both. In 1965, he recorded *Bringing It All Back Home* with a nine-piece half-electric, half-acoustic band. This album included two of his most popular mainstream hits, "Tambourine Man" (which was soon covered by the Byrds in the new folk-rock genre) and "It's All Over Now, Baby Blue." Dylan's own attempts to move out of acoustic folk to electrified rock were not initially welcomed, best expressed in his being booed off stage at the 1965 Newport Folk Festival.

In the subsequent album *Highway 61 Revisited*, he included "Like a Rolling Stone," which, at more than six minutes, was the longest "45" record ever released and reached number two on the Billboard singles chart. Dylan continued to record but was increasingly overwhelmed by pressures and in 1966, he had a near-fatal motorcycle accident, which allowed him to retreat to the solitude of his home in Woodstock, New York, with his wife Sara.

When Dylan returned to recording, he recorded in a country style, including the albums *John Wesley Harding* and *Nashville Skyline.* In the years that followed, Dylan released multiple albums, some commercial or critical successes, and some not. By 1998, he had written more than five hundred songs released in forty-three albums. In 1998, he won three Grammy awards, including best album for *Time Out of Mind.* Before that, he had won or shared in only four minor Grammys. Reviewing Dylan's impact, Jay Cocks wrote that Dylan represented a

> series of dreams about America as it once and never was. It was folk music, deep within its core, from the mountains and the delta and the blacktop of Highway 61. Rhythm and blues, too, and juke joint rock 'n' roll, and hymns from backwoods churches and gospel shouts from riverside baptisms. He put all that together, and found words to match it.[4]

In 2001, Dylan won an Oscar for best song for his "Things Have Changed," a song he had written for the movie *Wonder Boys.* Jennifer Lopez, who announced the award, commented that "in a sense, [the song] mirrors the ongoing career of Bob Dylan." In his acceptance speech, broadcast from Australia where he was on tour, Dylan said, "I'd like to thank the members of the academy who were bold enough to give me this award for this song. It's a song that doesn't pussyfoot around or turn a blind eye to human nature."[5]

Still writing, recording, performing, and touring, Dylan continues to honor his musical roots. In an interview in 2005, he explained, "I know there are groups at the top of the charts that are hailed as the saviors of rock 'n' roll and all that, but they are amateurs, they don't know where the music comes from. . . . I was lucky. I came up in a different era. There were these great blues and country folk artists around, and the impulse to play 'those sounds' came to me at a very early age. I wouldn't even think about playing music if I was born in these times."[6] Displaying his characteristic sense of humor, he closed the interview describing how he currently feels by saying, "Any day above the ground is a good day."[7]

[4] Cocks, Jay. Time 100/Most Influential Folk Musicians: The Folk Musician BOB DYLAN Master poet, caustic social critic and intrepid, guiding sprit of the counterculture generation. 06-08-1998.

[5] "Bob Dylan Wins Oscar for Best Song" Posted by Song Bird, March 26, 2001.

[6] "Bob Dylan: Interview from the Tour Program." http://www.artsandopinion.com/2005_v4_n1/dylan.htm (Accessed 02-20-05).

[7] Ibid.

the urban folk music movement. Soon he helped bring it to an end. In 1964, Dylan was on tour in Great Britain where he met and talked with members of the Beatles, the Rolling Stones, and other rock groups. These groups and other British stars were becoming so popular that their success was titled "The British Invasion." Furthermore, a new kind of hybrid was developing: folk-rock. In 1964, the British band, The Animals, released an electric version of "The House of the Rising Sun," a folk song that had been discovered in Kentucky in 1937 by Alan

Break-Out Six

PROFILE *Ben Harper*

Ben Harper was born and raised in Claremont, a small college town in southern California. His father was African American and his mother was white, and they were both musicians. His mother, an accomplished singer/guitarist in the Urban Folk Revival tradition, was the parent who raised him. Ben's maternal grandfather owned a shop that specialized in the collection and restoration of acoustic stringed instruments. From an early age, Ben was allowed to play many different kinds of contemporary and historical stringed instruments but he eventually settled on playing acoustic slide guitar.

He grew up listening to folk, blues, soul, and reggae. When he was nine, his mother took him to a Bob Marley concert, in which Peter Tosh joined Marley for an encore version of "Get Up, Stand Up," the reggae classic that urges the oppressed to fight for their rights. It was a pivotal experience for Harper, who later said,

> "It was almost like watching a crucifixion. . . . That guy, he was another coming of something. To me, he's proof of divinity. He just kept getting better all the time. . . . His life was music. A lot of these cats, they want to be famous . . . it puts a really bad taste in your mouth. But Bob was always Bob. Humbleness and humility were the foundation of his person, which always kept the music close to the root. And the closer to the root, the sweeter the fruit. Just an eternal sense of inspiration."[8]

Harper began writing his own songs, many of which focused on themes of personal freedom and social injustice. He performed regularly in the Los Angeles area before he was even a teenager. In 1994, he recorded and released his debut album, *Welcome to the Cruel World.* This was followed by the politically intense *Fight for*

[8] Weiss, Neil. "Musical Prophet in Training." LAUNCH. 4-20-03. http://launch.yahoo.com/read/interview/12047796 (Accessed 2-20-5).

Lomax. And in early 1965, an American group called the Byrds made their debut with an electric version of Dylan's "Mr. Tambourine Man." This trend toward folk-rock continued in the music of other increasingly popular musicians, including Donovan, the Lovin' Spoonful, and the Mamas and the Papas.

At the Newport Folk Festival in 1965, with a record attendance of eighty thousand, Dylan came on stage with an electric guitar to sing "Maggie's Farm" and "Like a Rolling Stone." Many members of the audience responded with open hostility, booing, and hissing. Even though Dylan returned later that evening with an acoustic guitar, the message was clear. With a performance of "It's All Over Now, Baby Blue," Dylan signaled his personal and artistic evolvement away from folk music to a new style that was more introspective (abandoning the folk tradition's "spokesperson for a community" orientation) and a style influenced by rock and roll.

THE FOLK REVIVAL ENDS

In 1967, the first "pop" festival was organized at Monterey, California, modeled after festivals such as the Newport Folk Festival. San Francisco – based bands such as Janis Joplin with Big Brother and the Holding Company and the British group The Who created a sensation. The concept of a pop/rock festival was emulated in different parts across the country, culminating in the Woodstock Music and Art

Your Mind in 1995, and *The Will to Live* in 1997. (In this recording, he introduced a backup band, the Innocent Criminals, which included a bassist, drummer, and percussionist.) Although Harper eschewed the commercialism of the music industry mainstream, his music became a mainstay on college and alternative radio stations. Although he never had a "hit album," his constant touring (opening for groups such as R.E.M., Radiohead, Metallica, Pearl Jam, the Fugees, and Dave Mathews, as well as performing as his own headliner) combined with critical acclaim has helped him to build a large and dedicated fan base.

Throughout his career, he has retained a strong spiritual and political orientation, and, for example, played in both the 1997 and 1999 Tibetan Freedom Concerts. In 2001, he released *Live from Mars*, a double disc that demonstrated his artistic evolution to include electric and acoustic material. In 2003, he released the worldbeat-inspired *Diamonds on the Inside* and then, after a European tour with the Gospel group, Blind Boys of Alabama, in 2004 released a collaborative album with them titled *There Will Be Light.*[9]

Harper says that he lives for his music, explaining, "I write songs because I *need* to write songs. That's what I'm supposed to do, that's what I have to do, and that's what I'm here to do."[10] But like folk music itself, Harper continues to absorb new influences. He views his later music not as "departures" from his essentially urban folk roots but, rather, as his personal and artistic evolution, stating,

> If I don't have the potential to write in different styles and sing in different voices and play in different ways, I won't stay inspired. I refuse to make uninspired music. . . . If I'm inspired and music inspires me, then I will continue to play it. But I would never insult the people that love this music and I would never insult the blessing of music in my life and I would never insult myself by playing uninspired music.[11]

[9] Wilson, MacKenzie. "Ben Harper Biography." http://launch.yahoo.com/ar-250855-bio—Ben-Harper (Accessed 02-19-05).

[10] Ibid.

[11] Farinella, David John. "Sit Down and Shine." LAUNCH. 09-28-1999. http://launch.yahoo.com/read/interview/12026800 (Accessed 02-20-05).

Fair held in 1969. The Woodstock music festival drew an audience of approximately four hundred thousand to a farm at White Lake in New York State. Some of the musicians who performed at this festival, including Joan Baez and Woody Guthrie's son Arlo, were folksingers. But the festival favorites were clearly the new acid rock 'n' roll artists such as The Jimi Hendrix Experience, Jefferson Airplane, and Santana. Between 1967 and 1970, thirty major rock festivals were held across the country, attracting audiences of at least 2.5 million. In 1970, the Newport Folk Foundation decided not to hold a festival and, in 1971, the festival was canceled again and its license revoked. Although several musicians continued to sing both traditional folk music and what was by then referred to as "contemporary" folk music, and even though several prominent musicians such as Judy Collins, Joni Mitchell, Simon and Garfunkel, and James Taylor maintained for many years styles strongly influenced by folk music, the folk music revival had come to an end.

CONCLUSION

When Joan Baez sang "Joe Hill" at the first Woodstock Music Festival, the immense popularity of folk music had already given way to a new youth movement and counterculture that had emerged revolving around rock 'n' roll. By 1970, many of the popular folk artists who had filled concert halls only a few years earlier were no longer being offered recording contracts. But even though the folk music revival had come to an end, the folk music tradition continued to influence the music scene. Several members of popular psychedelic rock groups had begun as folk musicians, including Joe MacDonald of Country Joe and the Fish, Roger McGuinn of the Byrds, Jerry Garcia of The Grateful Dead, members of Crosby, Stills and Nash, and even the more recently popular Bruce Springsteen. Several generations of singer-songwriters, beginning with musicians such as Joni Mitchell, Carly Simon, and Cat Stevens and, later, including Emmy Lou Harris, Nancy Griffith, Mary Chapin Carpenter, and Jewel, have drawn heavily from folk backgrounds. Many of the best contemporary songwriters, such as Ben Harper, John Mayer, and Jack Johnson, would not be writing in their current style without the innovations of Urban Folk Revival poet-musicians such as Bob Dylan and Joni Mitchell.

Perhaps as a desire to offset the potential anonymity of a densely populated world, many musicians are also turning to their ethnic roots to find musical inspiration. Examples include Van Morrison and Peter Townsend, who have made important recordings and performances with the traditional Irish group, The Chieftains. The popularity of "unplugged" recordings such as *Clapton Unplugged* also may signal a widespread desire to humanize an increasingly technical world with the simpler acoustic traditions of folk music.

Today, folk music reflects the increased ethnic diversity and the shift toward a global community that generally characterize American society. At a contemporary folk festival, one will typically encounter a variety of music that might include Cajun and zydeco bands, calypso and reggae, Celtic songs, Taiko bands, and New Acoustic fusion groups as well as performances by traditional folksingers. Although it is not in the commercial limelight like modern rock, hip-hop, and other popular music, it continues to thrive. Each year there are more than one thousand folk and traditional music festivals and camps across the nation. Folk music organizations such as *Sing Out!*, founded in 1950, still print and distribute publications to a large readership. Regular columns provided by Pete Seeger, Tony Trischka, and Faith Petric help forward *Sing Out!*'s mission "to preserve and support cultural diversity and heritage of all traditional and contemporary folk music and to encourage making folk music a part of our everyday lives."[12] American folk music has changed, because American folk have changed. But as long as there are folk, there will be folk music and, just like the people it celebrates, it will continue to shape and be shaped by the larger society.

Bibliography

Baez, Joan. *And A Voice to Sing With: A Memoir.* New York: Summit Books, 1987.

Baggelaar, Kristin and Donald Milton. *Folk Music: More Than a Song.* New York: Thomas Y. Crowell Company, 1976.

"Bob Dylan: Interview from the Tour Program." http://www.artsandopinion.com/2005_v4_n1/dylan.htm (Accessed 02-20-05).

"Bob Dylan Wins Oscar for Best Song" Posted by Song Bird, Monday, 26 March 2001. www: On Express Yourself. Associated Press Los Angles (March 25, 2001, 11:39 p.m: EST).

Bronson, Bertrand Harris. *The Singing Tradition of Child's Popular Ballads.* Princeton: Princeton University Press, 1976.

———. *The Traditional Tunes of the Child Ballads.* Princeton: Princeton University Press, 1959–1971.

Chase, Gilbert. *America's Music: From the Pilgrims to the Present.* Third Edition. Urbana and Chicago: University of Illinois Press, 1987.

Child, Francis James. *The English and Scottish Popular Ballads.* Five vols. Boston and New York: Houghton, Mifflin Company, 1882–98.

[12] "The Sing Out Pages" http://www.singout.org/ (Accessed 02-17-05).

Cocks, Jay. Time 100/Most Influential Folk Musician: The Folk Musician BOB DYLAN Master poet, caustic social critic and intrepid, guiding spirit of the counterculture generation. 06-08-1998.

Coffin, Tristram P. *The British Traditional Ballad in North America.* Philadelphia: The American Folklore Society, 1963.

Denisoff, Serge R. *Sing a Song of Social Significance.* Bowling Green, OH: Bowling Green University Popular Press, 1972.

———. *Great Day Coming. Folk Music and the American Left.* Urbana: University of Illinois Press, 1971.

Dilene, Benjamin. *Romancing the Folk: Public Memory and American Roots Music.* London: University of North Carolina Press, 2000.

Farinella, David John. "Sit Down and Shine." LAUNCH. 9-28-1999. http://launch.yahoo.com/read/interview/12026800 (Accessed 02-20-05)

Graves, Anna Hunt. *Folk: The Life, Times, and Music Series.* New York: Friedman/Fairfax Publishers, 1994.

Greenway, John. *American Folksongs of Protest.* New York: Octagon Books, 1970.

Guthrie, Woody. *Bound for Glory.* New York: Dutton, 1943.

Hamm, Charles. *Music in the New World.* New York: W.W. Norton and Company, 1983.

Heylin, Clinton. *Bob Dylan: Behind the Shades, A Biography.* New York: Summit Books, 1991.

Hood, Phil, editor. *Artists of American Folk Music: The Legends of Traditional Folk, the Stars of the Sixties, the Virtuosi of New Acoustic Music.* New York: Quill, 1986.

Kingman, Daniel. *American Music: A Panorama.* New York: Schirmer Books, 1979.

Klein, Joe. *Woody Guthrie: A Life.* New York: Alfred A. Knopf, 1980.

Landy, Elliott. *Woodstock Vision: The Spirit of a Generation.* New York: Continuum, 1994.

Lomax, John, and Alan Lomax. *American Ballads and Folk Songs.* New York: The Macmillan Company, 1934.

Nettl, Bruno. *Folk Music in the United States: An Introduction.* Third Edition. Detroit: Wayne State University Press, 1976.

Miller, Jim. Editor. *The Rolling Stone Illustrated History of Rock and Roll: A New Edition of the Best and Most Complete History Brought Up-to-Date and Expanded.* New York: Random House, 1980.

Sandburg, Carl. *The American Songbag.* New York: Harcourt and Brace, 1927.

Seeger, Pete. *Where Have All the Flowers Gone.* 1993. A Singer's Stories, Songs, Seeds, Robberies, Peter Blood (Editor) Sing Out Publications.

Seeger, Pete. *The Incomplete Folksinger.* Jo Metcalf Schwartz (Editor). New York: Simon and Schuster, 1972.

Sharp, Cecil J. *English Folk Songs from the Southern Appalachians.* Maud Karpeles (Editor). London: Oxford University Press, 1932.

Shelton, Robert. *No Direction Home: The Life and Music of Bob Dylan.* New York: Da Capo Press, 1997.

Szatmary, David P. *Rockin' in Time: A Social History of Rock and Roll.* Englewood Cliffs New Jersey: Prentice-Hall, Inc., 1987.

Weiss, Neil. "Musical Prophet in Training." LAUNCH. 4-20-03. http://launch.yahoo.com/read/interview/120-47796 (Accessed 02-20-05)

Westrup, J.A. and F. Ll. Harrison. *The New College Encyclopedia of Music.* New York: W.W. Norton and Company, 1960.

Willoughby, David. *The World of Music.* Third Edition. Madison, WI. Brown and Benchmark Publishers, 1995.

Wilson, MacKenzie. "Ben Harper Biography." http://launch.yahoo.com/ar-250855-bio—Ben-Harper (Accessed 2-19-05)

Chapter Twelve

Rock 'n' Roll

During the mid-1950s, an entirely new genre of music appeared in America that eventually became the most popular music form of the twentieth century: rock 'n' roll. Rock 'n' roll was created out of a synthesis of several music traditions, the most important being rhythm 'n' blues, country, Gospel, and the popular vocal and instrumental styles of "Tin-Pan Alley." More than just a music genre, rock 'n' roll became a social phenomenon, influencing clothing, hairstyles, language, lifestyles, and politics. Once dismissed by its detractors as a fad, it is now clear that any survey of American music would be incomplete without some coverage of the social, political, and economic force of rock 'n' roll.

Overview of Rock 'n' Roll's Music Characteristics

From its emergence in the mid-1950s, rock 'n' roll developed into several different stylistic categories. These categories will be discussed as they developed historically. Each category constructs its style through unique treatment of various music characteristics. Some writers have stated that the only characteristic shared by all rock music styles is that it is loud. Nevertheless, the following describes the general manner in which rock 'n' roll deals with the structural building blocks.

Melody, Rhythm, and Harmony

Melodies are clearly shaped and easily remembered. Rhythm is emphasized, with quadruple meter dominant and emphasis on the "backbeats" (beats two and four). The rhythm is layered such that, beneath the strong macrorhythm, there are complex counter-rhythms. Harmonies are derived from the major/minor system, and there is frequent use of seventh chords. Rock 'n' roll often uses a melodic, rhythmic, harmonic, or lyric pattern that is catchy and functions as a "hook" to attract the listener to want to listen to the rest of the song and to want to hear it (and immediately recognize it) again.

Texture, Instrumentation, and Form

Texture is homophonic, and in some styles there is extensive use of call-and-response. The "core" rock instrumentation is drums, electric rhythm and lead guitar, and electronic keyboard supporting a lead singer with backup singers. The most frequently used form is the blues or the thirty-two-bar song form, a combination of four eight-bar phrases with the same melody and a "bridge" or chorus, represented by the letters AABA.

Rock 'n' Roll in a Historical and Social Context

As with any rapid societal change, the emergence of rock and roll occurred within a complex context of larger events and changes that allowed for and fostered its development.

Changes in the 1940s and 1950s

Beginnings of Desegregation and Expanded American World View

In the years immediately following World War II, a proud and grateful American public welcomed home its returning veterans. These veterans represented a wide range of races and ethnicities. The desegregation of the armed forces by President Harry Truman in 1948 was the beginning of the federal government's slow process to eventually mandate total desegregation at all levels of society.

Having fought in battles abroad, the returning GIs (the abbreviation for "Government Issue" that was used to refer to U.S. soldiers) had seen more of the world than earlier generations. When they came home, they shared their broader worldview, discoveries, and experiences with their friends and families. Many soldiers brought brides home with them from overseas. Literally and figuratively, Americans had become "more worldly." These factors contributed to a subtle but growing interest in other cultures, and the prior tendency to separate and insulate peoples of different races and backgrounds began to change.

The Booming Postwar Economy

The post–Word War II economy in America was booming, and there was a growing belief that education was the key to future success. The federal government responded in two important ways. First, there was the passage of the "GI Bill," with funds to support veterans financially as they pursued their education. Second, there was funding set aside both at the federal and the state levels to build colleges and universities. At one point, community colleges were built at the rate of one per week.

Elizabeth Eckford, 15, bravely perseveres despite cruel taunts from white bystanders as she attempts to attend as one of the first black students at Central High in Little Rock, Arkansas.
Source: AP Wide World Photos.

Furthermore, there was a philosophical shift to providing higher education opportunities for all people, regardless of their socioeconomic class. Before the war, a college education was the privilege of the upper classes and upper middle classes. Now, with many "open access" institutions built in local communities, college was available to everyone, and in many institutions, for little or no tuition.

An increased awareness of the value of completing high school and continuing on to college was replacing the earlier tendency for many young people to leave school and go to work, often at a family farm or business. The combination of a thriving economy and memories of the dreary and demoralizing Great Depression of the 1930s reinforced a collective hope in 1950s' adults to create a better world and future for their children. Consequently, large numbers of young people had greater freedom to make decisions for themselves than had previous generations. They had more time for socializing, and formed close bonds of friendship with their peers and in loosely organized social groups.

The Emerging Youth Culture and Economic Power

In contrast to the economic depression of the 1930s or the war years of the 1940s, the 1950s were a time of relative peace and prosperity. With hard work and a little luck, white middle-class Americans could look forward to owning a car, a home, and even a television. Of course, the 1950s also had a less pleasant side: tensions over the Cold War were high—students watched training films over what to do in case of the explosion of an atomic bomb—and Americans of color still lived within oppressive racial segregation and discrimination. But for many Americans, the new prosperity trickled down to teenagers whose earnings were no longer an essential component of the family's financial support. Parents wanted their children to enjoy economic and material comforts. Many teenagers were now given an allowance or allowed to keep money earned from after-school jobs. In the vernacular of capitalism, teenagers now had discretionary income, and with that income, they carried economic clout.

The entertainment business, heretofore the domain of adults, turned its attention to young people. The first teen movies, such as *The Wild One*, *Rebel Without a Cause*, and *The Blackboard Jungle*, catered to this youth market. The first generation of American "teenagers" was created, and with it, a teenage identity separate from adults. This teenage identity included its own clothes, hairstyles, slang, and, perhaps most important, its own music, rock 'n' roll. Perplexed and dismayed parents now witnessed a "generation gap," a division between generations that would grow to become a cultural revolution in the 1960s.

Rock was everything teenagers wanted. It was loud, raucous, and sexual. The subject matter of rock lyrics was not profound—dancing, dating, love, cars, school—but it spoke directly to teens. Performers were closer to their age, and dealt with issues important to teenagers. In many ways, rock 'n' roll was the antithesis of their parents' bland and nonthreatening songs from "Tin-Pan Alley."

Growth in the Music Industry

The technological conditions and developments of the post–Word War II era also had a profound impact on the music industry in peacetime America. The recording and broadcasting industries in the United States were intact, unlike those of countries whose industrial and manufacturing infrastructure had been devastated by war. The broadcast range of radio had been greatly expanded, and stations that had previously played exclusively to regional audiences were now accessible to many distant and diverse listeners, particularly at night when the airwaves were less crowded. The advent of television was soon to give the new rock 'n' roll stars a visual presence in the hearts and minds of teens. It is within this complex context of social, economic, and technological influences that rock 'n' roll was born.

The Birth of Rock 'n' Roll

By the late 1940s, black rhythm 'n' blues was attracting a wider audience, many of whom were young white teenagers. This phenomenon is called a crossover, which is a record intended for one market that succeeds in another. In 1951, a white disk jockey named Alan Freed, who had been influential in attracting white teenagers to the music, called the music "rock 'n' roll." The name was coined from a popular African-American slang phrase for sex that had appeared in many rhythm 'n' blues lyrics such as the song, "My Baby Rocks Me with a Steady Roll." Thus by the early fifties, black rhythm 'n' blues records were crossing over, making their way to the bottom of the white pop charts.

Influential record producers who observed the success of rhythm 'n' blues songs began to search for successful hits to "cover" by white musicians. A cover is a recording made subsequent to the original version that may or may not follow the style or lyrics of the original. Most of the early rock 'n' roll recordings were covers by white artists of black artists' previous rhythm 'n' blues recordings. The usual pattern was that an unknown rhythm 'n' blues song, by an unknown black group, on an unknown label would break into the national pop charts and would then be covered by white artists in a pop version that would be released by a major record company. Many, many songs in early rock 'n' roll were created in this manner, including "Sh-Boom" by The Chords (covered and made popular by The Crewcuts), "Shake, Rattle, and Roll" by Joe Turner (covered by Bill Haley and the Comets), "Earth Angel" by the Penguins (covered by the Crewcuts), "I'm Walkin'" by Fats Domino (covered by Rick Nelson), and "You Ain't Nothin' But a Houndog" by Big Mama Thornton (covered by Elvis Presley).

These covers and crossovers were central factors in the erosion of racially based music boundaries. Covers and crossovers also brought new stylistic influences. Hence early rock 'n' roll soon drew on several established music traditions: rhythm 'n' blues, Gospel, country, and the vocal and instrumental styles of Tin-Pan Alley.

The Primary Musical Influences on Early Rock 'n' Roll

Early rock 'n' roll reflected multiple influences.

Rhythm 'n' Blues

Rhythm 'n' blues refers to the transformation in the late 1940s and early 1950s of blues forms into music that was used primarily for dancing. This style of blues was especially popular in big urban centers with large African-American populations such as Detroit and Chicago. Urban blues grew in popularity with audiences who were finding the intense and complex bebop jazz styles too difficult to dance to and too hard to understand and appreciate. More and more blacks turned to bands that were playing blues-derived music with simpler harmonies and a more obvious and danceable rhythmic beat.

The instrumental ensemble consisted of several electric and amplified instruments, including guitar, organ, and bass. Although rhythm 'n' blues included a vocal line, because the primary purpose was dance music, the words were often employed for their rhythmic properties rather than their meaning. In the accompaniment, various patterns that had developed out of blues piano style were used and the rhythmic structure emphasized the offbeat stress on the "weak beats" (two and four in a quadruple meter).

A few companies such as Okeh and Columbia had controlled recordings of blues music and they segregated the marketing of this "black" music under the category of "race records." Following World War II, when this racially based segregation was seen as increasingly offensive, the record companies developed the term "rhythm 'n' blues" to replace the older term. Nevertheless, rhythm 'n' blues remained African-American recordings aimed at African-American audiences and the term became a generic rubric for various styles of music created by urban black musicians.

Gospel

Black Gospel music developed after the Civil War from the same roots as the blues. It was religious music that displayed the characteristics of slave camp meetings and spirituals, using the African traditions of call-and-response, improvisation, and the vocal stylings, rhythmic complexity and harmonic language that so frequently characterize African-American music. With the emotional involvement of the preacher and the congregation in the religious message, the music was characterized by exuberant handclapping, shouting, and dancing. Although originally sung by the congregation, professional Gospel choirs also were founded. Several well-rehearsed and professional Gospel choirs toured and recorded in the 1930s and 1940s.

COUNTRY

Country music had developed out of the folk music traditions of immigrants from the British Isles who had settled into the mountain regions of what is now the southern and southwestern United States. In addition to songs, these immigrants had brought various kinds of dance music such as the jig, reel, and waltz that were played by a fiddle or string band. With the invention of radio and the growing importance of recording technology in the late 1920s and the 1930s, this music was recorded and called "hillbilly" music and was made popular through various radio programs such as the Grand Ole Opry. During the subsequent decades, country music developed into several styles, and the styles that most influenced early rock 'n' roll were western swing (which originated in Texas as a fusion of country and jazz) and honky-tonk (the amplified, danceable hard-edged style made popular in the bars and dance houses).

TIN-PAN ALLEY

"Tin-Pan Alley" was the name for a section in New York City on West 28th Street between Broadway and Fifth lined with publishers specializing in popular songs. Before radio recording, and certainly before the birth of rock 'n' roll in the 1950s when the performance of a song became more important than the song itself, a song's popularity was determined by how many copies of sheet music it would sell. In order to make money, publishing firms hired lyricists and composers to create songs, and then they would employ various techniques to promote the songs. One of their marketing techniques was to hire pianists and singers to "plug" a song (called song pluggers). These musicians would play and sing that publishing firm's songs on request by any customer who walked in the store. According to legend, the songwriter-journalist Monroe Rosenfield coined the phrase "Tin-Pan Alley" between 1900 and 1903 because the clanking and clinking of cheap pianos sounded to him like the rattling of tin pans. The term eventually was used for all the pop music from the late nineteenth century through 1950s. Rock 'n' roll's use of records replaced sheet music and signaled the end of "Tin-Pan Alley," but the legacy of light and easy to listen to pop music designed to be "popular" with a general audience endured.

But there were additional influences even beyond these four. The music historian Robert Palmer also has noted that "the Bo Diddley beat" was Afro-Cuban, taken from a Cuban son record. The "screaming, athletic saxophone playing" was from big-band jazz. And several early hits, especially by Chicano artists such as Richie Valens, contained traditional Mexican rhythms. In Palmer's own words, "Rock & roll proved an All-American, multi-ethnic hybrid, its sources and developing substyles too various to be explained away. . . . "[1]

Two Examples of the Fusion of Styles

Each of the influential styles identified above was a distinct genre with a separate audience, but due to covers and crossovers in the late 1940s and early 1950s, the boundaries were eroding. Carl Perkins, Elvis Presley and Buddy Holly combined elements of rhythm 'n' blues with country. Jerry Lee Lewis

[1] Palmer, Robert, "The Fifties," *Rolling Stone*. April 19, 1990, p. 48.

and Little Richard brought in elements of Gospel. Pat Boone, Paul Anka, and Frankie Avalon stressed elements of Tin-Pan Alley. Borders were also blurring due to the crossovers of black rhythm 'n' blues performers such as Fats Domino and Chuck Berry who were now marketed as rock 'n' roll musicians to white audiences. All of this caused considerable turmoil in the recording industry, with one example of the industry's confusion being that sometimes both the original and its cover were on the pop chart at the same time. This happened, for example, with Fats Domino's "Ain't That a Shame" and Pat Boone's cover version of the same song. Although all of the music was soon categorized as rock 'n' roll, some of the styles, such as rockabilly and doo-wop, more clearly manifested the fusion of specific traditions.

Rockabilly

"Rockabilly" is the term given to one of the earliest versions of rock 'n' roll arising from a fusion of "hillbilly" country music and rhythm 'n' blues. It is exemplified by the first recordings of Elvis Presley at Sun Records. The standard accompaniment was electric lead guitar, acoustic rhythm guitar, string bass, and drums. The "hillbilly" or country characteristics included the steady, even duple or quadruple metrical rhythm patterns and the manner in which the lead guitarist played sliding notes up the strings similar to country's steel guitar. Other "country" characteristics were the way the string bass player slapped the strings against the fingerboard, the use of simple triads, and the vocal organization in which the second voice from the highest part carried the melody. The "rock" characteristics were from rhythm 'n' blues and included the use of a drummer and the manner in which the drummer emphasized the backbeats. Furthermore, many of the songs were covers by white musicians of rhythm 'n' blues recorded by African Americans.

Doo-Wop

The African-American vocal groups that had begun singing secular versions of Gospel music used a lead singer who was accompanied by other singers who responded to the lead singer's lines. The responses included repeating a few words of the line, or singing "nonsense" syllables. "Doo-Wop" was the term for this kind of music, and it referred to the nonsense syllables that the backup singers used. Early examples of the doo-wop style from the 1940s were The Mills Brothers, The Ink Spots, and The Ravens, but the style became more generally popular with mainstream audiences in the song "Crying in the Chapel" (1953) by the African-American group The Orioles. Interestingly, the Orioles' version was a cover of a recording made earlier by a white singer named Darrell Glenn. The most successful doo-wop recordings, however, were covers of African-American recordings by white groups, such as The Crew-Cuts' (a white group from Canada) version of The Chords' recording of "Sh-Boom" (1954). The style was continued by the Platters, Drifters, and Coasters.

Rock 'n' Roll's First Stars

Bill Haley

Bill Haley was one of rock's first stars, and his music reflects the cross-influences of the different styles. His band, the Saddlemen, were initially country western, but they were interested in rhythm 'n' blues. During performances, they would sometimes slip in some rhythm 'n' blues songs they performed in country style to avoid alienating their white audience. Changing their name to Bill Haley and the Comets, they later consciously blended country and western with rhythm and blues, and with this hybrid style achieved their first of several big hits, "Rock Around the Clock." Buoyed by its inclusion in the film *Blackboard Jungle*, it was the top-selling record in 1955. This recording was the first important breakthrough for white rock 'n' roll. The music's compelling dance rhythms, its lyrics, which spoke about teenage issues and concerns, and its rebelliousness and challenge to authority were very appealing to teenagers. Because teens now had the money and the power to buy the records, a major new industry was born. But Haley was pushing forty, somewhat rotund, and his "duck's-tail" hairdo looked a little silly over his receding hairline. What was needed was someone younger and more dangerous, a musical equivalent of James Dean. In 1953, that someone walked into Sam Phillips's Sun recording studio in Memphis, Tennessee, to make a record "for his mama": a young truck driver named Elvis Presley.

ELVIS PRESLEY

Elivs Presley was born in 1935 in Tupolo, Mississippi. He was nineteen years old when he walked into Sam Phillips's recording studio. Phillips had achieved notoriety recording black rhythm 'n' blues on his Sun Records label, but he was frustrated by the limited exposure available to black artists. Phillips felt that the potential market was enormous. What was needed was a Southern white performer who could convincingly deliver black rhythm 'n' blues. Presley came from a poor "white trash" family, which in the 1950s meant that the Presleys lived on the wrong side of the tracks, side by side with African Americans. Elvis not only knew traditional white genres such as pop and country, he also knew and loved black music, especially Gospel and rhythm 'n' blues. His early recordings reflected both influences. For example, one of his first singles was his cover of black blues singer Arthur "Big Boy" Crudup's "That's All Right (Mama)" on one side, and a rockabilly version of white country singer Bill Monroe's "Blue Moon of Kentucky" on the other side. After Elvis had achieved some local success following his recordings at Sun Records, Sam Phillips sent him to audition for the *Grand Ole Opry.* Elvis failed the audition—he was too "black" for the *Opry.* But he was also too "white" for the rhythm 'n' blues audiences.

Presley apparently learned his sexually suggestive hip gyrations from the black performers he had seen, and he incorporated these movements into his stage presence. His overt sexuality and his mixing of black and white music elements outraged conservative adults, thereby assuring his success with teenagers. Presley became a phenomenal success, and known as "the King," it was he who truly introduced the concept of rock 'n'

In 1956, Elvis performs at the Memphis state fair using moves he had seen used by local African-American rhythm and blues artists. *Source: Getty Images. Inc.-Hulton Archive Photos.*

roll star as a cultural hero. Without him, rock 'n' roll might have just been the fad its detractors had predicted. His versatility offered something for everybody. He could shout rhythm 'n' blues or croon a sentimental ballad. Girls liked his sex appeal and good looks, while boys liked his sullen demeanor and hoodlum dress. Parents, despite their antipathy to rock 'n' roll, had to admit that he was polite, patriotic, and believed in God. He was a tremendous commercial success, and would sell over five hundred million albums by the time of his death.

Little Richard

The self-proclaimed founder of rock 'n' roll is Little Richard, who exemplified rock's extroverted, raucous side. Richard Wayne Penniman was the third of twelve children in a poor and deeply religious African-American family. Richard was torn between hell-raising and God-fearing religion. Friends would tell of awaking from a postconcert party to the sound of Richard reading to them from the Bible, and he took up and left the ministry several times. His frenetic performance style, in which he sweated, danced, and generally worked the audience to frenzy, was not unlike that of a Pentecostal preacher. In 1957, he retired from performing to marry and pursue his religious calling. Neither lasted very long, but during a comeback tour of England, he deeply influenced two newly formed rock groups, the Beatles and the Rolling Stones. One of rock's most influential figures, his wild performance style, homosexual hype, self-promotion, and controversial persona influenced subsequent artists from James Brown to David Bowie and Prince.

Jerry Lee Lewis

Another important figure in early rock was Jerry Lee Lewis. He is often called a white counterpart to Little Richard, and the two did have remarkably similar upbringings and styles. Jerry Lee's stardom, however, was much briefer, and his career ended for many years because of a scandal over his marriage to a thirteen-year-old cousin. Despite the brevity of his stardom, his blend of Gospel, country, and rhythm 'n' blues combined with his flamboyant performance style influenced a number of subsequent musicians.

Chuck Berry

Chuck Berry's roots were in blues and rhythm 'n' blues, with a singing style influenced by country and western. His own music, however, was clearly rock 'n' roll. He even helped define rock's style in both his playing and his lyrics in the 1957 hit "Rock and Roll Music." He solidified the guitar as the most important instrument in rock and roll. Most of his numerous hit songs were in twelve-bar blues form, with lyrics tailored to such teen issues as dating, cars, and school. His real legacy is his guitar solos, distinctive—particularly the intros—and much imitated.

Conflicting Reactions to Rock 'n' Roll

Rock 'n' roll's merging of the music traditions of African Americans and whites was a manifestation of the eroding racial barriers that had begun in other areas of American society. For example, the 1954 Supreme Court decision of the case known as *Brown v. Board of Education* stated that equality could not exist when people were separated, and mandated that public schools be integrated. But the battle against rock 'n' roll was not exclusively on racial grounds. Parents worried about the music's emphasis on sexuality, freedom, and resistance to authority. Given the generally conservative context of the 1950s—the era of McCarthyism, the Cold War, and intense pressure for conformity—it is not surprising that rebellious teenagers would embrace a musical style that the establishment condemned. In a chapter cleverly titled, "The Empire Strikes Back,"[2] the music historian Reebee Garofalo explains,

[2] Garafalo, Reebee. *Rockin' Out: Popular Music in the U.S.A.* Upper Saddle River, NJ: Prentice Hall, 2005, pp. 123–145.

Break-Out One

LISTENING GUIDE *"Whole Lotta Shakin (Going On)"*

Performing Artist: Jerry Lee Lewis

Jerry Lee Lewis, born in 1935, grew up in Louisiana listening to both country and blues singers. After hearing Elvis Presley's Sun label recordings, he traveled to Memphis and recorded covers of African-American blues songs. "Whole Lotta Shakin" was released in 1957 and is a cover of a recording made by Big Maybelle in 1955. The lyrics are full of the sexual references that characterized much of rhythm 'n' blues and the rock and roll that evolved from it. Lewis was a great performer, and used a dramatic honky-tonk piano style of playing that earned him the name "The Killer."

Jerry Lee Lewis at the piano, singing.
Source: Corbis/Bettmann.

Rhythm	Quadruple, with honky-tonk piano style emphasizing rhythmic foundation.
Melody	Blues pattern of AAB
Harmony	Listen to the blues progression.
Texture	Homophonic with some implied call-and-response between singer and guitar.
Form	Blues AAB
Instrumentation	Male vocal lead with piano, guitars, drums.

> . . . rock 'n' roll had become the focal point for all of society's fears of miscegenation, sexuality, violence, juvenile delinquency, and general moral decline. In the eyes of many, the danger was not simply that the music was urban, sexual, and black; such music had been around for a long time. The danger was that it was no longer contained "on the other side of the tracks." Rock 'n' roll's biggest sin was to bring styles of music that were considered class- and race-specific into the mainstream and in so doing to redefine our conception of popular music.[3]

Some whites, particularly in the South, resisted the changes that were occurring, and rock 'n' roll became a target of many attacks. Rock 'n' roll was denounced as "the Devil's music" and as being part of a communist plot to undermine the morals of America's younger generation.

ASCAP/BMI AND THE PAYOLA SCANDAL

There also was a business and economic basis to the fight against rock 'n' roll. The American Society

[3] Ibid., p. 140.

American rock 'n' roll musician Chuck Berry plays guitar and sings on stage in the mid-1950s, c. 1955. *Source: Getty Images, Inc.-Hulton Archive Photos.*

of Composers, Authors, and Publishers (ASCAP) was an organization that had been formed in 1914 along with unions in other labor fields. The purpose of the organization was to collect royalties for the composers and publishers that were its members whenever their music was performed in concerts. Few rock musicians were members of ASCAP, and belonged instead to a rival organization called Broadcast Music, Inc. (BMI). BMI was formed in 1940 to collect royalties for its members for music that was broadcast over the radio or on television. BMI was founded largely out of resistance to the fees that ASCAP had been imposing and because musicians resented the monopoly ASCAP had on business. As radio and television broadcasting became an increasingly dominant performance medium, BMI became wealthier and more influential, and ASCAP was looking for ways to discredit the music BMI was handling.

One strategy for attacking BMI was to request that a congressional committee examine the practice of "payola." Payola was the process of paying a disc jockey to play new records on the radio. It was not specifically illegal at the time, but it was considered a conflict of interest and a breach of ethics in broadcasting. The investigation, which occurred in 1958, was known as the "payola scandal," and it put many small record companies and disc jockeys out of business. The record companies and disc jockeys most affected by the investigation were those who had promoted music by African-American performers, including the disc jockey Alan Freed, who had coined the phrase "rock 'n' roll."

ROCK 'N' ROLL AT THE END OF THE 1950S

By the end of the 1950s, rock 'n' roll was in danger of dying out. The "payola scandal" had put many record companies and disc jockeys out of business. Buddy Holly, Richie Vallens, and "the Big Bopper" were killed in an airplane accident. Eddie Cochran was killed in a car accident, and Carl Perkins had been severely injured in one and did not resume his career. Elvis Presley had been drafted into the army. Jerry Lee Lewis had been informally "blacklisted" because of his marriage to his young teenage cousin. Little Richard had left rock for the ministry. Chuck Berry had been arrested and was on trial for allegedly transporting a minor over state lines (many believed he had been framed).

Subsequent musicians began to put out more formula ridden music written and performed by professional writers and musicians that had less of the raw energy of early rock 'n' roll.

Described by historian Reebee Garofalo as "Schlock Rock,"[4] the music was dominated by white middle-class "teen idols" such as Fabian, Frankie Avalon, Bobby Rydell, Bobby Darin, and Annette Funicello. (This style was maintained in the next decade by stars such as Del Shannon, Gene Pitney, Ricky Nelson, Paul Anka, and Lesley Gore.) All produced safe, pop-based music. Just when critics were giving rock its final rites, several new and distinctly different but white-based styles emerged in the early 1960s: folk rock, "the British Invasion," and surf music.

Folk Rock

Teenagers in the 1950s became young adults in the 1960s, and with their growing maturity, many wanted music of greater sophistication. Just as Americans in the 1920s and 1930s looked to folk music as an alternative to mainstream commercial songs, so did young adults turn to folk music in the 1960s. Responding to this rekindled interest, folk songs were enhanced by sophisticated arrangements that appealed to college-age students. Typical of this movement was the Kingston Trio, with its clean-cut appearance and nonpolitical folk-style songs.

The folk movement was given further impetus by two societal crises that dominated the 1960s: the Civil Rights movement and the Vietnam War. The commercial folk music of the Kingston Trio gave way to more political folksingers such as Joan Baez and Bob Dylan, who aligned themselves with these and other political causes. Rather than music to dance to, this became music to listen to and to motivate one in the pursuit of social justice, world peace, and racial equality. Inspired by urban folk singers/activists Woody Guthrie and Pete Seeger, Bob Dylan was the most influential in carrying the political message.

Dylan's song "Mr. Tambourine Man" was not a political song but, rather, written to evoke the sounds and images of a Mardi Gras festival in New Orleans that Dylan had seen. When he recorded it, he sang it as a solo accompanying himself on the guitar in the folksinging tradition. Roger (Jim) McGuinn, the leader of a band called The Byrds that had been comprised of musicians who had been involved in various folk groups, decided to record it in a manner that fused both folk and rock characteristics. The singing by the group was in close, folk-styled harmonies, but the backup band included the electric guitars and drums as well as McGuinn's distinctive twelve-string acoustic guitar. The Byrds' recording of the song became a national hit, and they followed it with additional folk-rock fusions, including a version of Dylan's "All I Really Want to Do" (1965) and Pete Seeger's "Turn, Turn, Turn" (1965). Other groups, such as the Turtles, Simon and Garfunkel, The Buffalo Springfield, and Crosby, Stills, and Nash continued the folk rock tradition.

The British Invasion

The Beatles were a British group from Liverpool, England. They had begun by imitating American music styles in the early 1960s. By 1963–1964, they had achieved extraordinary commercial success and almost complete domination of the record market. The success of the Beatles ushered in a whole series of other English groups, with the most important and long-lasting being the Rolling Stones. The Rolling Stones also began their musical careers imitating American music. But, unlike the Beatles, who played "skiffle" (an imitation of American white folk music combined with jazz), the Rolling Stones played rhythm 'n' blues. In fact, in a letter to the BBC in which Brian Jones (an early founding member who drowned mysteriously in his swimming pool in 1969) was trying to get the new group airtime, Brian Jones said the band played authentic

[4] Garafalo, Reebee. *Rockin' Out: Popular Music in the U.S.A.* Upper Saddle River, NJ: Prentice Hall, 2005, p. 132.

Perhaps the most influential band in history was the Beatles, a British group who started their career creating their own versions of American pop music styles. Many of their songs continue to score high on lists from American-based television and radio programs. *Source: Getty Images, Inc.,-Hulton Archive Photos.*

Chicago blues in the style of Howlin' Wolf and Muddy Waters. (They were rejected because they sounded "too black.")

The success of the Beatles and the Stones ushered in many other British groups, giving the entire phenomenon the term "the British Invasion." The Beatles were interested in innovations and continued experimenting from 1965 to 1969 with instrumentation, textures, forms, rhythms, melodic designs, and lyrics. With their contributions, rock 'n' roll evolved into music of greater complexity and breadth that was now known as "rock."

Surf Music

Another style developed in California: surf music. Although folk and folk rock strove for honesty and the greater good of society, surf music was about girls, cars, and having fun. Centered in southern California, it emerged out of the sport of surfing and its surrounding subculture. Its early stars were Dick Dale and the Deltones, and Jan and Dean (Jan Berry and Dean Torrence). Dick Dale and his band members had worked closely with Leo Fender, the inventor of the first solid-body electric guitars, and created an intense, amplified style characterized by driving ostinatos and reverberation. Jan and Dean had "Top Forty" hits fifteen times. Their careers ended when Jan was nearly killed in an automobile accident. The real stars of surf music, however, were the Beach Boys. The group started in 1961 as a family affair—brothers Brian, Carl, and Dennis Wilson, their cousin Mike Love, and friend Al Jardine. "Surfin Safari" (1962) was the first of a "wave" of hits that also included slow ballads such as "Surfer Girl."

Brian Wilson was the leading force, and under his guidance the band moved into their postsurf stage with "Good Vibrations." "Good Vibrations," the result of ninety hours of studio time, was musically and technically one of their most sophisticated rock songs to date and became a million-seller. Encouraged by the success of "Good Vibrations," Brian continued into a more experimental realm, but the rest of the group was reluctant and worried about its commercial appeal. Only the Beatles were experimenting along such lines at this time and, ironically, the Beach Boys were paralleling them in many ways. Ultimately, the Beach Boys were typecast, and could never successfully break out of the naïve and simple style that launched their careers.

Later Developments of Rock

Rock music continued to absorb other influences and spawn new styles, signaling innovations on many fronts and often simultaneously. The earlier instrumentation of saxophone, piano, amplified guitar, and drums expanded to several guitars, electronic keyboards, a variety of other instruments (including world instruments), and an increasing reliance on electronic technology. The separation of composer and performer gave way to the merging of the single performer-composer. New forms were added to the original forms of the twelve-bar blues and the thirty-two-bar song form. Song lyrics used to deal only with teenage love and adolescent concerns; lyrics now included everything from social commentary to sophisticated free-association poetry.

As it has continued to evolve, it has hybridized such that the term "rock" has been joined with many other terms. Thus, "Country Rock" describes music that represents the fusion of rock with country music elements. "Christian Rock" describes rock music with Christian-inspired lyrics. Terms have been devised to describe and classify rock-based music using a variety of criteria. For example, Hard Rock/Soft Rock distinguishes the music based on its energy and volume. Classic Rock/Modern Rock distinguishes it on its historical placement. "Glam Rock" describes groups such as David Bowie's Ziggie Stardust and The New York Dolls that emphasized tongue-in-cheek glamour and sexually ambiguous costumes, makeup, props, and attitude. "Goth Rock" describes bands such as Dead Can Dance and Marilyn Manson, who embraced morbid "Gothic" imagery. "Jam Rock" is a term sometimes used to describe bands that emphasize improvisation, such as the Dave Matthews Band, Phish, and Ben Harper, as "jamming" is a term used to describe musicians gathering to improvise and create music.

"Rock" is now such a vague term and could be used to categorize the work of so many different musicians that its power as identifying a genre of music is fairly meaningless. Nevertheless, what follows is an attempt to describe the most significant and easily recognizable broad genres, adopting the organization, definitions, and representative artists provided by Audiogalaxy (http://www.audiogalaxy.com) in 2005. It addresses only white-based rock (as distinguished from African-American and Latin-based genres that are covered in other chapters) and does not include coverage of styles such as disco, pop, and electronica that developed in parallel to the main currents of rock evolution.

Acid and Psychedelic Rock, New Psychedelia

"Acid" is the nickname for LSD, an illegal hallucinogenic drug made from lysergic acid that became very popular in the 1960s along with the hippie culture. One of the earliest departures from the conventional rock groups, "Acid Rock" evolved out of the LSD-inspired bands that flourished particularly (although not solely) in the San Francisco area. Prominent San Francisco-based bands include Janis Joplin and the Holding Company, Jefferson Airplane, The Grateful Dead, Country Joe and the Fish, and the Quicksilver Messenger Service. Groups from other places also made important contributions to this genre, such as The Jimi Hendrix Experience, The Doors, Led Zeppelin, and Cream. In its earliest forms, acid rock blended amplified, bluesy-based rock with drugs, using various techniques to manipulate the music (such as rapid note repetitions or distortions) that enhanced psychedelic perceptions. In the 1990s, renewed interest in this approach led to a genre called New Psychedelia. New Psychedelia musicians emerged primarily in Athens, Georgia, with a loosely organized but prolific group of musicians called the Elephant 6 collective. Released under names such as Dressy Bessy, Elf Power, the Minders, and Beulah, these groups emphasize an ecstatic approach with a love for unusual instruments and synethsized sounds.

Metal

"Heavy Metal" evolved out of Acid Rock, and is a name that is said to have been devised by a British journalist who described early Led Zeppelin as sounding like heavy metal crashing to earth. Heavy Metal is characterized by power, volume, and aggressiveness, often combined with technical speed and virtuosic musicianship. Early bands that were influential in this genre include AC/DC and Black Sabbath. Later metal groups, such as Alice Cooper and Kiss, made their performances even harder and heavier by incorporating animal rituals, pyrotechnics, and gender-bending androgyny through the use of elaborate costumes and makeup. Later still, Jon Bon Jovi brought in elements of romance, which softened metal and extended its appeal to female audiences. (Because of Bon Jovi's elaborate hair, his style has been called "Hair Metal.") As a reaction to this "lightening" up of metal, Speed/Thrash Metal emerged on the West Coast with Metallica, Slayer, Anthrax and Nuclear Assault. These groups "cranked" up the music's speed as well as the hostility and menacing quality of the lyrics, sometimes incorporating themes of justice and environmental concern. As with so many other broad genres, the basic approaches of metal music were combined with other influences to create several different subgenres such as Industrial Metal, Nu Metal, and Death Metal.

Punk, Grunge, and Post Punk

Punk rock emerged as a defiant reaction against the heavily produced Disco and Glam Rock music in the late 1970s. Outraged by the bloated egos, artistic excess, and expensive production requirements that seemed to characterize these dominant styles, punk emerged nearly simultaneously in New York with the Ramones and in London with the Sex Pistols. Other punk groups included Dead Kennedys, Clash, and The Misfits. In an attempt to regain the energy and accessibility that characterized rock 'n' roll's earlier years, punk musicians reduced rock to the essentials: three-guitar riffs, loud and fast beats, and angry lyrics. Although there were occasional mainstream hits, it primarily remained underground, subdividing into subgenres such as Hardcore Punk, Art Punk, Cow Punk, Pop Punk, and Ska Punk, until the term "punk" lost much of its descriptive power. Groups such as Green Day and Smashing Pumpkins are examples of punk-influenced groups. In the late 1980s, bands that combined punk attitude with emphasis on drug use to create a kind of fuzzed out, buzzy, stop/start aesthetic were called "Grunge." Most of these bands came out of the Seattle area, with Nirvana being the most famous. More commercially friendly bands that followed Nirvana include Pearl Jam, Creed, Stone Temple Pilots, Bush, and Everclear. Bands such as U2 and The Fall, who continued to experiment by abandoning the standard rock instrumentation and incorporating synthesizers and guitars to create lush, layered sounds, have created music that is sometimes referred to as Post Punk.

Art, Jazz, and Experimental Rock

Starting in the late 1960s, several musicians attempted to "elevate" the quality of rock music by incorporating various aspects of classical or jazz music. Groups such as The Moody Blues, Pink Floyd, Emerson, Lake, and Palmer, Jethro Tull, and Yes incorporated synthesizers, "quotations" of classical compositions, and "classical art music elements" such as orchestral instruments and complex treatment of formal elements. Other groups, such as Chicago, Blood, Sweat, and Tears, and Steely Dan continued with Miles Davis's experimentations of fusing rock with jazz elements, especially in the way the groups dealt with instrumentation, harmony, form, and improvisation. In

Break-Out Two

IN-DEPTH FOCUS *John Mayer and the Search for Superstars*

In "Packaging Pop Trends: The Search for the Next Big Thing," the music historian Reebee Garofalo describes the music industry's current search for superstars. "In its current form, the music industry needs stars—superstars, really—like fish need water. Superstars are what make everything else work for the industry—the formidable marketing apparatus, radio promotion, music videos, and live performance touring circuits. The major labels are prepared to risk millions of dollars in search of that one artist or group who will make up for dozens of others who, according to record company accounting, lose money."[5] Garofalo further explains that if a single artist can sell forty million units, it is less expensive than forty artists selling one million units each because the industry does not have to duplicate the marketing and promotion costs forty times. Thus, it is in the industry's financial interests to promote as few artists as possible.

One of the most successful of the new "superstars" is John Mayer. Mayer briefly attended Berklee College of Music in Boston, and then settled down in Atlanta, where he performed regularly at local clubs. He released his debut solo album, *Inside Want Out*, on an independent label in 1999. Consisting of solo singing with acoustic guitar accompaniment, the album demonstrated Mayer's exceptional guitar technique and songwriting ability. In 2000, his performance at the South by Southwest Music Festival generated a recording contract with Aware Records, a small label owned by Columbia.

Produced by John Alagia, who had previously worked with Dave Matthews, the new *Room for Squares* album featured a full electric band. Columbia re-released the album adding one bonus track in 2001. Mayer's intense worldwide touring schedule combined with word-of-mouth helped him acquire a large and dedicated fan base. By 2003, the album had gone triple-platinum and had remained in the Billboard "Top One Hundred" for more than eighty consecutive weeks. Spawning three hit singles, the album also generated his first Grammy award for "Best Male Vocal Performance" with the song "Your Body Is a Wonderland." Another successful live album, *Any Given Thursday*, was followed by the much anticipated *Heavier Things*, released in 2004.

[5] Garafalo, Reebee, *Rockin' Out*, pp. 379–380.

more recent years, musicians who have retained the essential rock components but experiment extensively with new sounds and production techniques on a consistent basis have been classified as "Experimental Rock." Bands such as Oingo Boingo, Sonic Youth, and Pram exemplify this category.

ALTERNATIVE AND INDIE ROCK

The broad and vague term "Alternative" was originally used to describe any nonmainstream rock groups. But the lines between alternative and mainstream pop became blurred in the early 1990s when formerly alternative bands such as Nirvana, Sonic Youth, and the Red Hot Chili Peppers became commercially successful. Soon pop bands started adopting alternative characteristics, and alternative bands were marketed to pop music audiences. Currently, anything not immediately recognized as "pop"—from Rock of Soundgarden to Smashmouth—is typically labeled "alternative." Within "Alternative" there are several subgenres. For example, "Adult Alternative" emerged in the mid-1990s as a reaction to the growing mainstream acceptance of earlier Alternative bands. Representative groups include Counting Crows, Hootie and the

Fully conscious of the pressure, Mayer commented, "In some ways the stakes get higher when you make a second major-label record and everyone's looking. And in some ways, absolutely nothing is different, because your voice still sounds the same and your hands still feel the same on the guitar. You just write your songs. You're just a guy with a guitar putting in a Thai food order at 9 P.M."[6]

Guitarist and singer John Mayer performs at the Fleet Pavilion in Boston, July 17, 2002.
Source: CORBIS-NY. Photo by Steven Tackeff. © Steven Tackeff/ZUMA/CORBIS. All Rights Reserved.

Heavier Things was recorded in New York and finished in Los Angeles, produced by Jack Joseph Puig. Puig had worked with Sheryl Crow, the Black Crowes, Hole, and Jellyfish. In Mayer's words, "Jack understood what I wanted to do next. . . . He understands the romance of making records. Jack and I pushed each other to the limits of our knowledge, and that's why the record is as fresh as it is. There are raw decisions made out of the comfort zone of past achievement."[7] The song "Daughters" from this album earned him another Grammy, this time for "Song of the Year."

In a 1979 interview reprinted in 2005 after his death, Johnny Carson commented, "Rock stars have not been able to handle the fame and money thrown at them."[8] It is interesting that in the CD liner inserts for Mayer's *Heavier Things*, the track listings are presented in a graphic of a game spinner wheel and that the opening track, "Clarity," includes the lyrics, "I worry . . . and I will wait to find if this will last forever, and I will wait to find that it won't and it won't because it can't (it's not supposed to)." Whether or not Mayer can continue to preserve a sense of personal balance and artistic integrity under such intense industry pressure is yet to be seen.

[6] "About John Mayer." http://www.johnmayer.com/flash/index.html (Accessed 02-23-05).
[7] Ibid.
[8] "The King of the Night," *Rolling Stone*, February 24, 2005, p. 35.

Blowfish, and the Gin Blossoms, and later groups such as Third Eye Blind and Matchbox Twenty.

Derived from the term "Independent, " "Indie Rock" is used to describe the bands who continued to resist the increasing commercialism of punk-inspired music and the coopting of alternative music. Rather than a specific sound, it is used to describe a guitar-based, "Do-It-Yourself" aesthetic of musicians who record on independent labels. Groups such as Sebadoh, Guided by Voices, Superchunk, Beat Happening, Shellac, and Dashboard Confessional are examples of prominent "Indie" rockers.

Conclusion

Originally the marginalized musical expression of a rebellious youth culture, rock music now has widespread mainstream acceptance. Its emergence in the 1950s signaled a move away from the dominance of European-based culture to a culture that clearly incorporates the influences of other ethnic and racial groups, particularly those of African Americans. Its history is also closely intertwined with significant shifts in other social and cultural areas. Before rock 'n' roll, popular music was not age-specific. Rock 'n' roll helped herald in the increasing consumer and cultural clout of youth. Earlier music genres were acoustic. Rock music helped launch increasing musician dependence on technology. Finally, as one of the most powerful American influences on the rest of the world, it has helped herald our transition from a national to a global community.

Bibliography

"About John Mayer." http://www.johnmayer.com/flash/index.html (Accessed 02-23-05).

Barnard, Stephen. *Rock: An Illustrated History.* New York: Schirmer Books, 1986.

"Berry, Chuck," in *Contemporary Musicians: Profiles of the People in Music.* Michael L. LaBlanc (Editor). Detroit, MI: Gale Research, Inc.; vol. 1, pp. 22–25.

DeWitt, Howard A. *Elvis, the Sun Years: The Story of Elvis Presley in the Fifties.* Ann Arbor, MI: Popular Culture, Ink, 1993.

Du Noyer, Paul, consulting editor. *The Story of Rock 'n' Roll: The Year-By-Year Illustrated Chronicle.* New York: Schirmer Books. 1995.

Garafalo, Reebee. *Rockin' Out: Popular Music in the U.S.A.* Upper Saddle River, NJ: Prentice Hall, 2005, p. 132.

Harris, James F. "Listen to the Music: The Meaning of Classic Rock," *The World & I.* http://www.elibrary.com/s/edumark/getdoc.cgi?id+195291447x12 . . . :US;EL&dtype=0~0&dinst= (Accessed 05-07-01).

"The King of the Night," *Rolling Stone*, February 24, 2005, pp. 33–35.

Palmer, Robert. "The Fifties," *Rolling Stone.* April 19, 1990, p. 48.

Palmer, Robert. *Rock & Roll: An Unruly History.* New York: Harmony Books, 1995.

"Presley, Elvis," in *Contemporary Musicians: Profiles of the People in Music.* Michael L. LaBlanc (Editor.) Detroit, MI: Gale Research, Inc.; vol. 1, pp. 175–179.

Rock & Roll Generation: Teen Life in the 50s. Editors of Time-Life Books; with foreword by Dick Clark. Alexandria, VA: Time-Life Books, 1998.

Rollingstone Encyclopedia of Rock & Roll. Jon Pareles (Consulting Editor). New York: Rollingstone Press/Summit Books, 1983.

"Songwriter Nil Lara Builds Music by Bridging Cultures". (discussion) (*Morning Edition- (NPR)*) host Bob Edwards; http://www.elibrary.com/s/edumark/getdoc.cgi?id+195291447x12 . . . :US;EL&dtype=0~0&dinst= (Accessed 05-07-01).

———. "Today in Music: A Look Back at Popular Music." United Press International via COMTEX. http://www.elibrary.com/s/edumark/getdo . . . rn:bigchalk.com:US;EL&dtype=0~=&dinst=0 (Accessed 05-07-01).

Waksman, Steve. *Instruments of Desire: The Electric Guitar and the Shaping of Musical Experience.* Cambridge, MA: Harvard University Press, 1999.

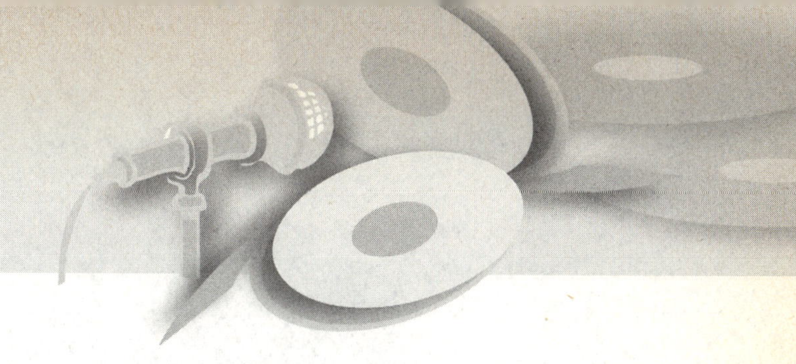

Chapter Thirteen

Soul, Motown, and Funk

For African Americans, the 1960s were marked by both despair and celebration. Building on efforts of the 1950s, the tumultuous decade opened with attempts to integrate the still racially segregated schools and public facilities in the South. On February 1, 1960, four African-American students in Greensboro, North Carolina, sat down at the segregated lunch counter in Woolworth's, waiting all day without being served. Their patient courage inspired eighty-five demonstrators to join them over the following two days. The year 1961 brought the "freedom rides," where two buses carrying black and white passengers traveled throughout the South to test the segregation of interstate bus terminals. They met only minor problems in some states, but in Alabama one of the buses was burned and the riders were attacked as they attempted to flee the bus. Several were beaten severely, as the police had refused to protect the freedom riders. In 1963, in a demonstration in Birmingham, Alabama, the city's commissioner of public safety ordered police to chase demonstrators with dogs and use fire hoses to blast them against buildings. Later that year, a quarter of a million people, black and white, marched to the Lincoln Memorial in Washington, DC, to listen to Martin Luther King Jr. deliver his "I Have a Dream" speech and sing "We Shall Overcome."

In July 1964, the mounting anger and frustration of African Americans erupted in violent riots in New York's black ghettos in Rochester, Harlem, and Brooklyn. Before the riots subsided, two hundred people, most of them African Americans, were killed. On August 11, 1965, the Watts neighborhood in Los Angeles, California, also exploded. Rioting, looting, and arson spread through the community for two days until the National Guard came in and occupied the neighborhood on August 14 and 15. Three more years of racial unrest followed, including riots in Detroit, where forty-three people died and blocks of buildings blazed on fire. During this period of civil disturbance and the fight for civil rights, several new genres of African-American music emerged that are of critical importance to American music: Soul, Motown, and Funk.

Overview of the Musical Characteristics of Soul, Motown, and Funk

Soul Music

Soul music was created by and for African Americans through the merging of black Gospel with rhythm 'n' blues that began in the late 1950s. Most of the artists that performed soul music were

Members of the Mississippi Freedom Democratic Party are led by Fanny Lou Haner in a song as they protest at the National Democratic Convention in August 1964. *Source: Photo by George Ballis. Take Stock—Images of Change.*

Gospel singers and instrumentalists who combined some of the traditions of the black church (emotional singing, call-and-response, the stress on the backbeat, and rhythmic complexity) with the secular traditions of popular music (primarily the subject matter of the lyrics and the performance venues). Soul music represented an authentic "blackness" that supported and reinforced the Black Power and Civil Rights movement. Soul singers sang of social injustice, black militancy, and racial pride. The music also preached a message of nonviolence and love. It celebrated the growing Black Consciousness Movement, a time of struggle as well as unprecedented gains. Soul music was tangible evidence that the psyche and attitudes in the black community were changing. The civil rights movement was empowering black people, and the new soul music celebrated rights finally won and expressed hope for the future. Soul music spoke of a determination to "Move on Up" and get "Respect," and it encouraged the black community that "Our Day Will Come."[1] Major soul artists include Ray Charles, Sam Cooke, Jackie Wilson, Aretha Franklin, Wilson Pickett, Otis Redding, Jerry Butler, Nina Simone, Marvin Gaye, and Al Green.

Police in Birmingham, Alabama, used dogs, fire hoses, and nightsticks to break up a civil rights demonstration in 1963. *Source: AP Wide World Photos.*

[1] These are titles to soul songs by Aretha Franklin and Ruby and the Romantics.

Motown

The Motown sound was the creation of Berry Gordy Jr., through his record company "Motown," established in Detroit, Michigan. From the beginning, Gordy intended to create crossover hits that would appeal to mainstream white Americans as well as African Americans. Many of the most popular songs were the products of the songwriting and production team Holland-Dozier-Holland. The various artists and vocal groups were accompanied by sophisticated arrangements played by the jazz-trained studio backup band known as The Funk Brothers. This core group of musicians was augmented as needed by other rhythm 'n' blues and jazz instrumentalists, and even classical string ensembles. Except for the use of call-and-response and the complex polyrhythmic foundations created by the Motown percussionists (who often used nonstandard instruments and sources to create their rhythmic textures), African-derived music characteristics were downplayed in favor of a more popular crossover style. The songs used a variety of forms besides the standard AABA, and always had a catchy melodic hook. Major Motown artists include the Supremes, the Temptations, The Miracles, Marvin Gaye, the Marvellettes, Martha and the Vandellas, Stevie Wonder, The Jackson Five and later Michael Jackson, The Commodores, and Lionel Richie.

Funk

Begun by the soul singer James Brown in the mid-1960s, "funk" is a style of music that uses characteristics derived consciously and emphatically from African traditions. One of the most important of these characteristics is polyrhythm, in which each instrument or instrument group repeats its own simple rhythmic pattern, creating complex rhythmic textures by overlaying these patterns. In funk, even instruments such as the horns that in other music genres are used to play melodies, play repeated rhythmic patterns or punctuate the rhythm. The harmonies focus on a few simple chords that are also repeated, contributing to the development of a strong "groove." Additionally, call-and-response between the singers and the audience reflects the African roots. Important funk artists include James Brown, Sly and the Family Stone, Earth, Wind, and Fire, George Clinton, and Kool and the Gang.

Soul, Motown, and Funk in a Historical and Social Context

Soul Music

Background of the Term "Soul"

The term "soul" had been used in the late 1950s by African Americans to represent black identity. Beginning in 1957, a series of jazz bebop musicians used *soul* in the titles of their recordings. The horn player Lou Donaldson recorded *Swing and Soul* (1957), the saxophonist John Coltrane released *Soultrane* (1958), and the trombonist Bennie Green cut *Soul Stirring* (1958) and *Hornful of Soul* (1959). In the 1960s, collard greens, black-eyed peas, and sweet potato pie became "soul food," and fellow blacks became "soul brothers" and "soul sisters." The influential Black Panther Eldridge Cleaver wrote the book *Soul on Ice*, and referred to the shifts from bop to hard bop as "soul music." But the term in relationship to music did not really come into common usage until the middle-to-late 1960s, by which time it was used to refer to a new kind of popular music that had evolved out of the merging of black Gospel with rhythm 'n' blues.

Early Soul Music

The earliest soul music was created in the late 1950s and early 1960s with artists such as Ray Charles, Sam Cooke, Jackie Wilson, and James Brown.

Ray Charles

Ray Charles Robinson (1930–2004) was blinded by glaucoma when he was six years old. He had already started learning to play the piano, and when he could no longer see, he continued to learn other instruments, including trumpet, saxophone, and clarinet. He also learned to read and write music notation in Braille. When he was fifteen years old, he was orphaned and began to make his living by playing music. Ray Charles had grown up listening to Gospel music as well as rhythm 'n' blues, and he started to fuse elements of both of these traditions. One way he merged the traditions was simply to incorporate Gospel characteristics into his rhythm 'n' blues songs, such as in his 1956 hit "Hallelujah, I Love Her So." Another way was to take an actual Gospel song and secularize it, primarily by changing the topic of the lyrics. For example, "I've Got a Woman" (1955) is derived from Alex Branford's Gospel song "I've Got a Savior," and "This Little Girl of Mine" is a remake of the Clara Ward Singers' version of "This Little Light of Mine." Naturally, this practice of taking songs that were sung in the church and turning them into worldly secular pop hits was resented by many religious people. The first recording to be identified as "soul" was his "What'd I Say" (1959). It contained call-and-response patterns and used an electric piano that simulated the church organ sound.

SAM COOKE

Sam Cooke (1935–1964) began to sing professionally in 1951 when he accepted the lead vocal role in the already established Gospel group the Soul Stirrers. To avoid upsetting the religious community when he decided to perform secular music, he assumed the name Dale Cooke for his recording of "Lovable" (1956). By 1957, he felt secure enough in his secular identity to record "You Send Me" under his own name. This hit launched his career as a pop idol and he went on to score nineteen "Top Forty" hits, including "Chain Gang" (1960), "Another Saturday Night" (1963), and "Shake" (1964). Cooke achieved considerable success, even forming his own publishing company and being one of the first African Americans to be signed by the major record label, RCA. Unfortunately, his life was cut short when he was shot to death under suspicious circumstances in a motel room in 1964.

JACKIE WILSON

Jackie Wilson (1934–1984) began his career in 1953 as lead vocalist for the Dominoes. Wilson had been a gospel singer and had a versatile voice that easily crossed over into pop. He later worked with Motown's founder Berry Gordy Jr. to influence Motown and other styles of the sixties. He made many hit records, and performed in an energetic style that garnered him a large fan following. In 1975, he suffered a heart attack on stage and lapsed into a coma, in which he remained until his death in 1984.

JAMES BROWN

While Ray Charles, Sam Cooke, and Jackie Wilson sang soul in a style that crossed over to white audiences, James Brown intended his music for blacks. James Brown was born in 1928 in Macon, Georgia. His mother had left him in the care of her sister when he was five years old, and James helped in the financial support of his aunt by dancing on street corners for tips. When he was a little older, he started singing Gospel in the August Baptist Church in Augusta, Georgia. Later, arrested and sent to prison, he formed a musical combo with a small group of inmates who used a modified washtub as a string bass and pocket combs for harmonicas. In his early twenties, he returned to his Gospel roots and was accepted into the group The Swanees. In the mid-1950s, when the Swanees moved to secular music with Brown as the lead singer, they changed their name to the Famous Flames. With the Flames as his backup band, he recorded the hit "Please, Please, Please" in 1956, and with just one word sung in a shouting, squealing, howling style, the song became a hit. James Brown had a style of singing that was very forceful and incorporated energetic vocal embellishments.

He made his concerts even more powerful with his physically dynamic stage presence, which involved rhythmic dance steps, leg splits, and drops to the knees. Part of his performance was to collapse on stage from the emotional fervor of his singing, something that he had seen African-American

Break-Out One

LISTENING GUIDE *"Say It Loud: I'm Black and I'm Proud"*

Performing Artist: James Brown

James Brown (born in 1928) started performing simply to make money to survive. When he was five years old, his mother left him to be raised by her sister. Brown earned money to help support his aunt by dancing on street corners. As a youth he sang Gospel in church and in his early twenties he was accepted into the Gospel group, The Swanees. This group changed their name to the Famous Flames when they began to sing nonreligious music, and released their first hit song "Please, Please, Please" in 1956, a Gospel-styled secular song. During the Civil Rights era, Brown delivered preacher-like messages addressing African-American pride in several of his songs. This song, released in 1968, was one of these important contributions.

Rhythm	Quadruple, with backbeat accented by guitar and horns. Polyrhythms created among the horns, bass, and the drums with each instrumental group maintaining their own rhythmic pattern that is simple but repetitious.
Melody	Emphasizes rhythmic speech.
Harmony	Notice the emphasis of a single chord for long sections, emphasizing rhythm as the foundation for the piece.
Texture	Listen to the call-and-response and complex rhythmic texturing.
Form	Repetitious single phrases.
Instrumentation	Solo male voice with chorus; emphasis on guitar, drums, horns.

preachers do during particularly intense worship services. His use of a very prominent horn section, call-and-response performance texture, and charismatic showmanship made him a star in the black community as well as Europe and England in the mid-1960s. His various titles include the "Godfather of Soul," "Soul Brother Number One," and "Mr. Dynamite." In the mid-1960s, he shifted to a style called "funk" that celebrated black heritage even more emphatically. Several of his songs became anthems for the Black Power movement, including songs such as "Black Is Beautiful," "Say It Loud (I'm Black and I'm Proud)," and "I Don't Want Nobody Givin' Me Nothin' (Open Up the Door, I'll Get It Myself)." His *Live at the Apollo*, Vol. I, became one of soul music's biggest hits and was on the *Billboard Charts* for sixty-six weeks. In keeping with the concept of the black community helping itself in the 1960s, James Brown helped raise millions of dollars for charity and owned five radio stations.

Geographical Centers for Soul Music

There were three geographical areas in which soul music developed and flourished: Chicago, Detroit, and Memphis.

Chicago Soul

Chicago, long a center for blues, developed its own style of soul music that is best exemplified by Curtis Mayfield and the Impressions.

Break-Out Two

PROFILE *Aretha Franklin*

Aretha Franklin, known to many as "Lady Soul," began her musical career as a young girl singing in her father's church in Detroit, Michigan. Her father was one of the most successful black preachers in the North and, through his ministry, she was exposed to the best Gospel music of the day. Not only was her mother reputedly a superb Gospel singer, but Aretha also heard some of the greatest professional Gospel singers who were traveling on the evangelical circuit. In 1960, when she was eighteen, Aretha decided to try to make it as a popular singer and went to New York to work with the legendary producer and talent scout John Hammond of Columbia Records.

American Soual singer Aretha Franklin, a star on the motoron record label, May 1968. *Source: Getty Images, Inc.-Hulton Archive Photos.*

John Hammond had been involved with African-American artists for years. In fact, it was he who is often credited with bringing Gospel music into popular culture through his show "From Spirituals to Swing" that he had presented at Carnegie Hall in New York City back in 1933. Over the years he had recorded, produced, and promoted many of the most famous black singers, including Bessie Smith and Billie Holiday. Aretha's first single, "Today I Sing the Blues," was created in this tradition, treated as a "race record," and marketed and distributed only to black audiences.

In an effort to increase her success, Columbia executive Mitch Miller (the host of the popular television program, "Sing Along with Mitch") decided to try to widen her appeal by transforming her into one of the growing number of crossover artists such as Dionne Warwick and Nancy Wilson. To accomplish this, he arranged for Aretha to receive voice lessons and hired

Curtis Mayfield and the Impressions. Born in Chicago in 1942, Curtis Mayfield began writing music when he was eleven, and he sang with the Northern Jubilee Gospel Singers as a teenager. His soft, high-pitched tenor voice was easily recognizable, and as the lead singer with the Impressions, he created a style that was distinctive and inspirational. He developed a reputation as a thoughtful lyricist who was able to articulate the problems of race in particular and the nation in general. Songs such as "Keep On Pushing," "This Is My Country," "Choice of Colors," and "We're a Winner" were both motivational and overtly political. He stressed that he had two main messages, faith and inspiration, and he attributed his positive outlook to the upbringing he received by his grandmother. In 1961 he sang the lead on the Impressions' recording of "Gypsy Woman," which incorporated flamenco-styled rhythms and castanets. He also produced the Impressions' recording of "Amen" that became a hit and was a featured song in the movie *Lilies of the Field* (1963). Later, Mayfield

famous musicians such as Bob Mersey (who also worked with Barbra Streisand) to arrange for her show tunes and jazz standards. These recordings forced her to abandon much of her Gospel traditions—not only was she no longer able to accompany herself on the piano, but she was also required to sing in a cool, precise and controlled manner that was the antithesis of the free and emotional style characteristic of Gospel singing. The records were only moderately successful, and by the end of 1966 she was deeply depressed and in debt to Columbia Records.

When Aretha's contract expired with Columbia, she went to work for Atlantic Records in their studios in Muscle Shoals, Alabama. Here, white musicians Jerry Wexler and Rick Hall, who had been accustomed to working with black artists in the more purely African-American music tradition known as soul, allowed her much more freedom in the recording studio. She was allowed to choose her own songs, and was also able to work out the arrangements she preferred with the studio band. The first album she released for Atlantic Records, *I Never Loved a Man the Way I Love You*, and its opening cut, "Respect," exploded on the scene in 1967. For the next three years, she became one of the most popular black musicians, with nine million-selling singles and three million-selling albums, including hits such as "Dr. Feelgood," "A Natural Woman," "Baby, I Love You," "Chain of Fools," and "Think." She was named the Best Female Vocalist of the Year and in 1968, Detroit mayor Jerome Cavanaugh declared a special day, "Aretha Franklin Day."

But by 1969, "soul" music was on the decline and with it, Aretha Franklin's popularity began to wane. She returned to Columbia Records, abandoned her soul style and attempted to retrieve the mainstream pop and jazz style of her earlier career. Recording songs such as the Beatles' "Eleanor Rigby" and, with Duane Allman of the Allman Brothers, "The Weight," she attempted—and failed—to appeal to the post-Woodstock counterculture crowd. Although she continued to record, she was still considered "Lady Soul" of the 1960s. With the passage of that decade, she became a culturally displaced musician as both whites and African Americans moved on to new and different musical styles.

In 1972, Aretha went back to church and delivered what many consider to be her greatest performance. With her Baptist minister father, the Reverend C. L. Franklin, guiding her, she joined another of her mentors, the Reverend James Cleveland and his Southern California Community Choir, to rework the Gospel songs and spirituals of her childhood. These songs were issued as the double album *Amazing Grace* and released by WEA/Atlantic. *Amazing Grace* went on to become a gold record, and it is considered one of the best church recordings by one of the greatest singers of all time. Aretha is now heralded as the undisputed queen of rhythm 'n' blues, has won an amazing fifteen Grammy awards, and holds the record as the woman with the most Grammy nominations (thirty-nine). In 1985, she became the first woman in history to be inducted into the Rock 'n' Roll Hall of Fame.

wrote the score for the movie *Superfly* (1972). This soundtrack, as well as his album *Back to the World* (1973), achieved gold record status.

DETROIT

Detroit, Michigan, was not home of a particular soul style, but it was the hometown of several soul musicians, the most important being Aretha Franklin.

Aretha Franklin. The "Queen of Soul," Aretha Franklin, was born in 1942. Aretha was the second of six children whose father was a minister in Detroit. By the age of fourteen, she was traveling throughout the Midwest singing Gospel music in various churches. The great Gospel singer, Mahalia Jackson, was a major influence in Aretha's life. When Aretha's mother died when Aretha was ten, Mahalia became a surrogate mother to the family. After Aretha turned eighteen, she went against the advice and wishes of Mahalia and joined a soul circuit, touring with artists such as Sam Cooke, Mavis Staples, and Lou Rawls, all of whom came from a Gospel music background. Her recording titled "Respect" was so popular during the riots of 1967 that the time became known as the summer of "'Retha, rap, and revolt."[2]

MEMPHIS SOUL

The more "down home" of the three areas was the "Southern Soul" music issued by the Stax/Volt label in Memphis, Tennessee. Memphis had been an important musical center for early rock 'n' roll with Sam Phillips and his "Sun Records" label that had recorded many early rhythm 'n' blues and rock 'n' roll artists, including B. B. King and Elvis Presley.

The Stax/Volt Recording Label. In the 1960s, Stax was founded by Jim Stewart, a white banker, and his sister Estelle Axton. The first two letters of their last names were the basis for the name Stax. Part of the reason Stax was important was because the musicians, staff, and production crew were racially integrated, not a common phenomenon in the tumultuous period of the early sixties in the South. Volt was a companion label to Stax (thus the Stax/Volt label) and most of the Memphis soul artists began their careers recording for these two labels. In 1965, Stax appointed Al Bell, a former DJ and Stax's first black executive, to head up sales. Bell's promotional savvy resulted in Stax expanding to about one hundred acts by 1967.

Booker T. and the MGs. Memphis soul recordings used a consistent backup instrumental group called Booker T. and the MGs. The organist/arranger of the group was Booker T. Jones, but the name also served to honor the important African-American educator and inventor Booker T. Washington. The "MGs" stood for "Memphis Group." Steve Cropper, one of two white musicians in the group, played guitar and also became an important songwriter. In addition to the organ, bass, and drums instrumentation provided by Booker T. and the MGs, the recordings frequently used horns.

Wilson Pickett. One of the important solo performers for Memphis Soul was Wilson Pickett. Pickett was born in Alabama but moved to Detroit where he sang Gospel music with the Violinaires. He later abandoned Gospel style to sing rhythm 'n' blues with the Falcons. He returned to his Gospel style when his producer, Jerry Wexler, sent him to record with Stax in Memphis. It was there that in 1965 he recorded "In the Midnight Hour" (co-written at the recording session by Pickett and Cropper), which had overt Gospel music characteristics.

Otis Redding. The main artist and biggest-selling singer at Stax was Otis Redding. Redding was born in 1941 in Macon, Georgia (birthplace of Little Richard and James Brown). In 1962,

Otis Redding (1947–1967) was a soul singer whose powerful, Gospel-based singing also was popular with white audiences. Studio portrait, c. 1965.
Source: *Getty Images, Inc.,-Hulton Archive Photos.*

[2] Haskins, James. *Black Music in America: A History Through Its People.* New York: Thomas Crowell, 1987.

Redding drove some friends (Johnny Jenkins and the Pinetoppers) to the Stax studio to record. When they were finished, they had thirty minutes of recording time left and Otis asked if he could record a song. He sang a song in the style of Little Richard, and the Stax president, Jim Stewart, told him the world didn't need another Little Richard. Redding instead recorded the Gospel song "These Arms of Mine." Stewart issued Redding a contract, released the recording and it became Redding's first hit. Redding's recordings of "Try a Little Tenderness" and "Dock of the Bay" sold millions, and he was one of the first soul music artists to have real commercial success with white audiences. He and several members of his band died in an airplane crash in 1967.

Motown

Precursors to Motown

The Motown sound was conceived and developed by Berry Gordy Jr. Born the seventh of eight children to Bertha and Berry Gordy Sr. in 1929, Berry dropped out of high school to become a boxer. After a short stint in the army, he opened a jazz record store with the financial backing of the Gordy family. The record store failed. In Berry's own words, most blacks had by this time shifted their interest away from bebop jazz to rhythm 'n' blues. Berry began working for one of the automobile manufacturing plants, which were the largest employers in Detroit, and which earned the city the moniker the "motor city." While working as a chrome trimmer on the assembly line, Berry was consistently writing songs and submitting them to magazines and contests. Jackie Wilson recorded Berry Gordy's first successful song in 1957, titled "Reet Petite." He and Wilson had four more hits from 1957 to 1959, and it was also in 1957 that Berry Gordy discovered The Miracles.

The Lincoln-Mercury assembly line was the model for Gordy and his vision of a business operation that he conceived of as "Hitsville, U.S.A." With his help, he hoped that young artists who had come into the front door unknown, would be polished performers and stars by the time they came off the "assembly line." By 1958, Gordy had put together a team of writers and producers of great talent consisting of "Smokey" Robinson and the brothers Brian and Eddie Holland. In 1959, Gordy started his own record label called Tamla, whose release of Marv Johnson's "You Got What It Takes" was the first of his many hits.

Founding of Motown Records

In 1960, Gordy formed his second recording label and called it Motown, a play on words honoring Detroit's role as "motor city." It was on this label that he issued the Miracles' third release, "Way Over There," followed by another hit, "Shop Around." Encouraged by these hits, Gordy signed other young black Detroit musicians. Eventually, his artists would include an amazing lineup of stars who flourished in a consistent series of major pop hits. His artists at Motown included the Supremes, the Temptations, The Miracles, Marvin Gaye, the Marvellettes, the Four Tops, Martha and the Vandellas, Stevie Wonder, The Jackson Five (with the young Michael Jackson), Junior Walker and the All Stars, The Commodores, and Lionel Richie. Motown would also expand to include several record labels beyond Tamla and Motown, including Gordy, Soul, VIP, Mowest, and Melody. He also founded a music publishing company called Jobete, using the first letters of the names of his three daughters Joy, Betty, and Terry.

Berry Gordy Jr.'s Commitment to Crossover and Community

Through the period of riots and racial unrest, Gordy had his artists sing of love and the human concerns to which people of all races could relate. The company slogan was "the sound of young America." Most of his performers were from the Detroit area and had come from difficult and poor backgrounds, such as the Supremes who came from the Brewster-Douglass housing project in Detroit's ghetto. In order to ensure crossover hits to the mainstream white audience, Gordy minimized the African-American characteristics in the music and performance style of his singers, aiming to produce clean-cut, fast-selling, crossover pop hits.[3] When other rhythm 'n' blues artists were performing in simple dresses or pants, Gordy's performers wore elegant evening gowns and tuxedos. He established a "finishing school" called "International Talent Management Incorporated" to train his performers to drop African-American modes of walking, speaking, and dancing so that they would be able to move smoothly in upper-class white society. Although financial and contract disputes eventually disrupted the sense of community at Motown, most of the early Motown artists cherished the sense of family that Gordy had created. In the words of Otis Williams, "Joining Motown was more like being adopted by a big loving family than being hired by a company. This isn't just nostalgia talking either. It really was a magical time."[4]

One of the examples of the sense of community was the Motown Revue, which toured the South by bus late in 1962. Memories of the 1961 Freedom Rides and the violent racist attacks on the bus riders were still fresh in people's minds. For the Motown Revue, a lineup including Mary Wells, the Supremes, the Miracles, the Temptations, Edwin Starr, Marvin Gaye, "Little Stevie" Wonder, the Marvelettes, and Martha and the Vandellas played a grueling itinerary in which they performed ninety one-night concerts. Most of the time, they slept on the crowded bus. Gordy had warned them that they would be representing not only Motown records but also all of Detroit. The performers encountered gas station attendants who refused to let them use the toilets, restaurants that would feed them only through a small window in the back by the garbage cans, and even gunfire at the tour bus. In Memphis, they accepted racially separate seating areas, singing each song twice, once to the white audience on one side of the auditorium and once to the black audience on the other. Gordy hoped and believed that his Motown singers were helping in the fight against racism, and made generous donations to established civil rights groups, expressing his respect for "all people who were fighting against bigotry and oppression."[5]

Additional efforts to assist in the struggle for civil rights included the Gordy label release in 1963 of two albums of Martin Luther King Jr.'s speeches, *Great March to Freedom* and *Great March to Washington.* In Gordy's words, "I saw Motown much like the world Dr. King was fighting for—with people of different races and religions working together harmoniously for a common goal. . . . While I was never too thrilled about that turn-the-other-cheek business, Dr. King showed me the wisdom of nonviolence."[6] The Motown Revue survived and thrived during the tour, and Martha Reeves, who remembered Gordy as being a "very spiritual" man with "visions far beyond any of our imaginations," said Motown was "an exciting place where magic was created."[7]

Motown in the 1970s and 1980s

By 1970, Motown had become more aware of the necessity to more publicly recognize its black roots and formed a new label, Black Forum, which released spoken word recordings by black poets such as Margaret Danner and Langston Hughes, and speeches by political activists such as Stokely Carmichael (who had coined the phrase "Black Power" in 1966). Along this same venue, in 1971, Marvin Gaye was given more creative control of his recordings. The result was his hit album *What's Going On.* He wrote, produced, sang, and played most of the instruments. Gordy was

[3] Szmatmary, David P., *Rockin' in Time: A Social History of Rock and Roll.* Englewood Cliffs, New Jersey: Prentice Hall, 1987, p. 145.

[4] Werner, Craig, *A Change Is Gonna Come: Music, Race and the Soul of America.* New York: Penguin, 1999, p. 22.

[5] Ibid. p. 27.

[6] Ibid. p. 27.

[7] Ibid. pp. 21–22.

Break-Out Three

PROFILE *Brian McKnight*

With over sixteen million records sold over an eight-album/twenty-three-singles career, Brian McKnight is one of the most successful contemporary artists in a style sometimes described as "neoclassical soul." Like many soul and funk artists, Brian McKnight grew up in a musical family, singing Gospel in the local church choir. His grandfather was the director of the choir, and his older brother, Claude, was a member of a successful doo-wop/Gospel vocal group that recorded with the Reunion Label. As a young teenager, Brian started composing his own music in an "easy listening" jazz style. By eighteen, he had formed a band and was performing in local venues. His demo tape attracted the attention of Mercury Records' president Ed Eckstine, who offered Brian a recording contract. McKnight's first single, "The Way Love Goes," was released in 1991 and peaked at number eleven after nineteen weeks on the Billboard R & B charts. Two follow-up singles did not do as well, barely making the chart's "Top Sixty." Finally, "Love Is," a duet with Vanessa Williams featured on the television show *Beverly Hills 90210*, rose to number three on Billboard's Pop Charts, introducing McKnight to a crossover audience.

McKnight recorded two more albums for Mercury before transferring to Motown in 1998. His first album with the Motown label was a Christmas collection called *Bethlehem*, followed by *Back at One* in 1999 (triple platinum). Several albums followed, including *Superhero* in 2001 and *U Turn* in 2003. After taking some time off from music to deal with personal issues as well as play guard for the California ABA basketball team the Ontario Warriors, McKnight returned to music, releasing *Gemini* in 2005. By February, the album was the number four–selling album in the country, and included two hits "What We Do Here" and "Every Time You Go Away," which reached number one on the Adult R & B charts and earned him a Grammy nomination. Although his main fame has ultimately been as a solo singer, his talents as a songwriter and producer also have been in demand, and over the years he has helped other major artists, including Nelly, Mariah Carey, and Justin Timberlake.[8]

[8] Lytle, Craig. "Brian McKnight" All Music Guide. http://www.vh1.com/artists/az/mcknight_brian/bio.jhtml (Accessed 02-26-05) and "Brian McKnight: Official Site" http://www.brian-mcknight.com/ (Accessed 02-26-05).

reluctant to release the album, fearing that the political and socially critical lyrics would alienate his Motown fans, but eventually Gordy relented. The album sold over a million copies with three of the songs on the album becoming number one hits: "Inner City Blues (Make Me Wanna Holler)," "Mercy, Mercy Me (The Ecology)," and "What's Going On?" This was different from any album previously released by Motown and brought attention to the new influence of the importance of album sales as well as the singles that had been the lifeblood of Motown.

Motown announced the closure of its Detroit offices in June 1972 as Gordy shifted his emphasis to making movies and working in the TV industry. Gordy resigned as president of Motown in 1973, and became chairman of the board of Motown Industries. This same year, Stevie Wonder's *Innervisions* album on the Motown label won five Grammy awards. His *Songs in the Key of Life* won four Grammy awards in 1976. Other artists who later signed with Motown were Rick James, Lionel Richie, and The Commodores.

Berry Gordy sold Motown in June 1988 to MCA Records, retaining the rights to the Jobete Publishing catalog. He had guided Motown into becoming one of the largest black businesses in the United States. He and many of his artists were financially successful to degrees hardly dreamed of in the early 1960s, and there has never been another company that has exceeded the number of top ten hits that Motown had in the 1960s and 1970s. Motown Records still exists and proudly displays its motto: Motown: Artistic Integrity—Our Legacy, Our Future! It continues to sell records and memorabilia of its past, but it also records and promotes new artists such as Brian McKnight, Erykah Badu, Remy Shand, and Kem.

Funk

In 1965, James Brown released "Papa's Got a Brand New Bag" which, with its rhythmic intensity and polyrthymic layering, issued in a new style called "Funk." Emphasizing the basic four beats of a quadruple meter, and then using the rest of the instruments—drums, guitars, keyboards, and horns—to layer rhythmic patterns on top of each other, the music was extraordinarily visceral and compelling. In this new style, Brown created a series of hypnotic and kinetic hits, which were added to the black anthems of his soul period, including "I Got You (I Feel Good)" (1965), "Let Yourself Go" (1967), and "Say It Loud, I'm Black and I'm Proud" (1968). In these masterpieces, rhythm became the absolutely essential musical fabric, and these recordings are considered by many to be the keystone of the next major development in African-American music, hip-hop and rap.

Conclusion

For two years after Martin Luther King Jr.'s speech, "I Have a Dream," despair mingled with a sense of accomplishment. The optimism generated by the March on Washington was shattered with the assassination of President John F. Kennedy three months later in November 1963. In the next two years, however, President Lyndon Johnson, deeply committed to social equity, forced through several important pieces of legislation, including the Civil Rights Act of 1964 and the Voting Rights Act of 1965. Johnson's "War on Poverty" launched additional federal legislation to expand health insurance and assist education. These efforts moved the United States further toward the vision of an end to racial injustice, but in the second half of the 1960s, attention shifted to other concerns, primarily the Vietnam War. Some members of minorities turned their back on integration to fight for separate group power, and younger white Americans dropped out of mainstream society to become "hippies" in the emerging counterculture. In 1968, Martin Luther King Jr. was assassinated in an act of pure racial hatred, triggering another round of violence in black ghettos in Chicago and Washington, DC. These developments brought about corresponding changes in American music, most noticeably the emergence of psychedelic acid rock for whites, and hip-hop and rap for blacks.

Bibliography

Charlton, Katherine. *Rock Music Styles: A History.* Second Edition. Madison Wisconsin: Brown and Benchmark, 1994.

De Curtis, Anthony and James Henke, editors. *The Rolling Stone Illustrated History of Rock and Roll.* New York: Random House, 1980.

Goldfield, David, et al. *The American Journey: A History of the United States*, Combined Volume. Upper Saddle River, New Jersey: Prentice Hall, 2001.

Gordy, Berry. *To Be Loved: The Music, the Magic, the Memories of Motown.* New York: Warner Books, 1994.

Haskins, James. *Black Music in America: A History Through Its People.* New York: Thomas Y. Crowell, 1987.

Lytle, Craig. "Brian McKnight" All Music Guide. http://www.vh1.com/artists/az/mcknight_brian/bio.jhtml (Accessed 02-26-05) and "Brian McKnight: Official Site" http://www.brian-mcknight.com/ (Accessed 02-26-05).

Neal, Mark Anthony. *What the Music Said: Black Popular Music and Black Public Culture.* New York and London: Routledge, 1999.

Southern, Eileen. *The Music of Black Americans: A History.* Third Edition. New York: W.W. Norton & Company, 1997.

Stambler, Irwin. *The Encyclopedia of Pop, Rock, &Soul.* Revised Edition. New York: St. Martin's Press, 1989.

Szatmary, David P. *Rockin' in Time: A Social History of Rock and Roll.* Englewood Cliffs New Jersey: Prentice Hall, 1987.

Werner, Craig. *A Change Is Gonna Come: Music, Race and the Soul of America.* New York: Plume, 1999.

Chapter Fourteen

Salsa, Reggae, and Caribbean Latino Music

On September 1, 2004, the fifth "Latin" Grammy awards were presented to musicians from the Latin American world. The term "Latin America" refers to the Spanish-based culture of people from North, Central, and South America as well as the Caribbean, Spain, and Portugal. This culture-based definition is relatively easy to comprehend; understanding what is meant by "Latin music" is more of a challenge. The U.S. record industry defines Latin music as simply any release with lyrics that are mostly in Spanish. But just as "Latin America" includes multiple national identities from over twenty different countries, each with its own history and cultural traditions, so does "Latin music" include a wide variety of unique musical styles.

The Latin Grammy awards have brought attention to some of the difficulties within the Latin music community. One area of tensions was highlighted when two U.S. record labels boycotted the Latin Grammys because they believed the awards did not sufficiently honor Mexican or Mexican-American musicians. Another area of stress surrounds the attendance and participation of Cuban artists. Juan Vila, spokesman for the national Cuban-American organization *Junta Patriotica Cubana,* expressed concerns that the Latin Grammy awards and record profits had become a vehicle for supporting Castro's communist regime in Cuba.[1]

Despite the tensions, the Latin Grammy awards have become an important means for creating greater public awareness of the excellence and cultural diversity of Latin recording artists. It is also the first prime-time English-, Spanish-, and Portuguese-language telecast on U.S. television. Distributed in more than one hundred international markets, it is arguably the most high-profile American celebration and broadcast of Latin culture.

[1] "Protests Over Latin Grammys." BBC News: Entertainment. September, 7, 2001. http://news.bbc.co.uk/1/hi/entertainment/music/1530199.stm (Accessed 03–03–05). Attendance by Cuban artists has continued to be problematic. For the award ceremony in 2003, none of the twelve Cuban acts nominated for awards were able to attend because they did not get visas. A similar situation occurred in 2002, when none of the twenty-two nominated musicians received visas in time. U.S. State Department spokesman said this was because the applications arrived too late to be processed; Cuban representatives say that they did not receive visas in time partially because of pressure from Miami-based Cuban exiles. "Juanes Shines at Latin Grammys." *CBS News: The Early Show.* March 28, 2004. http://www.cbsnews.com/stories/2004/03/28/earlyshow/leisure/music/main609077.shtml (Accessed 03-03-05).

During the Carnaval Miami, costumed dancers participate in a parade that is part of a two-week celebration of Hispanic culture. *Source: Photo by Nick Wheeler. Corbis/Bettmann. © Nick Wheeler/CORBIS.*

Many of the artists who have been honored in the Latin Grammys have been musicians with Caribbean roots, including Ricky Martin, Marc Anthony, Linda "La India" Caballero, Gloria Estefan, Jennifer Lopez, Tito Puente, and Ibrahim Ferrer, the star of the film *The Buena Vista Social Club.* It is also the Caribbean-based music that is meant by what has become a catchall term for Latin dance music, "salsa." Although in the next chapter we will focus on Mexican-based Latin music, in this chapter, we concentrate on Caribbean-based Latin music.

Defining "The Caribbean"

The "Caribbean" refers to a series of islands called the Antilles archipelago located in the Caribbean Sea, which is situated southeast of Florida between the Atlantic Ocean and the Gulf of Mexico. This archipelago includes several islands and countries. Cuba is the largest and the closest, just ninety miles away from Miami, Florida. But there is also Jamaica, Haiti, the Dominican Republic, the Commonwealth of the Bahamas, and Puerto Rico. Each of these countries has its independent and unique history, although they are joined together by the common heritage of European colonialism and slavery.

Cuba was the location for the original landing of Christopher Columbus on October 27, 1492, and Cuba remained a Spanish colony until 1898. The United States, restricted by its own law to respect Cuban self-determination, could not annex Cuba as it did Puerto Rico, Guam, and the Philippines. Instead, the United States installed a governor who was eventually replaced by Cuban presidents. Cuba's assets were increasingly placed into foreign hands. For example, by the 1920s, U.S. companies owned two thirds of Cuban farmland, imposing tariffs that crippled Cuba's own manufacturing industries. Discrimination against blacks was institutionalized, and tourism based on drinking, gambling, and prostitution flourished. In 1959, a young lawyer named Fidel Castro led a revolution, and in 1959, Cuba became the only communist country in the Americas. Because of the U.S. involvement in the "cold war" with the United Soviet Socialist Republic (USSR) and Cuba's close ties with the USSR, the relationship between the United States and Cuba has been strained for many years. This difficult relationship was highlighted in 2000 with the case of six-year-old Elián

Gonzales, the only survivor of a boat that capsized that was carrying his mother and friends escaping Cuba to emigrate to the United States. Elián made it to Miami by clinging to an inner-tube, but his survival prompted a custody battle between the boy's great uncle in Florida and his father in Cuba. U.S. officials enforced a court order returning Elián to Cuba.

Another of the important islands in the Caribbean is Puerto Rico, a self-governing territory of the United States. Like Cuba, it was one of the first places to be conquered by Columbus, who arrived there on his second voyage in 1493. Also like Cuba, Puerto Rico remained a Spanish colony until 1898, when it was ceded to the United States by Spain at the close of the Spanish-American War. Unlike Cuba, Puerto Rico is actually part of the United States, and Puerto Ricans are U.S. citizens. Because of this close connection to the United States, and because it provides the second largest Latino population born in the United States (with twice as many people as the third largest group, Cuban Americans), we will look in more depth at the history, social context, and music traditions of Puerto Rico.

Overview of Caribbean Music Traditions

As indicated earlier, "Latin music" is a broad term encompassing several different musical styles. One component of the various styles is the rhythms. There are many different rhythmic styles, each with their own name such as *mambo*, *guaracha*, *bomba*, and *merengue.* Before we look at what distinguishes the different subsets, let us look at the characteristics that unify much of Latin music.

Structural Characteristics Unifying Caribbean Music

Rhythm: Clave

One of the most elemental characteristics of Latin music is the rhythmic pattern known as clave (pronounced klah-veh). The clave rhythmic pattern is often played on an instrument known as "claves," which are two round, polished sticks that are struck together. But the clave rhythm can also be played on any percussion instrument. The pattern

The documentary film *The Buena Vista Social Club* brought the intense sounds and complex rhythms of Cuban Latin jazz to mainstream America. *Source: Photo by Christian Charisias/REUTERS. © Reuters New Media, Inc./CORBIS.*

itself consists of a two-measure rhythmic phrase that is united by a pulse. The rhythmic pattern is created on top of this pulse and consists of a measure of three notes and another measure of two notes. The order of these notes can be switched, organized as "three-two" or "two-three." Additionally, there are two types of clave, *son* and *rhumba.* In the more traditional *son* clave, the final pulse falls on the beat, whereas in the rhumba clave, the final pulse falls off the beat (or on the four-plus side). Although this rhythmic change may seem minor, since all of the rhythms in a given arrangement are based on *clave*, it has a major impact on the rhythmic nature of the piece. The clave is the foundation of Caribbean rhythms, and all other rhythmic patterns and melodic phrases revolve around it. This characteristic rhythmic pattern can be traced directly back to the rhythmic patterns of Africa, particularly the Yoruba culture of Nigeria.

Caribbean music has other important rhythmic elements derived from African traditions, such as *polymeter*, where duple and triple meters are played simultaneously, and polyrhythms, where accents and syncopations give the illusion of polymeter, but the rhythms are all unified by a central pulse.

Texture: Coro-Pregon

Another unifying characteristic of Caribbean music is the performance texture of *Coro-Pregon*, a vocal call-and-response descended from African musical style. In a salsa arrangement, the fixed sections of the song are separated by *montunos,* where the lead singer (Pregonero) improvises lyrics. The *montunos* alternates with the fixed response of the *Coro*, which is generally sung by the other members of the group. In modern salsa, the improvised lyric is gradually being replaced with fixed lyrics, but experienced Latin musicians can still improvise *Pregon.*[2]

Instrumentation

Caribbean music makes extensive use of percussion instruments, especially drums, bells and shakers—another reflection of African musical tradition. The *Timgales* are a central element of the contemporary ensemble. *Timgales* are two metal cased tuned drums enhanced with woodblocks, bells, and cymbals. The timgales are an instrument created in the islands, reportedly by cutting the bottom off of European tympani. A defining characteristic that distinguishes timgales from European percussion is that the metal shell of the drum is as much a part of the instrument as the head. The timgales are played with thin sticks and usually keep a steady pattern on the shell punctuated with the head. The bell (actually a refined cowbell) is very important, and signals the ensemble and dancers that a section change has occurred (such as moving into the *montuno* section, or *coro-pregon).* The bell is normally played by the *bongo* player, who also serves as a main member of the *coro.*

Perhaps the most interesting musical element of much of Caribbean music is the role of the piano and bass. The piano normally plays in a highly arpeggiated style that is also known as *montunomo* (although the piano style known as *montunomo* should not be confused with the improvised *montuno* section of the song in which the *coro-pregon* and instrumental solos take place). The bass plays a *tumbao*, a repeated pattern that emphasizes beats two-plus and four, along with the *congas.*

Son

The *son* is perhaps the most important influence on contemporary salsa. A popular dance among the working class, the Caribbean *son* is roughly equivalent to the Mexican *son*, which is the generic term for peasant or rural music that originated in the songs brought over by the Spaniards. The Caribbean *son* emerged around the turn of

[2] A fine example of *Coro-Pregon* performed by older *Salseros* is "El Cuarto de Tula" from *The Buena Vista Social Club.* This recording is a *Descarga* (an extended jam), which features the *Soneros* Ibrahim Ferrer, Manuel Licea, and Eliades Ochoa improvising lyrics juxtaposed with the fixed *Coro* response.

Break-Out One

IN-DEPTH FOCUS *Reggae to Ragga*

Out of the tiny island of Jamaica comes reggae, one of the most influential Caribbean music genres. Like the other Caribbean islands, Jamaica had been home to a number of plantations that functioned through the exploitation of African slaves. Even after slavery was officially abolished in 1838, planters continued to devise methods that kept blacks in essentially slave conditions. In the 1920s, Marcus Garvey—a Jamaican laborer who had emigrated to the United States in 1917—became a powerful spokesman for black unity. Garvey led a pan-African movement advocating for the return of all African descendants who had been scattered throughout the world due to slavery to return to Africa. In one of his pamphlets, he urged Africans in the Americas to look to Africa for a new prince that would be their leader.

Some Jamaicans decided that the new leader was Haile Selassie I, the Emperor of Ethiopia from 1930 to 1974. Selassie's original name was Tafari Makonnen, but he went by the title "Ras Tafari." Ras Tafari claimed descent from Solomon (a king of Israel from about 970–930 B.C.E., who was honored for his wisdom in both Judaism and Christianity). Members of the Rastafarian messianic movement that developed in Jamaica in the 1930s believed that Ethiopia was the true Zion (the "House of God" derived from one of the hills on Jerusalem on which the city of King David was built). They proposed that Ras Tafari was the reincarnation of Jesus, and that white Christians had perverted biblical scripture to hide that Adam and Jesus were black.

Rastafarians believe that spirituality is individual and personal, and that any person's spiritual views are valid as long as they are possessed of the Spirit of Jah (God). Jah is a living force on earth and enables otherwise disparate humanity to unite. To embody this sense of unity in speech, Rastas refer to each other as "I." Thus, "I" means I; "I" means you, and "I and I" means we. Rastas believe that all individuals of African descent who are living outside of Africa are awaiting repatriation to Africa. The largest of the Rastafarian gatherings are called grounations. Here Rastas talk collectively about religious, social, political, and livital (life) issues and participate in rituals that involve Bible reading, drumming, singing hymns, and smoking marijuana (called *ganja*). Rastafarians also forbid the cutting of hair, and have made popular a style in which long strands of hair are twisted closely from the scalp down to the tips and called "dreadlocks."

the century in Cuba. *Son* spawned several important hybrid styles in the Caribbean just as it had in Mexico, including *son-montuno*, *son-pregon*, *guajira-son*, and *afro-son*. The distinctive sound of *son* is defined by a stringed instrument derived from the Spanish guitar. In Mexico, this was the *jarana*. In Cuba, the stringed instrument is the *Tres*, with three or four double strings that are played with a pick. The Puerto Rican version of this instrument is the *cuatro*.

DANZA

At the basis of Caribbean music is dance music, and the Caribbean islands have provided the world with some of its most popular dance rhythms. One category of dance music is called *danza* and it has its roots in the traditions of the European colonists. These were slow, refined dances that were adaptations of nineteenth-century European aristocratic dances such as the waltz and mazurka. Puerto

In the 1970s, producers and musicians in Kingston, Jamaica, were looking for a new beat, and decided to fuse two music trends already in existence. The first music trend was *mento*, a rural, drum-based folk music style dating back to plantation slaves' Saturday night social gatherings that used rebellious, topical, and witty lyrics. The second music trend was "rock steady," a successor to *ska* (a style that had developed in the mid-1960s fusing fast R & B with a series of off-beats). The combination formed *reggae*, from the Jamaican word *rege-rege*, meaning to quarrel.

These changes in music corresponded to shifts in society. Emperor Haile Selassie had visited Jamaica in 1966, encouraging a huge growth in Rastafari. One of the many ska groups that helped shape the development of reggae was a group called the Wailers, consisting of Bob Marley, Peter Tosh, and Bunny Wailer. Marley was the son of a black mother, Cedella, and a white ex-British army officer from Liverpool. Raised in the tough Trench town ghetto of West Kingston, Marley was an adamant Rastafrian. Marley's messages of strength and social unity became international hits. In 1976, Marley was the victim of a political assassination attempt when seven armed men broke into his home on the eve of an election concert. Marley sang at the concert anyway, but then went to Miami until it was deemed safe to return to Jamaica. In 1978, he returned for an historic performance in which he linked arms with the opposing political leaders and sang "One Love," a hymn to peace and brotherhood.

The "One Love" concert also commemorated the twelfth anniversary of Selassie's visit to Jamaica. Marley's second most famous concert was in 1980, celebrating the independence of Zimbabwe. The new Zimbabwean flag consisted of Rasta colors: yellow for sunshine, red for bloodshed, green for the jungle, and black for the African people. Thirteen months after this concert, Marley died of cancer and his funeral brought ten thousand people onto the streets of Jamaica. In the twenty years following Marley's death, Jamaican reggae has become a huge international influence, especially in Africa, where Marley's message of struggle, peace, and pride remains powerful.

In the United States, reggae continues to flourish in Jamaican communities in cities like New York and Miami. During the 1980s, several studios/labels were launched that specialized in reggae sung by Jamaican émigrés. By the 1990s, when musicians in many genres were experimenting with computerized rhythms, reggae evolved into "ragga," a fusion that is "ragamuffin" (a child dressed in tattered clothes who roams the streets), incorporating eclectic elements, particularly hip-hop and rap. Important ragga stars include Shinehead, Shaggy, Born Jamaicans, and Red Fox.[3]

[3] "Jamaica: The Loudest Island in the World." *World Music, The Rough Guide.* vol. 2. London: Rough Guides, Ltd., 2000, pp. 430–456.

Rico's anthem, "La Borinqueña," is a *danza. Danzas* were played by small orchestras known as *charangas* and were comprised of strings and flute with a rhythm section. *Danza* later led to the development of *danzon*, which added a fourth section called a *mambo.* The *mambo* section was an open vamp (where musicians repeat a simple harmonic formula) over which solos could be improvised. Although this form is essential to the development of modern salsa, it is the *plena* that provide the core component of Puerto Rico's popular music.

Specific Music Traditions of Particular Importance to Puerto Rico

Plena

Plenas apparently first appeared in Puerto Rico at the end of the nineteenth century, when two English-speaking singers and their daughter arrived from Barbados or St. Kitts and settled in one of the

Break-Out Two

PROFILE *Puerto Rican Roots: Ricky Martin, Jennifer Lopez, and Marc Anthony*

Ricky Martin, born in Puerto Rico, was the only child of Enrique Martin, a psychologist, and Nereida Morales, an accountant. Although he had been working as a member of the teen group Menudo for many years and also had appeared both on Broadway (in the production of *Les Miserables*) and ABC's soap *General Hospital*, Martin became an international superstar with his performance of the soccer anthem "La Copa de la Vica" at the 1998 World Cup and his megahit "La Vida Loca."

Jennifer Lopez was born in the Bronx, New York, to Puerto Rican parents. She started out acting in musical theatre and made her film debut when she was sixteen in a little-known film, *My Little Girl.* She continued to perform in a variety of roles, including as one of the "Fly Girls" in the TV series *In Living Color*, and in the films *Money Train*, *Mi Familia*, *Jack*, and *Blood and Wine*, until she landed the title role in 1997's *Selena.* Co-starring with George Clooney in 1998's *Out of Sight,* Lopez became the highest-paid Latina actress in Hollywood history. That summer, she released her debut pop album, *On the 5*, with the hit single "If You Had My Love." She has continued to release albums as well as act. Her most recent album, *Rebirth,* was released in 2005.

Marc Anthony, born Marco Antonio Muniz, was named by his musician father after a famous Mexican singer of the same name. He changed his name professionally to avoid being confused with the legendary singer. Marc was instructed in music theory and composition by his father, and grew up listening to rock, R & B, and Latin music. When he was twelve years old, he and his sister were "discovered" by a producer of demos and commercials, and Marc began his dual career in acting and singing. He sang background on albums by Menudo, Safire, and the Latin Rascals, and also sang "house music" in English in dance clubs in New York. He has acted in Broadway productions (including Paul Simon's Capeman) and also in films such as *Bringing Out the Dead*, *Man on Fire*, *The Substitute*, *Big Night*, and *Hackers.*[4]

[4] Harris, Craig. "Marc Anthony," from All Music Guide. http://www.vh1.com/artists/az/anthony_marc/bio.jhtml (Accessed 03-01-05).

black ghettos of Puerto Rico's southern port of Ponce. They played guitar and the *pandereta* (a small hand-held percussion instrument similar to the tambourine, but without the cymbals attached) and composed and sang songs commenting on the daily life of the local black working-class people. Possibly derived from the Spanish version of "play now," the songs became known as *plenas.*[5] Eventually, the *plena* ensemble included two or three *panderetas*, conga and bongo drums, the *guiro* (a scraper that is one of the sole surviving instruments of the Taino Indians), and a small, four double-string guitar called the *cuatro.* Many of the *plena* ensembles were rural musicians, called *jíbaro*, and *jíbaro* artists were very popular in the 1930s and 1940s.

Plena ensembles such as Rafael Hernandez's Trio Borinquen and Manuel Jiménez's (known as "Canario") became great stars in New York's thriving Puerto Rican community. Canario was the first to augment the traditional *plena* with the piano, bass, and brass instruments that had become so popular in jazz bands. Thus, two strands of music

[5] Steward, Susan. *Musica*. London: Thames and Hudson, Ltd., 1999, p. 95.

Teaming with producer and disc jockey Little Louie Vega, Anthony recorded his debut album, *When the Night Is Over,* in 1991. In a Latin hip-hop style, the album featured a guest appearance by salsa superstar Tito Puente. Reciprocating later that year, Anthony was the opening act on a show at Madison Square Garden that celebrated Puente's one hundredth album release.

Anthony's manager had suggested he sing in Spanish, but Marc wasn't interested until, driving in Manhattan, he heard a song called "Hasta Que Te Conoci" by Juan Gabriel. "It ripped me apart," he explained. "I don't know why and I don't want to know why. I called my manager and asked if I could record it in salsa."[6]

Anthony recorded it in 1993, and brought the musical tracks to Radio y Musica, a Latin music convention to which his manager had sent him to perform. Dressed in borrowed clothes, he recalled that one person clapped when he went on stage. When he was finished, he left the stage so quickly that his manager had to stop him and point out that he was receiving a standing ovation. Several disc jockeys were dialing their cell phones, and Anthony heard one say, "Find this kid's CD. I threw it out this morning; it's in the trash. Find it, and play it!"

Later that day, he appeared on a television show called "Carnaval Internacional." The show was broadcast all over the world, and Anthony later said, "That changed my life forever. I mean in one day. It seemed like years before I was ever in New York again. I was booked and booked and booked: Panama, Ecuador, Argentina, Colombia, Puerto Rico, Miami, Los Angeles. I woke up once in the middle of the night in a hotel and I didn't know where I was. I called my brother's room and said, 'Where are we?' All I could see was a city at night. Tokyo. I thought, 'How did this happen?' "[7]

In 1999, he released his debut English-language pop CD, titled *Marc Anthony,* which has since been certified triple-platinum, its success largely because of the single "I Need to Know." This song earned Marc a Grammy nomination for Best Male Pop Vocal Performance and the song "Dimelo" (the Spanish-language version of the song) won a Latin Grammy for Song of the Year.

On Valentine's Day, 2000, an HBO special titled, "Marc Anthony: The Concert from Madison Square Garden," showcased Anthony's English-language hits along with the Spanish-language hits that established him as a top-selling salsa singer. In June 2004, he and Jennifer Lopez were married. He has continued to win many awards, including the 2005 Grammy for Best Latin Pop Album for Amar Sin Mentiras, and four Premio Lo Nuestro Awards.

[6] http://www.marcanthonyonline.com/ (Accessed 03-01-05).
[7] Ibid.

evolved: the rural, traditional, string instrument *jíbaro* style performed by Puerto Ricans in New York such as Los Pleneros de la 21, and the urban, modern, nightclub sound of pan-Latin groups backing big-name singers such as Bobby Capó, Daniel Santos, and Rafael Cortijo.

In 1990, a *plena* revival was led by a twelve-piece band called Plena Libra. As with so many ensembles at the end of the twentieth century, Plena Libra combined traditional elements of *plena* with the newer, dynamic salsa-influenced style and staging. Although salsa and *merengue* are more commercially successful forms of contemporary Latino music, *plena* is still an important music tradition for Puerto Ricans. In the series of megaconcerts with which Puerto Rican superstar Ricky Martin launched the new millennium, he closed the concerts with a *plena* finale performed by a group of *pleneros* from New York.

BOMBA

Another one of the important Puerto Rican musical styles, *bomba*, refers to both a rhythmic style and to the drum on which it is played: a barrel-shaped drum similar to the conga drum but shorter. Traditionally, *bomba* drummers sit in a line. Each drummer plays a different sized drum that provides rhythmic counterpoint to smaller drums (*subidors*), maracas, and wooden sticks (*palillos*). The *bomba* is characterized by its own unique rhythmic pattern, called a *cuá*, which is similar in function to the clave. It is distinct in that it is a one-measure phrase, as opposed to the two-measure clave phrase, and the rhythmic accent consistently falls on the fourth beat. In Puerto Rico, *bomba*'s principal artists have been the Cepeda family (who perform as well as lead workshops) and the group Paracumbé. In New York, *bomba* is performed by the salsa-jazz band Orquesta Libra.

Other Caribbean Music Traditions

Merengue

Merengue was created on another Caribbean island, the island of the Dominican Republic, where *merengue* musicians are treated as celebrities. As with *bomba*, *merengue* is identified by its rhythmic pattern. It is an aggressive, unsyncopated, strongly accented duple meter that accompanies a fast-paced two-step dance in which the dancers step sideways from left to right. Traditional *merengue* music was performed by acoustic instruments, with an accordion playing lead and backed up by a bass, *guira* and a two-ended tambora drum (which is held by one hand and played with a stick by the other hand). But in contemporary *merengue* music, the piano replaces the accordion and the groups generally utilize a large saxophone and brass section, with these instruments playing fast, virtuosic riffs in a complex, highly polyphonic texture.

Cumbia

Cumbia's origins are in Colombia. *Cumbias* were initially a slow, sensual dance performed by African slaves and Indians as a courtship ritual. Over the years, it evolved in a manner similar to *merengue* in the Dominican Republic. Originally a folk dance, in contemporary society it can reflect its rural origins and be played on acoustic instruments such as the accordion and guitar, or it can be urbanized and played by electric ensembles in flashy stage performances. In the dance that is coordinated with the music, couples hold each other's hands at waist level and out to the side. The upper part of the body stays stiff, whereas the lower body shifts with sensuous hip movements. There are three steps, two with one leg and one with the other that are performed against a solid duple meter.[8] As with so many other Latin music styles, in the 1930s, *cumbia* bands incorporated the brass instruments characteristic of jazz swing bands.

Rumba

Rumba developed in Cuba, again out of slave traditions. The dance steps, rhythms, and instruments of the slaves' religious rituals eventually became secularized and the basic entertainment of slaves on Sundays, their day off. In terms of instruments, *rumba* is played on conga drums accompanied by hand percussion (*guiros* and claves). Many African rhythms were used, but today these various rhythms have been distilled down to three: *guaguancó*, *yambú*, and *columbia*. Each of these rhythms corresponds to specific dance steps.

The *guaguancó* is a fast, erotic couple dance in which the man dances around the woman, lunging and thrusting with his pelvis, symbolically representing a rooster performing a courtship ritual around a hen. The woman dances in such a way as to avoid contact, particularly in the pelvic region, as she wraps her skirt around herself to protect her. The *yambu* rhythm accompanies a slower couple dance, with the sexual component downplayed because the dance is supposed to be a symbolic representation of old people. It is danced with a set of shuffly moves. The *columbia* rhythm is the fastest and most exciting *rumba* and is designed as a showcase for a single male performer.

[8] Steward, Susan. *Salsa*. 1999, p. 15 and pp. 132–133.

Sometimes there is confusion between the terms *rumba* and *rhumba*, which is a ballroom dance that developed in the swing era and was not a true *rumba*. One of the most famous *rhumbas* is the 1939 song "La Cucaracha" ("The Cockroach"), which became an international hit.[9]

Conga

Congas, also from Cuba, originated in Cuba's carnival parades. In these parades, various musicians were grouped together in ensembles called *comparsas*. When this parade-based dance came on to the dance floor, participants would alternate between dancing together in couples and separating and reforming in a human chain. Desi Arnez introduced the *conga* to the United States through his performances in Miami and New York. In 1988, Gloria Estefán and the Miami Sound Machine made famous a Latino-disco version of the dance with "Conga," the theme of Miami's Cuban Carnival that year. At that carnival, 119,986 Latin Americans and tourists danced their way through Little Havana and into the Guinness Book of Records.[10]

Mambo

Mambo, also from Cuba, developed in the 1930s out of *danzon* and apparently (although this is debated) was invented by a Cuban band led by Antonio Arcano. Arcano's band was a popular *danzón* orchestra in Cuba called Las Maravillas del Siglo (The Miracles of the Century). The rhythm section of the band featured three brothers, Jesús, Israel, and Orestes López, who also helped in the writing and arranging of music for the band. In 1938 Orestes composed a tune that he called "Mambo" that incorporated a new African rhythm that he referred to simply as the *nuevo ritmo* (new rhythm). At first this rhythm was too African for the sophisticated Havana *danzón* crowd, and it was even banned by the radio stations for six months. *Mambo* was eventually accepted in Cuba, but it never became as popular there as it did elsewhere.[11]

Reggae

One of the most generally known Caribbean-based genres emerged in Jamaica in the late 1960s as a fusion of two earlier Jamaican styles: *mento* (a rural folk music tradition dating back to slave social gatherings) and "rock steady" (a late *ska* style). Musically, reggae combines elements of rock, calypso (dance music originating in Trinidad that is often played by a steel band), and soul. Its most readily distinguished feature, however, is its slow tempo and accentuation of the second and fourth beats (the "off-beats") of a four-beat bar. Reggae is closely associated with Rastafarian, a nondoctrinal religious group that stresses black culture and identity. The lyrics of reggae songs reflect this association and often focus on spiritual and political concerns. The musician responsible for catapulting reggae to international popularity was Bob Marley, a member, along with Bunny Wailer and Peter Tosh, of an earlier ska group called The Wailers. Since Marley's death in 1981, the reggae tradition has been maintained by his son, Ziggy, as well as musicians such as Peter Broggs, Luciano, Kashief Lindo, and Lucky Dube.

Caribbean Music Traditions Within a Historical and Social Context

Pre-Conquest and Establishment of Spanish Colonies

Taino Indians and Spanish Conquest

Before European invasion and colonization, the Caribbean islands were home to thriving indigenous tribes. The most recent of several different

[9] Ibid., p. 31.
[10] Ibid., p. 33.
[11] Ibid., p. 35.

Indian peoples on the island of Puerto Rico were the Taino Indians. The Taino lived along the shores of the island and called the island Borinquen, "land of the valiant and noble lords." They had a complex social structure, a sophisticated stone sculpture tradition, and supported themselves by fishing and farming. They were artisans and talented musicians, who apparently lived peacefully and without crime, poverty, warfare, or disease.

After Columbus arrived and claimed the land for Spain, he renamed the island San Juan de Bautista and named the best natural harbor of the island "Puerto Rico," meaning "rich port" or "doorway to riches." Eventually, Puerto Rico became the name of the island, and San Juan de Bautista its capital city. A Spanish soldier named Ponce de Leon was appointed the governor over the first Spanish colony in 1508. The Taino Indians were horrifically brutalized and, although a few escaped to safety in the hills or on to other islands, most died due to torture, murder, and disease brought by the Spanish.

Importation of African Slaves to the Caribbean

By the middle of the sixteenth century, the Spanish had established large sugar plantations. To replenish the Indian labor force that had been reduced so significantly, the Spanish began importing African slaves, who subsequently became an important component in the sugar cane economy. Because of slavery, Africans became the third major ethnic group in Puerto Rican culture, intermingling with those of native Indian descent and with the people of Spanish descent. As time went on, the three groups intermixed to such an extent that Puerto Ricans (and other Caribbean island countries) now enjoy a rich variety of skin colors and ethnic mixtures. But because Puerto Rico is one of the smallest islands, much smaller for example than Cuba or the Dominican Republic, it simply did not have as many large sugar plantations as the larger islands and hence, it had a smaller African slave population. As a consequence, its culture, including its music, has stronger Hispanic elements than African ones.

The Spanish-American War and U.S. Annexation of Puerto Rico

In the seventeenth, eighteenth, and early nineteenth centuries, Great Britain and other European powers tried to take Puerto Rico from Spain. When the United States and Spain became involved in the Spanish-American War of 1898, Americans invaded the island, defeated the Spanish, and annexed Puerto Rico and other territories to the United States. Puerto Ricans are now born U.S. citizens, and Puerto Ricans can travel to and from the mainland without going through immigration. In *Census 2000*, Puerto Ricans were the second largest "Hispanic" group, with 3.4 million.

Puerto Rico as an American Territory

Migration to the United States: 1900–1930

Puerto Ricans immigrated to the United States even when Puerto Rico was a Spanish colony. Craftsmen and merchants who settled in New York were called Nuyoricans. But the greatest migration began when Puerto Rico became part of the United States, and this migration has continued to increase ever since. Mostly Puerto Ricans have moved to the mainland for practical reasons. Between 1900 and 1925, the island's population had doubled and this growth seriously taxed the economy. Furthermore, devastating hurricanes struck in 1928 and 1932. During the "Great Depression" in the United States, prices for Puerto Rico's principal crop—sugar—declined and many people lost their jobs.

Puerto Ricans left the island by hundreds of thousands and settled into an area north of Central Park and south of Harlem, transforming this neighborhood into "El Barrio," also known as "Spanish Harlem." The immigrants brought with them their music traditions and scores of small ensembles sang the *plenas* and performed the various *danzas*. Employment was available in the New York City docks, and in tobacco factories, laundries, and "sweatshops." Spanish-language radio stations that broadcast live performances from local nightclubs united the community. The new record companies sent talent scouts into the Caribbean to find musicians to perform Cuban *son* and Puerto Rican *danzas* and *plenas*.

Integration with Jazz Styles in the 1930s and 1940s

When the United States raised the minimum wage to 25¢ in 1935, Puerto Rican needlework factories laid off thousands of Puerto Rican women. This, combined with changes in agricultural practices on the island, motivated more people to emigrate. In Cuba, many musicians such as Desi Arnez and Miguelito Valdés fled to the United States to escape the civil war against the Cuban dictator General Machado. Cubans often created the music styles that became the popular trends, but most of the musicians performing the music were Puerto Ricans.[12]

By 1940, soaring population combined with lack of employment opportunities motivated thousands of Puerto Ricans to move to the mainland, particularly New York City, to look for a better life. The city was pulsing with the sound of big band jazz and blues. Tour buses took visitors to "Black Harlem's" Savoy Ballroom and the Cotton Club and then a few blocks south to "Spanish Harlem" to hear music in cafés and bars with names like "Flor de Borinquén" and "El San Juan." Because of color segregation, the black, white, and Latin dancing crowds frequented clubs only in their own territories, but the musicians frequently crossed boundaries and played in mixed race ensembles.

In the early 1940s, a new style of music emerged as César Concepción merged the rural *plena* of Puerto Rican folk music with the big-band jazz format. Also in the 1940s, a young Puerto Rican named Tito Rodriguez (one of the three "Mambo Kings") arrived in New York as a seventeen-year-old with his older brother Johnny. He sang with several bands and then eventually formed his own group called the Mambo Devils. Within the close-knit Latin community, Tito Rodriguez also met Tito Puente, the teenaged drummer for a big Cuban orchestra led by José Curbelo.

In 1949, Federico Pagani opened a new club called the Palladium on the corner of Broadway at 52nd Street, right in the center of Manhattan. This club became an all-Latin showplace drawing not only the greatest Latin musicians but also Hollywood's most glamorous stars such as Marlon Brando, Kim Novak, and Eartha Kitt. For almost two decades, the Paladium helped consolidate the musical identity of Latin New York.

Influence of Rock 'n' Roll in the 1950s

In the 1950s, rock 'n' roll influenced the Latin community, and musicians attempted to integrate its stylistic characteristics into traditional Latin music. One of the styles of early rock 'n' roll was called doo-wop, and one of the most successful "doo-woppers" was Frankie Lymon and the Teenagers, comprised of two black Americans, two Puerto Ricans, and a Dominican. In 1955, the group had a top ten hit with "Why Do Fools Fall in Love?" Their manager, George Goldner, established the Tico label to record musicians who were fusing the doo-wop style with their Latin bands.

Cuban Musicians and Charanga

Another example of fusion that became very popular in the 1950s was a mix of big-band style with Puerto Rican *bomba*, perfected in a hit by a band called Rafael Cortijo's Combo titled "La Bombon de Elena." By the end of the 1950s, hundreds of Cuban musicians moved from Havana to New York City and settled in Spanish Harlem and other Hispanic communities in Brooklyn and the Bronx. One of these Cuban musicians, Gilberto Valdés brought a new kind of ensemble to New York: the *charanga*. *Charanga* orchestras used flute and

[12] Ibid., p. 47.

Break-Out Three

PROFILES *From Cuba: Tito Puente and Gloria Estefan*

A central figure in twentieth-century American music, the late Tito Puente has been honored with many titles, including "The Mambo King" and "The King of Latin Jazz." Born in 1923, he had intended on becoming a professional dancer, but he tore a ligament and shifted his attention to music. He eventually became accomplished on piano, saxophone, and a wide range of percussion instruments as well as excelling as a composer, arranger, and producer. After serving in World War II, he took advantage of the GI Bill to attend the prestigious Julliard School of Music in New York. By the time he enrolled in the school, he had already had a long career as a professional musician, having begun in 1937 with the Cuban bandleader José Curbelo. In 1949, he achieved a crossover hit "Abaniquito" with his Tito Puente Orchestra. In the 1940s and 1950s, he made recordings of *mambo* and *cha-cha-cha* with his long-standing music partner Celia Cruz that are still dancing hits today. But he continued to create contemporary hits well into the 1990s, including the fusions of jazz and rap in the *NuYorican Soul* project (1996) and the tribute *50 Years of Swing* (1997), in which he drew together tunes by the men and women who have dominated Latin music in the twentieth century.

Although Puente began his career in the first half of the century, Emilio and Gloria Estefan became highly influential in the latter half. Emilio Estefan is known as the "godfather" of Latin pop music. A Cuban immigrant and drummer who pulled together a band called the Miami Sound Machine in the early 1980s with his then-girlfriend lead singer, Gloria Estefan, the group made a smash hit in 1985 with "Conga." This hit transformed Gloria Estefan into a superstar. While she continued to work as a performer, Emilio began to explore work as a songwriter and as a producer. In 1995 he created a new recording company under the Crescent Moon label and started recording Latin musicians that the major labels were ignoring.

Emilio Estefan went on to receive several Grammy nominations and to work with other non-Latino artists such as Madonna and Will Smith, who wanted to add some Latino musical characteristics to their songs. Before his death, he managed a multimillion-dollar empire that included

Multitalented Latin music superstar Tito Puente. *Source: Ricardo Bentacourt/Ralph Mercado Management. Universal Music Latino. Ricardo Bentacourt/RMM/Universal Music Latino.*

violin and played intensely rhythmic arrangements. Valdés's own band was powered by Afro-Cuban conga player Mongo Santamaría. A later addition to the group was Johnny Pacheco from the Dominican Republic, who played drums as well as accordion and even the Cuban flute. The highly rhythmic nature of bands like this was perfect for dancing and encouraged the formation

music publishing and real estate, and was investigating producing sitcoms for television and movies. He was one of the leaders in bringing Latin performers to the mainstream and likened his own work to that of Berry Gordy with Motown: "I think what happened with R 'n' B at Motown is what's happening with Latin music now. It's like a sleeping giant waking up all over the world."[13]

Gloria Estefan rose to international fame with the 1985 hit "Conga." *Source: Photo by John Bellissimo. Corbis/Bettmann.*

[13] Farley, Christopher John. "Latin Music Pops." *Time*, May 24, 1999, p. 76.

of other *charanga*-style bands. Another Cuban musician, Celia Cruz, left Cuba in 1959 and settled in New York and began recording with Tito Puente and other top bandleaders. She went on to win several Grammy awards and other honors, eventually becoming the "Queen of Salsa."

Increased Migration to Mainland and Assimilation Issues in the 1960s

In the 1960s, the island of Puerto Rico became more independent and was allowed more self-rule. But many Puerto Ricans were still migrating to the mainland, particularly New York. Even though they were U.S. citizens, they were often not treated well and were victimized by discrimination because they were poor, came from rural backgrounds, had a wide range of skin colors, spoke Spanish, and came from a tropical, island culture. Some of these issues were highlighted in the musical and movie *West Side Story*. Assimilating into the urban New York culture was difficult, but they continued to develop support systems of organizations and communities to assist immigration efforts. Although New York was originally the main destination, Puerto Ricans soon branched out into other areas, including Chicago, Philadelphia, Milwaukee, Detroit, Miami, San Francisco, and Los Angeles. Although many moved to the cities, others moved to the rural areas and were employed as migrant field hands.

Challenges at the Beginning of the Millennium

In tropical Puerto Rico, many people work in the sugarcane fields where the agricultural season's schedule begins in January and ends in June or July. On the mainland, however, the agricultural season is on a different schedule, and Puerto Ricans can find year-round work by moving back and forth between the island and the mainland. About twenty thousand of these contracted "migrant" farm workers come to the mainland each year. With the opportunity to view the more opulent American lifestyle, many farm workers have tried to move permanently to the mainland. Moving to small cities and towns close to the farms where they worked, and taking jobs in unskilled or semiskilled labor industries such as garment making and service businesses, they often become the targets of discrimination. Recently, many of these industries have moved to areas outside of the United States, and the number of these kinds of jobs for Puerto Ricans has been reduced. Today, most Puerto Ricans are still at the lowest socioeconomic classes and struggle socially, economically, and politically.

One of their challenges continues to be the language barrier. The educational system was generally not supportive of Spanish-speaking students, but for the last two decades, many urban schools have hired bilingual teachers and established special programs to assist Puerto Rican immigrants. While continuing to deal with the language issues, Puerto Ricans on the island also will need to resolve their relationship with the United States. Some Puerto Ricans want to become America's fifty-first state; others want to become an independent country or part of a Caribbean commonwealth; still others want to maintain the existing arrangement as a U.S. territory.

The Development of Salsa

The Birth of "Salsa"

Salsa, like the term "jazz" or "rock," is a broad term encompassing a wide variety of music. The term itself was devised out of the Spanish word for "sauce" in New York in the 1960s by the record industry in order to help market and sell the music coming out of the Caribbean. Salsa also refers to a hot sauce, a common ingredient in many Caribbean and Latin American cuisines, and "salsa" seemed an appropriate term for the "hot" new music from these areas. The term became very popular in the mid-1970s to describe the music being created by New York–based Latin musicians who reworked the big-band arrangements during the "mambo" era adding influences from rock, funk, and other contemporary styles.

Salsa, like all Caribbean music, is a melting pot of African, indigenous, and European musical characteristics. Various stylistic elements have been fusing since the sixteenth century when the Spanish first colonized the area, with the consequence that Caribbean music contains a complex blend of instruments, rhythms, and melodic stylings as well as a wide range of dance steps that were a key element for the music.

African and European Influences on Salsa

African Influences

An important component in salsa is its emphasis on drumming. This emphasis is a direct heritage of the enslaved African peoples who were brought to the area and who were able to maintain, in varying degrees, the sacred and secular drumming traditions of their homelands in Africa. This emphasis on drumming is a dominant factor in all Afrocentric music. A second inheritance from Africa is the close bond between music and language. Many African languages were tonal and communication could be extended from the voice to instruments, particularly drums. From this extension the "talking drums" developed. The central texture of call-and-response singing is also present in salsa. Finally, and in some ways most important, there is the close connection between music and dancing. Salsa is Latin dance music, and every musical style within salsa has a characteristic rhythmic pattern that directly correlates to a dance step.

European Influences

Because of its role in colonizing the Caribbean area, the music of Spain is the most important European musical influence. By the sixteenth century, Spanish music itself was already an amalgamation of European, Arabic, Gypsy, Nordic, Indian, and Judaic influences. Like Mexico, the urban music of the Caribbean was influenced by the "cultivated" or "classical" music traditions of the Spanish court and Roman Catholic Church. The rural music was influenced most strongly by the folk-style musics of Spain, specifically the country folk songs and dances. Spanish dances combined with African dances to become an essential ingredient in Caribbean culture.

Salsa's Increasing Popularity

Fania Records

Fania Records was established in Manhattan in 1964 but became very important in the 1970s under the direction of its founder, musician-producer Johnny Pacheco. Originally from the Dominican Republic, Pacheco had been playing with big New York bands since the 1950s. In the late 1960s and throughout the 1970s, a team of multiethnic producers at Fania released a series of records that included both traditional and updated Caribbean music. In 1971, the record company created a wildly popular show called *Fania All Stars*, with a Puerto Rican New Yorker called Izzy Sanabria hired as master of ceremonies. Sanabria encouraged the audience to shout "salsa" as he introduced the soloists.

The basic ensemble for salsa was much the same as during the earlier mambo era, with *orquestas* (big bands) divided into brass sections accompanied by a rhythm section of piano, bass, and drums. These bands back up a lead singer, called a *salseros*, who participates in a call-and-response with the *coro* (chorus) sung by members of the band.

The percussion section is the powerful foundation for the music, performing a complex combination of rhythms. All of these sections interplay in such a manner that they compete in a call-and-response style reminiscent of both African vocal styles and 1940s big-band riffing. "Salsa" is a catchall term that includes multiple styles, each possessing the characteristics of a certain region or area of the Caribbean as well as the current style. For example, Puerto Rican bands such as La Sonora Poceña emphasized a *conjunto*, trumpet-led ensemble style. But Ritmo Oriental and Los Van Van from Cuba developed a salsa style drawn from the *charanga* instrumentation, which pitted three violins against three trombones. Then, in the 1980s, particularly with the *merengue* bands from the Dominican Republic, synthesizers were included eventually leading to the development of technomerengue in the 1990s. Musicians such as Rubén Blades led these kinds of salsa-electronic fusion groups that integrated electronic instruments and samples with traditional instruments such as the *guiro* (scraper).

Salsa and Latino Music in Miami

Although New York is absolutely central to the development of salsa, Miami, Florida, also has had a significant role. The city itself was often referred to as "Old Cubans' Town" until the early 1980s, when an influx of Colombians followed by waves of immigrants from Central American countries

Break-Out Four

LISTENING GUIDE *"Menea La Cintura"*

Performing Artist: Kaos

This is a party song that emphasizes that the band "Kaos" is the hottest band around to motivate people to get up and dance.

Rhythm	Quadruple but with polyrhythmic layering
Melody	Simple and repetitive
Harmony	Basic chord progressions but with jazz-influenced chords
Texture	Notice the *coro-pregon*; the vocal call-and-response descended from African musical styles; notice the fixed response of the *coro* known as the *montunos*
Form	Repetition of call-and-response
Instrumentation	Extensive use of percussion instruments with piano and bass and brass instruments

such as Nicaragua and El Salvador diversified the Latin mix of the population. Nevertheless, even today almost half the population of Miami has family roots in Cuba.[14] Miami became home to its own sound, called the "Miami Sound," a blend of salsa, rock, and pop. Two of the most successful Latin artists in mainstream America, Emilio and Gloria Estefan, have created music incorporating a wide range of Latin styles, including more-or-less mainstream salsa ("Conga" and "Doctor Beat") and, in 1990, the albums *Mi Tierra* (*son*) and *Abriendo Puertas* (*merengue*).

The success of Fania soon inspired the founding of rival record companies, and these companies, established in Miami, Puerto Rico, and New York, helped shape salsa as the broad-based term for all Latin music. As Fania began to decline in the 1980s, two new labels, Rodven and RMM, took up the market. RMM, particularly, housed in New York, has helped salsa become more integrated with other American music. An economic recession in the Dominican Republic in 1988 served as a catalyst for half a million Dominicans to move to the United States, settling primarily in New York. Dominicans brought with them a passion for *merengue,* and *merengue* soon dominated the Latin club season.

Salsa was revived by Sergio George, who joined RMM and began creating a new sound that emphasized trombones, reminiscent of salsa's *mambo* roots. His first hit was made by a Japanese group called Orquesta de la Luz, but additional success came as he developed an in-house RMM group. This in-house group contained long established superstars such as José Alberto, Celia Cruz, and Tito Puente as well as new younger singers such as Marc Anthony, Victor Manuelle, and La India.[15]

CONCLUSION

Today, salsa and other forms of contemporary Latino music are among the most popular music styles in the country. Many new magazines, television programs and films are being established that

[14] Ibid., p. 120.

[15] Steward, Susan. "Salsa: Cubans, Nuyoricans and the Global Sound" *World Music, The Rough Guide.* pp. 488–501.

incorporate various aspects of "hot" Latin music. Latin dance classes and clubs introduce people of all races and ethnicities to salsa steps and routines. Meanwhile, Latin music as a whole continues to evolve and reflect current cultural influences. For example, a young trio called Dark Latin Groove has fused salsa with soul and rap. Their style and success inspired salsa singers to create other salsa to hip-hop fusions, such as merenge-house, and salsa-merenge. Ricky Martin, Marc Anthony, and Linda "La India" Caballero have created what some have referred to as "salsified pop," in which they fuse various styles and record both in Spanish and English, appealing both to Hispanics and to mainstream American audiences. At the same time, traditional music performed by older musicians such as Ibrahim Ferrer with the *Buena Vista Social Club* is also attracting new audiences. With people of Hispanic descent now comprising the largest ethnic minority in the United States, Latin music styles will continue to thrive and become an increasingly influential force in American music.

Bibliography

Burton, Kim. "Colombia: El Sonido Dorado." *World Music, The Rough Guide,* vol. 2. London: Rough Guides, Ltd., 2000.

"Cuban Americans are 1.2 million . . ." in *San Jose Mercury News*, May 10, 2000.

Fairley, Jan. "Cuba: Troubadours Old and New." *World Music, The Rough Guide*, vol. 2. London: Rough Guides, Ltd., 2000.

Fairley, Jan. "Cuba: ¡que rico bailo yo! How Well I Dance." *World Music, The Rough Guide*, vol. 2. London: Rough Guides, Ltd., 2000.

Farley, Christopher John. "Latin Music Pops." *Time Magazine,* May 24, 1999, pp. 74–79.

Greene, Granville. ¡Sabrosa! *American Way*, August 15, 1999, pp. 53–58.

Harvey, Sean and Sue Steward. "Merengue Attacks." *World Music, The Rough Guide*, vol. 2. London: Rough Guides, Ltd., 2000.

Haubegger, Christy. "The Legacy of Generaion Ñ," *Newsweek*, July 12, 1999.

"Jamaica: The Loudest Island in the World." *World Music, The Rough Guide*, vol. 2. London: Rough Guides, Ltd., 2000, pp. 430–456.

"Juanes Shines at Latin Grammys." CBS News. The Early Show. March 28, 2004. http://www.cbsnews.com/stories/2004/03/28/earlyshow/leisure/music/main609077.shtml (Accessed 03–03–05).

Larmer, Bnrook. "Latino America." *Newsweek*, July 12, 1999, pp. 48–60.

Mauleón, Rebeca. *Salsa Guidebook for Piano and Ensemble.* Petaluma, CA: Sher Music Co., 1993.

Manuel, Peter with Kenneth Bilby and Michael Largey. *Caribbean Currents: Caribbean Music from Rumba to Reggae.* Philadelphia: Temple University Press, 1995.

"Protests Over Latin Grammys." BBC News: Entertainment. http://news.bbc.co.uk/1/hi/entertainment/music/1530199.stm (Accessed 03-03-05).

Steward, Sue. *Musica!: The Rhythm of Latin America.* San Francisco: Chronicle Books, 1999.

Steward, Sue. "Salsa: Cubans, Nuyoricans and the Global Sound." *World Music, The Rough Guide*, vol. 2. London: Rough Guides, Ltd., 2000.

Steward, Sue. *Musica!: Salsa, Rumba, Merengue, and More.* San Francisco, CA: Chronicle Books, 1999.

Sweeney, Philip. "Puerto Rico: Not Quite the 52nd State." *World Music, The Rough Guide*, vol. 2. London: Rough Guides, Ltd., 2000.

Chapter Fifteen

Tejano, Banda, and Contemporary Mexican-American Music

The murder of pop star Selena Quintanilla-Pérez in 1995 and the 1997 movie *Selena* about her life brought national attention to the music traditions of Mexican Americans. For the first time, many members of the mainstream culture were exposed to the term "Tejano," a word that translates as Texan and that is used to describe a musical style that originated in South Texas around the turn of the twentieth century. Tejano has its roots in the music of primarily Mexican-American farm workers, who took music that was popular with immigrant Germans, Poles, and Czechs and blended it with the traditions of Mexico. But Tejano did not originate with Selena, nor did it disappear with the death of its brightest star. Furthermore, Tejano is only one of several styles of Mexican-American music. Like musicians of other races and ethnicities, Mexican-American musicians have been reconciling their ethnic heritage with contemporary culture for years as they create music in a wide variety of styles.

Mexican-influenced rock—Rock Espagnol—was popular in the earliest stages of rock history, including number one hits such as "Tequila," released in 1958. Richie Valens (Valenzuela), of Mexican American and Native American descent, was the first influential Hispanic rock 'n' roll star. One of his biggest hits, "La Bamba," was a rock version of a traditional Mexican folk song. Carlos Santana, a Mexican American who was born in Mexico and moved to San Francisco in 1961, has been an iconic force in music since his exhilarating performance at the original Woodstock Festival in 1969. In 2000, Santana won nine awards including Album of the Year, Best Rock Album, and Record of the Year for his multistyled, fusion album *Supernatural.* At the Latin Grammy Awards in 2004, Santana was honored as the Latin Recording Academy Person of the Year for his significant professional, cultural, and social accomplishments.

Other well-known or rising Mexican-American rock musicians include the members of Los Lobos, the Latin Playboys, and Ozomatli. The Latin Playboys are a cutting-edge recording group that is pushing the boundaries fusing contemporary alternative rock and traditional Mexican music style characteristics. The band Ozomatli, formed in Los Angeles in the mid-1990s, blends salsa, urban hip-hop, and jazz funk, and won the best Latin/Rock Alternative Grammy for its album *Street Signs.*

Tejano star Selena was achieving crossover success when she was murdered in 1995. Here, she is singing at the Cunningham Elementary School in Corpus Christi, Texas, on November 14, 1994. *Source: AP Wide World Photos.*

There are also prominent musicians whose Mexican ethnicity is less well known and who have risen to stardom in other genres. Joan Baez, whose father was of Mexican parentage, became the undisputed "Queen" of folk music during the Urban Folk Revival and has continued to record and perform in a wide range of folk and folk-derived styles. Linda Ronstadt, also of Mexican-American heritage, is a popular music superstar who has recorded in many styles, ranging from her roots ranchera album *Canciones de Mi Padre* to rock 'n' roll, country, and even classical. These artists are only some of the most famous Mexican-American musicians who have adapted their heritage to thrive in contemporary culture.

Overview of Twentieth-Century Mexican-American Music Traditions

Throughout the first half of the twentieth century, Mexican Americans continued to create and listen to the *sones, mariachi, corridos*, and *canciones* that were such a vital part of their Mexican musical heritage. But these traditional styles were soon augmented by new developments known as Norteño/Tex-Mex, Tejano, and Banda.

Stylistic Categories

Norteño/Tex-Mex and Conjunto

Known as *norteño* ("northern") below the border, and Tex-Mex above the border, this is the overall category name for a musical style that was created when musicians incorporated the button accordion of the German, Czech, and Polish immigrants into the *corrido*-singing *son* ensembles. The music is characterized by consistent use of the polka duple meter and a style of singing that includes the nasal singing of the ballads and frequent extending of the final notes of the phrases in a manner that is characteristic of the *ranchera.*

A subset of the Norteño/Tex-Mex musical genre is *conjunto*, the Spanish word for "group." *Conjunto* music has been a very popular style in Texas and the term *conjunto* has come to mean the specific style of accordion-led dance music that is similar to *norteña* with the distinction that the emphasis is on the dance beat rather than on the singing of the ballads. The traditional *conjunto* band consists of a small group of instrumentalists playing the *bajo sexto* (the twelve-string guitar), bass, drums (usually the congo and bongos), and the button accordion.

Tejano

"Tejano" literally means "Texan," as this style originated in South Texas. From the Eastern Europeans that had migrated into the area, the Mexicans and Mexican Americans assimilated the accordion and popular dances such as the waltz and polka. Later, they also incorporated pop and country western dance tunes that they combined with their own Mexican traditions of *cumbias* and *huapangos.* Tejano is also characterized by an emphasis on singing, with songs in traditional Mexican lyrics. It is essentially the urban form of the rural *conjunto* but with added voice.

BANDA

Banda music uses brass band instrumentation to create fiery, brilliant, and complex renditions of *norteño* dances, *ranchera* ballads, and unique versions of *cumbia, merengue*, and *salsa* from the Latino music traditions of countries outside of Mexico. Banda's roots are in the European concert band tradition. Thus, banda is the Mexican equivalent of the American concert or marching band. The traditional instrumentation, which includes tuba as the bass instrument, is being gradually augmented and sometimes replaced by electronic keyboards. Many banda pieces are in triple meter, a direct connection to the European dance tradition.

Structural Characteristics

MELODY, RHYTHM, AND HARMONY

The melodies tend to be essentially European in style, based on major and minor scales with simple chords providing harmony. With styles that fused elements of other styles (such as banda's incorporation of jazz characteristics), the melodies and harmonies will reflect these other influences. The rhythm for Mexican-American styles in general is very metrical, with the dance-derived music emphasizing the rhythms associated with specific dances.

INSTRUMENTATION, TEXTURE, AND FORM

The instrumentation is specific to the style. For example, norteño/Tex-Mex is distinctive because of the use of the accordion, banda is characterized by the brass instruments, and Tejano for the amplified instruments and drums of rock 'n' roll. Some of the uniquely Mexican kinds of instruments include the *guittarun* (a large bass guitar), *bajo sexto* (the twelve-string guitar), and *jaranas* (little guitars). The texture is primarily homophonic, but with the more complex styles incorporating polyphony. Form tends to be strophic, or strophic with verses.

TWENTIETH-CENTURY MEXICAN-AMERICAN MUSIC WITHIN A SOCIAL AND HISTORICAL CONTEXT

The First Half of the Twentieth Century

POLITICAL AND SOCIAL CONTEXT OF THE 1900–1930S

During the first decades of the twentieth century, the population of Mexican Americans grew steadily, augmented continually by new immigrants. Many of the people coming from Mexico were migrant workers who worked as farm laborers during part of the year and then lived in cities during the agricultural "off-season." In the cities they created their own communities or *barrios.* The need for American men in the military during World War I left labor vacancies that created an even greater demand for Mexican workers. The Department of Labor eased the rules that had earlier limited the employment of Mexicans, and because industry promised higher wages and was less physically exhausting than agriculture, many Mexicans and Mexican Americans moved to northern and northwestern cities. Here they joined the expanding urban economy in industrial and construction jobs.

After World War I, the demand for unskilled labor continued to grow because of limits on immigrants from Asia and Eastern Europe. Between 1920 and 1929, six hundred thousand Mexicans entered the United States. For example, during the 1920s, the number of Mexicans in Los Angeles tripled to nearly one hundred thousand, with segregation confining them to areas within east Los Angeles. Most entered the United States on permanent visas, settling in Texas, California, and other southwestern states. These visas granted them legal residence but not citizenship, and, by 1929, a million people from Mexico lived in America.

Although many immigrants came into the United States legally, thousands of Mexicans also entered without visas. In 1924, the United States set up a border patrol to prevent unlawful entry, but Mexicans easily crossed America's poorly guarded two-thousand-mile border. In 1929, when the stock market crash shattered the American economy and initiated the Great Depression, unemployed Anglos began taking jobs previously held by Mexicans. Unable to find new jobs, eighty five thousand Mexicans returned to Mexico.

WORLD WAR II AND SOCIAL ACTIVISM IN THE 1940S

Hundreds of thousands Mexican Americans enlisted in World War II and fought alongside whites. To some extent, earlier ethnic stereotypes began to change after the war, as Mexican Americans became some of the war's most decorated heroes, earning forty-nine Congressional Medals of Honor. After World War II, the social and historical context for Mexican Americans began to change. Several political organizations were established to secure equal rights and opportunities for the Mexican-American community, and these organizations stressed the need for Mexicans to develop their American identity. The League of United Latin American Citizens (LULAC) founded in Texas in 1928, and the GI Forum, founded in Texas in 1948, were the most important of these groups. They pushed Mexican Americans to learn English and to assimilate into American society. They fought to improve education for Mexican Americans and they strove to acquire political power through voting. LULAC successfully pursued two legal cases that anticipated *Brown v. Board of Education,* and, in 1948, the Supreme Court upheld court rulings that declared segregation of Mexican Americans unconstitutional.

THE DEVELOPING NORTEÑO AND TEX-MEX STYLES

Throughout the first half of the twentieth century, Mexican Americans continued to create and listen to *sones*, *mariachi*, *corridos*, and *canciones*, but these traditional styles were soon augmented by new styles.

At the 1973 convention of the United Farm Workers, Dolores Huerta and César Chávez confer, trying to build a united union that welcomed all ethnic backgrounds, even though most of its leaders and members were of Mexican heritage. *Source: Wayne State University Archives of Labor and Urban Affairs. Walter P. Reuther Library, Wayne State University.*

Norteño and Tex-Mex. The corridos that told the stories of everything from the colonial revolution against Spain to the war between the United States and Mexico laid the foundation for a style that developed in the northern areas of Mexico and along the Mexican-American border. These "northern" bands are less familiar than mariachis, but they have also played an important role in contemporary Mexican and Mexican American music. Known as *norteño* ("northern") below the border, and Tex-Mex above the border, musicians incorporated the button accordion of the German, Czech, and Polish immigrants into the *son* ensembles.

Conjunto. *Conjunto* music is a subset of Tex-Mex and has been an integral music style in Texas for many decades. It is currently experiencing great popularity among Mexicans and Mexican Americans. Although literally translated as "group", *conjunto* has come to mean the specific style of accordion-led dance music that is similar to *norteña* with the distinction that it is dance music. The traditional *conjunto* band consisted of four instrumentalists, one each playing the *bajo sexto* (the twelve-string guitar), bass, drums, and the button accordion. Musicians in the traditional *son* string groups had appreciated the accordion's volume (so important for dancing) and versatility (it could play both melody and harmonic accompaniment). *Conjunto* bands combined the song traditions of the Mexicans and Mexican Americans with the rhythms of European dances such as the polka and waltz. The polka was dominant because this was the dance so popular with the German and Polish immigrants. It was characterized by a duple oom-pah, oom-pah beat; the waltz was characterized by a triple oom-pah-pah, oom pah-pah beat.

Created in the rural communities of Texas, the songs that were sung by vocalists in *conjunto* bands contained lyrics that concerned hard work, class struggle, and longing for something more in life or different in love. When the early American labels of Victor, Columbia, and Okeh were searching for various folk musics in the late 1920s, they made the first recordings of *conjunto* bands with musicians such as Bruno Vilareal, Narcisco Martínez, and Don Santiago Jiménez.

Break-Out One

LISTENING GUIDE *Corrido El General Santa Cruz*

Performing Artist: Antonio Federico, vocal; Frank Moreno, accordion; Paul Romero, guitar; Alfonso Molina, guitarrón

This traditional corrido—a song that tells a historic story—is set in the small border village of Sasabe, west of Nogales, New Mexico. No one living remembers the battle referred to in the text or any of the names of the people mentioned.

Rhythm	Waltz time (3/4).
Melody	Simple, with emphasis on singing and lyrics in Spanish.
Harmony	Basic emphasis on primary triads.
Texture	Homophonic; lead vocal on melody, with accordion fills "responding" to vocal lines.
Form	Strophic
Instrumentation	Typical Tejano band accompainment, with accordion playing the melody harmonized in thirds with simple guitar accompainment; the guittarón handles the bass part.

The Second Half of the Twentieth Century

CHANGES IN THE 1950S AND 1960S

After World War II, *conjunto* bands continued to flourish. Valerio Longoria, an accordionist from San Antonio, integrated three innovations into conjunto style. He brought in romantic bolero melodies that he sang and also played on the accordion, he added drums, and he introduced the Colombian cumbias.

In the 1950s, the accordionist Tony de la Rosa incorporated another innovation: he transformed the acoustic *conjunto* band by integrating elements of rock 'n' roll, specifically electric guitars and drums. He also slowed the tempo down and modified the music to create a more sophisticated, urban genre. As a virtuoso accordionist, he was also able to incorporate complex solos into the ensemble music. His technical ability combined with soulful singing made him a phenomenal success in the early 1960s, and he played to packed houses and recorded more than seventy-five albums during his lengthy career.

Another accordion player also soared to stardom in the 1960s and continues to be active: Esteban Jordan (also known as Steve and even "El Parche" because of the patch over his right eye). Jordan began playing with his brothers in a relatively traditional *conjunto* band called Los Hermanos Jordan. But under the influence of rock 'n' roll, he started to improvise solos on the accordion that were reminiscent of the improvisations of Jerry Lee Lewis on the piano and Jimi Hendrix on the guitar.

THE 1970S AND 1980S

In the 1970s and 1980s, two sons of Santiago Jiménez (who had recorded traditional *conjunto* in the 1920s) continued the *conjunto* tradition. Santiago Jiménez Jr. retained the folksy, older rural style, whereas his brother, Leonardo "Flaco" Jiménez, continued the new accordion style with a faster, flashier, more virtuoso style. In 1990, Flaco Jiménez and Tejano singer Freddie Fender became the Tex-Mex supergroup known as "The Texas Tornados."

Today norteño/Tex-Mex remains popular throughout Mexico and the southwestern areas of the United States. The ballads that are sung include lyrics that are updated to reflect current issues such as crossing the border or getting busted for drugs. Norteño bands such as *Los Tigres del Norte* and *Los Cadetes del Norte* keep an eye out on the local newspapers to convert new stories into ballads. Los Tigres has become the most successful group of this genre and records both in the United States and in Mexico, having achieved stardom on both sides of the border.

TEJANO

"Tejano," which means "Texan," is essentially the urban form of the rural *conjunto.* The style began developing in the 1950s as the *orquestas Tejanas* (Texan big bands) catered to the needs of the more affluent Mexican Americans who wanted sophisticated music for ballroom dancing. Whereas Selena with her band, Los Dinos, are the most well-known Tejano musicians, other popular bands and artists include Roberto Pulido, Tropa F, and Los Dos Gilbertos.

The first musician credited with creating this new style was the jazz band director Isidro Lopez, who decided to add the essential characteristic of *conjunto*—the accordion—to his big swing jazz band. This innovation of Lopez, along with listening to rock 'n' roll, influenced a musician who formed a band called Little Joe and the Latinaires. They combined the glittery costumes and choreographed dance steps of early rock 'n' roll with the *orquesta Tejana* style. Eventually, the *orquesta* aspects faded and mainstream pop became dominant. By the 1960s, two styles dominated in Tex-Mex music: the rural, folksy *conjunto* and the urban, sophisticated, pop-style *Tejano* bands such as Little Joe, Sunny Ozuna, and Augustine Ramirez.

Tejano in the 1970s–1990s. As the decades continued, *Tejano* bands adapted to reflect the characteristics of the era. For example, in the

Break-Out Two

PROFILE *Carlos Santana*

Carlos Santana was born in the village of Autlan, Mexico, in 1947 and then moved with his family in 1955 to the border town of Tijuana. Carlos's father was an accomplished mariachi violinist, and he exposed Carlos to traditional Mexican music from an early age. Santana also listened to other genres of music, particularly the blues as played by African-American guitarists John Lee Hooker, T. Bone Walker, and B. B. King. In 1961 he moved to San Francisco, the undisputed epicenter of the cultural change that is now simply and collectively referred to as "the Sixties." In 1966, Carlos formed his first band, the Santana Blues Band. It was this first blues band that, under the guidance of rock promoter Bill Graham, went on to perform in Graham's historic Fillmore West and that gave such an electrifying concert in the original Woodstock Festival in 1969.

Carlos Santana is perhaps the most famous Mexican-American musician and has created music that has incorporated many different music styles. Here he is in concert in Mexico City, promoting his album *Supernatural*. *Source: Photo by Daniel Aguilar/REUTERS/Corbis/Bettmann. © Reuters New Media, Inc./CORBIS.*

1970s, band members had long hair and wore bell-bottom jeans. In the 1980s, they added heavily synthesized tracks and the MTV-style "concert performance" attributes of rock theatrics. Two other important successes in the 1980s also set the stage for future Tejano stars. The first was the recording *Canciones de Mi Padre* by the pop superstar Linda Ronstadt, which contained a collection of primarily *rancheras* in the *conjunto* style. The second was the band Los Lobos, who became hugely successful with the soundtrack to the movie *La Bamba*, a commercial film about the first Mexican-American rock star, Richie Valens.

Clearly one of the most popular figures in the early 1990s was Selena. Selena grew up in Corpus Christi, Texas, and began singing as a child in her family's restaurant. She spoke English, and her idol was the 1970s' disco star Donna Summers. But her father insisted that she learn to speak Spanish and that she stay true to her Mexican roots. She won her first Tejano music award when she was only fifteen years of age. In 1995, just when she was experiencing true "crossover" success with songs such as "Amor Prohibido," she was shot in the back by her fan club manager. Current prominent Tejano stars include Bobby Pulido, Elsa Garcia, Jennifer Peña, and the band Cómo Te Extraño, led by Pete Astudillo.

The Late Twentieth Century

In the last decades of the twentieth century, Mexican immigrants continued to pour into the United States. These immigrants ensured that Mexican-American music was constantly reinforced and influenced by developments in Mexico. One of these developments was the popu-

Bill Graham encouraged the band to constrain their loose jamming style of extended improvisations and to incorporate distinct beginnings and endings that worked better both for recording and for radio play. The band released its first album in 1969, which went double platinum and featured the hit single "Evil Ways." This self-titled album contained Santana's early signature fusion style of rock with congas, timbales, maracas, and Latin rhythms along with expert guitar work. In November 1970, Santana issued the album *Abraxas* in which he included Tito Puente's "Oye Como Va" and a remake of Fleetwood Mac's "Black Magic Woman." Both songs became huge pop hits.

For the next thirty years, Santana continued to create music fusing his unique, virtuosic guitar playing with a wide variety of styles, including rock 'n' roll, blues, Afro-Cuban, and global music idioms which have been released in fourteen gold and nine platinum albums. These albums have earned him multiple Grammys and Bammys (Bay Area Music Awards). In 1997 he was named Latino Music Legend of the Year by the Chicano Music Awards, and he was part of a select inaugural group (along with Bill Graham and Jerry Garcia) to be inducted into the Bammy Hall of Fame. In 1998 he was inducted into the Rock and Roll Hall of Fame. In 2000, Santana was further honored by winning nine Grammy Awards for his thirty-sixth album *Supernatural.* In 2004, Santana was honored as the Latin Recording Academy Person of the Year for his significant professional, cultural, and social accomplishments. Carlos Santana is arguably the most important and famous Mexican-American musician in history, and in the spirit of the twenty-first century, he continues to transcend ethnic, racial, and cultural barriers as he creates powerful music that reconciles his Latin roots with the music of the global village.

larity of the updated *norteño* sound that had laid the foundation for a new music style that became the rage in the 1990s, *banda* music.

Banda

Banda music fused *norteño* style with brass band instrumentation in fast and virtuosic renditions of *norteño* dances, *ranchera* ballads, and unique versions of *cumbia, merengue*, and *salsa. Cumbia* music is dance music that has its roots in Colombia as a fusion of African and Indian music, and it is a specific kind of dance accompanied by music that is characterized primarily by a rhythm in which the offbeat is emphasized by the drums, shakers, and cymbal. Just as *cumbia* is the national music of Columbia, *merenge* is the national music of the Dominican Republic. Like *cumbia, merengue* is identified by its rhythmic pattern, an aggressive and unsyncopated duple beat juxtaposed against a counter rhythmic pattern. "Salsa" is a more generic term, referring to the intensely rhythmic music brought into the United States by immigrants from the Caribbean, particularly Cuba. All of these musics are discussed in more depth in the earlier chapter on Caribbean music, but it is these various international "Latin" styles that formed the basis for *banda.*

One of the classical *banda* ensembles is *Banda del Recodo*, led by the late Don Cruz Lizárraga, who died in 1996. The leadership of the group passed on to his two sons, Germán and Alfonso. Another prominent current banda group is Juan Gabriel Y Banda Recodo. *Banda* music currently dominates most television programs, and it is the sound of the *bandas* that fill local Mexican and Mexican-American stadiums and village halls. *Banda* music has also led to a proliferation of new dances, including the *quebradita*, but the *cumbia* remains the basic dance that forms today's banda repertoire.

A Sampling of Various Contemporary Fusions

The success of Mexican-American musicians such as Linda Ronstadt and Los Lobos inspired Mexican Americans to feel that perhaps they could retain their Mexican roots and traditions while still assimilating fully into "American" mainstream culture. Many younger musicians attempted to reconcile the various influences by creating new fusions of style.

A. B. Quintanilla. Selena's brother, A. B. Quintanilla, spent a year trying to sort things out after Selana's death, but returned to the music field when a friend asked him to produce a song for Thalia, another Latin pop star. He subsequently formed a new band, the Kumbia Kings, and released an album, *Amor, Familia y Respeto*, in 1999 followed by *Shhh* in 2001. *Shhh* contains a combination of cumbias, reggae, pop, rap, and R & B, and the lyrics are sung in both Spanish and English to succeed on both sides of the border. In response to the bilingual character of the album, Quintanilla responded, "That is what is so beautiful about being Latino and American. You get the best of both worlds."[1] Another example of this kind of contemporary border disappearance is Rapper Sinful, born and raised in Long Beach, California. He emerged as a "Spanglish" rap artist as one of two members of The Mexakinz and released their album *Zig Zag* in 1993 with a new album released in the summer of 2001.

Tish Hinojosa. Born in San Antonio to Mexican immigrants, Tish Hinojosa absorbed traditional Mexican music styles along with the rock 'n' roll and urban folk revival music of the socially conscious 1960s. Learning guitar as a teenager, she sang folk and pop songs in local clubs, eventually moving to New Mexico, then Nashville, releasing her own cassette titled *Taos to Tennessee* (eventually released as a CD). In 1988 she moved to Austin, Texas, with the hope that her unique blend of roots music would find a good reception in the local, thriving music scene there. In 1992, she released *Culture Swing*, an album reflecting her multiple Mexican-based, folk-derived influences, and the album was named the Folk Album of the Year by the National Association of Independent Record Distributors. In 1995, she worked with the Rounder label to produce *Frontejas*, an overview of Texas/Mexico border music that was highly acclaimed in the Latin music community. She continues to perform, record, and advocate for both Latin and women's rights.[2]

Ozomatli. In the mid-1990s, a group of primarily Mexican-American musicians in Los Angeles started merging Latin salsa, urban hip-hop, and jazz-funk to create a unique fusion. Eventually settling into a basic ten-member band, Ozomatli performed for several years in the local club scene. They released their debut album in 1998, followed by *Embracing the Chaos* in 2001, *Coming Up* in 2003, and *Street Signs* in 2004. Their multicultural blends, exceptional musicianship, and intense national and international touring helped attract a large fan base.

Peter Mogt. One final example of music crisscrossing the border is a new style called "nortec" that mixes traditional norteño with electronically synthesized music called techno. The style emerged in Tijuana under the leadership of Pepe Mogt, who was looking for something that was more current than the *norteño* music of his parents that he found *naco* (cheesy). Mogt took various outtakes of *norteño* that included accordion, drum, and tuba riffs from a local studio's demo tapes, fused them with a compelling

[1] Lopez, Jessica Y. "A.B. Quintanilla III and the Kumbia Kings." *Ritmobeat*, June 2001, p. 26.

[2] Huey, Steve. "Tish Hinojosa." From All Music Guide, http://launch.yahoo.com/ar-252219-bio—Tish-Hinojosa (Accessed 03-08-05).

Tejano star Tish Hinojosa is a singer and songwriter who grew up listening to traditional Mexican-American music. Here she is singing folk and border songs at the Irving Plaza, New York City, on May 5, 1995. *Source: Jack Vartoogian.*

polyrhythmic drumbeat, and processed the samples through various analog and digital synthesizers to release "Polaris." The track started out as a hit at local parties, but soon spread quickly to other parts of Mexico and into the United States. In February 2001, their music was distributed and released by an American label, Palm Pictures, as the *Tijuana Sessions, Vol. 1.*

Conclusion

On June 11, 2001, *Time* magazine released a special issue titled *Welcome to Amexica*, with the cover byline "The border is vanishing before our eyes, creating a new world for all of us."[3] Various essays discuss ways in which the border between the United States and Mexico is dissolving as a result of trade (soon Mexico will pass Canada as the top trading partner of the United States) and multiple political agreements. But the main focus of the issue is on the cultural interchange of Mexican and American people. With eight hundred thousand individuals from both countries going back and forth over the border legally every day, there is bound to be the exchange of ideas, attitudes, values—and music—that steadily erodes politically imposed national distinctions. Added to these individuals are the forty-six hundred people who cross illegally[4] each day (some staying, others returning voluntarily or being caught by border guards). With numbers of this magnitude, it is easy to see why the last census shows that Hispanics have overtaken African Americans as the country's largest minority. Fifty-eight percent of Hispanics are from Mexico and retain strong ties to their Mexican cultural and ethnic heritage. It is clear that the extensive demographic presence of Mexican Americans will have an increasingly important influence on American mainstream music.

[3] *Time*, June 11, 2001; "Welcome to Amexica," vol. 157, no. 23.
[4] Ibid., "A Whole New World," by Nancy Gibbs, pp. 38–45.

BIBLIOGRAPHY

Campa, L. Arthur. *Hispanic Culture in the Southwest.* Norman: University of Oklahoma Press, 1979.

Geijerstam, Claes af. *Popular Music in Mexico.* Albuquerque: University of New Mexico Press, 1976.

Gibbs, Nancy. "A Whole New World." *Time,* June 11, 2001, vol. 157, no. 23, pp. 38–45.

Goldfield, David, et al. *The American Journey: A History of the United States.* Second Edition. Upper Saddle river, New Jersey: Prentice Hall, 2001.

Huey, Steve. "Tish Hinojosa." From All Music Guide, http://launch.yahoo.com/ar-252219-bio—Tish-Hinojosa (Accessed 03-08-05).

Tanner, Helen Hornbeck, editor. *The Settling of North America: The Atlas of the Great Migrations into North America From the Ice Age to the Present.* New York: Macmillan, 1995.

Turino, Thomas. "Music in Latin America." *Excursions in World Music.* Bruno Nettl, Charles Capwell, Isabel K. F. Wong, Thomas Turino, Philip V. Bohlman. Third Edition. Upper Saddle River, New Jersey: Prentice Hall, 2002.

Tyrangiel, Josh. "The New Tijuana Brass." *Time,* June 11, 2001, vol. 157, no. 23, pp. 76–78.

Young, Kristen. Tejano brings flavor of Mexico to Texas A&M-area Music Scene, *University Wire.* http://www.elibrary.com/s/edumark/getdo . . . rn:bigchalk.com:US;EL&dtype=0~0&dinst=0 (Accessed 05-03-01).

Chapter Sixteen

Asian American Music

Asian Americans are the third largest ethnic and racial minority in the United States. In *Census 2000*, Asian Americans accounted for 3.6 percent of the total population. Although they represent a much smaller subpopulation than blacks or Hispanics (accounting respectively for 12.1 and 12.5 percent), they are also one of the fastest growing minority groups. In 1980, the population of Asian Americans was 3.7 million. By 2000, the number had almost tripled to 10.1 million. Demographically, Asian Americans constitute an important and distinctive panethnic minority in the United States.

There is even some evidence that Asians, specifically the Chinese, may have been the first ethnic group to arrive in North America besides the indigenous peoples we now refer to as Native Americans. There are two legends in Chinese history, one dating back to the fifth century and the other to 2250 B.C.E., of Chinese travelers to a country far to the east. The earliest record is a compilation of books entitled *Shan Hai Jing* (*Classic of Mountains and Seas*) compiled by a man named Yu that describes the geographical characteristics of a land across the "Great Eastern Sea." The later record is the story of the travels of Hui Shan, a Buddhist priest, who informed the Chinese court of his journeys to a far-away country called "Fu-Sang," which some scholars believe is present-day Mexico.

Yet, despite the numbers and possible evidence of ancient Asian presence in the United States, there is no "Asian American" music genre, per se. On a Web site devoted to a discussion of Asian-American culture,[1] someone asked why American popular music contained so many genres that reflect the influences of Latinos and African Americans but none of Asian Americans. Forum moderator Ada Lio acknowledged the absence of "a decidedly Asian contribution," and suggested that "maybe a solution lies in going back to the roots of our ancestors and inventing a new style." The discussion on this Web site is a window into some of the complex issues surrounding Asian Americans and Asian-American music.

[1] About Us, 2001. About.Com,Inc. *Asian-American Culture.* "When Will Asian-American Music Get Its Turn?" Moderated by Ada Lio.

Challenges and Issues in Discussing Asian Americans and Asian-American Music

It is true that the other broadly based ethnic constituency groups have produced, through their interaction with one or more of the other groups, a readily identifiable uniquely American music genre. For example, the interaction of African Americans and European Americans produced blues, Gospel, and jazz. Hispanic Americans (already an ethnic and racial blend of indigenous, African, and European peoples) have produced mariachi, salsa, and Tejano. Asian Americans have not yet produced a recognizable, uniquely American music that is equivalent to jazz or Tejano, but such an observation does not take into account several critical issues. To begin to develop some understanding of the complexity of these issues, we must first identify what is meant by "Asian American."

Origin of Term "Asian American"

The term "Asian American" was first adopted in the late 1960s at a time when two thirds of the Asians in the United States had been born here. (Today the statistics are reversed, and over two thirds of Asians are foreign-born immigrants.) Having been born here, they felt more connected to their "Americaness" than to their ancestral homelands. The term also developed within the context of the Civil Rights movement. In the 1960s, it had a political resonance that implied progressive social goals and a stand against U.S. involvement in Southeast Asia. The Chinese-American and Japanese-American communities, which had been socially and politically distant from each other since World War II (during which time China and Japan were enemies), began a dialogue using the title "Asian American" to imply a common ground. As time progressed, Asian American came to suggest not a political vantage point, but rather that the person so designated was of Asian heritage. Yet, what constitutes the boundaries of Asia is confusing and disputed, and from any vantage point, includes a large number of distinctly different countries. Immigrants from these countries find the term "Asian American" odd, as they don't necessarily see or feel much kinship with immigrants from other Asian countries.

Diversity of Asian Americans

The title "Asian American" is currently used in the United States to define a wide range of ethnic groups that have arrived in America from "Asia." Asia is the largest of the earth's seven continents, covering about one third of the world's total land area and containing about three fifths of the world's population. Because of its great size and diversity, it is often further divided both geographically and culturally. The five major geographic subdivisions include over thirty distinct nations. For example, "East Asia" includes the nations of China, Korea, and Japan. "Southeast Asia" consists of nations such as Vietnam, Indonesia, Cambodia, Thailand, and the Philippines. "South Asia" includes nations such as India and Pakistan. Southwest Asia includes Iran, Iraq, Israel, and Saudi Arabia. Finally, "North Asia" includes the nations of the former Soviet Union. Culturally, some of these nations (such as China and Japan) are considered "Asian," whereas others (such as Russia and Israel) are not. Significantly, Australia and New Zealand are geographically located in Asia, but no popular definition includes these nations as part of Asia.

Thus, "Asian Americans" are extremely diverse, and although there is a large Asian-American population, it is not necessarily a "community." The obstacles to drawing them together range from language and religion to historical rivalries and experiences immigrating to the United States. Asian-American leaders have been frustrated by the lack of solidarity that is often found in black and Latino communities. This also has an impact on music, as each of the various subgroups have their own music traditions, and hence, there is not a single "Asian" music style that can fuse with other ethnic traditions to create a new American genre.

"NEWNESS" OF THE ASIAN-AMERICAN COMMUNITY

Perhaps one of the most critical issues pertaining to the development of a uniquely Asian-American music genre is the relative newness of Asians in America. Although there are some Asian-American families who have been in the United States for many generations, the majority of individuals have immigrated within the last three decades. Thus, Asians in America are predominantly first generation. It is not surprising, therefore, that a distinct musical style has not yet emerged. Jazz, too, didn't develop overnight. To understand why the Asian-American community is so small and generally "new," it is important to review the major immigration policies that have governed Asian immigration to the United States. Asian immigration can be roughly divided into three periods: 1849–1882, 1882–1965, and 1965 to the present.

The Three Periods of Asian Immigration

1849–1882: THE PERIOD OF UNRESTRICTED IMMIGRATION

Before and during this period, several Asian groups arrived on the shores of North America. The earliest groups were primarily Filipinos brought on Spanish ships in the early 1700s, who settled in Louisiana, and Chinese sailors, merchants, and artisans arriving in the ports of New York City, Boston, and Philadelphia. But the first large wave of immigration from Asia occurred during the Gold Rush of 1849. Like pioneer immigrants from other countries, thousands of mostly male Chinese came to what they called *Gum San*—"the Gold Mountain"—to seek their fortunes. After the Gold Rush slowed and development in the West continued, men were recruited from their villages in southern China to become contract laborers primarily in the mining industry and in railway construction. Most of the laborers did not intend to move permanently, but rather to advance their economic status and then return to their ancestral villages.[2] Many did return, but others chose to stay or were not able to earn enough money to pay for their trip back.

In 1865, an estimated twelve thousand Chinese laborers were brought to America for the building of the transcontinental railroad. As the mining and construction industries declined, Chinese laborers moved into fishing and in to agricultural areas. Coming from the Canton River delta area, they knew how to transform the Sacramento River delta area into rich farmland and to channel the water into a sophisticated irrigation network. During the 1860s, anti-Chinese sentiment grew as a reaction to labor conflict, economic depression, and targeted racial bias. In 1870, rioters on the West Coast demanded the deportation of the Chinese and destroyed Chinese neighborhoods. Anti-Chinese sentiment led the U.S. Congress to pass very harsh laws discriminating against the Chinese, including the first restrictive immigration law. This law, known as "The Chinese Exclusion Act," was passed in 1882 and prohibited the entry of Chinese laborers for ten years and barred Chinese from becoming American citizens.

1882–1965: THE EXCLUSION PERIOD

During this second period, only Asian diplomats, merchants, and students and their dependents were allowed to come into the United States. Members of the "Mongolian race" were also denied the right to become naturalized American citizens. The Chinese Exclusion Act was extended for another ten years by the Geary

[2] This was reflected in their refusal to cut their long hair, required by Manchus to be worn in a braid (or be beheaded) called a "Queue." If a man were to cut his Queue, this would represent that he was disobeying the emperor and therefore would not be able to return to China. So even though non-Chinese ridiculed these men, they didn't dare cut their hair, as that would indicate that they had detached themselves fully from the emperor and their homeland.

Chinese immigrants working in California were attracted to Gum San (the "Gold Mountain") during the 1849 Gold Rush. Mines and minings. This picture shows gold mixers with Chinese laborers at the Seed of Auburn Ravine, California, in 1852. *Source: California State Library. Courtesy of the California History Room, California State Library, Sacramento, California.*

Act of 1892. In 1904, exclusion was extended indefinitely. In 1905, President Roosevelt extracted a promise from the government of Japan (called "The Gentlemen's Agreement") that it would not permit the emigration of laborers to the United States. In 1923, Congress also enacted a general immigration law that included a provision prohibiting the entry of aliens ineligible to citizenship. This included Chinese, Japanese, Koreans, and Asian Indians. Occasional loopholes (such as for World War II war brides and selected refugees) allowed some to enter, but basically Asian immigrants were prevented from entering the country and those that were already here were confined largely to segregated areas called "Chinatowns" or "Japantowns" in major cities throughout the country. Although the exclusion act was repealed in December 1943 (when China became an ally of the United States in World War II), the quota for Asian immigrants was still very low. For example the quota for Chinese was set at 105 persons per year. The Civil Rights movement in the 1960s, particularly the changes in the immigration laws, reopened American doors to Asian immigrants.

1965–Present: Immigration on an Equal Basis

The Immigration Act of 1965 abolished the discriminatory national origins quota system, beginning July 1, 1968. Asian immigrants since 1965 have come largely in three categories. The first consists of well-educated intellectuals, scientists, and engineers who came to the United States for advanced degrees and decided to stay. They have made significant contributions to the United States, most notably in the areas of science and technology. The second category consists of tens of thousands who came to escape political instability or repression. A third category was created by the 1965 changes in immigration policy that gave high priority to family reunification. This greatly increased an

In this engraving, Thomas Nast attempted to raise sympathy for Chinese immigrants. Here, Columbia, a symbol for American ideals, attempts to protect an immigrant crouched in front of anti-Chinese slogans and an angry mob. Cartoon by Thomas Nast, 1871.
Source: Stock Montage, Inc. Historical Pictures Collection.

immigration pattern known as "chain migration," in which people sought to join relatives already in the United States.

Historically, the sum effect of these immigration laws was to keep the Asian-American communities small, marginalized, and exploitable primarily only as labor. But the abolishing of the discriminatory quota system after 1965 meant that Asian immigration to the United States could start to be equivalent to other immigrant groups. Although Chinese Americans remain the single largest Asian-American group, Asian Americans have become very diversified, beginning with a large influx of Japanese between 1898 and 1907. Asian immigrants quickly became the fastest growing immigrant group, with more than 1.5 million arriving during the 1970s as opposed to about eight hundred thousand from Europe.

Current Asian Communities in the United States

Today, Asian-American communities are some of the fastest growing in the United States. The most current national census data show that the largest groups of Asians living in the United States, in descending order of population size are: Chinese 2.43 million, Filipino 1.85 million, South Asian/Indo-American 1.68 million, Vietnamese 1.12 million, Korean 1.08 million, and Japanese 796,700. They share a common profile in that a small portion of the community, referred to as "The First Wave," has been in the United States for generations. For example, some Chinese-American families have now been in America for six generations. But the greater portion of Asian immigrants, the "Second Wave," has arrived in the last few decades. This means that although some Asian Americans have culturally assimilated to the mainstream of American life, for the most part, many Asians in America are first generation. Their musical tastes and habits are as diverse as the Asian-American population; some prefer the classical or art music of their own country or of European classical music, others the international styled pop music in their own language, and yet others the mainstream popular music of the United States.

Acknowledging the number and diversity of Asian-American communities, for the purposes of this chapter we will focus on the six largest groups of Asians in the United States in order of population size. With apologies to those groups not listed, an attempt to include every Asian group represented in the United States is beyond the practical scope of this chapter. Because Chinese Americans are the largest and oldest Asian-American group, we will start there, looking in slightly more depth at their music traditions. We will follow this with a brief look at the history and music of the other five largest groups in the United States.

Asian-American Music within a Social and Historical Context

Chinese Americans

In the 1990 census, there were 1.6 million Chinese Americans, making them the largest Asian-American group in the United States, with 40 percent living in California. But even this relatively concise category of "Chinese Americans" obscures considerable diversity. China's population is approximately 93 percent "Han" Chinese. The 7 percent non-Han ethnic minority consists of more than seventy million people further subdivided into fifty-six ethnic minorities distinguished by history, language, religion, and culture. The Chinese language consists of more than a dozen major spoken dialects, although all writing is done using the same characters that have been in use for more than three thousand years. Most prewar Chinese immigrants to the United States spoke the various dialects of Cantonese. Cantonese-speaking communities are thus common in the United States, but are actually a minority in China. In 1955, the Chinese Communist government established Putonghua ("common speech")—the dialect of the northern province known to Westerners as "Mandarin"—as the official spoken language, and now many Chinese immigrants speak this language.

The immensity of China's geographical size, population size, and ethnic and cultural diversity is a complex subject even for scholars who have made it their life's study, and therefore it is inaccurate and inappropriate to make broad generalizations. Nevertheless, a few comments can be made regarding structural characteristics.

Break-Out One

IN-DEPTH FOCUS *The Chinese Lion Dance*

Every language and dialect group of "Overseas Chinese" in the United States has musical, dance, instrumental, and singing groups, mostly of amateur status, who practice and perform for their own community. But there are two large groups who have come to the United States. The first group is the Cantonese of the southern, Guangdong province and their subdialect groups. These were the earliest immigrants to the United States. For historical and geographical reasons, Cantonese-speaking communities are common in the United States but are actually a minority in China. The second group is the National Dialect groups such as the immigrants from the Republic of China (or Taiwan) and the northern provinces of the People's Republic of China.

One of the Chinese musical traditions that is popular with members of both groups is the Lion Dance. Generally connected with the martial arts, Lion Dancing is also the most accessible performance to observers from outside the Chinese community. The performance has a small but loud percussion ensemble that consists of a large drum (*Da Ku*), a bronze gong (*Da Lo*), and a pair of cymbals (*Nan Po*). Seen by both the Cantonese and National dialect-speaking Chinese as a good luck ritual that brings prosperity and drives away evil influences, Lion dancing is normally performed at special events. These events include the opening of a new store, a community festival, or the traditional new year's day of the Chinese calendar. This New Year begins with the second new moon after the winter solstice, which occurs between January 21 and February 19. Both for Overseas Chinese and in China, this is a traditional time of celebration.

Structural Characteristics of Traditional Chinese Music

Melody, Rhythm, and Harmony. Melodic contour, especially vocal melodies, is closely correlated to Chinese language. Rhythmic organization can be free, additive, or divisive/metrical depending on the style. Traditional melodies draw on the primary Chinese pentatonic scale, the most common of which arranged in an ascending order are equivalent in terms of relative pitch to C–D–F–G–A.

Instrumentation, Texture, and Form. The most important chordophone instruments include two categories of zithers: the *zheng* (a small, high-pitched zither with movable bridge) and the *Qin* (a zither with seven strings that is used to perform sophisticated, introspective music). Another important cordophone is the *pipa* (a pear-shaped lute with four strings that are plucked). There is also the *Erhu* (the category name for many regional variations of two-string bowed fiddles). Idiophone and membranophone percussion instruments were also very important, and include bells, gongs, cymbals, clappers, and wooden-framed barrel drums. One of the most popular is the *Yunluo*, which is a frame of ten gongs. Aerophone instruments include both wind instruments such as the *Dizi* (a transverse flute in which the performer blows across a hole in the flute, but containing a membrane that gives it a buzzing, nasal tone) and reed instruments such as the *Sona* (a flared bell instrument originally from the Middle East). One of the most interesting and oldest of the reed instruments is the *Sheng*, which is a type of mouth organ usually with seventeen pipes played by blowing through a mouthpiece at the side. Texture can be monophonic, homophonic, heterophonic, or polyphonic and formal structures can be simple patterns of folk music to highly complex structures in opera.

Influence of Confucian Philosophy on Chinese Music

For thousands of years, the most profound influence on Classical music in Chinese culture has been Confucian philosophy. The Confucian concept proposes that music and rituals must be played, sung, and performed in exactly the correct manner and with the proper attitude, or there will be serious consequences. Certain sounds, ritual movements, and numbers have symbolic importance. For example, the five-note pentatonic scale was associated with the five basic elements of earth, metal, wood, fire, and water as well as other significant organizations of five, for example, colors (red, blue, yellow, white, and black) and directions (center, north, east, south, and west). The misapplication or neglect of this symbolism was believed to have negative results. This matter was considered of such great importance that the emperor himself was responsible for performing many yearly rituals, accompanied with the correct music, to ensure the welfare of the nation.

Peking/Beijing Opera

Chinese opera, of which there are several regional schools and styles, for centuries had as their subject matter the ancient and popular myths, legends, and the histories of the previous dynasties. Without proper instruction and study of the conventions, hand gestures, character facial painting, and stylized singing, many of these forms can be completely bewildering to outsiders. The most well-known style of Chinese opera is Peking opera. Peking opera developed in the late eighteenth century when various acting companies came to Peking to celebrate the eightieth birthday of the emperor. The performances were so successful that soon this style became dominant. Following are some of the characteristics of Peking opera.

Originally, Peking opera was provided as entertainment to the rich, and audiences were not expected to keep quiet but rather to socialize and converse during the performance. The opera consists of dialogue sections interspersed with singing and instrumental sections. It contains a variety of action, including stylized battle scenes typically featuring extraordinary acrobatic skills, as well as dance, comical slapstick, dramatic acting, and virtuosic singing. The repertory is divided into two groups of plays, distinguished by subject matter and style of performance. The *wu* refers to military subjects that are based on old stories and legends that emphasize heroic action and intrigue. They often contain spectacular battle scenes, and sometimes they concern gangsters and thieves. *Wen* are civic and love stories and deal with daily social problems. Sometimes the two styles are combined in a single play. Actors in a Peking opera are primarily categorized by character (as opposed to vocal range, which is the norm for European opera). There are the Sheng (the main male characters), the Dan (the female characters), the Jing (the warriors, bandits, statesmen, or gods), and the Chou (the male comic roles).

Changes After the Establishment of the People's Republic of China

Peking opera was one of the main targets for reform after the establishment of the People's Republic of China in 1949. Mao Zedong believed that art should serve the "workers, peasants and soldiers" and not the aristocracy. Art should be used to help convert the masses to socialism and should contain particularly patriotic themes. The reformers changed opera texts and conventions such as kowtowing and other gestures of humiliation while also developing modern operas on contemporary themes such as stories from the Chinese Revolution or class struggle.

Concurrent with the modifications of Peking opera in the last half of the nineteenth century was a revival of traditional, regional folk forms that were seen as the true "people's" music. Additionally, there has been a movement to involve more amateurs in musical performance. One outcome of this revival was an active campaign to develop and standardize the manufacture of musical instruments while modifying them to accommodate Western tonality and harmony. Hence, some instruments were given frets or keys in order to achieve this. A second outcome was to introduce instruments into a Western-style orchestral performance. Yet another strong development at this time was the establishment of Western-style conservatories of music, largely influenced by China's relationship with the Soviet Union. By the early 1960s, the cultivation of Western music had reached high standards and many performers began to win prizes at international festivals in Russia and Eastern Europe. These developments have also affected U.S. immigrants and Chinese Americans. Many important classical musicians are now ethnic Chinese, and the children of Chinese immigrants study Western classical music in the United States and they play a dominant role in youth orchestras.

Today, every language and dialect group of Overseas Chinese in the United States has musical, dance, instrumental, and singing groups, mostly of amateur status, who practice and perform for their own community. Also, for many arriving immigrants in the last several decades, recordings of popular music from Hong Kong, Singapore, and Taiwan constitute the music of choice and these recordings are, except for the lyrics that are sung in a dialect of Chinese, for the most part indistinguishable from the international popular music of other cultures.

Filipino Americans

The modern history of the Filipinos is closely tied to the fact that their country was a Spanish colony for four hundred years and then an American territory for many years. During the period spent as an American territory, American teachers transferred the American educational system to the Philippines. Filipinos were taught American English, to pledge allegiance to the American flag, and to sing the U.S. national anthem in school. After achieving independence in 1945, educated Filipinos in the cities have been in constant contact with American mainstream culture through films, books, and, now, television programs. This, coupled with the fact that many Filipinos have Hispanic surnames, has led to smoother, but far from trouble-free, transition into American culture for Filipino immigrants. The Philippines is a nation composed of thousands of islands. There are many language and dialect groups in these islands, but the language of *Tagalog*, mixed with a smattering of English and Spanish words, is most commonly heard in the United States.

Music in the community can be divided into three areas: (1) the indigenous music of pre-Spanish Filipino culture (including the music of the Moro Islamic minority of the southern islands); (2) Spanish colonial musical forms; and (3) popular Filipino-American music. Because of their outward appearance of assimilation, many observers assume that some of the popular singers and performers of Filipino-American heritage represent Filipino-American music, but as with several other groups of Asians, they have become adept at popular American music forms such as Broadway show tunes, rock, and rap. Their ability and familiarity with American popular music is a testimony to their long and close ties with the United States and its entertainment media.

There are a small number of Filipino musicians and dancers who have chosen to study and perform a pre-Spanish musical form known as *Kulingtang*. Consisting of a series tuned brass gongs struck with wooden mallets, along with a number of drums and other percussion instruments, *Kulingtang* gives us the most accurate insight into indigenous Filipino music before the arrival of the Europeans. Others have adopted the study and performance of Spanish Colonial–period songs and dances played on fretted string instruments originally imported from Spain such as the guitar and the *Bandurria* (a twelve-string fretted instrument). Both of these groups represent a portion of the Filipino-American population that pursue historical forms in an effort to maintain a clear Filipino identity in their music and culture. Filipino Americans also have been very successful in American music forms such as Broadway musicals, jazz, and other popular mainstream music styles.

Indian and Pakistani Americans

India has been called "a continent within a country." A nation with a population that competes with the People's Republic of China for largest in the world, it is the world's largest democracy and is composed of a wide spectrum of religions, cultures, languages, customs, and history. To begin with, there is no single Indian language. The Indian constitution recognizes fifteen languages with over seven hundred dialects. Most of the major languages have their own alphabet. On most Indian currency, thirteen languages are printed. The religions of India include Hindu, Muslim, Christian, Sikh, Jain, Buddhist, Parsi, Jewish, and Zoroastrian, as well as others. The diversity of languages, combined with India's position as a British colony, led to the use of British English as a common language. The classical music of the subcontinent is generally divided into two systems: the North Indian or Hindustani, and the South Indian or Karnatak. The music of some of the larger groups in India is so complex that it would be impossible to describe them in detail in less than several volumes. Instead, we will take a look at the basics and what is available in the United States at this time.

The classical music of India is essentially melodic (derived from *ragas*) with an often-complex rhythmic accompaniment (derived from *talas*). Rather than scales, Indian music is composed of a number of melodic schemes called "*raga*." These *ragas* provide the melodic building blocks out of which performers improvise. Musicians expand, embellish, and "draw out" the possibilities inherent in the melodic embryo of the *raga*. Each *raga* can have an association with a human emotion, a time of the day, and a season of the year. The other musical component is *tala*, a recurring arrangement of rhythmic patterns. The schools and systems of Indian classical music traditionally require long apprenticeship with a guru or teacher, and instruction using mnemonic syllables. This enables the student to sing simple and complex *ragas* or *talas* from memory without the aid of an instrument. Schools and teachers of the various musical systems and styles abound in the Indo-American community and present a full yearly calendar of concerts and recitals. Packaged shows of pop stars and religious artists on tour from India and Pakistan are common and draw large crowds from the community.

The Indo-American community also supports and encourages the study of Indian instruments and their music. One of the most familiar instruments to mainstream America is the *sitar*, associated by most Americans with artist Ravi Shankar. The sitar and its music became a "fad" in the rock scene of the 1960s, especially after George Harrison of the Beatles began to study it and include it in the Beatles music, beginning with the *Revolver* album. Other instruments include the *veena*, an ancient double resonator lute; the *bansuri* or bamboo flute; the *harmonium*, a popular British import consisting of a small hand bellows keyboard organ; and the *tabla*, or tuned hand drums. Lessons on and performances of these instruments by Indo-Americans fill local community newspapers and periodicals. Instruction in singing offered in Indo-American papers include *ghazal* ("love lyrics") and *bhajan* (the descriptions of the lives of Hindu Gods Rama, Krishna, or Siva). The popular music of the "Bollywood" Indian film industry adds to a host of devotional styles for every taste and interest.

A surprising crossover in recent years has been the art of the devotional music of Qawwal. A religious form of music used by mystics of the Sufi sects of Islam in Pakistan, it has gained fans in the United States who are drawn to the hypnotic drone of the harmonium and percussion and the ecstatic vocal improvisations of the singers. Often consisting of Persian poetry sung in Urdu or Punjabi, the form has been used in Western film scores such as Martin Scorsese's film *Last Temptation of Christ* and Oliver Stone's controversial film, *Natural Born Killers*. It has made "pop" stars of singers such as the late Nusrat Fateh Ali Khan.

Vietnamese Americans

As a by-product of the U.S. military involvement in SouthEast Asia, several Asian groups have immigrated to America in the last thirty years. The largest of these, the South Vietnamese, include tribal ethnic minorities such as the Hmong and Mien. Most immigrants arrived after the fall of the Saigon government and the evacuation of the American forces in 1975. Others, such as the ethnic Chinese who had lived in Vietnam for generations, were forced to flee because of political upheavals and persecution in the decades following the end of the war.

Though politically independent, Vietnam was drawn into a Chinese sphere of influence as early as the Han dynasty (207 B.C.E.–220 C.E.), and its ruling class for much of its history was frequently Chinese or Chinese educated. As a result, the oldest classical Vietnamese court music is a reflection of the Chinese court music of that period. Vietnamese folk music is characterized by the use of string instruments. These include the *Dan Tranh* (a sixteen to twenty-one-string zither), the *Dan Nguyet* (a moon-shaped fretted lute), and the *Dan Nhi* (a two-string spike fiddle). One of the most ancient instruments is the *Dan Bau*, or monochord, on which a skilled player, by adjusting the tension of the single string while performing, can produce a surprisingly wide range of notes. A form of Vietnamese opera, *Cai Luong*, is still popular with many older Vietnamese. *Cai Luong* is a reformed version of an older, classical theatre called *Hat Bo*. It began in the 1920s, and its plots are simple, filled with action, humor, and lots of songs and music.

Vietnam became a French protectorate in 1884, and under French rule, Chinese script was dropped and a phonetic alphabet was adopted. Christianity and the French language became the fashion among the powerful and ruling class, and Vietnam's popular music was strongly influenced by French culture. After a war of independence from France that ended in 1954, there was a disastrous war between South and North Vietnam, which did not end until 1975. In the last days of the American military involvement, the evacuation of more than ninety-six thousand Vietnamese took place. This was followed by a second wave of refugees called the "Boat People" because they escaped through a very dangerous and desperate manner by crowding on to small boats. The Vietnamese-American community suddenly grew beyond the few hundred listed as living in the United States in 1965. Popular music among Vietnamese Americans today is roughly divided between *Nhac Ngoai* or Western songs sung in Vietnamese-language versions, and *Nhac tru tinh* or slow ballads.

Korean Americans

Koreans have a distinctive language, culture, and customs that have at times been influenced by, but are still always separate from, their nearest geographical neighbors, China and Japan. The Korean language is a member of the Ural-Altaic family, which includes languages such as Mongolian, Finnish, and Hungarian. Known to its inhabitants as "The Land of the Morning Calm," it currently is separated into two countries, North and South Korea. The first Koreans to arrive in the United States, some eight thousand between 1903 and 1920, came as the Empire of Japan was in the process of annexing their homeland in 1910. Under Japanese rule, Korean immigration to the United States virtually came to a halt. After World War II, a Democratic government was founded in 1948 and reconstruction began. From 1950 to 1953, a war between North and South Korea involved the U.S. military as members of the United Nations' forces. This led to a number of "war brides" and orphans being admitted to the United States in the 1950s, but immigration from Korea was not to begin again in earnest until the late 1960s. The tiny Korean-American population, which had been here since the turn of the 1900s, grew several times after 1970 and can be found primarily in Southern California and New York City.

The primary difference between Korean music and that of its neighboring countries is the fact that traditional Korean music is usually in triple meter. In 109 B.C.E., the Chinese emperor Wu annexed what was to become Korea and for the next four hundred years it was ruled by China. At this time, Classical Korean music was strongly influenced by China's culture and arts. Folk music in Korea is noted for its hardy and rugged style. Minstrel songs are referred to as *P'ansori* and folk songs as *Minyo.* Each province of Korea has its own distinctive *Minyo* or folk song tradition.

The number of Korean Americans involved in Western classical music is substantial and represents the aspirations of an arriving immigrant group to enter a respectable middle-class position as educated and skilled participants. There is a sizeable industry in Korea that produces a version of international pop music for listeners both in Korea and among the overseas Korean communities. With the exception of some singers whose work is influenced by classical Korean singing style, as a general rule, this music differs from other examples of international pop music only in the language of its lyrics.

In recent years, as community-sponsored Korean-American youth groups attempt to maintain a connection with their cultural roots, the forming of *Samulnori*, a modern derivative of *P'ungmul* (a rural percussion tradition), has become very popular. *Samulnor* ensembles consist of four instruments: the *Puk* (double-headed barrel drum), the *Jing* (large gong), the *Chang-go* (hour-glass-shaped drum), and the *Kengari* (a small hand-held gong). This exuberant music is played at festivals such as *Ch'usok* (the Harvest Moon Festival). Activities during these festivals include the playing of traditional games and performing folk dances. Like other Asian groups, educated young Korean women are often encouraged to join traditional dance groups to gain poise and grace. This training often includes instruction on musical instruments such as the *Kumango* (a plucked zither), the *Chang-go*, or the *Puk*. In addition to performing on these instruments, they also learn to sing the classical Korean songs.

Japanese Americans

Because of historical factors such as Japan closing its borders to outsiders from 1640 to 1853 and the fact that modern Japan is a wealthy industrialized nation, there has never been a large-scale immigration from Japan to the United States. The community itself defines its members in a loose system that consists of counting how many generations that person's family has been in the United States. For instance, *Issei, Nisei, Sansei*, and *Yonsei* label the first, second, third, and fourth generations of Japanese Americans. The community can be loosely divided into two groups, the Japanese Americans who have been in America since the turn of the 1900s and the new immigrants from Japan, called *Shin Issei.*

Noh Theater developed as entertainment for the wealthy class and became very formal and stylized. Kita Noh Theater Co., *Momiji-Hari.* *Source:* *Jack Vartoogian.*

Arriving primarily from Hawaii during a brief window of opportunity from 1898 to 1924, the early Japanese-American community was primarily rural and agricultural. The *Issei* (first generation) brought with them the traditional and popular Japanese music of the day, and even the busiest farmer might belong to an arts group that practiced forms of Japanese poetry such as *Waka* or *Haiku*, or play a musical instrument such as the *shakuhachi* (an end-blown bamboo flute). The *Nisei* (second generation) in the 1930s and 1940s quickly adopted popular forms of American music such as jazz.

The traumatic effect of the incarceration of the 110,000 West Coast Japanese Americans into concentration camps in the interior of the United States during World War II is a major factor when considering the music, or indeed any aspect, of the culture of the Japanese Americans. In fact, one of the respites from the dreariness of the internment camps from 1942 to 1945 was entertainment sponsored by detainees. These included the traditional music and dance performances for the older *Issei*, and also big band dances where young Japanese Americans moved to the sounds of camp amateur swing bands playing all the latest mainstream hits. When first released from the U.S. interment camps in 1945, many Japanese Americans were sensitive to the fact that their loyalty to the United States had been questioned. As a consequence, a sizeable number of Japanese Americans chose to reject anything not seen by the mainstream public as culturally 100 percent American. By contrast, other Japanese Americans continued the practice of sending young boys to judo class and girls to learn the *Koto* (a Japanese zither).

In the late 1960s and early 1970s, a movement among Japanese *Sansei* (third generation) began to explore their identity through music, literature, film, and art. One by product was renewed interest in a traditional instrument and form called Taiko. Historically a part of the outdoor festivals, notably the Buddhist Festival of the Dead (*O-Bon Odori*), *Taiko* groups were seen by Buddhist temples and Japanese Christian churches as a way to regain the interest of young Japanese Americans who were drifting away from the community. The perfect performance venue for this large collection of drums of different sizes is an outdoor event. This, and the fact that with a little instruction and practice the average person could play well enough to perform in just a few months, has made *Taiko* a mainstay of Japanese-American events in less than one generation. Today, there are about one hundred *Taiko* groups registered in the United States and Canada, of which approximately 98 percent are listed as amateur or community-based organizations.

Jazz, in all its forms, has had a special fascination for Japanese and Japanese Americans. The number of Japanese Americans and Japanese nationals living in the United States working as professional jazz musicians is much larger than their fractional percentage of the American population would suggest. These two factors have produced several attempts to fuse Japanese traditional music and Western jazz music. The most commercially successful example is the jazz-rock fusion band from the Los Angeles area known as Hiroshima who use the conventional Western jazz instruments (such as the saxophone, bass, and keyboards) but also include the *Koto*, *Taiko*, and *Shakuhachi* in their arrangements.

Asian-American Music in the Last Half of the Twentieth Century to the Present

In the late 1960s to the early 1970s, a student movement with the participation of established artists and writers began to explore the idea of what the title *Asian American* could mean. Asians, like Latinos, Africans, and others in the United States, were challenging old stereotypes about themselves and seeking new roles and images. Books, plays, graphics, and music were used to express this search. Proponents of this new self-image proposed that the two choices then available to people of Asian descent living in America were inadequate. The first was a strict adherence to traditional Asian culture and acceptance of the role of "perpetual foreigner." The second was complete assimilation into mainstream American life at the cost of cultural surrender. The proponents of the new image conceived of a third, the *Asian American.* This American citizen of Asian heritage would be able to comfortably blend Asian and American influences in a single lifestyle to the benefit of both cultures.

With this in mind, several musicians consciously attempted to create something that they felt could accurately and legitimately be labeled Asian-American music. The first record album of the music that reflects this belief was *A Grain of Sand*, produced in New York City in 1973 by Barbara Dane for Paredon Records. It contained the music and songs of three artists: Nobuko Miyamoto, Chris Iijima, and Charlie Chin. The collection was the culmination of three years of writing and touring the Asian-American communities of the United States. Using acoustic guitars and simple "folk" song arrangements, the song lyrics were concerned with issues of identity, racial stereotypes, political change, and social justice. These songs were Western in musical style but "Asian American" in terms of the political and social content of their lyrics.

A Sampling of Fusions

Since the 1970s, there have been various musicians of Asian ethnic heritage who have experimented with blending Asian music characteristics with Western-styled music. Artists such as the pianists Jon Jang and Benny Yee, the saxophonists Fred How and Francis Wong, and several others have attempted to create contemporary American music and still keep Chinese traditional influences in their work.

Cibo Matto is the name of a Japanese-American female duo from New York. The duo is comprised of vocalist Miho Hatori and producer Yuka Hondam, and their album *Viva! La Woman* was released in 1996. Described as a fusion of hip-hop with acid jazz, the first cut includes spoken Chinese in the background. Hondam's mix of sampled sounds and music from jazz orchestras and movie sound tracks is combined with guitar, brass, voices, and funky bass.

The Far East Side Band consists of Jason Hwang (violin), Yukio Tsuji (percussion and Japanese shakuhachi), and Sang Won Park (kayagum and other Korean instruments). In their album *Urban Archaeology*, released in 1996, they add Joe Daley (tuba) and electronically processed sounds. Their music is described as ranging from East Asian traditional music solos to "Asian Dixieland jazz."

The Asian American Jazz Orchestra (AAJO) also has done much to define contemporary Asian-American music. Originally assembled in 1998 for a national touring project on the internment of Japanese Americans during World War II, AAJO is comprised of musicians who are experts in the jazz tradition and who also possess fluency on a variety of Asian instruments.

Asian Americans and "Classical" Music

Asian-American composers are also asserting a strong presence in contemporary American art or "classical" music. In 1999, Hseueh-Yung Shen, a Chinese-American composer, won the top prize in the American Composers Orchestras 1999 competition. Shen competed against six other

Break-Out Two

PROFILE *Yo-Yo Ma*

One of the foremost Asian-American musicians is Yo-Yo Ma, an internationally famous cellist in the Western European "Classical" music tradition. Born in Paris in 1955, his father was the musicologist Hiao-Tsun Ma, who had emigrated from China in the 1930s. In 1963, the father moved his family to New York City, where Yo-Yo began studying at the Julliard School of Music. While Yo-Yo studied there and also later at Harvard University, he performed with both student and professional groups. In 1978, he won the Avery Fisher Prize, which brought engagements with major performing ensembles such as the New York Philharmonic orchestra. In 1984, he recorded the *Six Bach Suites for Unaccompanied Cello*, which won him a Grammy Award. The next year, he won a second Grammy award. Yo-Yo Ma has continued to expand musical horizons, participating in a variety of fusion and experimental endeavors.

Edgar Meyer, Mark O'Connor, and Yo-Yo Ma worked together to create the fusion CD *Appalachian Journey*. Here the three are playing on November 7, 1966 at New York's Bottom Line. *Source: AP Wide World Photos.*

In 1999, he joined the country music fiddler Mark O'Connor and string-bass virtuoso Edgar Meyer to produce the video and CD "Appalachian Journey." This album uses the three string players as the core, but then adds special guests singer/songwriter James Taylor and fiddler/vocalist Alison Krauss. The recording includes various American genres from traditional Anglo fiddle tunes to Stephen Foster songs. In interviews, Yo-Yo Ma has explained that often disparate types of music have very deep and surprising connections, and that "it's part of the same flow."[3]

One of Ma's goals is to explore music as a means of communication, and as a vehicle for the migration of ideas around the world. This interest led to his establishment of the Silk Road Project, which studies the cultural, artistic, and intellectual traditions along the Silk Road trade route that connected the Mediterranean Sea to the Pacific Ocean. This project is an umbrella organization and resource for many cultural and educational programs, participating in several festivals, including the Smithsonian Folklife Festival in 2002.

Ma has collaborated with musicians from many different genres and cultural traditions. In 2004, he released *Yo-Yo Ma Plays Morricone*, his reimagining of themes from Ennio Moriccone's award-winning film sound tracks. The idea for this recording began during the Academy Awards in 2001, when Ma was performing the award-winning score for *Crouching Tiger, Hidden Dragon* and met Morricone. Having won fifteen Grammy awards and released over sixty albums, Yo-Yo Ma remains one of the best-selling and most widely known musicians in the classical field.

[5] Schaefer, liner notes, *Appalachian Journey*, Sony Music Incorporated, 1999. Yo-Yo Ma, Edgar Meyer, Mark O'Connor. Catalog # 66782.

Break-Out Three

LISTENING GUIDE *"Hard Times (Come Again No More)"*

Performing Artists: James Taylor with Yo-Yo Ma, Edgar Meyer, and Mark O'Connor

"Hard Times" was written by Stephen Foster (1826–1864), who, as a young composer living in Pittsburgh, used to listen to the black stevedores at the Pittsburgh levee. He became very interested in black music and even attended services at a black church. In 1849 he wrote the song "Susannah," which became popular with miners in the Gold Rush. Foster's songs were frequently sung in minstrel shows, but he strove to make his music more universal and resisted the caricatures of blacks often found in minstrel shows. The lyrics for "Hard Times" encourage people to be mindful of the hungry and poor who remain on the fringes of society right outside our doors. This recording was made in 1999 by one of the foremost Asian-American musicians, Yo-Yo Ma, in collaboration with the country music fiddler Mark O'Connor, the multiple-genre string-bassist Edgar Meyer, and the urban folk star James Taylor. It represents a fusion of many American elements that are all "part of the same flow."

Rhythm	Duple
Melody	Simple and memorable
Harmony	Basic triads
Texture	Homophonic with counter melodies provided by fiddle and string bass
Form	Strophic
Instrumentation	Solo male voice with guitar, string bass, and fiddle accompaniment

finalists, one of whom was Ken Ueno, of Japanese ancestry. This was not an isolated incident, for in the last decade, Asian-American composers have won many coveted prizes and fellowships, including the Lili Boulanger Award (Chen Yi), the Grawemeyer Award (Chinary Ung), Guggenheim Fellowships (Zhou Long, Bright Sheng), and the Rome Prize (Bun-Ching Lam and P.Q. Phan). These composers mix Asian and American elements in their work.[4] To what extent the music created by all or any of these fusions can be identified as "Asian American" is worthy of discussion. For example, even if these musicians are immigrants themselves (and were not born and raised in the United States), one cannot presume that they know Asian musics or aesthetics, since during the first half of the twentieth century, most music schools in China, Japan, and Korea taught only eighteenth- and nineteenth-century Western art music.

CONCLUSION

Fundamentally, America is a multiethnic society of immigrants from all over the world, who "listen to music with cultural and ethnic ears."[5] When Asian-American musicians explicitly or implicitly mix Asian and American elements in their music, they not only offer us new sounds,

[4] Lam, Joseph. "Exotica for Sale or the New American Music? How Should We Listen to Music by Asian-American Composers?" *American Composers Orchestra* Web page. http:// www. americancomposers.org/

[5] Ibid.

but they also challenge American ears and minds with what the music means. Is it a personal expression of the musician's individual sense of ethnic identity or aesthetics? Does it profess as one of its goals to address and reflect the experience of Asians in America in general? Is it an attempt primarily to create something that will appeal to an audience and hence be a commercial success? Does its reference to Asian ethnicity make any difference in the music aesthetically? Or is it the beginning of a new American musical genre that will eventually take its place alongside jazz and Tejano? Only critical listening, and the passage of time, will tell.

BIBLIOGRAPHY

About Us, 2001 About.Com,Inc. *Asian-American Culture.* "When Will Asian-American Music Get Its Turn?" Moderated by Ada Lio. April, 2001. http:// www.about.com/(Accessed 2001).

Araki, Nancy K. and Jane M. Horii, *Matsuri: Festival, Japanese American Celebrations and Activities*. Heian International Publishing Company, 1978.

Berger, Donald Paul. *Folk Songs of Japan.* New York: Oak Publications, 1972.

Chaitanya Deva, B. *An Introduction to Indian Music,* Publications Division, Ministry of Information and Broadcasting, Government of India, 1973.

Cordova, Fred. *Filipinos: Forgotten Asian Americans,* Demonstration Project for Asian Americans, Division of Special Programs of the National Endowment for the Humanities, 1983.

Feng, Theo-dric. Adapted from reviews posted by Amplitude, a Washington, DC–based magazine put out by the Asian American Arts and Media, Inc. Asian/Asian American Music. http://members.tripod.com/˜tfeng/ (Accessed 03-10-05).

Jones, Stephen. "China: Han/Traditional." *World Music: The Rough Guide*, vol. 2. London: Rough Guides, Ltd., 2000, pp. 33–44.

Kim, Ryan. *San Francisco Chronicle* Staff Writer. "Asians pursue a united state/Fastest growing population finds community building of a continent's people an elusive American dream." http://www.sfgate.com/cgibin/article.cgi?file=/chronicle/archive/2001/08/02/MN125464.DTL

Kishibe, Shigeo, *The Traditional Music of Japan.* Tokyo: The Japan Foundation, Ongaku No Tomo Sha, 1966.

Korea National Tourism Organization, *Korea.* Seoul, Korea: Korea Tourist Information Center, 1996.

Lam, Joseph. "Exotica for Sale or the New American Music? How Should We Listen to Music by Asian-American Composers?" *American Composers Orchestra* Web page. http://www.americancompusers.org

Law, Joan and Barbara E. Ward, *Chinese Festivals.* Hong Kong: South China Morning Post Publications, 1982.

Liang, Prof. Tsai-Ping. *Chinese Musical Instruments & Pictures.* Taiwan: Chinese Classical Music Association, Taipei, 1970.

"Ma, Yo-Yo," in *Encyclopedia of World Biography Supplement*, vol. 20. Gale Group, 2000. Reproduced in *Biography Resource Center.* Farmington Hills, MI: The Gale Group. 2001. http://www.galenet.com/servlet/BioRC (Accessed 05-07-01).

Ma, Yo-Yo in *Contemporary Musicians*, vol. 24. Gale Group, 1999. Reproduced in Biography Resource Center. Farmington Hills, MI: The Gale Group. 2001. http://www.galenet.com/servlet/BioRC (Accessed 05-07-01).

Mackerras, Colin P. "China: Drama," *The New Grove Dictionary of Music and Musicians.* Stanley, Sadie. (Editor). Fifth Edition, 1980. Volume Four. pp. 23–259. Macmillan Publishers Limited, London *Grove's Dictionaries of Music*, Inc., New York, NY.

MacDougall, Bonnie S, editor. *Popular Chinese Literature and Performing Arts in the People's Republic of China, 1949–1979.* Berkeley and Los Angeles: University of California Press, 1984, pp. 112–143.

Malm, William P. *East Asia: China: In Music Cultures of the Pacific, the Near East, and Asia.* Second Edition. Englewood Cliffs, NJ: Prentice Hall, 1977.

Mingyue, Liang. *Music of the Billion: An Introduction to Chinese Musical Culture.* New York: Heinrichshofen, 1985.

Otake, Gary. "Thoughts on Asian American Music." E-mail to Elizabeth Barkley; August 29, 2001.

Pian, Chao Rulan. "China, General." *The New Grove Dictionary of Music and Musicians.* Stanley Sadie. (Editior). Fifth Edition, 1980. Volume Four, pp. 245–250.

Popley, Herbert Arthur. *The Music of India.* Delhi, India: Low Price Publications, 1921.

Takaki, Ronald. *Strangers From a Different Shore: A History of Asian Americans*. Little, Brown, and Company. 1989.

Thornberry, Barbara E. *The Folk Performing Arts: Traditional Culture in Contemporary Japan.* Albany: State University of New York Press, 1997.

Wellesz, Egon, editor. "Ancient and Oriental Music." *New Oxford History of Music*, vol. 1, London: Oxford University Press, 1957.

Wong, Deborah. "I want the microphone: Mass mediation and agency in Asian-American popular music." Cambridge, MA: TDR, Fall 1994, v38 n3, p. 152(16). Full Text: Copyright New York University & Massachusetts Institute of Technology, 1994.

Wong, Isabel K.F. "The Music of China." *Excursions in World Music*, Second Edition. Bruno Nettl, Charles Capwell, Isabel K.F. Wong, Thomas Turino, and Philip V. Bohlman. Upper Saddle River, New Jersey: Prentice-Hall, 1997, pp. 69–102.

Chapter Seventeen

Hip-Hop and Rap

When the Sugarhill Gang released "Rapper's Delight" in 1979, few people could have predicted that hip-hop and rap would become the most important music forces of the late twentieth and early twenty-first centuries. "Rapper's Delight" drew on trends that had originated in New York several years earlier. Brought to the United States by the Jamaican immigrant Kool Herc, and elaborated on by Grandmaster Flash, hip-hop started with disk jockeys "rapping" words in a rhymed and rhythmic patter. This practice of rapping over records was done live at parties and on radio programs before it was actually recorded and eventually released as a piece of music by the Sugarhill Gang. But rhythmic musical speech had been in existence for centuries. Furthermore, it was an integral part of African oral traditions, and had manifested itself in African-American culture in everything from black preaching and "signifying" to rhythm 'n' blues and funk. What made rap and hip-hop so powerful was that now this form of rhythmic speech and the sounds that provided the accompaniment, "spoke to" and became the voice of a whole generation. Although it had begun in the culture of young African Americans, it was soon embraced by youths of all races and ethnicities. The focus of the furor in the 2001 Grammy Awards, for example, was about the music of Eminem, who is white.

Criticisms and Defenses of Rap

What eventually made rap so incendiary was that many people, including many African Americans, did not like what was being said in one style of rapping, the extreme "hard core" or "gangsta" rapping. Rather than the fun, witty party lyrics initiated by the earliest rappers, the language of this style of rapping used obscenities, displayed racism, made violent and derisive remarks about homosexuals, promoted misogyny, and encouraged crimes, including murdering police. Parents feared that rap made ghetto life look attractive, luring impressionable middle-class youths into a ghetto fantasy in which they would adopt the values and attitudes of depraved street thugs. Critics voiced concern that the offensive language both glorified and incited violence. Its defenders said that this kind of rap simply described the harsh realities and problems that were (and still are) occurring in some segments of American society.

A group of demonstrators protest Time Warner when one of their groups released a single entitled "Smack My Bitch Up." Beverly Hills, CA. *Source: Photo by Reuters. Corbis/Bettmann.*

Others said that at least some of the lyrics were intended to be humorous.

Criticisms also focused on the music itself. As one writer said, "I think the phrase 'rap music' has replaced 'jumbo shrimp' as the ultimate oxymoron. Perhaps calling it street poetry would make sense, but to call it music is to refuse to acknowledge that the emperor has no clothes."[1] The "clothes," of course, are "melody" and "instruments," two of the traditional building blocks of music. Defenders responded by citing other examples in which these same structural characteristics were absent. Even in "classical" music, for example, there are no conventional melodies in percussion compositions or in the early-twentieth-century German opera technique of "Sprechstimme." And in terms of instruments, using records as instruments was not so far removed from using synthesized sounds in other genres of contemporary electronic music.

Ultimately, hip-hop and rap have challenged conventional definitions of music, composition, and performance. Furthermore, their popularity represents a realignment of culture, race, and ethnicity in America. Rap, particularly, has given the formerly invisible underclass a loud and powerful voice. Even with the success and talent of other contemporary musicians and artists, it is clear that rap has continued to engage audiences and to speak for a generation of young people in a way that other pop styles have ceased to do. Hip-hop and rap music now have global appeal, and are being created by musicians from all over the world. One of the first tasks to better understand its popularity is to differentiate between the words "Hip-Hop" and "Rap."

Overview of Hip-Hop and Rap Music Traditions

Defining Hip-Hop and Rap

Hip-Hop Culture

Hip-hop is the name for the culture of which rap is simply a part. Hip-hop culture initially had four main elements: emceeing (rapping), break dancing, graffiti art, and dj'ing. Eventually, it included the new styles of language and fashion that were popular among rappers and their fans.

[1] Philip Barnett, "The Battle Over Rap." (*Newsweek*); 10-30-2000.

Rap

Rap is a vocal style of rhythmic speaking in rhyme. The voice is used as a percussive instrument while delivering messages in complicated verbal rhythms. The actual speaking is called "rapping," or, "MC'ing." Early rap artists wanted their lyrics to be clearly understood, and the patter format seemed to achieve this clarity. Initially, rapping was simply chants and call-and-response rhymes over a DJ's manipulations of records. It became one aspect of a cultural phenomenon called "hip-hop," apparently from early rap lyrics such as "Say hip, hop, you don't stop."[2]

Hip-Hop as Background Music for Rap

"Hip-hop" was originally used to refer to the background music for rap. Several techniques developed to make this background music more interesting. For example, an early technique called "scratching," involved playing a record but changing the direction of rotation back and forth rapidly to create a rhythmic pulse. A variation was to use a second turntable to play the same record straight through while one scratched the record in a rhythmic counterpoint on the first turntable. In addition to "scratching," another technique used multiple turntables to insert sections from one recording into another called "cutting." A related technique was to move between recordings, and if the recordings had different tempos or speeds, use a varispeed control mechanism to maintain a constant beat pattern to blend the different songs. These are just some of the techniques that evolved to create the background music.

The first people to do this were disc jockeys, and so they used records that already existed. Early hip-hop artists maintained this practice of using existing records when they began to take excerpts, or "samples," from recordings to create the background for their raps. They would take these samples, and repeat them or combine them in different ways in a technique called "looping." Because many of the artists whose music was "sampled" viewed this as stealing, lawsuits ensued. Eventually, rap artists needed not only to acknowledge the sources from which they took their samples, but they also had to pay these sources royalties. This became expensive, so vocalists started to create completely new compositions to serve as their accompaniment. Drum machines, synthesizers, and computers provided the technology both to isolate precisely the samples from existing records and to generate new sounds and rhythms to create their music.[3]

Hip-Hop as a Distinct Musical Style. Hip-hop also has been used to refer to the musical style in which a kind of patter-song vocal technique is used that is somewhere in between, or combines elements of, rapping and singing a melodic melody. Singers in this style also use an electronic-generated and highly rhythmic music texture as backup. As rap became more associated with social and political messages, hip-hop tended to maintain the earlier party atmosphere associated with reggae and the funk DJ's who had initiated the style.

Stylistic Categories of Rap

Old School

This describes both the earliest hip-hop and rap recordings and current recordings that emulate the older styles that were created using two turntables and a microphone.[4] It emphasizes simple beats, perhaps only a sampled bass line, and straightforward party rhymes. Kool Herc, Run DMC, and the Beastie Boys are the true Old

[2] Light, Alan. "Rap and Soul: From the Eighties Onward," in *The Rolling Stone History of Rock and Roll*, p. 682. Although these words were used in other songs, they also were used in the first rap recording to make it on to radio charts, "Rapper's Delight."

[3] Charlton, Katherine, *Rock Music Styles: A History*. Second Edition. Iowa: Wm Brown, 1994.

[4] The definitions and representative artists for Old School, Turntablist, and the various hip-hop subcategories were taken from Audiogalaxy (http://www.audiogalaxy.com) in 2005.

School, and Mos Def/Black Thought is an example of contemporary artists experimenting with the same kind of sound.

Hard Core or Gangsta Rap

Rather than "party lyrics," some rap vocalists began to rap more political lyrics, addressing issues of racism, life in ghettos, including drug use, injustice, gang warfare and street violence. Some rappers provoked serious controversy, such as Ice-T (Tracy Morrow) in his song "Cop Killer" (1992), that warned he would go out and "dust off" some cops, slitting a policeman's throat and watching his family mourn. As reprehensible as this sentiment is, it should be remembered that this was Ice-T's response to the highly publicized police beating of Rodney King in Los Angeles, and the fact that these policemen were acquitted. Ice-T was from the same area, and he and other rappers had witnessed, experienced, and talked about police brutality for years. It was hard for him and others to accept that despite the video documentation of the beating, the police were found "not guilty of excessive violence."

The language of this more extreme style of rapping that focused on violence and rage in urban life also used obscenities, and sometimes displayed overt racism against other ethnic and racial minorities, such as Jews and Asians. Some rappers encouraged intolerance of homosexuals, and routinely referred to women as "bitches" or "hos" (whores). Many people condemned these rappers for their offensive language, which they feared promoted violence. For example, Black Women for Political Action were among many groups that pressured Time-Warner to sell the rap label under which Ice-T had recorded and distributed "Cop Killer."

Turntablist or DJ

Evolving from Kool Herc's original DJ'ing, Turntablist is "live" performance featuring the DJ and his or her turntables, sometimes in competition settings. Turntablists use scratchings, mixing, and transforming techniques to create unique combinations that may or may not include rapping. The earliest rap artists such as Grandmaster Flash and Afrika Bambataa were the original Turntablists, but more contemporary artists such as the X-ecutioners, Cut Chemist and Peanut Butter Wolf, and The Mixologists have maintained the basic style. Most Turntablists are musicians who, because their compositions are extemporaneous and not typically recorded, achieve local fame but are not part of the standard recording-based music industry.

Independent or Underground Hip-Hop

Analogous to Indie Rock, this genre includes artists who produce and distribute their music independently of the mainstream music industry. Released from industry pressures to create music that has wide audience appeal, these artists emphasize their resistance to compromise. Kook Keith, Latyrx, Mos Def, and Jurassic 5 are examples of Independent Hip-Hop.

Bass and Southern Hip-Hop

Developing out of the Electro Funk approach of Africa Bambataa, Bass music is a club-based genre that features fast, bass-heavy dance music with chanted vocals that are highly sexual. This genre has been primarily centered in Miami and other areas of the Deep South and is represented by artists such as Quad City Djs, Magic Mike, and Tag Team. Southern Hip-Hop emphasizes a heavy bass line. Sometimes considered a derivative combination of Miami Bass and Gangsta Rap, it fuses the slow funk, bluesy feel of the former with the abrasiveness and intensity of the later. Artists such as OutKast, Goodie Mob, and Dead Prez have been described as Southern Hip-Hop artists.

Nonviolent and Pop Rap

All rap is not gangsta rap focusing on violent subjects. In fact, some writers have suggested that one of rap's primary dangers is that it leads people to think that all blacks, or all blacks living in ghettos, subscribe to the hard-core "gangsta" worldview. Illustrating this point is Afrika Bambaataa (Nathaniel Hall), one of the Bronx creators of hip-hop, who founded Bam's Zulu Nation, today known as The Universal Zulu Nation. This international hip-hop movement promotes social activism and urges people to uphold principles of "knowledge, wisdom, understanding, freedom, justice, equality, peace, unity, love, and respect."[5] Bam's rap lyrics celebrate the sense of brotherhood in the community, and the desire to build relationships with women that are based on shared love and mutual respect.

M. C. Hammer's rap "Help the Children" urged people to assist in efforts to improve the life of children in harsh urban environments. Artists recording under the general title "The Native Tongues Posse" used their lyrics to display pride in their African roots, and the songs stressed the optimism and unity that they experienced in black neighborhoods. Several rappers formed a coalition in 1990 to record "We're All in the Same Gang," which preached against violence. Even Tupac, who was a leader in gangsta rap and who lost his life to urban violence, rapped on a wide range of topics. His song,"Dear Mama," for example, was a moving, tender testimonial to his love and respect for his mother, who as a single mother addicted to drugs, worked hard to create a loving family environment for Tupac and his sister. More recently, hip-hop that contains the fun and hooks but without the "danger" is described as Pop Rap, and includes some of the work of Coolio and Puff Daddy.

Rap also split into two geographically based styles: East Coast Rap and West Coast Rap.

East Coast Rap

The lyrics of rap artists on the East Coast tended to focus on racism against African-American communities, including the attitudes of police and government agencies. One of the earliest examples was Grandmaster Flash and the Furious Five's description of problems in the ghetto, called "The Message" (1982). In a later example, the lyrics of Public Enemy's "911 Is a Joke" (1990), described how calling 911 in an emergency is a cruel trick because the rescue squads don't care about people, especially those in African-American neighborhoods. Important East Coast rappers include Run-DMC, Public Enemy with Chuck D., LL Cool, 2 Live Crew, and the late Notorious B.I.G.

West Coast Rap

On the West Coast, N.W.A. (Niggaz With Attitude), with their lead rapper, Ice Cube (O'Shey Jackson), are credited with creating "gangsta rap" with their release in 1989 of *Straight Outta Compton*, produced by Dr. Dre. West Coast rappers focused on street violence and gang-related issues. The West Coast rapper who garnered a lot of attention was Tupac Shakur, with the record company Death Row. Shakur's style included vocals and more song style rapping. He also crossed over into film acting. His style popularized a form of rap that was aligned with the oral tradition of the black community, storytelling and signifying. Competition and hostility between artists on the rival coasts are said to have been the motive behind the shooting of Tupac in 1996.

Internationally famous rap artist Tupac Shakur was murdered in 1996.
Source: *AP Wide World Photos.*

[5] Fernando, S. H., Jr. "Back in the Day: 1975–1979." *The Vibe History of Hip-Hop*, p. 15.

WOMEN RAPPERS

To some extent, in direct contrast to hard-core rap, women rappers such as Queen Latifah (Dana Owens) wrote from a women's perspective, and talked about the importance of respect, community, and developing strength of character. In "Unity" (1993), she challenged, "Who you callin' a bitch?" and urged women, "You gotta let 'em know, you ain't a bitch or a 'ho'." The first successful female hip-hop group, Salt-N-Pepa, was a trio comprised of Salt (Cheryl James), Pepa (Sandy Denton), and DJ Spinderella (Dee Dee Roper). Their lighter approach and their almost "girl group" singing integrated with the rap puts them more in the genre of hip-hop. In 1999, Lauryn Hill was nominated for ten Grammy awards (she won five) for her hip-hop album *The Miseducation of Lauryn Hill* and was featured on the cover of the February 1999 *Time Magazine*, which included an eleven-page cover story on hip-hop and rap.

The important female rap artist, Queen Latifah, promotes positive goals in her lyrics. *Source: Photo by Gary Gershoff. Retna, Ltd.*

RAP AND OTHER RACIAL/ETHNIC GROUPS

The popularity of rap extended to other ethnic and racial groups. In 1987, three white ex-punk musicians who called themselves the Beastie Boys released *Licensed to Ill* with the song "(You Gotta) Fight for Your Right (to Party!)." This song became a hit at parties and introduced the sound of hip-hop's sampling techniques to a wide audience. Kid Frost, growing up in the Chicano community of Los Angeles, used his raps to address brutality against Chicanos. In his music, such as *Hispanic Causing Panic* (1990) and "Lowrider (on the Boulevard)" from *Latin Alliance* (1991), he used Latin rhythms and samples from Mexican-American musicians such as Santana. Musicians such as Molotov have continued Latino rap, often rapping in a mix-language dialect called "Spanglish." Rap groups are also prominent in the international pop scene, such as Korean bands Noise, Rula, and Taiji Boys, and Haitian bands Zin and Top Vice.

In 2001, rap and hip-hop constituted almost 13 percent of all domestic sales in the United States, and there are many individuals and groups who have played, or currently play, an important role in its success from either a business or a musical perspective. Some examples of people or groups not yet mentioned include Sean "Puffy" Combs, Wu-Tang Clan, Snoop Doggy-Dog, EPMD, Sister Souljah, DMX, Sarah Jones, Blaque, and Roots.

RAP AND HIP-HOP IN A SOCIAL AND HISTORICAL CONTEXT

Roots of Rap in African and African-American Oral Traditions

Rhymed and rhythmic speaking has always been an integral part of African-American cultures. For example, James Brown, the "Godfather of Soul" and the originator of funk, had used a speaking style on message songs of the 1960s, including "Say It Loud—I'm Black and I'm Proud." Louis Jordan had used rhythmic speech in songs such as "Saturday Night Fish Fry" in the 1940s. Rhythmic and rhymed speech can be traced in a steady line from musicians in all genres of African-American music back through rhymed "signifying," storytelling, preaching, and eventually back to the griots and paralinguists of traditional cultures in West Africa.

Paralinguists and Griots

At a West African king's court, paralinguists were high-status poet-musicians who created poems that glorified rulers and ancestors or delivered the king's commentaries to the tribe in witty, elegant language. These poems were often accompanied by drums and horns. The traveling poets, called *griots*, functioned in a similar manner among the villages. Griots were able to recite lengthy poems that recalled historical events and precise genealogies while they accompanied themselves on a variety of lute-style string instruments. West African cultures also maintained important prose tales that told stories involving human characters, or animal characters who represented humans. Plots often centered on the ability of the weak to outsmart the larger and meaner antagonists, and these stories were retained by African Americans as allegories for the struggle between slaves and powerful white masters.[6] Prose stories were frequently relayed in a rhymed monologue called a "toast," and toasts thrived in the streets, army, prisons, and juke joints. These toasts sometimes turned up completely intact in various forms of African-American music, such as in James Brown's "King Heroin" in 1972.[7]

Syndesis

Rap and hip-hop's compositional technique of sampling is also seen as having African roots. In West African cultures, the interaction between youth, elders, and ancestors was grounded in a process called syndesis. The syndetic approach encouraged descendents to respond to previous works of art by taking elements of those works and incorporating them into their new creations.[8] This process is seen in instrumental "quotations" in both jazz and blues, and it is on some level also the basis of sampling. Furthermore, some scholars see the spirit of call-and-response in the syndetic approach, where young blacks honor their ancestors "call," yet respond with their own contribution that brings ancestral wisdom into the current world but does not view that wisdom as final. Although rhythmic speech and syndesis can be seen in many forms of African-American culture, it has found its strongest and most sustained expression in hip-hop and rap.

The Earliest Hip-Hop and Rap

Kool Herc

The "seeds" of hip-hop appear to have been planted in the United States in 1971, when the Bronx resident Cindy Campbell, who needed some back-to-school money, asked her brother Clive to throw a party for which people would pay admission.[9] The siblings charged 25¢ for girls and 50¢ for boys. Held in the recreation room of their high-rise housing project, the party was a great success. Clive knew how to generate a party atmosphere. In his hometown of Kingston, Jamaica (in which he had grown up in the ghetto called "Trenchtown," as did reggae artist Bob Marley), he had seen partiers hire DJs with big sound systems who would "toast" in a singsong voice before and at the beginning of each song, creating "dub poetry." When he was thirteen years old and had moved to the

[6] Hine, et al. *The African-American Odyssey*. Upper Saddle River, New Jersey: Prentice Hall, 2000, pp. 20–21.

[7] Light, Alan, *The Vibe History of Hip-Hop*, p. 8.

[8] Werner, Craig, *A Change Is Gonna Come: Music, Race and the Soul of America*, p. 334.

[9] An alternative "beginning," as relayed in Alan Light's *The Vibe History of Hip-Hop* (p. 14), says that this was a birthday party and that it did not occur until 1973.

Break-Out One

LISTENING GUIDE *"The Breaks"*

Performing Artist: Kurtis Blow

Kurtis Blow (b. 1959) is one of the most influential of "old-school" hip-hop and rap artists, inspiring Run D.M.C., Whodini, and many other MCs who emerged in the 1980s. He grew up in Harlem and began his rapping career as early as 1976 in a club known as Charles Gallery. By 1977, he had acquired an inner-city fan cult that followed him in his ever-expanding club appearances. His first national exposure occurred in 1979 when he was one of the first rappers to record for a major label (Mercury). His broad-based popularity began with the release of his second single, "The Breaks," in 1980. "The Breaks" moved to number four on the R&B singles chart, and was certified gold by RIAA. With the shift to more social commentary and gangsta rap in the later 1980s, Kurtis Blow's style started to sound dated, but he is known as one of hip-hop's most influential pioneers. In 1997, he contributed the liner notes to Rhino's series "The History of Rap." The lyrics to "These Are the Breaks" reflect the fun, party lyrics that predated "gangsta" and more socially critical lyrics.

Rhythm	Duple
Melody	Early sing-song, rhythmic speaking on pitch
Harmony	Simple, repetitive chords with pronounced bass line
Texture	Notice the call-and-response between Blow and the background chorus
Form	Series of repeated, rhymed phrases alternating with "that's the breaks, that's the breaks"
Instrumentation	Primary male voice, guitar, prominent bass line, drums, including steel drums and piano

Grandmaster Flash in 1981. *Source: CORBIS-NY. Photo by S.I.N. c S.I.N./CORBIS. All rights Reserved.*

United States, he focused his energies on building up his own sound system so that he could do the same DJ function. Because New Yorkers were not into reggae at this time, he used the funk records that were so popular with the young blacks and Hispanics of the Bronx area in which he lived. With the success of Cindy's party, Clive went on to do more parties. In 1973, he gave his first block party, by this time using the moniker "Kool Herc."[10]

[10] "The Arts/Music/Hip-Hop Nation: Hip-Hop Nation There's more to rap than just rhythms and rhymes." Christopher John Farley with reporting by Melissa August/Washington, Leslie Everton Brice/Atlanta, Laird Harrison/Oakland, Todd; 02-08-1999.

Herc had been expanding on his technique, for example, concentrating on the "break" segment of the song, which was the section in between vocal choruses and verses where just the instruments, especially the percussion, took over. Knowing the popularity of this part of the song with partiers, he decided to use two copies of the same record on two different turntables and cut back and forth between them in order to make the break last longer. This produced the "breakbeat," the sound that became the starting point for much hip-hop and later techno. The people who became his most serious devotees were the dancers who saved their best moves for the break section in the song, and it was through this that they became known as "break boys," or simply "b-boys," and the style became known as break dancing.

Grandmaster Flash and Afrika Bambaataa

Grandmaster Flash (Joseph Sadler) had grown up in the Bronx and idolized Kool Herc. Like Herc, he had Jamaican roots, but he also had been tinkering with electronics as a student in a nearby vocational school. With this training, he constructed a cue monitor, which enabled him to hear one record through the headphones while the other was playing for the audience.

With this technological advantage, and the supreme hand–eye coordination that had earned him his nickname, he soon surpassed Herc in popularity.[11] He and his crew also developed other technological innovations, including the technique of working the needle back and forth rhythmically that became known as "scratching." Yet another modification was using multiple MCs (masters of ceremony, or microphone controllers) simultaneously to engage the crowd. Known as Grandmaster Flash and the Furious Five, the group interacted with each other rapping out catchphrases such as "Clap ya hands to the beat," as well as rapping out complicated routines of back-to-back rhyming. Another early important DJ was Bronx DJ Afrika Bambaataa, with his crew of DJs called Zulu Nation. His record, "Planet Rock," was one of the seminal presentations of scratching, electronic additions, high-tech beats, cutting rhythms, and highly processed vocals that became "hip-hop." By 1978, groups of MCs such as the Furious Five and Zulu Nation had become more popular than single DJs.

The Cold Crush Brothers and the Sugar Hill Gang

One of the Bronx groups that expanded on Grandmaster Flash's approach was the Cold Crush Brothers, managed by Henry "Big Bank Hank" Jackson. Jackson also worked at a pizzeria in Englewood, New Jersey. One day, while rapping along to a Cold Crush tape, he was approached by Sylvia Robinson. Sylvia was a former rhythm 'n' blues singer who had several independent record labels that she ran with her husband, Joe. One of the labels was Sugar Hill, named after an area in Harlem that had been home to many black musicians, poets, and artists. Sylvia had become intrigued by rap, and asked Hank if he was interested in joining a group she was putting together. Although Hank had not been an MC himself, he agreed, and went back to the lead vocalist for the Crush Brothers, "Grandmaster Caz," who helped him by giving him his book of rhymes. Over a rhythm track taken from a recent number one disco record called "Good Times" by Chic, Hank, and two other guys rapped Caz's rhymes and recorded "Rapper's Delight" as the Sugarhill Gang. It was "Rapper's Delight" that was the immediate, commercial catalyst for subsequent recordings of hip-hop and rap.

The Context for the Rise in Popularity of Rap

The End of Disco

Rap music allowed young, urban New Yorkers to express themselves in an accessible art form that

[11] Fernando, S.H., Jr., "Back in the Day: 1975–1979" in *Vibe History of Hip-Hop*, p. 18.

offered unlimited challenges. There were no definite rules, it did not require purchasing and learning how to play an instrument, and it did not require an ability to sing. One had only to be original and to be able to rhythmically rhyme. Rap was also a response to disco, the music style that dominated popular radio, and that to many young urban blacks was a watered down and insipid version of the soul and funk music that had been popular in the 1960s. During the summer of 1979, anywhere from five to seven of the top ten singles in America were disco. The genre became overexposed, the market was saturated, and the backlash began. When "Good Times" (the record that provided the rhythm track for "Rapper's Delight") debuted in the Top Ten in July 1979, six of the other ten records were disco. When it reached number one on August 1, only three disco records remained in the Top Ten. By the time it fell out of the Top Ten on September 22, no disco records remained and the press declared that the disco era was dead. When "Good Times" fell out of the Top Forty in late October, "Rapper's Delight" was introduced and eventually peaked at number four.

RETURN TO SEGREGATED RADIO PROGRAMMING

The fast and dramatic death of disco had an important impact on popular radio. Two charts for tracking record success had existed for some time: Billboard's pop singles chart and the rhythm 'n' blues chart. When "Rapper's Delight" was introduced in 1979, nearly half of the records that were popular across the country were found on both charts. But by the first half of 1980, only 21 percent were on both charts, and by 1982, the amount of crossover was 17 percent. During a three-week period in October 1982, not one record by an African American was on the Top Twenty of the pop singles or albums charts, a polarization that had not occurred since the 1940s.[12] Programmers, anxious to move away from anything that sounded "disco," sought out alternatives, but from two entirely different recording repertoires. This new wall between black and white music encouraged rap to develop separately from the white mainstream, produced by blacks for a black audience.

White kids were not listening to hip-hop, and the sound was so foreign that when Grandmaster Flash and the Furious Five opened for the English punk group Clash in New York City in 1981, audience members who pelt them with plastic cups drove them from the stage.[13] In the meantime, the Sugar Hill label continued to release influential hip-hop hits (including many by Grandmaster Flash) that rose to prominence on the rhythm 'n' blues charts, leading larger labels to search for and release their own competitive rap recordings.

Shift in Rap from Party Music to Social Commentary

In 1982, Grandmaster Flash released "The Message," which shifted rap to more social commentary. The record described the desperation and rage felt in the black community, where hopes and dreams were reduced to efforts to survive: "It's like a jungle, sometimes it makes me wonder, How I keep from going under." The words also described someone being sent to prison for 8 years, who is "used and abused" by his cellmates until he commits suicide by hanging himself. Sugar Hill did not initially want to release "The Message," fearing that the departure from the party image would be commercial suicide. "The Message" did not make it at all on to Billboard's Top Forty, but it soared to number four on the rhythm 'n' blues charts and was honored as "single of the year" in critics' polls for both the *Rolling Stone* and *Village Voice*.

When Run D.M.C. released their first album (1984), they continued the tradition of incisive rhymes, delivered in a harder-edged manner

[12] Greenburg, Steve, "Sugar Hill Records," in *Vibe History of Hip-Hop*, pp. 24–25.
[13] Ibid., p. 27.

with the backup music stripped to its essentials. Others followed their lead, and although some of these rappers were not from the ghetto, it soon became clear that being "real" and "hard" were the new values. Also founded in 1984, Def Jam records became a label that found great success with new artists. LL Cool J was the most prominent of this new group of rappers, and his performance of "I Can't Live Without My Radio" was sharp and spare. Used in the movie *Krush Groove*, LL Cool became the archetypal B-boy. Creating four platinum albums by 1991, and giving a searing performance backed by an acoustic band on *MTV Unplugged*, Cool became the first superstar of rap.

Hip-Hop and Rap Become More Mainstream

The hip-hop culture was steadily being brought to mainstream attention. Charlie Ahearn's 1982 film, *Wild Style*, showed break dancing, graffiti art, and the styles of language and fashion of the B-boys. Break dancing became a national fad and was shown in everything from television commercials to fashion magazines. But except for the anomalous "Rapture" by white new-wave group Blondie in 1980, rap music remained out of the mainstream until the late 1980s. The group largely responsible for rap's crossing over was Run D.M.C., who collaborated with the white group Aerosmith, to make a new version of Aerosmith's "Walk This Way" (1977). The song was released on their *Raising Hell* album (1986), and became number four on the Billboard pop charts.

The white group Beastie Boys' party song, "(You Gotta) Fight for Your Right (to Party)," was even a greater success, and the first rap album to hit the top of the Billboard charts. Other rap hits followed, such as DJ Jazzy Jeff and Fresh Prince's lighthearted pop rap, "Parents Just Don't Understand" (1988). De La Soul's *3 Feet High and Rising* (1989) further broadened rap's base, as they sampled recordings by Steely Dan and Johnny Cash, and created lyrics that ranged from humorous absurdity to social commentary. Queen Latifah's *All Hail the Queen* (1989) brought a woman's perspective into the genre. Fusion efforts uniting hip-hop beats with more traditional rhythm 'n' blues created Keith Sweat's "I Want Her" (1987) and Johnny Kemp's "Just Got Paid" (1988), both produced by Teddy Riley and given the name "New Jack Swing." This fusion style continued with Riley's own group in *My Prerogative* (1989) and in the sound for Michael Jackson's *Dangerous* (1991). The growing popularity of hip-hop and rap was also reflected in the 1988 founding of the hip-hop magazine, *The Source*, by two Harvard undergraduates. *The Source* was the first of several publications that now cover the contemporary rap scene. In August 1989, the cable music video channel MTV debuted *Yo! MTV Raps*, which quickly became the station's most popular program.[14]

The Growth of Hard-Core Rap

Meanwhile, rap with a more political and social tone was evident in the high success of Public Enemy, who released *It Takes a Nation of Millions to Hold Us Back* (1988), and emphasized black nationalist pride. As this style of rap grew, and obscenities, rage, and violence characterized more of the lyrics, rap became more controversial. In 1989, N.W.A. (Niggaz with Attitude) released *Straight Outta Compton*, which contributed to the development of hard-core rap, referred to as "gangsta" rap. On that album, the track "Gangsta, Gangsta" began with gunshots. Another track on the album, "Fuck tha Police," attracted the attention of the FBI, who sent a letter of warning to the record company.

[14] The success of *YO! MTV Raps* and music video in general led to marketing a recording that includes the production of a music video release as well. The rise of rap music videos opened a creative avenue of expression for black visual artists, set designers, and other technical staff. This has generated a body of technicians who are ultimately having an impact on black film production, which had been a nonexistent creative field for them and other black visual artists.

THE OBSCENITY TRIAL OF 2 LIVE CREW

The controversial element of rap was foregrounded in the national media with the 1990 obscenity trial of Miami's 2 Live Crew. The trial was sparked by the arrest of Charles Freeman, a record store owner in Florida, who was picked up for selling Crew's album, *Nasty As They Wanna Be* (1989). The album had been brought to the attention of a federal court judge in Fort Lauderdale earlier by an antiporn crusader from Miami, and the judge had pronounced the recording "obscene." This was particularly newsworthy, as this was the first time in the history of the United States that a federal court had set down such a ruling about a recording.[15] The album was banned in Florida as well as in other states. Although Freeman was found guilty in trial, 2 Live Crew was acquitted. Sales of the album skyrocketed, and the group even celebrated the notoriety by naming their next album *Banned in the U.S.A.* (1990), which was a play on Bruce Springsteen's album *Born in the U.S.A.* (1990).

GANGSTA RAP BECOMES MAINSTREAM

Mainstream America was becoming more and more aware of rap, but primarily of the extreme, high-profile gangsta rap. It also was clear that this was the kind of rap that was achieving great commercial success. In 1991, N.W.A.'s second album, the searing, violent, and misogynistic *Efil4-zaggin* ("Niggaz 4 Life" backward) entered Billboard's pop chart at number two. This was followed four months later by similarly successful Public Enemy's *Apocalypse 91: The Enemy Strikes Black*, and Ice Cube's solo album *Death Certificate*, which also debuted in the number two slot. Another hard-core rap CD, Snoop Doggy Dog's *Doggystyle*, immediately rocketed to the number one spot on the charts (1993).

Critics became alarmed, stressing that not only was this type of rap focusing almost exclusively on pathologies within American culture, particularly black ghetto communities, but also that it was glorifying ghetto life and inciting violence. Albums with sexually explicit or violent lyrics were required to post a "Parental Warning" logo on the CD covers. Despite of (or because of) attempts to curtail it throughout the 1990s, hard-core gangsta rap continued to increase in popularity. In the words of one writer, "after the smoke clears, gangsta rap will be identified as the most influential style in all of pop music in the '90s."[16] Real-life violence overshadowed recorded violence when, in 1996, "West Coast" superstar Tupac Shakur was murdered by gunmen in Las Vegas. Then, in 1997, "East Coast's" Notorius B.I.G. was shot as well. As much of the rap world was stunned by these losses, and criticism intensified on the dangers of hard core rap, Sean "Puffy" Combs renewed his commitment to maintaining it: "We can't let this music die."[17] In 1997, with his *Beats by the Pound* production associates, he began a prolific series of CDs containing tunes made for consumers now known as "No Limit" fans.

RAP AT THE END OF THE MILLENNIUM

In 1998, rap became America's top-selling musical format, selling more than eighty-one million CDs, tapes, and albums and increasing by a stunning 31 percent from 1997 to 1998. This percentage can best be appreciated when rap is compared with country music, previously the fastest growing format, which in the same period grew by only 2 percent. Increase in the music industry as a whole was only 9 percent. Furthermore, even though hip-hop and rap were genres started in black America, in 1999 whites purchased 70 percent of hip-hop albums.[18] In the first year of the new millennium, rap accounted for 12.9 percent of all domestic record sales.

[15] Green, Tony. "The Dirty South," in *Vibe History of Hip-Hop*, p. 268.

[16] Alvarez, Gabriel. "Gangsta Rap in the '90s," in *Vibe History of Hip-Hop*, p. 286.

[17] Hunter, James. "Master P," in *Vibe History of Hip-Hop*, p. 390.

[18] "The Arts/Music/Hip-Hop Nation: Hip-Hop Nation There's more to rap than just rhythms and rhymes." Christopher John Farley with reporting by Melissa August/Washington, Leslie Everton Brice/Atlanta, Laird Harrison/Oakland, Todd; 02-08-1999.

Break-Out Two

PROFILE *Jay-Z*

Jay-Z was born and raised in the Marcy Projects, a rough area of apartment buildings for low-income families in Brooklyn, New York. Jay-Z was still a child when his father left his mother, and was soon spending lots of time on the streets where he earned a reputation as a fledgling rapper. His nickname, Jazzy, evolved into Jay-Z. He started to hang around with another New York rapper, Jaz-O, who mentored Jay-Z in the rap industry. With friends, he created Roc-a-Fella Records in order to cut out the middleman. In 1996 he produced his debut album, *Reasonable Doubt.*

As Jay-Z cranked out a series of albums, he built up Roc-a-Fella Records into a successful business enterprise, developing a roster of talented rappers (e.g., Beanie Sigel, Cam'ron, M.O.P) and producers (Just Blaze, Kayne West) as he also expanded to clothing (Roca Wear), tours, and even films (*Paid in Full, State Property*). In the meantime, his music continued to develop a strong fan base. His earlier works were in the gangsta rap genre, but by 1997, Jay-Z released *In My Lifetime*, which reflected a shift to a more pop-rap style. *Vol 2, Hard Knock Life*, released in 1998, furthered this shift, featuring well-crafted hooks and trendsetting beats and garnering extensive airplay. More albums followed, including *Vol 3, Life and Times of S. Carter* (1999) and *Dynasty Roc l Familia* (2000). By 2001 with the release of *The Blueprint*, he had solidified his position as one of New York's top rappers. Billed as a sequel, *The Blueprint: The Gift and the Curse* was released in 2002, and like so many of his previous albums generated a number of singles. The most famous was his cover of 2Pac's "03 Bonnie & Clyde," which he performed with Beyoncé Knowles. In 2005, his single "99 Problems" from *The Black Album* won him Best Rap Solo Performance.

Rap artist Jay-Z performs at the 1st annual Black Entertainment Television Awards at the Paris Las Vegas Hotel-Casino in Las Vegas, June 19, 2001. Jay-Z won the award for Best Male Hip-Hop Artist. *Source: CORBIS-NY. Photo by Ethan Miller. C Ethan Miller/CORBIS.*

The 2001 Hip-Hop Summit

In 2001, music executive Russell Simmons, one of the cofounders of the Def Jam hip-hop and rap empire, announced a "Hip-Hop Summit." He invited major artists, recording industry insiders and executives, members of Congress, academics, civil rights groups, and the leader of the Nation of Islam, asking them to return to rap's roots, City of New York, to discuss a variety of issues. For over two days, people talked about getting artists and the entertainment industry "to take responsibility for

LL Cool J in 1997, was one of the most successful rap artists to come out of the Def Jam record label. *Source: Black Bear Productions, Inc. By Wayne Maser. Courtesy Black Bear Productions, Inc. By Wayne Maser/Starfish Management.*

themselves," to establish mechanisms for conflict resolution among artists, and to closely examine artist development and marketing in order to identify strategies to "elevate the art form."[19] Minister Farrakhan addressed the gathering for two hours, urging artists to harness their power to more enlightened lyrical expressions to combat injustice, racism, and exploitation. He also challenged critics to reach out to artists and help change the conditions that "spawn offensive lyrics." Martin Luther King III exhorted attendees that it was time for the hip-hop community, civil rights activists, and the business community "to come together to forge an agenda to move the nation forward."[20]

Conclusion

The twentieth century was enriched extraordinarily by the music contributions of African Americans. It is almost impossible to imagine what music would be like without spirituals, jazz, Gospel, blues, and rhythm 'n' blues. Now, added to this list, are hip-hop and rap. These latter styles, particularly, will certainly frame our memories of the last decades of the twentieth century. Begun three decades ago, an entire generation of American youth—blacks, whites, Latinos, Asians, and Native Americans—has grown up immersed in the hip-hop culture. Doug Century, who has studied the hip-hop culture, has predicted that white acts will eventually dominate rap, just as white musicians have eventually dominated other black musics. "It's possible that in fifteen years, all hip-hop will be white."[21] By contrast, American culture is in a constant process of reinvention. Just as it was impossible to predict the ultimate growth and popularity of hip-hop and rap when "Rapper's Delight" first appeared on the national pop charts in 1979, we most likely will be amazed when we look back sometime in the future, to see how the youth culture has, once again, transformed itself and its music.

Bibliography

Alvarez, Gabriel. "Gangsta Rap in the '90s," in *The Vibe History of Hip-Hop.* Alan Light (Editor). New York: Three Rivers Press, 1999.

"The Battle Over Rap." (*Newsweek*); 10-30-2000.

Birchmeier, Jason. "Jay-Z." From Artist Main. http://www.vh1.com/artists/az/jay_z/artist.jhtml (Accessed 03-15-05).

[19] Muhammad, Richard and Saeed Shabazz. "Hip Hop Summit Convenes in New York." http://www.finalcall.com/national/rapsummit (Accessed 06-26-2001)

[20] Ibid.

[21] "The Arts/Music/Hip-Hop Nation: Hip-Hop Nation There's more to rap than just rhythms and rhymes." Christopher John Farley with reporting by Melissa August/Washington, Leslie Everton Brice/Atlanta, Laird Harrison/Oakland, Todd; 02-08-1999.

Public Enemy's Chuck D discusses the history of Hip-hop culture and rap music. http://www.theherald.org/herald/issues/032399/chuck.f.html

The History of Hip Hop http://www.daveyd.com/raphist2.html

Charlton, Katherine. *Rock Music Styles: A History.* Second Edition. Madison Wisconsin: Brown and Benchmark, 1994.

De Curtis, Anthony and James Henke, editors. *The Rolling Stone Illustrated History of Rock and Roll.* New York: Random House, 1980.

Fernando, S.H., Jr. "Back in the Day 1975–1979," in *The Vibe History of Hip-Hop.* Alan Light (Editor). New York: Three Rivers Press, 1999.

Goldfield, David et al. *The American Journey: A History of the United States*, Combined Volume. Upper Saddle River, New Jersey: Prentice Hall, 2001.

Greenberg, Steve. "Sugar Hill Records," in *The Vibe History of Hip-Hop.* Alan Light (Editor). New York: Three Rivers Press, 1999.

Greenberg, Steve. "The Dirty South," in *The Vibe History of Hip-Hop.* Alan Light (Editor). New York: Three Rivers Press, 1999.

Hager, Steven. *Hip Hop: The Illustrated History of Break Dancing, Rap Music, and Graffitti.* New York: St. Martin's, 1984.

Haskins, James. *Black Music in America: A History Through Its People.* New York: Thomas Y. Crowell, 1987.

Hine, Darlene Clark, et al. *The African-American Odyssey.* Upper Saddle River, New Jersey: Prentice Hall, 2000.

Hunter, James. "Master P," in *The Vibe History of Hip-Hop.* Alan Light (Editor). New York: Three Rivers Press, 1999.

Light, Alan. *The Vibe History of Hip-Hop.* New York: Three Rivers Press, 1999.

Neal, Mark Anthony. *What the Music Said: Black Popular Music and Black Public Culture.* New York and London: Routledge, 1999.

Rose, Tricia. *Black Noise: Rap Music and Black Culture in Contemporary America.* Hanover and London: Wesleyan University Press, 1994.

Werner, Craig. *A Change Is Gonna Come: Music, Race and The Soul of America.* New York: Plume, 1999.

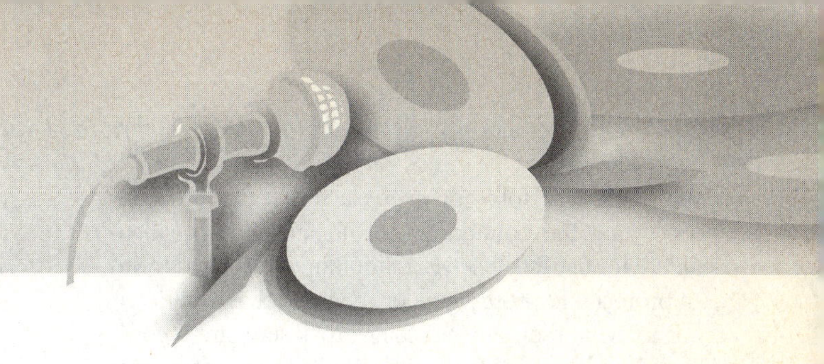

Contemporary Fusions and Looking Toward the Future

Popular music today is an international, multibillion-dollar business. Music is so pervasive it would be difficult for most Americans to experience a day without hearing it somewhere. As a result of tremendous advances in communications technology, we are at a unique point in history: just as the world has become a "global village," so has music become a worldwide soundscape. Musicians and music listeners currently have access to musical styles from previous eras as well as music from around the world. Many music listeners are eclectic in their tastes, enjoying different kinds of music depending on the context or their particular mood at the time. Most contemporary musicians are no longer focused on a single style—they pick and choose elements from an extensive array of styles to craft their own personal musical expression. The tracks on a single artist's CD might include a variety of genres, or a single track might contain elements of multiple genres. Fusions abound, and the possibilities for different combinations are virtually limitless.

This almost dizzying array of choices can be extraordinarily exciting, and it also can be alarming. In this book we have explored a wide variety of American musics, including folk music, blues, jazz, Cajun, zydeco, Gospel, rock and roll, Motown, soul, funk, rap, salsa, reggae, and Tejano. We looked at how each style has roots in the ethnic traditions of a specific immigrant group and how it evolved into a uniquely American music. We examined both the elements that make that style distinctive from a purely musical perspective as well as the context that originally created that style. The thread that has woven all of this together is that each music developed as an expression of a specific subculture within the larger mainstream American culture. Some people worry that extensive intermingling of styles will result in the loss of important heritages. But music is not static. It must change to reflect changing circumstances. To be anything more than an historical artifact, music must evolve into new forms that retain vitality and relevance in contemporary society.

The popular music historian Michael Campbell[1] proposes that we are currently experiencing two contradictory trends. One trend favors cross-pollination, encouraging musicians to incorporate stylistic elements from around the world and to blend today's

[1] Campbell, Michael. *The Beat Goes On: Popular Music in America.* Second Edition. Belmont, CA: Thomson Schirmer, 2006.

pop, rock, jazz, folk, and even classical music so seamlessly that the boundaries are no longer distinguishable. He suggests there is a simultaneous second trend to protect and preserve older styles: Native Americans are reviving their ancient songs; rock stars are recording decades-old "standards"; individuals and entire organizations are actively conserving styles of previous eras. These trends may seem at odds, but Campbell suggests they complement each other and help our culture to maintain a healthy balance. Although one trend seems to lead forward and another seems to move backward, both trends represent two directions down the same road. In order to appreciate where we are and where we are going, we must understand and honor the places from whence we came. It is likely that experiments with various fusions will continue to characterize popular music of the future, and it is equally probable that we will maintain our interest in understanding and preserving the past. We can look down the road in either direction and still rejoice, as it is clear that the development of popular music in America has been, and continues to be, a remarkable journey.

Name Index

Subject Index

Songs and Albums Index

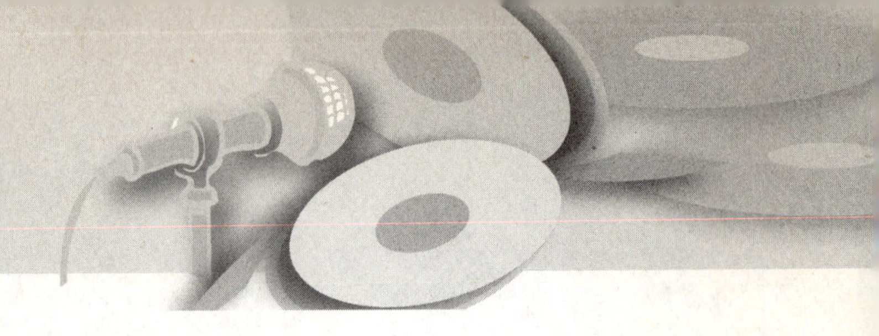

CROSSROADS

The Multicultural Roots of America's Popular Music, Second Edition

ELIZABETH F. BARKLEY

Companion Compact Disc

1. Traditional: Rabbitt Dance (a)
2. Traditional: Barbara Allen (b) J.B. Cornett
3. Traditional: Barbara Allen (b) Jean Ritchie
4. Traditional: Barbara Allen Pete Seeger
5. Traditional: Drum Rhythms (c) Dan Musicians
6. Traditional: La Llorona (b) Suni Paz
7. Johnson: Cross Road Blues Robert Johnson
8. Ellington-Strayhorn: Take the A Train Ella Fitzgerald with Duke Ellington and his Orchestra (d)
9. Ward: How I Got Over Mahalia Jackson (m)
10. Guillory: Zydeco Queen Ida & Her Zydeco Band (f)
11. Bryant: Rocky Top The Osborne Brothers (g)
12. Traditional: Barbara Allen Joan Baez (h)
13. Williams, David: Whole Lotta Shakin' Jerry Lee Lewis (i)
14. Brown: Say It Loud - I'm Black and I'm Proud (j) James Brown
15. Corrido El General Santa Cruz (b) Federico, Moreno, Romero, Molina
16. Torres: Menea La Cintura (l) Kaos
17. Foster, arr: Taylor, Ma, Meyer, O'Conner: Hard Times Come Again No More (m) James Taylor with Yo-Yo Ma, Edgar Meyer, Mark O'Conner
18. Blow/Ford/Miller/Moore/Simmons/Smith: The Breaks (n) Kurtis Blow